# Justice Beyond Borders

*A Global Political Theory*

SIMON CANEY

OXFORD

UNIVERSITY PRESS

# OXFORD
UNIVERSITY PRESS

Great Clarendon Street, Oxford OX2 6DP
United Kingdom

Oxford University Press is a department of the University of Oxford.
It furthers the University's objective of excellence in research, scholarship,
and education by publishing worldwide.
Oxford is a registered trade mark of Oxford University Press in the UK
and in certain other countries

© Simon Caney 2005

The moral rights of the author have been asserted

Reprinted 2013

British Library Cataloguing in Publication Data
Data available

Library of Congress Cataloging in Publication Data
Data available

ISBN 978-0-19-929796-2

To
Joanna, Eleanor, and Isabel

# Contents

Four additional points should be made. First, as the above six issues make clear, my concern is with questions in political philosophy. This book does not seek to provide an explanatory account or theory of how the global system operates.[1] This does not, however, imply that we can ignore factual and explanatory accounts of the global order. Any defensible global political theory must rely on factual statements about the world. As we shall see at various stages throughout the book, a number of arguments are vulnerable precisely because they rest on indefensible empirical propositions or implausible explanatory theories.

Second, it is important to explain why this book refers to *global* political theory and eschews the more frequent term *international political theory*. The latter phrase is almost always employed to refer to the ways in which states should treat other states.[2] To frame the questions examined in this book thus is misleading in a number of ways. First, since the term *international political theory* is used to refer to relations between states, it misleadingly equates nations with states. This equation is misleading because, as we shall see shortly, the two concepts are quite distinct. Second, it presupposes that there should be states rather than non-sovereign forms of political organization. The state, as we shall see in Chapter 5, is a very specific type of political regime and it is by no means clear that it is the best available. Third, the term *international political theory* suggests not only that states are the bearers of duties but also that they have these obligations to other states. It suggests that the subject should be about how states treat other states. This, however, unreasonably restricts the subject by excluding individuals or other non-state entities from being the objects of moral concern. Finally, the term *international political theory* narrows the subject considerably and ignores important questions such as how international institutions such as the European Union or United Nations or World Bank or International Monetary Fund should act.

Third, it is worth emphasizing that this book examines global *political* theory. As such it differs from what one might term global *ethics*, where this focuses exclusively on the moral obligations owed by individuals (Dower 1998: 4). This work is concerned with the obligations of individuals but it also explores the moral nature and rights and duties of political institutions including not just states but also supra-state institutions. Its concerns are, thus, not reducible to individual morality.

Fourth, and finally, we can distinguish between three different levels at which a global political theory may operate. The first level is the most abstract: a global political theory must be able to say how a 'global political theory' relates to 'domestic political theory'. Should the principles that apply in the domestic realm (whether that is defined as the 'nation' or the 'state') be adopted at the global level? Or are the realms disanalogous in a morally relevant way? If so, how? A second level concerns principles: a global political theory must be able to provide guidance as to what principles should be adopted and which institutions should be put into practice. The third level is more concrete: this involves the application of principles to specific issues (such as, for example, whether the war against Iraq initiated in 2003 was justified). This book operates primarily at the first and second levels. The third, note, can be performed only by integrating principles (i.e. level-2 analysis) with an enormous amount of empirical detail and by concentrating on specific issues in a case-by-case way. Rather than focusing on any specific case-studies, this book seeks to identify what principles should be applied at the global level (level-2) and in the process of doing so to examine how a global political theory relates to the values and norms that we think should apply in the domestic realm (level-1).

Having outlined the subject matter of this book, I now want to make clear the aims of the book. These are twofold. *Justice Beyond Borders* seeks, first, to provide a defence of what is commonly termed a *cosmopolitan political morality* and to apply it to the six issues cited above. It argues that cosmopolitanism provides the most plausible position on human rights, distributive justice, political institutions, war, and intervention. Second, it aims to explore in depth and to evaluate competing philosophical perspectives on these issues. As such it seeks to provide a comprehensive analysis of all the leading and important contributions to these topics.[3] Each chapter, thus, aims both to defend a cosmopolitan outlook and to evaluate prominent contributions to the debates examined.

My view is that these two aims complement each other. Consider the first aim: I think that the best way to defend a particular perspective is not only to outline the reasoning underlying it but also to deal with the objections posed by other perspectives (C. Jones 1999: 17). Consider too the second aim: I am not sure it is altogether possible to analyse prevalent perspectives and not reveal one's hand. Attempts to provide a wholly neutral account of other approaches fail and a person's views inevitably emerge. Given this, better then to make absolutely clear where one stands.

To examine these six issues, it is, I think, useful to begin by drawing attention to four competing approaches to global political theory—namely, what I shall call *cosmopolitanism, realism, the 'society of states'* tradition, and *nationalism*. These provide a useful framework within which to examine the six issues and to stake out and defend a cosmopolitan approach. I shall say more about the rationale for referring to traditions of thought (and the important limits on doing so) shortly (Section VII). In the meantime, I want to outline the four perspectives, beginning with cosmopolitanism.

# I

Cosmopolitanism is well defined by Thomas Pogge, who writes:

Three elements are shared by all cosmopolitan positions. First, *individualism*: the ultimate units of concern are *human beings*, or *persons*—rather than, say, family lines, tribes, ethnic, cultural, or religious communities, nations, or states. The latter may be units of concern only indirectly, in virtue of their individual members or citizens. Second, *universality*: the status of ultimate unit of concern attaches to *every* living human being *equally*—not merely to some sub-set, such as men, aristocrats, Aryans, whites, or Muslims. Third, *generality*: this special status has global force. Persons are ultimate units of concern for *everyone*—not only for their compatriots, fellow religionists, or such like (1994a: 89, cf. further p. 90).[4]

Cosmopolitans, then, generally affirm three principles: the worth of individuals, equality, and the existence of obligations binding on all. These tenets are affirmed by contemporary theorists such as Brian Barry (1998: 146; 1999: sec. IV, esp. pp. 35–6), Charles Beitz (1994: 124–5; 1999c), Martha Nussbaum (1996: 2–17), and Peter Singer (1972: 229–43; 2002). These thinkers are conventionally described as belonging to an 'analytical' approach. In this light it is worth noting that a cosmopolitan ethic is not the preserve of analytical philosophers alone and some philosophers not conventionally classified as analytical, such as Jacques Derrida, also espouse a cosmopolitan ethic of hospitality to all (Derrida 2000, 2001). Finally, we might record that cosmopolitanism is also affirmed by many religious thinkers and indeed many religions assert the equal moral worth of all individuals, emphasizing our duties to everyone. In addition to its modern defenders, cosmopolitanism also has a long intellectual history. Earlier proponents include, for example, Diogenes the Cynic who famously described himself as 'A Citizen of the world' (Laertius 1905: 240–1). Cosmopolitan ideals are also affirmed by Stoic philosophers like Cicero. In his *de Officiis*, for example, Cicero outlined the ideal of a community of mankind and argued that persons have duties to all other humans (2001 [44 BC], bk. 1, secs 22 [pp. 9–10], 50–52 [pp. 19–20]; and bk. 3, secs 21–22 [pp. 91–92], 28 [p. 93], 31–32 [p. 94], 69 [p. 107]). That cosmopolitanism is affirmed by some Cynics and Stoics is frequently stressed. It is, however, worth noting that similar ideas can also be found in other cultures. For example, the Chinese philosopher Mo Tsu defends recognizably 'cosmopolitan' ideals. Mo was a contemporary, and critic, of Confucius. He defended an impartial and broadly consequentialist morality which judges practices by their outcomes.[5] The foundation of his philosophy was the principle of 'universal love' (Mei 1974 esp. bk. I, ch. IV, pp. 13–16; bk. IV, chs XIV–XVI, pp. 78–97). One aspect of this doctrine of universal love was a repudiation, and critique, of partiality (Mei 1974, bk. IV, ch. XVI, pp. 87–97, esp. pp. 87–92). Moving on from these early cosmopolitans we might note that later cosmopolitans include Enlightenment thinkers such as Voltaire, Jeremy Bentham, and Immanuel Kant. Bentham, for example, defended the idea of an international court to resolve conflicts in his 'A Plan for an Universal and Perpetual Peace' (1962 [1786–9]). Most famously, Kant defended a universal moral philosophy. He also affirmed a universal right to 'hospitality' (1989 [1795]: 105–8]). However, Kant's position is complex (and illustrates a point made later about the permeable nature of traditions) for although his moral theory is cosmopolitan he is also well known for rejecting world political institutions (1989 [1795]).

A number of further clarificatory points should be made about cosmopolitanism. First, we should record that whilst all cosmopolitans affirm the above three claims they often differ considerably in their moral theories. Some, for example, take a utilitarian approach, believing that political morality requires that the utility of all sentient beings throughout the world should be taken into account and then maximized (Singer 1972: 229–43). Others, however, reject this utilitarian brand of cosmopolitanism, defending instead a cosmopolitan theory that is rights-based rather than consequentialist (Shue 1996a). Such an approach calls for the rights of *all persons* to be protected. These are but two of the many varieties of cosmopolitanism. The central point is that cosmopolitan tenets may be affirmed by a variety of very different political theories.

A second important feature about cosmopolitanism should be noted. To see this it is helpful to employ a distinction invoked by Charles Beitz between what he terms 'institutional' and 'moral' conceptions of cosmopolitanism (1994: 124–5). (Thomas Pogge (1994a: 90) makes the same distinction but uses the terms 'legal' and 'moral' cosmopolitanism instead). The three cosmopolitan claims given above all constitute aspects of moral cosmopolitanism. Institutional/legal cosmopolitanism, by contrast, maintains that there should be global political institutions. This distinction is important because cosmopolitans are fundamentally committed to the moral claims but are not thereby necessarily committed to the institutional ones. As we shall see in Chapter 5, some who affirm the moral claim *do* also embrace the institutional/legal claim: a case in point is Dante Alighieri in his tract *de Monarchia* (1949 [1313]). Other examples include H. G. Wells who defended a world state on the grounds that it was needed to protect civil, political, and economic rights (1940). A similar position has also been taken by the contemporary philosopher Kai Nielsen (1988).[6] Others, however, who affirm cosmopolitan moral claims reject a world state. They think that cosmopolitan moral claims are compatible with, or even require, states or some alternative to global political institutions. It is vital, then, to keep the distinction between the two doctrines clear since objections to institutional cosmopolitanism in themselves do not tell against moral cosmopolitanism. That is, critiques of a world state or global political authorities do not impugn the moral convictions that all persons are of equal moral worth and that everyone has duties to other human beings.

A third point concerns the relationship between cosmopolitanism and liberalism, where liberalism is a doctrine concerned with persons' equal liberty. Many leading cosmopolitans do defend a liberal outlook (e.g. Barry, Beitz, O'Neill, and Pogge).[7] Nonetheless it is conceptually possible for someone to endorse cosmopolitanism but reject liberalism. For example, although most cosmopolitan utilitarians seek to defend liberal rights it is possible for them to argue that maximizing total utility at the global level requires restrictions on freedom. Alternatively, some religious thinkers have argued for the equal moral standing of all persons but have argued for illiberal interpretations of these principles. Some indeed have embraced authoritarian or theocratic conceptions. A second important point to note here is that some who are committed to liberalism reject cosmopolitanism. A clear example of this is John Rawls who argues in *The Law of Peoples* (1999b) that liberal principles should not be applied to the world as a whole.[8] Thus, whereas many cosmopolitans defend a liberal conception of

*Discourses* that republics may employ any means—no matter how unjust or cruel—to defend themselves (1988 [1531], bk. III, sec. 41, pp. 514–15). There are, of course, realist strains also in Thomas Hobbes's *The Leviathan* (1996 [1651], ch. 13, paragraphs 12–13, pp. 85–6; ch. 30, paragraph 30, p. 235).[16]

To gain a better grasp of realism we should bear in mind four additional points. First, we should record that realists are sometimes ambiguous between the claim that morality has no place in international affairs, on the one hand, and the claim that states should (morally should) pursue the national interest, on the other hand.[17] What both share is a scepticism about reformist proposals and a hostility to utopianism, but they do differ importantly. Clearly the former is a more radical position, calling for the abandonment of moral norms in the international realm (cf. Art and Waltz 1983: 6; Kennan 1954: 47–9). The second, although critical of cosmopolitan conceptions of political morality, does at least agree with cosmopolitans that political institutions should observe moral norms. We find both views in Morgenthau's work. Sometimes he writes that moral principles should not be applied to foreign policy. His more considered position, however, allows moral norms to influence foreign policy in two ways. First, Morgenthau argues that moral norms can and should operate as a constraint on what states can do in their foreign policy (1985: 249–56, 274). As he writes '[t]ake any number of examples from history and you will see that time and again statesmen have refrained from certain actions on moral grounds, actions they could have taken physically and which would have been in their interests' (1979: 2). Moral values simply rule out certain courses of action. One example of this, for Morgenthau, is the ethics of warfare. Certain moral rules, he claims, are observed, although he does add that these are waning (1985: 252–60). Second, he maintains that states have a moral duty to further their national interest. As he writes in his work *In Defense of the National Interest*, 'remember always that it is not only a political necessity but also a moral duty for a nation to follow in its dealings with other nations but one guiding star, one standard for thought, one rule for action: THE NATIONAL INTEREST' (1951: 242).[18] Foreign policy is thus a moral business.[19]

A second important point, one that is raised by the preceding point, concerns the concept of the 'national interest'. A full understanding of realism requires a clear understanding of this concept.[20] As Alexander Wendt notes, one can distinguish between 'objective' and 'subjective' conceptions of the national interest (1999: 234). The former defines a state's national interest in terms of certain specified ends—say, wealth or military power. Wendt, for example, maintains that a state's national interest comprises four components: 'physical survival, autonomy, and economic well-being', and 'collective self-esteem' (1999: 235, cf. pp. 235–7).[21] This objectivist approach can be contrasted with a second, subjectivist, conception. According to this approach, a state's national interest is defined in terms of the goals that that state seeks to advance. Both are open to question. One question to pose to objectivists is an epistemological one: how can one ascertain the interests of a state independently of its own wishes? By what epistemological method can one discern where a state's interests lie? On the other hand, the subjectivist conception is also problematic. Some realists argue that states fail to further their national interest. Morgenthau, for example, criticized American foreign policy for subordinating its interests to idealistic moral ventures. To make this criticism, however, conceptually presupposes that a state's interest is distinct from what it thinks it is, which requires the rejection of a subjectivist approach. Related to this, realists urge the state to advance the national interest: if the subjectivist conception were true this would be pointless for states, tautologically, seek their own interests.

A third significant feature of realism that should be borne in mind concerns the empirical and explanatory claims made by realists and it is that different realists give different reasons as to why states will pursue their national interest. Waltz provided an interesting and instructive classification in his important work *Man, the State and War* (1959). He divided explanatory accounts of global politics into three types. First image theories explain international phenomena by reference to human nature. Second image theories explain international phenomena by reference to domestic factors: states' internal structure affects international affairs. Third image theories explain international phenomena by reference to the structure of the international system. Many realists adopt a first image approach. Morgenthau, for example, postulates that human beings have a desire for power (1985: 3–4, 31, 38–40) and tends to argue, on this basis, that foreign policy should not be governed by ethical considerations.[22] Others, by contrast, adopt a third image account. One problem with first image theories is that they cannot explain why humans can be moral in domestic politics but cannot be moral in another realm such as international politics. If human nature is the key variable, how can it be that persons can be moral in some areas of human life but not in others? An additional factor other than human nature is required to explain the divergence and this shows that a first image explanation is insufficient.[23] Waltz himself favours a third image explanation, arguing that states behave the way they do because they are driven to do so by the international structure. His influential and important work *Theory of International Politics* is, perhaps, the clearest and most sophisticated expression of this perspective (1979).[24]

A fourth point about realism that should also be noted concerns the relationship between the realist ethical claim, on the one hand, and realist empirical/ explanatory claims on the other. Clearly, someone may affirm both the empirical claims and the ethical claim. Indeed, as we have already seen, some arguments for the ethical claim may well rely on realist factual propositions (as well as additional moral claims). To return to an argument cited above, one rationale underlying the state's pursuit of its national interest is that it cannot trust other states not to attack it and hence it is entitled to maximize its own power. To give some additional examples, realist arguments for the pursuit of the national interest and against cosmopolitan normative proposals are often predicated on empirical claims such as that: cosmopolitan ideals are unlikely to be successful, or that the transnational institutions favoured by some cosmopolitans will prove to be ineffectual or the plaything of powerful states. We should nonetheless recognize that the two claims (empirical and ethical) are conceptually distinct and are not logically tied to each other. Accordingly, one can affirm either claim whilst repudiating the other. One might, for instance, affirm the empirical claim but deny the ethical claim. One might, that is, think that states ought to pursue cosmopolitan ideals but also believe that they will not do so (Dower 1998: 20). One might, conversely, deny the realist empirical claim but hold to the realist ethical claim. One might, that is, think that states ought to pursue the national interest but that sometimes they do not. Indeed this is a common strain in realist analysis of American foreign policy. Morgenthau, for example, decries American politicians for being misled into idealistic and utopian moral missions that were catastrophic and counter-productive. Better, he thought, for states to pursue their own interests. He makes clear too that he thought that it was morally better for them to do so: as we have seen above, his view is that they have a moral obligation to further the national interest (1951: 242). So, although the rationale for realist ethical claims may sometimes draw on realist empirical claims, the two are logically independent of each other.

One final observation about most, if not all, realists concerns the relationship between domestic politics and international politics. Broadly speaking realists tend to think that states can adopt moral norms in the domestic realm but not in the international realm: there is then a clear demarcation (Morgenthau 1979: 10–11, 13; 1985: 13–16). As we have seen above, this claim is problematic for first image explanations of international relations for it is hard to see how a theory that explains conduct solely in terms of human nature can maintain that humans can cooperate within the state and yet also assert that they cannot cooperate at the international level. Nonetheless, many realists do want to maintain this difference. Realist thought in general emphasizes a strong contrast between the domestic and the international. To employ the terminology introduced above, we might say that realism's level-1 analysis can be contrasted with cosmopolitan approaches which are far more suspicious of the domestic/international distinction and which ask why the principles we hold in the domestic realm should not apply in the global realm too.

## III

A third perspective that we will encounter in this work is what I have termed the 'society of states' approach. This approach maintains that a just global order is one in which there are states and the states accept that they have moral duties to other states. It prescribes an ideal in which independent and equal states respect other states' right to independence and observe a norm of non-intervention. One important defender of this vision is Hedley Bull who articulates this ideal in his influential work _The Anarchical Society_ (1977; cf. also 2000a, b, c). Bull is a representative of what is sometimes referred to as the English School, a term used to refer to some primarily British based international relations theorists who argued for the promotion and preservation of a society of sovereign states bound together by a commitment to some common rules.[25] Other defenders of the society of states include Terry Nardin who in *Law, Morality and the Relations of States* argues against both realist and cosmopolitan conceptions of international political morality. He draws a distinction between purposive and practical conceptions of international politics (1983). Under the former, states should pursue and promote cosmopolitan ideals. Under the latter, however, states should abjure such goals and should respect other states' sovereignty. Nardin favours the practical approach, arguing that it provides order and protects diversity. Other important representatives of the society of states are Robert Jackson who, in *The Global Covenant*, defends a world of states (2000) and Mervyn Frost who provides a different vindication of the society of states in his work *Ethics and International Relations* (1996). Aspects of these works will be evaluated in later chapters and so I shall refrain from analysing them more here.

Before proceeding further, it is worth drawing attention to one other thinker who takes a broadly similar approach. In his Amnesty Lecture on the Law of Peoples and in his subsequent book with that title, Rawls defends what he terms a 'society of peoples' (1993*a*, 1999*b*). He makes clear his rejection of realism and cosmopolitanism and calls for a world constituted by decent well-ordered peoples (1999*b*: 46–8, 119–20). Rawls himself, it should be noted, would resist the term a 'society of states' for he distinguishes between 'peoples' and 'states' and rejects a system of states in favour of a society of well-ordered peoples. Rawls's distinction between 'peoples' and 'states' is, however, not clear. Two versions of the distinction can be found in his work. Sometimes, the distinction concerns the legal powers at their disposal. Rawls says that states have two legal powers: 'the right to go to war in pursuit of state policies' (1999*b*: 25) and the right to 'unrestricted internal autonomy' (1999*b*: 27). Neither legal right is possessed by peoples (1999*b*: 25–7). At other times, Rawls distinguishes between states and peoples, not in terms of the legal powers they possess, but in terms of their motivations. States, he avers, are motivated by their 'rationality' alone and lack a sense of 'reasonableness'. Peoples, by contrast, are 'reasonable' (1999*b*: 27–9) and, unlike states, possess 'moral motives' (1999*b*: 17). These two conceptions of the distinction are, of course, distinct and not coextensive. A political regime may possess the two legal powers (and hence be a state according to the first version) and yet be reasonable and not driven wholly by its rational ends (and hence not be a state according to the second version). In addition, a political regime may not possess the legal powers to wage war for its own gain and to treat its subjects as it wishes (and hence not be a state on the first version). It may, however, exceed its legal powers and be thoroughly unreasonable in its foreign policy, subordinating others in its pursuit of its rational self-interest (and hence be a state on the second conception).[26]

Neither version of the distinction is, however, sustainable. The first is implausible: the assertion that states necessarily possess the two powers Rawls

or national self-determination. Nationalism also clearly contrasts with the two statist perspectives since it argues for the primacy of the *nation* rather than the *state*. It does not, for example, call for a society of states: it calls for national autonomy. Nationalists will thus be critical of a system of states that does not grant nations autonomy, either in the form of their own state or in the form of devolution. In addition, by contrast with realists, nationalists tend to think that the global realm should be governed by moral principles. It is not an amoral realm.

To gain a better understanding of nationalism we need a clear understanding of the concept of a 'nation'. What, then, is a nation? As a number of commentators have noted, one can find within nationalist writings three conceptions of the nation: what one might term the *statist*, the *ethnic,* and the *cultural* conception.[34] Let us examine each in turn. On a *statist* conception, a nation is a state. As is commonly recognized, in ordinary usage people often equate nations and states. Terms such as 'the United Nations', 'international relations', and the 'national interest', for example, all use the term 'nation' to refer to a 'state'. One might add that on one variant of this *statist* position, nations are not strictly speaking states but are, rather, the people who belong to a state. On this construal of nationality, the French nation refers to the citizens of France.

Statist conceptions suffer from two problems. The first is that to define a nation as a state leads to some absurd conclusions. For instance, on a statist conception, the concept of a multi-national state must be translated as a 'multi-state state' which is clearly incoherent. In addition, on a *statist* conception, the familiar concept of a 'nation-state' would have to be translated as a 'state-state', which is simply repetitive and adds nothing to calling it a state. However, when someone describes a country as a nation-state they are saying more than that it is a state: they are saying that it is a particular kind of state and the *statist* conception clearly cannot capture this. The first problem then is that the *statist* conception cannot provide plausible definitions of straightforward notions like a nation-state or a multi-national state. A second problem with the *statist* conception is that it is not true to the usage of nationalist political philosophers or to national independence movements. The latter are committed to securing greater autonomy for a non-state community. They are not arguing for the autonomy of the state but for the autonomy of a group of people.

Let us consider then a second conception of the nation, that which defines a nation in terms of a group of people who share a common ethnic identity. This *ethnic* conception is, however, no more plausible than the previous one. Two considerations tell against it. First there are many relatively uncontroversial cases of nations that share no common ethnicity. To be American, for example, is not to belong to any one ethnic group. The same might be said of many other nations. Second, the members of an ethnic group can include members of a number of different nations. Ethnic groups, such as Jews, can and do straddle numerous nations. It is true that some members of a few nations claim that their nation is defined in ethnic terms. For example, at the turn of the twentieth century, some conceived of the French nation in ethnic terms and maintained that one could not be Jewish and French. However, that some believe that members of their nation share a common ethnic identity does not show that their nation does in fact do so: their belief may well be mistaken. Indeed, such beliefs are often mistaken and many are ignorant of the diverse ethnic origins of their nation.

In the light of the defects of these two preceding accounts of a nation, many contemporary nationalists advocate a third and final conception of nationality, what I have termed the *cultural* conception.[35] Tamir and Miller, for example, have both found the two preceding accounts unsatisfactory and have argued that nations should be defined in cultural terms: a nation, on this conception, is a group of people who share a common culture.[36] This is evident in Miller's definition of a nation as 'a community (1) constituted by shared belief and mutual commitment, (2) extended in history, (3) active in character, (4) connected to a particular territory, and (5) marked off from other communities by its distinct public culture' (1995: 27, cf. also pp. 22–7).[37]

At this point in the proceedings, it is worth noting one important consequence of the distinction between states and nations. Nationalists and statists both distinguish between the 'global' realm and the 'domestic' realm. However, they necessarily draw the line between the domestic and the global in a different way. For nationalists, obviously, domestic political theory is concerned with issues within the nation, whereas for statists, equally obviously, domestic political theory is concerned with issues within the state. The critical point is that given that the borders of nations frequently do not map onto the borders of states, it follows that their account of what is included in 'domestic' politics and what is included in 'global' politics will be different. Nationalists and statists thus have a different conception of the 'domestic' realm and a different conception of where non-domestic theory begins.

Having considered various definitions of nationality and contemporary exponents of nationalism we should complete the analysis by noting that there is a long tradition of earlier nationalist thought. This would include thinkers such as Guiseppe Mazzini and Johann Herder. Nationalist sentiments can also be found in liberal writers like John Stuart Mill and T. H. Green.

## V

This concludes my account of the four perspectives that will be employed at various points in this work. Before continuing further it should be noted that others provide other distinct typologies. Chris Brown (1992) and Janna Thompson (1992), for example, employ a twofold categorization, distinguishing between cosmopolitanism and communitarianism. Whilst like them, I think 'cosmopolitanism' is a useful category it is, I believe, helpful to disaggregate 'communitarianism' into realism, society of states, and nationalism. To do otherwise occludes important differences in values. To give one example, there is a great deal of difference between, on the one hand, those who extol the virtues of realpolitik and the pursuit of the national interest, and, on the other hand, those who emphasize the central moral importance of national identity and the rights of nations. First, there is, obviously, a clear difference in their fundamental values: Miller and Tamir are committed to the rights and duties of nations, not states. In addition to this, their critique of cosmopolitan views is not, by contrast with realist views, predicated on claims about the prevalence of power and the impossibility of moral conduct at the international level. Furthermore, we find that differences at the level of basic values generate differences at the policy level. Realists are, indeed, highly critical of the nationalist commitment to national self-determination on the grounds that it may lead to international instability. For these kinds of reasons it is unhelpful to subsume realism, nationalism, and 'society of states' theories all together under the heading of 'communitarianism'.

If we turn now to other taxonomies, we can see that some writers employ a threefold categorization. Martin Wight (1991), for example, differentiates between Kantians (revolutionists), Grotians (rationalists), and Hobbesians (realists).[38] Beitz, too, employs a tripartite division in his important work *Political Theory and International Relations* (1999c).[39] My categorization follows his in distinguishing between cosmopolitanism, realism, and the 'morality of states' (what I have termed the 'society of states'). My only disagreement with Beitz's categories is that I believe that it is useful to include 'nationalism' since none of the three other perspectives can capture the fundamental importance of *nations* that writers like Miller and Tamir emphasize.

# VI

Having outlined four competing traditions I want to make clear my position on the importance of identifying competing philosophical traditions. One might distinguish between three ways of writing on any set of related ethical issues. According to one approach one focuses on *thinkers* and assesses their work; according to a second, one focuses on *traditions of thought* and assesses the weaknesses and strengths of that tradition; and according to a third, one focuses on *arguments* for and against certain courses of action.

This work adopts the third approach. Basing one's analysis on the works of a number of great thinkers is no doubt instructive but it may be repetitive if two or more philosophers advance similar lines of reasoning. In addition, it is often incomplete because there is no guarantee that the philosophers selected cover all relevant considerations. If we turn now to the second approach this too is problematic. It relies heavily on being able to identify who is a member of a tradition and who is not. Furthermore, it makes sense only if the members of a tradition speak with one voice on all issues. This quite clearly is not the case: to take a domestic example, Rawls (1999c) and Robert Nozick (1974) are both liberals but there is a dramatic difference between them on matters of distributive justice. Neither of the first two methods thus serves the aims of this book. Given its aims—to defend certain conclusions and to analyse prevailing arguments on each of the issues listed above—this book falls into the third category. What I take to be of fundamental importance is the question 'what should we do?'

Such an approach, however, benefits from drawing on a knowledge of competing traditions of thought. This obtains for two reasons. The first is simply that arguments for and against certain propositions are located within philosophical traditions and we gain a better understanding of the arguments by understanding the tradition as a whole. The second is that a philosophical perspective may generate arguments that apply to one issue (such as civil and political rights) and also to another (like the ethics of warfare or the case for intervention). What we are witnessing then is not a series of unconnected arguments applying to these issues but, rather, the application of a tradition to a number of them. So, rather than see some separate arguments for human rights, say, and then some other arguments for global distributive justice, and then some distinct arguments for global political institutions, what we see is a philosophical tradition at work that draws on similar reasoning to speak to a number of issues. The arguments considered apply to more than one topic: they spread over a variety of them, without necessarily applying to everything. The philosophical examination of ethical issues can, thus, profitably draw on an account of various different traditions of thought.

This claim should not be misunderstood, however, and I want now to stress the limitations on the role that can be ascribed to traditions of thought. What the two preceding considerations do not entail is that one should seek to examine all the issues from each of the four perspectives. This holds for three reasons. First, in outlining these four perspectives, I am not claiming that each of them has a position on each of the six issues to be examined. We should not, for example, expect there to be a 'nationalist' line on all the issues to be examined. To think that there would be is to succumb to something similar to what Quentin Skinner has termed 'the mythology of doctrines', where the latter refers to 'the expectation that each classic writer (in the history, say, of ethical or political ideas) will be found to enunciate some doctrine on each of the topics regarded as constitutive of his subject'. As Skinner continues '[i]t is a dangerously short step from being under the influence (however unconsciously) of such a paradigm to "finding" a given author's doctrines on all the mandatory themes' (1988: 32, cf. pp. 32–8). As reported above, my two aims in this book are (a) to defend a specific cosmopolitan political morality and (b) to provide a comprehensive analysis of six pressing issues and the arguments adduced in the debates on these issues. Issues, then, are in the driving seat and a philosophical tradition will be examined only if it sheds light on a specific issue. My point about the four traditions given above is that they speak on many, if not always all, of the subjects examined in this book.[40]

Second, too much concern with philosophical traditions leads to a fruitless obsession as to whether philosopher X is, say, really really a cosmopolitan or not. The four traditions sketched above are intended as a rough rule of thumb. There are two points here. First, we should not lose sight of the fact that what matters above all is the *arguments for and against* certain courses of action or political proposals. What matters is what we should do (what are the arguments for and against certain courses of action) and not which side won. Second, to concentrate on appraising philosophical perspectives assumes a chimerical precision so that one can say that Bull, for example, definitely is not a realist. As is widely recognized, and my characterizations above have made clear, traditions are not normally characterized by such clearly demarcated borders. We should avoid a narcissism that is concerned not with what should be done but with which 'tribe' someone belongs to.

Finally, we should note against a tradition-driven approach, that this encourages people to think that traditions are monolithic entities that possess distinct and separate identities. It thus militates against the idea that traditions may overlap or even converge on some issues. As such it tends to obscure commonalities.

Traditions, then, should play a role in our understanding of the ethical issues explored by *Justice Beyond Borders* but they should not be employed uncritically and they should not dominate our thinking. What the preceding analysis of four traditions has, hopefully, achieved then is to set out the intellectual context in which many of the arguments to be examined are located. Further, it has provided clear definitions of concepts that are employed throughout the rest of the book—including concepts such as a 'nation', a 'people' (as defined by Rawls), the 'society of states', and the 'national interest'.

## VII

Having outlined the aims of the book and its method, let us turn to its structure. The book is structured as follows. First, any global political theory must start by asking whether there are indeed universal moral values. Our analysis begins, then, in Chapter 2, by addressing precisely this question. It considers three unconvincing arguments in defence of universal moral values before developing two more persuasive arguments. It also examines but rejects nine arguments for cultural relativism, arguing that they are either unconvincing or they collapse into a brand of universalism.

Having argued that there are universal moral values, the next logical step is to ask what these universal moral values are. This question is pursued in the next two chapters. Chapter 3 examines claims that there are what I shall term universal principles of *civil and political justice*. By the latter, I mean those principles that specify what rights people have to what freedoms. The questions examined, then, include: what civil and political human rights, if any, are there?, what are the most persuasive arguments for such rights?, and what are the objections against civil and political human rights? The chapter presents an analysis of human rights, criticizes three cosmopolitan arguments for civil and political human rights, and then defends a fourth cosmopolitan argument. It then examines an alternative defence of civil and political human rights developed by Rawls before evaluating four challenges to civil and political human rights. Chapter 3 thus argues for universal human rights to certain civil and political liberties.

The book then moves from *civil and political justice* to *distributive justice*. Chapter 4 accordingly examines what universal principles of distributive justice (if any) there are. It begins with an analysis of three types of argument for cosmopolitan principles of distributive justice before suggesting and defending four principles of cosmopolitan distributive justice. The chapter then considers five objections, some of them outlined by Rawls and others by nationalist political thinkers like Miller. It concludes with an appraisal of, and response to, realist analyses of global distributive justice.

Having argued that there are cosmopolitan principles of *civil and political justice* and cosmopolitan principles of *distributive justice*, this leads logically to the question 'if one affirms cosmopolitan principles of justice, what kind of world order should one accept?' Should there be a system of states? Or should there be global political institutions? And should nations have autonomy including even statehood? Chapter 5 pursues these questions. In doing so it develops a cosmopolitan perspective on political institutions, giving two reasons as to why we should accept a multi-level global order, including global political institutions, states, and sub-state political authorities (a 'cosmopolitan democracy'). Having defended this political framework, the chapter considers five challenges to this ideal before then exploring four arguments for national self-determination. It concludes that a cosmopolitan political order should grant a very heavily qualified role to national self-determination.

The preceding chapters have concerned ideal theory for they examine accounts of what justice requires and what the best institutional arrangements are. An account of global political theory would, however, be radically incomplete if it were silent on what should happen in non-ideal circumstances. We might divide non-ideal circumstances into two kinds—first, those where a political regime is wronged and, second, those where there is injustice within a political regime. Accordingly, the next two chapters explore these two kinds of non-ideal theory.

Chapter 6 examines whether a political regime may wage war if it, or its members are wronged by an external agent, where this might include other political regimes or international terrorists. (The phrase 'political regime' rather than 'state' is employed because it is more inclusive. The actors in question may not be a state: they might be an international organization like the United Nations. In addition the question at stake arises even in a world without states which is constituted by alternative distributions of power and authority.) Chapter 6 thus asks the following questions: 'when, if ever, may political regimes wage war?' and 'what means can they justly employ in waging war?' The chapter begins by discussing prevailing state-centric conceptions of the just war before moving on to analyse cosmopolitan contributions to just war theory and to construct and defend a cosmopolitan account of just war. It concludes with a critique of realist insights into the ethics of war.

Having examined one kind of non-ideal situation, we then examine in Chapter 7 a second kind, namely injustice within a political regime. The chapter focuses on the question of whether it is ever justified to intervene in the affairs of another political regime. To answer this question, the chapter begins with an analysis of humanitarian intervention before outlining a cosmopolitan argument for the right, and indeed duty, of humanitarian intervention. It then considers four arguments for a norm of non-intervention presented by 'society of states' theorists, realists, and nationalists. The chapter suggests, on cosmopolitan grounds, that humanitarian intervention is defensible under certain conditions.

In short, then, *Justice Beyond Borders* defends global norms of *civil and political justice* (human rights to civil and political freedoms) and *distributive justice* (subsistence rights, equality of opportunity, a principle of equal remuneration for equal work, and a priority for the poor). Drawing on these it defends a non-statist political order, calling for accountable global political institutions. It then supplies an account of the principles that should govern the relations between political regimes, generating principles that should guide the waging and conduct of war and principles that should guide the practice of humanitarian intervention. As I have said above, though, in reaching these conclusions, I hope also to have given a comprehensive analysis of the most significant philosophical treatments of the six issues examined.

# VIII

Before proceeding further, there is one additional preliminary point I would like to make. I have outlined two aims of this book. A third sub-theme I would like to emphasize is that the topics examined in this work are so closely intertwined that one cannot satisfactorily deal with some of the issues without also engaging with some of the others. Since this point is of great importance it is worth labouring it at some length. To see the way in which the issues are inextricably interlinked consider some examples. Consider, for instance, the topic of civil and political human rights (Chapter 3). To answer the question of whether there are human rights one needs to have an answer to the logically prior question of whether there are any universal values (the subject matter of Chapter 2). And a treatment of human rights leads naturally to the question of what if anything we can do to prevent human rights violations (the subject matter of Chapter 5) and also to the question of whether we can intervene to protect human rights (the subject matter of Chapter 7). It raises, moreover, the question of who should bear the costs of the international protection of human rights and this in turn raises questions of distributive justice (the subject matter of Chapter 4). In addition to this it also bears on the nature of just warfare (Chapter 6) for accounts of a just war generally ascribe certain rights to non-combatants (e.g. the right not to be directly attacked) and, more generally, to all persons (e.g. a right not to be tortured or napalmed).

The same interlinked phenomenon can be seen by examining other topics. Consider humanitarian intervention (Chapter 7). To evaluate the arguments for and against humanitarian intervention, one must consider whether there are civil and political human rights since one common argument for intervention is predicated on the need to protect such human rights (the subject matter of Chapter 3). One should, moreover, address arguments for global principles of distributive justice (the subject matter of Chapter 4) since some of the arguments for and against intervention presuppose a view about the nature of global distributive justice. It is, moreover, also hard to assess the arguments for and against intervention without evaluating more generally the nature and value of sovereignty (the subject matter of Chapter 5).

The examples could continue. For instance, consider Chapter 5, which examines what political structures are appropriate. It is implausible to maintain that this question could be satisfactorily addressed without considering what, if any, civil and political human rights (Chapter 3) or economic rights (Chapter 4) individuals are entitled to. Given the enormous impact that political institutions can have on people's rights it would be bizarre to consider what political institutions are appropriate in isolation from the question of what specific rights individuals have.

My point, then, is that the topics considered form an interlinked whole and it is artificial to separate them from one another. Indeed the later chapters presuppose the earlier chapters. Questions of global political morality are not neatly carved up into separate distinct questions—such as, 'is intervention ever justified?'—that do not bear on any other questions. This presupposes an artificial separation of realms.

Such a conclusion is, I think, not just true but it may also allay fears that this book seeks to undertake too much. Someone might argue that the subject matter of this book is unduly ambitious because one cannot hope to cover the six topics examined here in just one book. The earlier point, about the interlinked nature of global political theory, constitutes a partial reply to this concern: the subject matter *is* dauntingly complex but it is unavoidable to treat it in any other way.

A second, and related, point in response to the worry that one cannot give an adequate analysis of the six topics examined here in the space of one book is that much of the groundwork for some topics is done in other chapters. It is, for instance, misleading to think that Chapter 6, alone, deals with all the ethical issues surrounding warfare since it draws on analyses of consequentialism and individual rights (topics discussed earlier in Chapters 3 and 4) as well as analyses of the rights of political regimes (a topic examined in Chapter 5). Similarly, it is misleading to think that Chapter 7, alone, deals with humanitarian intervention for much of the analysis needed to evaluate humanitarian intervention is conducted in the preceding chapters, such as what human rights persons can claim (Chapters 3 and 4) and what criteria one can employ to judge the value of political regimes (Chapter 5).

A third point to make is that my aim in the book is to outline the general principles that should inform the issues considered (and in doing so to analyse how principles that pertain to the global realm relate to those that pertain to the domestic realm). It is not seeking to provide detailed definitive solutions to each of the questions addressed. To take one example, the analysis of intervention in Chapter 7 outlines the conditions that should be met if intervention is justified but does not apply this in depth to recent interventions, like the NATO intervention in Kosovo. It articulates the principles that must be met and their rationales but does not generate specific concrete conclusions. To use the terminology coined earlier, its primary concern is with level-1 and level-2 analysis and not with level-3 analysis.

Having given an overview of the aims, structure, and method of this book, let us now turn to the issues at stake.

## NOTES

1. It is also not an account of the history of political thought and international relations. For two excellent works which do provide analyses of previous political thinkers' treatment of international relations see Boucher (1998) and Doyle (1997).
2. See, relatedly, Martin Wight's definition of 'international theory' (1966a: 18).
3. I regret that I have been unable to engage with Allen Buchanan's recent work *Justice, Legitimacy, and Self-Determination* (2003). I came across this important book just before *Justice Beyond Borders* was due to be sent to the publishers. In the short time available, I have briefly noted in the text below some points of contact. His book promises to be a major contribution to the field and I hope, therefore, in later work to engage more fully with this book and to devote to it the attention that it merits.
4. I have omitted two footnotes from this quotation. The first [placed after the word *'persons'*] notes the difference between *persons* and *human beings*. The second [placed after the word *'equally'*] raises, but does not pursue, the question of the interests of past and future generations. See Pogge (1994a: 117, fns. 1 and 2).
5. For a powerful statement of his consequentialism see Mei (1974 [original date unknown], bk. XII, ch. XLVIII, p. 237).
6. For a history of earlier conceptions of cosmopolitanism and, in particular, institutional/legal conceptions see Derek Heater (1996).
7. On the affinities between liberalism and cosmopolitanism see Jones (1999: 15–16).
8. Rawls's theory is examined in some depth in Ch. 3, Sect. VIII and Ch. 4, Sects VII–VIII.
9. Although cf. also his later reassessment of this position: Waldron (2000: 227–8, 231–6).
10. Scheffler contrasts this kind of cosmopolitanism with a cosmopolitanism about justice (1999: 255–76).
11. See in this context Waldron's discussion (1992) for it is precisely in this context that he articulates his conception of cosmopolitanism.
12. This statement will be qualified later. Chapter 4 examines arguments for cosmopolitan principles of distributive justice that are predicated on certain claims about the extent of economic globalization (Ch. 4, Sect. III).
13. For useful discussions of realism cf. Donnelly (1992: 85–111; 2000, esp. pp. 161–92) and Michael J. Smith (1986).
14. See further Morgenthau (1951: 23–8, 92–113; 1985: 37–51). Cf. also (1951: 113–28).
15. Morgenthau, for example, writes: 'if you do not accept the principle that this is *homo homini lupus*, one man is to another like a wolf, then you will not survive' (1979: 11). Again: 'when society is no longer capable of protecting our survival, and we have to take care of that survival ourselves, the concrete moral principles by which we live are

bound to change. Otherwise, we will be killed by somebody who has fewer scruples than we have' (1979: 15).

16. These cursory characterizations are, of course, very crude. For good discussions of Machiavelli and Hobbes see Boucher (1998) and Doyle (1997).

17. This point is also noted by Darrel Moellendorf (2002*a*: 143). For an illuminating discussion of realists' equivocations and oscillations on this point see Donnelly (1992: 93–9, esp. pp. 96–9).

18. See also his discussion of 'the moral dignity of the national interest' (1951: 33, cf. pp. 33–9) and (1985: 12).

19. See, further, Morgenthau (1979: 1; 1985: 7). See also Kennan (1954: 61).

20. The very concept of the national interest as it is used by realists, note, elides the distinction between a nation and a state for they employ it to refer to the interests of the state.

21. Wendt draws on, and expands, an analysis of the national interest by George and Keohane. He draws from their paper the first three of the four interests listed in the text. For the reference see Wendt (1999: 235 fn. 124).

22. He does, however, also make second image claims. He argues, for example, that states are now less inclined to honour moral constraints on how to wage war. He explains this change in part in second image terms, arguing that many states before were governed by an aristocratic elite who believed in honour and chivalry but that with the democratization of the state (a change in the internal character of the state) this sense of honour no longer informed foreign policy (1985: 260–6). A second factor he adduces to explain this change is the rise of nationalism and he maintains that the latter is destroying international society (1985: 266–74).

23. For Waltz's critique of first image explanation see (1959: 26–41).

24. For other distinguished third image theories see Mearsheimer (1990: 5–56; 1995: 5–49).

25. For a good history of the English school see Dunne (1998). For an assessment of it see Caney (2001*b*).

26. Someone might doubt whether such a regime is possible on the grounds that states cannot perform actions which they are not legally empowered to perform. This doubt is, however, misplaced. It is perfectly possible for someone to act in ways that exceed her legal powers. She may, for example, vote twice in the same election if she impersonates someone else or she may purchase goods using a stolen credit card. In both cases she performs actions that she does not have the legal right or power to do.

27. Rawls seems to concede this (1999*b*: 27, 79).

28. For similar objections to Rawls's analysis of 'peoples' see Allen Buchanan (2000: 698–700); O'Neill (2001: 186–8). For an earlier discussion of this issue see Caney (2002*c*: 181).

29. Proponents of the 'society of states' themselves situate their approach in this way, cf. for example Wight (1991, esp. pp. 7–24). Bull also adopts this tripartite framework: cf; Bull (1977: 24–7; 2000*a*: 79–94). Bull credits this classification to Wight (1966*b*): cf. Bull (1977: 322 fn. 1).

30. See, further, Alderson and Hurrell (2000: 7–15); Dunne (1998: 142, 146–55); Wheeler (1992: 463–77); Wheeler and Dunne (1996: 91–101, 104–7).

31. See further Bull's distinction between an international system (where states interact) and an international society (where states share common values and recognize the sovereignty of other states) (1977: 9–16, cf. particularly pp. 13–16 on the society of states).

32. The phrase comes from the title of one of Miller's articles, 'The Ethical Significance of Nationality' (1988).

33. For a third important contribution to recent nationalist theory see Margaret Canovan (1996a). Cf. also her (1996b).

34. This classification combines two common distinctions, namely that between civic (what I have termed statist) and ethnic nationalism (cf. Smith 1991: 8–14) and that between political (statist) and cultural nationalism (Gilbert 1996: 102–18; Hutchinson 1994: 40–63). For further pertinent discussion on political and cultural nationalism see de-Shalit (1996: 906–20). This threefold distinction is explicitly invoked by Kai Nielsen in his article entitled 'Cultural Nationalism, Neither Ethnic nor Civic' (1996–7: 42–52).

35. For Miller and Tamir's repudiation of the statist conception see Miller (1995: 18–19) and Tamir (1993: 58–63). For their repudiation of the ethnic conception see Miller (1995: 19–21) and Tamir (1993: 65). In his 'Self-Government Revisited' Barry also criticizes statist and ethnic conceptions of nationality: see Barry (1991a: 168–70, 172–3) for why nationality is distinct from ethnicity and (1991a: 171–2) for why nationality is not equivalent to membership of a state. See further (1991a: 170) in particular on the nature of nationality.

36. In referring to this third conception as a cultural conception I am taking my prompt from Miller, Nielsen, and Tamir. All three consider ethnic and statist conceptions and, rejecting both, all invoke the concept of culture in their characterization of nationality. See Miller (1995: 25, 27), Nielsen (1996–7: 42–52), and Tamir (1993, esp. p. 67, but more generally 1993: 63–9; 1991: 572–80).

37. This conception is not without difficulty. One problem with defining nationality in terms of culture is that we then need to explain how national cultures and non-national cultures differ. (For a related observation see Mason 1995: 246).

38. See, further, note 27.

39. For another, but quite different, threefold categorization see Doyle (1997). Doyle distinguishes between realists, liberals, and socialists.

40. A note to the reader: the typology has least relevance to the issues discussed in Ch. 2. It will, though, inform to a much greater extent the discussion of the remaining chapters.

# 2

# Universalism

This chapter explores the question of whether there are universal moral values. Are there moral values that apply to all persons? Or is morality culture relative? If there are no universal moral values, what sort of moral values, if any, are there? These questions are clearly of considerable practical import. Many politicians and political activists assert there to be universal values and on this basis are highly critical of their own country and of other countries. They are joined in this by many moral and political philosophers. Onora O'Neill, for example, outlines and defends a universalist perspective in *Towards Justice and Virtue* (1996). Similarly, Brian Barry (1995*a*) and Jürgen Habermas (1986, 1992*a*, 1992*b*, 1993) both seek to ground a universalist political morality. Others, by contrast, eschew such a transcultural perspective, arguing that a universalist point of view is unattainable or, if attainable, highly undesirable. They canvass instead a relativist approach, according to which morality requires fidelity to the norms and values of one's community. According to this approach, we should adopt a more contextualist conception of moral argument and practical reason (cf. for example Walzer 1983).

Before giving more precise definitions of universalism and relativism and evaluating the arguments for and against them, it is important to make a preliminary point about the role of this chapter in relation to later chapters. It is common to contrast human rights, on the one hand, with cultural relativism, on the other. One might thus expect human rights and cultural relativism to be discussed together in the same chapter. In what follows, however, I will adopt a different approach. This chapter examines the general question of whether there are universal values or whether cultural relativism is correct. Its focus is on arguments for and against moral universalism *as a whole*. The next two chapters then examine two specific types of proposed universal values: Chapter 3 examines the plausibility of universal principles of civil and political justice and Chapter 4 examines the plausibility of universal principles of distributive justice. This chapter is, thus, a necessary backdrop to the later chapters.

The central reason for proceeding in this way stems from the fact that there are universalist theories which do not assert human rights and it is hence wrong to equate universalism with human rights. One might, for instance, be a universalist and affirm an authoritarian morality (such as an anti-liberal religion) which one thinks should be applied everywhere on this earth. Theories of human rights are, then, but some of the members of the class of universalist theories. With this in mind, we can discern three reasons for examining the arguments for and against universalism first before proceeding to consider the arguments for civil, political, and economic human rights. First, on a methodological level, it makes sense to consider if there are, as many think, any convincing arguments against universalism as a whole before moving on to consider specific universalist claims. If there is a compelling general argument against all universalist approaches then there is little point in examining whether any particular universalist claims are true. Second, the implications of the critiques of universalism are wider than the conclusion that there are no human rights. Accordingly, it would not fully recognize the significance of this conclusion to treat it *merely* as a refutation of human rights for it would be a more wide-ranging conclusion than that. A third reason for not discussing human rights and cultural relativism in the same chapter is, as we shall see later, that there are many critiques of human rights that are not relativist but which affirm universal values. Discussing human rights and relativism in separate chapters frees up room and thereby enables us to consider non-relativist challenges to human rights. A chapter that considered human rights and both relativist and non-relativist objections would be unmanageably large. For all these reasons it is useful to deal with universalism and cultural relativism first.[1]

This chapter takes the following form: Section I engages in a conceptual analysis of the terms 'moral universalism' and 'cultural relativism'. The following four sections then critically examine four arguments for moral universalism, finding three unpersuasive and one more promising (II–V). This is then followed by an analysis of nine challenges to moral universalism (VI–XIV). None of these challenges, it is argued, is persuasive. Some rest on implausible assumptions or misconceive the nature of universalism. Others, it is claimed, actually, on closer inspection, themselves rest on moral univeralism. In the course of examining the objections to universalism, the case for universalism is, it is claimed, strengthened further.

# I

Let us begin, then, by defining 'moral universalism' and 'cultural relativism', starting with moral universalism. Moral universalism, as I shall employ this term, maintains that there are some moral values that are valid across the world. If X is a moral universal then X applies to all persons: everyone is bound by, say, the duty not to murder or the duty not to rape. O'Neill provides a useful framework for defining universalism, identifying two key features. The first concerns 'form': universalists claim that the same values apply, without exception, to all members of a group. The second concerns 'scope': universalists claim that the relevant group is 'all persons'. Putting these two together, universalists claim that the same values apply, without exception, to all persons (1996: 11, 74).[2]

Thus defined, universalism is a familiar doctrine. O'Neill herself defends a universalist approach. She maintains that principles are valid if they can be universalized (1996: 51–9) and, drawing on this idea of universalizability, she argues that there should be universal principles prohibiting injury (1996: 163–8, cf. further pp.168–78). An alternative conception of universalism, defended by Brian Barry, claims that there are universally applicable principles of justice, where these are defined as those principles that cannot be rejected by any reasonable person, and on this basis he defends several civil, political, and economic human rights (1995*a*, esp. pp. 3–7).

Several points are worth noting about this characterization of universalism. First, it is of vital importance to distinguish between what Charles Larmore terms a 'universalist content', on the one hand, and 'universal justifiability', on the other (1996: 57, cf. generally pp. 57–9). The former refers to values that apply to everyone in the world and conforms to the definition of universalism introduced at the beginning of this section. We might term it 'universalism of scope and form', or more briefly 'universalism of scope'. The second brand of universalism, by contrast, refers to values that can be justified to everyone in the world in terms that they would accept. It claims that there are values that can be justified to everyone in the sense that everyone would accept the justification. We might term this 'universalism of justification'.[3] These two kinds of universalism are very different and are not coextensive. One way of seeing this is to note that we can combine a rejection of universalism of justification with an affirmation of universalism of scope. Consider, for example, someone who thinks that morality requires being faithful to one's traditions and who rejects the possibility of being able to persuade everyone of the rightness of their morality. Suppose, however, that the content of their moral scheme includes moral principles which are intended to apply to all (such as that all persons have rights). Such a person affirms one kind of moral universalism (universalism of scope) but denies another (universalism of justification): they 'affirm a set of duties binding on all without supposing they must be justifiable to all' (1996: 57). This is indeed Larmore's view (1996: 57–9).[4]

This distinction, we might note, is not particular to Larmore. Thomas Pogge draws a similar distinction.[5] In *Realizing Rawls* he points out that a moral ideal can be non-universal and parochial in two distinct ways. First, it might have a parochial source (it can only be justified to members of our culture). This is the opposite of universalism of justification. Second, an ideal might have a parochial (that is, non-universal) scope, applying only to members of one culture (1989: 212–13). This is the opposite of universalism of scope. As Pogge points out, these two are quite distinct for one may hold moral ideals grounded in the values of 'our' culture but which make claims about all persons. As he puts it, '[o]ur considered judgments support a conception of justice whose scope is universal, even though its present appeal is not' (1989: 270).[6]

This distinction—between universalism of scope and universalism of justification—is a pivotal one and, as we shall see, critiques of universalism frequently fail to distinguish between them. The key concept, for the purposes of this work, is universalism of scope, for it is this position that is affirmed by all universalists (although some may also affirm universalism of justification).

Religious universalists, for instance, think that their values should hold across the whole world. Similarly, as noted above, this is the kind of universalism affirmed by Barry and O'Neill, both of whom maintain that their principles of justice should apply to all. Another leading universalist, Martha Nussbaum, also affirms universalism of scope. Nussbaum identifies some key human goods that she claims are common to all human beings and, on this basis, defends principles of justice that include all in their scope (1992, 1993, 1999, 2000a, 2002). If we turn now from specific thinkers to more general concepts, we should also record that the concept of human rights is another example of universalism of scope. Proponents of human rights assert that one value (rights) should be applied, without exception, to all persons. They, thus, affirm a universalism of scope without necessarily being committed to universal justi-fication.[7] This point is brought out nicely by Beitz who writes: 'To say that human rights are "universal" is not to claim that they are necessarily either accepted by or acceptable to everyone, given their other political and ethical beliefs. Human rights are supposed to be universal in the sense that they apply to or may be claimed by everyone' (2001: 274). Another eminent example of a universalist theory is, of course, utilitarianism for it applies the same principle, without exception, to all persons (and indeed, all sentient beings). As such, it observes universal form and universal scope.

It should, of course, also be recorded that some universalists *also* affirm a version of universalism of justification. Contractarian thinkers like Scanlon (1998), for example, claim that correct moral principles are ones that no one can reasonably reject. Moreover, Barry, drawing on Scanlon's theory, maintains that correct *principles of justice* are ones that no one can reasonably reject (1995a).[8] Similarly, Jürgen Habermas, another eminent universalist, argues that valid moral norms are those that free and equal persons consent to in an 'ideal speech situation' (1986, 1992a, 1992b, 1993). He, therefore, endorses a univer-salism of scope (the principles of the ideal speech situation should apply to all) but also a universalism of justification (decisions are valid only if they command the consent of free and equal persons).[9] So the point of the distinction is not to dismiss universalism of justification. It is, rather, to note both that universalism of scope and universalism of justification are importantly different and that all the leading universalists affirm universalism of scope. Hereafter, the term universalism shall be used to mean 'universalism of scope'.

A second key feature of universalism is that it maintains only that some values are universal: it refrains from claiming that all are. This is in conformity with leading universalists such as Barry who, whilst stating that some values are uni-versal, insist that other moral norms may legitimately differ in different cultures (2001: 286–91).[10] Scanlon's claim that sound moral principles are principles that no one can reasonably reject (1998) represents another example of this kind of hybrid position. It is a universalist moral theory—the principle applies to all societies and all persons—but it sanctions cultural variety and diversity where no one can reasonably reject them (1998: 338–49).[11]

A third significant feature of universalism (as defined above) is that it maintains there to be some universal *values*. As such, moral universalism would be satisfied in a world in which people of different cultures observe the same (just) values even if they do so for different reasons and on the basis of different moral doctrines. Adopting a terminology created by John Rawls, a number of thinkers have argued that there is an international 'overlapping consensus' on some moral values.[12] By this they mean that people of different faiths or secular traditions (what Rawls terms comprehensive doctrines) can and do converge on some common moral values. There is thus an 'overlapping consensus' on values even though there is no consensus as to which moral theory is the most plausible. Note that if there is an overlapping consensus of this kind it would bring together universalism of scope and universalism of justification. It satisfies the former for it claims there to be values that should apply throughout the world and it satisfies the latter for it claims that these values can be accepted by all.

Fourth, it is worth noting what Scanlon terms 'parametric universalism'. The latter affirms a set of universal values but adds that they are applicable only when certain conditions are satisfied. As Scanlon writes, 'actions that are right in one place can be wrong in another place, where people have different expectations, or where different conditions obtain' (1998: 329). To give one example, one might follow John Stuart Mill (and many political scientists) in thinking that democratic institutions will function and flourish only when certain social preconditions are met (1977*b* [1861]: ch. 1, (esp. pp. 376–80), 413–21).[13] Bearing this in mind, one could affirm as a transcultural value the importance of democracy and yet, consistent with this, deny that every society should have democratic institutions right here and now. There is a universal value but its relevance depends on some empirical conditions being met. This, it should be emphasized, is not a cultural relativist claim for it is not argued that democracy is wrong simply in virtue of the fact that it does not cohere with the local values. The Millian can think that to the extent that the local values reject democratic institutions they are quite wrong. The local mores and conventions thus do not have fundamental moral authority: they are not constitutive of what is just or unjust. But they do, on a parametric universalist account, have importance and should not be neglected.[14] Put otherwise: the universalist component in parametric universalism is apparent when we recognize that on this account, any society that does meet the specified criteria should have democratic institutions and those that do not meet the criteria have reason to strive to bring them about.

An additional point should be made about universalism. It will be fairly clear from the above that all cosmopolitan thinkers are universalists. Utilitarian cosmopolitans, for example, aver that the same fundamental principle (to maximize utility) should apply to all sentient beings across the world. Cosmopolitans who embrace the notion of rights will, in a similar vein, maintain that this value should be applied universally to all. Since one fundamental cosmopolitan claim is that the values that apply to some persons should be applied to all, cosmopolitans are, of course, universalists. This much is obvious.

One might be tempted to think that thinkers who adopt a broadly communitarian perspective, such as nationalists, will necessarily accept a relativist perspective and repudiate moral universalism. Such a claim is, however, deeply mistaken in two ways. First, many adopt a universal account of the rights of nations, averring that all nations are entitled to be self-determining. The latter is a universalist claim in virtue of the fact that it exhibits a universal form (the *same* right is ascribed without exception) and a universal scope (it is ascribed to *all* nations). An example of this kind of universalism can be found in the later work of Michael Walzer, who defends what he terms 'reiterative universalism', where this affirms the universal right of all nations to be self-governing and to affirm their own values. Walzer contrasts this with what he terms 'covering-law universalism', where this identifies a blueprint that should be applied to each and every society (1990: 510–15). To see a second reason why it is wrong to assume that communitarians are necessarily anti-universalist, it is important to distinguish between different kinds of communitarian claim. Some communitarians defend a specific normative claim, arguing that community is an important human good. When contemporary Aristotelian communitarians, for example, argue that persons flourish by living and taking part in the polis they are making a universal claim about human flourishing that applies to all human beings. Such normative communitarian claims thus unsettle the common view that communitarian thinking is necessarily relativist.[15]

One final clarificatory point should be made. Universalism, it should be observed, is compatible with one sort of contextualism (Miller 2002*a*: 8; Pogge 2002*a*, esp. pp. 38–40). Many argue for a contextual approach according to which the rules appropriate for one domain (say the family) are distinct from the rules appropriate for another domain (say the marketplace) (Walzer 1983). A universalist can, of course, recognize *this* kind of contextualism and can happily accept that one rule should always apply to the family but that another, different rule should always apply to the marketplace. Both rules are universal in the relevant sense for both have a universal form and a universal scope.

Having analysed universalism, we may turn now to consider the main alternative to this, 'cultural relativism'. As defined here, cultural relativism maintains that correct moral principles are those that conform to a community's commonly held values. As Gilbert Harman writes, '[m]oral relativism denies that there are universal basic moral demands and says different people are subject to different basic moral demands depending on the social customs, practices, conventions, values, and principles that they accept' (1989: 371). A clear and emphatic statement of this view comes from Walzer in *Spheres of Justice*. Walzer famously maintains that '[a] given society is just if its substantive life is lived in a certain way—that is, in a way faithful to the shared understandings of the members' (1983: 313, cf. further 1987). We often think of etiquette or taste in a cultural relativist way (on which see Foot 2002): modes of greeting people are not uniform and universal but differ in different cultures. Another exponent of this particularist kind of reasoning is James Tully who in *Strange Multiplicity* argues against abstract universal principles (1995). He is critical of what, quoting Wittgenstein, he calls 'the craving for generality' (1995: 105). Instead, he defends a particularist conception of practical reason according to which the moral norms that bind people are those that issue from their practices and are the product of a historical process of negotiation and accommodation. As with universalism, we gain a fuller understanding of relativism by noting a number of distinctions.

First, it is useful to distinguish between the claim that all values are culturally relative and the more modest claim that some are. The latter claim is, of course, quite compatible with maintaining some values to be universal. One might, for example, think that there are some universal human rights but that there are other non-rights-related values that are culturally variable.[16]

Second, for a clear understanding of relativism we must have an account of the entity to which values are relative. As its name suggests, cultural relativism specifies that correct values are those values that accord with the commonly held values of a culture. The criteria of moral correctness for a person derive from his or her culture and the social practices in which he or she participates. This, however, requires further specification for we need to know what the culture in question is and how to identify the contours of a culture. Both tasks are difficult. In the first place, there is the question of which culture(s) someone belongs to. A person's identity might be defined in terms of their religion, gender, class, ethnicity, profession, nationality, region, or citizenship. If cultural relativism is to prove a viable moral theory it must be able to specify which of the above descriptions of a person's culture is the appropriate one and why. Second, it must be able to demarcate the borders of the relevant community(ies) and this is intensely problematic since the borders of cultures are notoriously inexact.

Prior to evaluating the arguments for and against moral universalism, we should make two preliminary points. First, it is useful to distinguish between two different kinds of argument for moral universalism and for cultural relativism. More specifically, we can distinguish between *normative* arguments, on the one hand, and *conceptual* arguments, on the other. A normative argument, as I define it, objects to moral universalism or to cultural relativism on the grounds that the latter entails some morally unacceptable implications. To give an example of a normative argument for universalism and against relativism: some maintain that cultural relativism is untenable on the grounds that it cannot condemn morally repugnant practices (Section II). Or to give an example of a normative argument against universalism: many argue that moral universalism should be rejected on the grounds that it suppresses cultural diversity (Section XII). By contrast with normative arguments, a conceptual argument, as I define it, objects to moral universalism or cultural relativism on the grounds that the latter fails to accommodate a key conceptual feature of a moral theory. To give an example of a conceptual argument against relativism: some argue that cultural relativism is conceptually incoherent for it contradicts itself (Sections III and IV). Or to give an example of a conceptual argument against universalism, some argue that morality must be able to motivate persons to comply with it and since universal principles cannot do so universalist conceptions of morality are untenable (Section VIII). Second, it is worth noting in advance that many of the critiques of universalism are motivated by a common source, namely the existence of considerable cultural diversity throughout the world. However, they differ considerably in their explication of how this diversity undermines moral universalism.

# II

Having conducted the necessary preliminary analysis, let us now consider four arguments for moral universalism. An appropriate place to begin is to consider a common normative argument against cultural relativism and for moral universalism. This argument contends that cultural relativism should be rejected because there are some cultures that hold repulsive moral views and cultural relativism would therefore sanction evil customs and traditions. Cultural relativism, it is argued, would, for example, condone slavery or the subjugation of women in cultures whose shared beliefs are, respectively, pro-slavery and in favour of the subjugation of women.[17] In a similar vein Jürgen Habermas criticizes those post-structuralist and post-modernist writers critical of moral universalism on the grounds that they are unable to provide and *justify* normative criteria by which to judge and condemn existing practices (1987: 283–6).

The philosophical source of this problem for relativism is well captured by Thomas Scanlon who observes that relativism is concerned with the reasons persons have to act and not with the point of view of the persons acted upon. As he puts it

those who defend relativism generally focus on how moral requirements could give agents reason to act, while those who oppose it focus on how these requirements could ensure that the victims of these actions have reason to accept their results. (1998: 406, fn. 11)

If Scanlon's suggestion is true (and it seems plausible) it would help explain the origin of the problem that the argument under scrutiny highlights. For if relativists concentrate on the reasons and motives that agents act upon and which guide their conduct rather than on the impact of these actions on other people then it would hardly be surprising if relativism yields outcomes that treat others unfairly. Against relativism, then, this argument draws attention to the victims of cultural traditions, such as subjugated women or homosexuals or individuals who dissent from the majority religion.

How might a cultural relativist respond to this line of reasoning? One common rejoinder is that it underestimates the possibility of internal social criticism. One need not rely on universal moral principles to criticize repugnant practices: cultures are always contested and, as such, it is always possible to draw on some existing social norms to criticize and reject others (Bell 1993: 64–5; Walzer 1987, esp. pp. 35–66). Cultures are, therefore, not necessarily wedded to morally grotesque outcomes.

This reply is right to point out that cultures are open to different interpretations. Where a culture is said to endorse a repugnant practice, there may indeed be other construals of the culture that do not condone (or even reject) the practice. However, it is not clear whether this response can fully absolve the relativist of the charge pressed against it. A culture may, for example, be so saturated with injustice that the prevailing concepts and perspectives are laden with it (O'Neill 1996: 22, cf. pp. 21–3). Furthermore, once we allow several rival interpretations of a culture we then face the problem of how we choose between them. On what grounds can a relativist claim in advance that in a community which contains traditions both of persecution and of tolerance the latter ones are the ones that count?[18]

A second response is to argue that the universalist criticisms are always too rash and fail to put the condemned practices into context. The claim is that when we gain a deeper knowledge and understanding of other cultures we appreciate that practices that might initially appear morally grotesque are not so.[19] As with the first response, there is some truth in this objection. Many are quick to condemn other cultures without bothering to acquire a sufficient understanding of them. However, whilst this response might show that some practices that seem evil are not so when inspected more closely, we have no reason to think that this strategy can work in each and every case where a culture adopts an abhorrent way of life.

Even if neither of the first two counter-arguments succeeds, however, the universalist argument is insufficient. Its problem is that it does not really amount to an argument against cultural relativism. It reports our view that such practices are intolerable but that does not constitute a justification for the condemnation. It says simply that 'we think that those practices are grotesque' but one needs to do more than this. One needs to be able to give reasons as to how and why the practice condemned is wrong and this presupposes that there are universally valid reasons. This argument therefore assumes that universalism is correct rather than vindicates it. The universalist argument is therefore inadequate (Caney 1999b: 22; cf. more generally, 1999b: 21–2).

## III

Having considered one normative argument against relativism and for universalism let us turn now to conceptual arguments. A second argument for universalism and against cultural relativism maintains that the latter is incoherent and self-defeating. Thomas Nagel advances this line of reasoning in *The Last Word*. He argues that a relativist has two options. First, she may contend that relativism is universally true. To this the reply is that relativism is self-defeating. Second, she may contend that relativism is relatively true. To this the reply is that those who are not initially persuaded of it have no reason to embrace it (1997: 15).[20] Either way, relativism cannot be stated in a coherent fashion. The point is put pithily by Tzvetan Todorov: '[t]he relativist inevitably ends up contradicting himself, since he presents his doctrine as absolute truth, and thus by his very gesture undermines what he is in the process of asserting' (1993: 389).[21]

This argument is, however, unconvincing for a relativist can reply that claims in some domains are universally valid but claims in other domains are not. He might then reason that the statement that all moral values are culturally relative belongs to the first category (that is universally valid claims) and, accordingly, that all moral judgements belong in a second category (that is, claims whose validity is culturally relative). Scanlon, who is no relativist, makes this point clearly (1998: 329–30). On this approach one can affirm a universally valid theory of morality with universally valid conceptual claims but also, as a consequence of this theory, maintain that there are no universally valid moral values. This response thus resolves Nagel's dilemma by denying the accuracy of the first horn of that dilemma. It claims, moreover, to do so consistently by making clear that not everything is relative: moral judgements are, but theories about the nature of morality are not.

A universalist might reply that this response is ad hoc. Why, it might be argued, are some claims universally true and other claims only relatively valid? Isn't such a division rather mysterious? Relativists can, however, respond to this objection in two ways. First, they can point out, on an *ad hominem* level, that almost all universalists think that some moral ideals are universal and that others are not. Hence they themselves are putting forward a two-tiered approach. Second, they can show that the proposed distinction on which the response rests is a commonplace and intelligible distinction that we accept elsewhere. Let me explain. Consider etiquette and courtesy again. Most people adopt a relativist position, thinking that the criteria of polite and courteous behaviour vary depending on which culture one is in. However, as such they are also affirming a universally valid claim about the nature of politeness. The thesis that the nature of polite conduct depends on cultural conventions is deemed to be universally valid. Nagel's dilemma is, therefore, flawed for it ignores a third option open to the relativist.

# IV

The first two critiques of relativism are, therefore, unpersuasive. Given this, let us consider a third critique of relativism, one that claims that relativism is self-refuting. The argument can be simply stated. It maintains that according to relativism correct moral values are those that match the shared understandings of their culture. But, it argues, the shared understanding of our culture and many others is that it is not true that the correct moral values for a person are those that match the shared understandings of their culture. Cultural relativism is thus self-defeating because the deep values of our culture and others are that cultural relativism is false. This argument is stated with particular clarity by Ronald Dworkin in his critique of Walzer's *Spheres of Justice*. As Dworkin put the point: 'it is part of our common political life, if anything is, that justice is our critic not our mirror . . . Walzer's relativism is faithless to the single most important social practice we have: the practice of worrying about what justice really is' (1986*b*: 219). Nussbaum makes the point with equal force:

> normative relativism is self-subverting: for, in asking us to defer to local norms, it asks us to defer to norms that in most cases are strongly nonrelativistic. Most local traditions take themselves to be absolutely, not relatively, true. So in asking us to follow the local, relativism asks us not to follow relativism.  (2000*a*: 49)

Relativism may therefore be rejected as conceptually incoherent.

A relativist might be inclined to challenge the empirical assumption made by this argument, arguing that the shared understandings of 'the people' are in fact relativistic. This claim will be explored in greater detail later in this chapter (Section X) but in the meantime we might raise a doubt about its truth. For example, according to many, people's religious convictions include beliefs and as such it would be inaccurate to comprehend their views as being culturally relative. Rather, it is claimed, persons maintain their beliefs to be true.[22]

Even if we grant, for the moment, this assumption to Dworkin and Nussbaum, the relativist may still deny the conclusion for she might argue that we can disregard people's meta-ethical beliefs as erroneous. According to this second reply, a culture's views about ethics (such as what distribution is just) are correct but its views about meta-ethical questions (such as whether relativism is true) are false and should be disregarded. This kind of view is, however, theoretically unstable and rather mysterious. How can it be that a community's shared views about justice including distributive justice, punishment, the treatment of women, and so on, are correct but its shared views about the nature of moral beliefs are profoundly mistaken? If shared understandings are constitutive of ethical correctness then why should this not apply to meta-ethics as well? Why would a culture's common meta-ethical views be more susceptible to error than its ethical views? It is hard to think of any reason why they should be.

Even if neither of the above relativist responses succeed, however, this argument is not a fully convincing defence of moral universalism. In the first place, to show that cultural relativism is self-defeating entails universalism *only if* these are the only two positions available. But this is not so: for example, one can be a moral sceptic. Furthermore, this argument does not tell us what any moral theory must tell us: how to derive these (universal) values. It works best, then, as a critique of relativism rather than a positive defence of universalism.[23]

## V

Having analysed three arguments for universalism, I want, in this section, to outline the beginnings of what I take to be a more persuasive argument for moral universalism. I shall term this the *General Argument for Moral Universalism*, or more briefly, simply the *General Argument*. The argument begins with (P1), the assumption that there are valid moral principles. (P1) simply denies a moral scepticism that rejects all moral principles. As such, (P1) is relatively uncontroversial.

Thoroughgoing moral sceptics are hard to find and they must provide a powerful argument as to why there are no moral principles.[24] The next step in the argument is (P2), the claim that the moral principles that apply to some persons apply to all persons who share some common morally relevant properties. (P2) is similarly hard to dispute: it simply affirms a truism. To this the argument then adds (P3), that persons throughout the world share some morally relevant similarities. (P3) maintains that, notwithstanding the many differences between different persons from different cultures, there are some morally significant commonalities. This, as we shall see, is the most controversial step in the argument and the ensuing discussion assesses its validity. If, however, it is correct, it is clear that there is a cogent argument for moral universalism. For given (P1), that there are some valid moral principles, (P2), that valid moral principles apply to all those who are similar in a morally relevant way, and (P3), that persons throughout the world are similar in a morally relevant way, it follows, (C), that there are some moral principles with universal form (the same principles apply) and universal scope (these principles apply to all).

Both (P1) and (P3) require further elaboration. Let us begin with (P3). Although controversial, this premise does possess some prima facie plausibility. Persons throughout the world have a significant number of morally relevant properties in common. First, they have some common *needs and vulnerabilities*. They suffer from physical pain, require food and water to survive, and are susceptible to disease, sickness, and malnutrition. This point is well made by Stuart Hampshire, who refers to 'the raw and basic necessities which are common to the whole species' (1983: 142, cf. pp. 128, 142, 143).[25] As he goes on to stress, these 'universal, species-wide requirements, derived from basic human necessities, are very unspecific; they are very general restraints which are compatible with many different conceptions of the good life for men' (1983: 143, cf. also p.155). The existence of needs common to all humans is also well brought out by John Kekes. As he records, some moral

requirements are set by universally human, historically constant, and culturally invariant needs created by human nature. Many of these needs are physiological: for food, shelter, rest, and so forth; other needs are psychological: for companionship, hope, the absence of horror and terror in one's life, and the like; yet other needs are social: for some order and predictability in one's society, for security, for some respect, and so on.   (1994: 49, cf. also p. 50)[26]

In short, then, persons have some common needs.[27]

Second, persons throughout the world have some common goods. Nussbaum develops this point persuasively, arguing for a specific list of human goods and capabilities. These include the following: 'life' (the ability to live a full life), 'bodily health' (the ability to live a healthy life with sufficient food and protection from the elements), and 'bodily integrity' (the ability to act on one's choices concerning sex and procreation without suffering from violence). Other goods include what Nussbaum terms 'senses, imagination, and thought' (the ability to employ these faculties), 'emotions' (the capacity for emotional bonds with other people), and 'practical reason' (the ability to choose and to reflect on one's conception of the good). They also include what she terms 'affiliation' (where this involves both 'friendship' and being treated with 'respect'), caring for 'other species', the capacity for 'play', and, finally, 'control over one's environment'— both 'political' and 'material' (2002: 129–30).[28] As Nussbaum stresses, these ten goods may take a variety of different cultural forms. Nonetheless, Nussbaum maintains, the above goods are universal human goods.

Persons throughout the world then have some common needs, common capacities, and common ends.[29] The preceding observations, needless to say, are tentative and suggestive. They do not constitute conclusive proof; but they do provide some prima facie support for the claim that persons throughout the world have some morally relevant properties in common (and hence that some of the principles that apply to some apply to all). (P3) can be strengthened further in two ways. First, it can be justified by defending some specific claims about the ways in which persons throughout the world share morally relevant properties. This task is undertaken in Chapters 3 and 4 which explore the rationale for universal principles of civil, political, and distributive justice. These chapters defend particular claims about persons' morally relevant commonalities and thereby support (P3). Second, (P3) can be supported further by considering challenges to it and exploring the ways in which such challenges are unpersuasive. Sections VI, VII, and VIII aim to do precisely this.

Prior to considering these challenges, it is worth now turning to (P1). As noted earlier, few will deny that there are some valid moral principles. However, (P1) is incomplete as it stands for it is silent on the methodological issue of how one can justify moral principles. It needs to be supplemented with an account of how one can defend some moral conceptions and criticize others. Following Rawls, I take it that the most plausible way of engaging in this enterprise is to strive for what he terms a process of 'reflective equilibrium' between moral theories and considered moral judgements. That is, one should take one's moral judgements and analyse them—seeking to eliminate bias, self-interest, and so on—and one should then test moral theories against such considered moral judgements, adjusting theory or judgements until they cohere. Through this process and through the critical scrutiny of moral judgements one can generate principles that are based on sound moral reasoning and not based on error or confusion (Rawls 1999*c*: 40–6). To this one should also add that any adequate moral theory must be able to cope with the objections that others may level at it, including objections from those from different cultures. This approach to moral justification, of course, has its critics (some objecting to any use of moral intuitions and some objecting to the use of moral theories) but space precludes a fuller examination (cf. for excellent discussion, Griffin (1996, esp. pp. 3–18, 123–36)). My aim, here, is not to defend this moral methodology but rather to make clear the approach that will be employed in the rest of the book.

Having outlined the General Argument it is important to make three observations. First, we should record that the General Argument is not simply an argument for moral universalism. It is not merely a sufficient condition for accepting universalism: it is also a necessary condition. The General Argument must hold if moral universalism is to be valid. Why? The answer is that if there are to be rules with a universal form (they apply without exception to all in the relevant group) and with a universal scope (the relevant group encompasses all humanity), then there must be some relevant commonalities (P3). To insist that the same values apply to all requires, if it is not to be wholly whimsical or arbitrary, that all have certain morally relevant properties in common. An argument of the above kind is therefore the only kind that can ground moral universalism. Moreover, if the above argument were false, moral universalism would be false. This means that the stakes are higher and that a refutation of the General Argument would constitute a refutation of the necessary presuppositions of moral universalism.

A second point worth recording has already been alluded to, namely that the General Argument, as outlined above, is not intended to defend any particular universal values (e.g. the right to freedom of expression or the right to have basic needs met). Rather, it outlines the logical structure of the rationale for a universalist position but does not specify its content. As such it needs then to be supplemented by additional arguments for specific individual universal values. This task is taken up in Chapters 3 and 4.

This leads to a third and final point about the argument: one implication of the General Argument is that any successful argument for a *particular* universal value (e.g. universal principles of civil and political justice, or universal principles of distributive justice) will have the same logical structure as the General Argument. It will, that is, identify a value and then show that the reasoning for it has universal force because all persons are similar in a morally relevant way (i.e. they will show that (P3) obtains). The General Argument, thus, provides the logical structure to which any specific individual universalist argument must conform. We shall return to this point in Chapters 3 and 4 when particular universal principles are considered and defended.

Having set out the basic structure that an argument must possess to vindicate moral universalism, the sections that follow explore nine challenges to moral universalism—during the course of which the plausibility of (P3) will be further assessed.

# VI

Let us begin with some conceptual arguments against moral universalism and in favour of cultural relativism. In this section and the following five sections, six conceptual arguments will be considered. These include the objection that universalism is: (1) flawed because committed to the idea of a common human nature; (2) too abstract and decontextualized to have relevance; (3) unable to provide an adequate account of moral motivation; (4) false to the experience of moral reflection; (5) unattainable because moral argument can take place only within historical traditions; and (6) vitiated by the existence of profound moral disagreement.

Let us consider the first argument. According to one anti-universalist argument, there is no common human nature and to subscribe to such a notion is to be guilty of an untenable essentialism. Richard Rorty, for example, opines that there is no common human nature.[30] If this were true it would be wrong to infer from the fact that some principles apply to some that they apply to all. (P3) is therefore incorrect and moral universalism rests on an implausible philosophical anthropology.

However, although many are critical of the idea of a common human nature, the reasons for dispensing with it are less clear.[31] Arguments against the concept tend to fall into one of three errors. The first error is to confuse *commonality* with *identity*. We might distinguish here between modest accounts of human nature, which maintain that persons hold a few properties in common (*commonality*), and ambitious ones, which ascribe a detailed and comprehensive account of what it is to be a human being (*identity*).[32] For instance, a modest account might ascribe to all human beings the capacity to feel pain. Such spare accounts of human nature can be contrasted with fuller accounts that define human nature in terms of a large number of essential properties. We should not think of this distinction as being one between two separate categories; rather, it makes sense to think of there being a continuum, at one end of which is the view that persons are identical and at the other end of which is the view that persons have nothing in common at all. Now this distinction is of critical importance because some argue against the notion of a common human nature that people can vary dramatically in their abilities, conceptions of the good, affiliations, motivations, and so on. The idea of a common human nature, it might be said, is incompatible with such enormous variations in people's norms, beliefs, behaviour, and desires. But such a line of reasoning is unpersuasive against the concept of human nature normally invoked by universalists (and against the account introduced in Section V) for it assumes that a common human nature entails *identity* whereas all that is required is the assumption of *commonality*. For example, the account outlined in Section V listed only several commonalities—such as some common needs and some common goods.

A second error is to move from objections to particular conceptions of human nature to a rejection of all conceptions of human nature. Many, for example, are critical of universalist moral theories on the grounds that their particular conception of human nature is ideological and biased. It is objected, for example, that the properties specific to one culture are treated as being universal (Foucault 1974: 173–4). The premise of this argument is true: but it hardly follows from the fact that *some* specific conceptions are biased that *all* are, and hence there is no such thing as a common human nature. The appropriate reaction to this concern is to construct an account of human nature and then to appraise it in the light of the observations and criticisms of other people of other cultures.

A third error is to assume that to posit a common human nature is to deny the historicity of persons. Again, though, this is misconceived for, as was noted above, to affirm a conception of human nature is to affirm some properties that persons have in common. As such it does not deny the many ways in which persons' membership of cultures render them different.

We have yet to see, then, why moral universalism (and (P3) of the General Argument for universalism) are flawed because reliant on the idea of a common human nature.[33]

## VII

In the light of the failure of the last argument, let us turn then to a second conceptual argument against universalism and for cultural relativism. For some the problem with moral universalism (and hence with the argument adduced in Section V) is not (or not simply) that there is no common human nature. It is, rather, that universal principles are inappropriate, if not useless, because they are too general and abstract to have much applicability. All the relevant work is done by local circumstance. What is needed is a contextualist approach that articulates principles appropriate for specific historical circumstances. We should take a more parochial and local approach if we are to arrive at principles that are valid and applicable. To put the point another way, one can distinguish between top-down and bottom-up approaches to moral issues, where the former articulate general and universal principles designed to cover all circumstances and the latter maintain that the principles to govern moral relations should be derived from within existing practices and conventions. Top-down approaches, the argument maintains, result in principles that are so attenuated and eviscerated that they lack local relevance.[34] The remedy for this failing is to look more to history and adopt a historicist or particularist approach which emphasizes historical context and specificity (cf. Dunne 1998: 190). This kind of point is pressed by James Tully who, in *Strange Multiplicity*, objects to abstract general principles and celebrates the sort of historical reasoning found, for example, in common law reasoning and casuistry (1995).

This argument, one might note, is directed specifically against what I have termed a universalism of scope. There should not, it claims, be principles with a universal jurisdiction. Rather the world should be a patchwork quilt in which members of different communities are governed by different historical conventions, principles, and practices. Moreover, the reason for this is that (P3) of the universalist argument outlined above is false. Persons face radically different situations and live in societies with different histories, contexts, and backgrounds.

This line of reasoning is flawed in several ways. First, it does not in itself establish the inappropriateness of universal principles. Rather, it shows that they should be combined with a proper recognition of historical and social circumstances. A universalist moral theory can be sensitive to context if it factors these into the application of its principles. To reject the view that valid moral principles are correct if they cohere with the traditions of a community is not to reject the importance of taking account of specific historical circumstances.

A second problem with the argument is that it mischaracterizes universalism. Universal principles are generally proposed to set parameters within which conduct can take place. They do not require the top-down application of blueprints that map out in precise detail what is to be done. They often specify background constraints on what can be done rather than detailed outlines of how society must be arranged down to the last detail (O'Neill 1996: 75, 78). Put otherwise: they might rule out some options (no murder, no deprivation, no racial discrimination) without requiring any particular options. Universalism, recall, stipulates that some ideals should have universal scope—not all ideals. As such, it is not vulnerable to the objection.

Finally, it is worth distinguishing between those ideals that have value only in certain situations and those that have value in a large number of situations. We can think of there being a continuum with, at the one end, values that are valid only in one specific state of affairs and, at the other end, values that are valid in all states of affairs. To illustrate the distinction, consider, again, the good of democratic government. As was noted above, it is widely held that democracy can flourish only where certain socio-economic and cultural conditions are satisfied. Other values, by contrast, have value in a wider range of circumstances. Consider, for example, the prohibition on torture. This injunction is much less dependent on historical circumstance for it has validity in all circumstances except, perhaps, extreme conditions where it is the only way to prevent a horrendous evil. With this distinction in mind, we can return to the anti-universalist argument. The argument has much more relevance against those ideals that depend on the realization of some very specific conditions. By contrast, ideals that are less dependent on specific historical circumstances are, *ex hypothesi*, more generally applicable and less vulnerable to modification and qualification by local circumstances. Hence the fact that there is very great diversity in social, economic, and political contexts does not undermine the applicability of these ideals. For these three reasons, universalism is not too abstract to have practical relevance.

## VIII

With the failure of the last argument, let us turn now to a third conceptual argument against universalism. Some challenge universalism—and would dispute (P3)—by arguing that moral principles apply to people only if they can motivate them and then arguing that universal principles cannot meet this condition. Walzer, for example, maintains that moral principles must resonate with those subject to them: they must be able to inspire them to comply with them. Culturally specific principles can do this and social criticism of practices that draws on local understandings can have an effect. As he puts it in *The Company of Critics*, '[c]riticism is most powerful . . . when it gives voice to the common complaints of the people or elucidates the values that underlie those complaints' (1988: 16, cf. also pp. 233, 235).[35] To be, what he terms, a 'connected critic' (1987: 39) is, thus, a valid form of moral enquiry. Universalistic moral reasoning, by contrast, is not. It is a form of what Walzer terms 'disconnected criticism' (1987: 64) and, as such, it does not speak to people or impel them to act. Alien abstract rules that are divorced from people's social norms and values stand little or no chance of meeting the motivational standards a morality must meet if it is to be practical. Similar claims are advanced by Daniel Bell. Drawing on Walzer, he argues in defence of a relativistic approach that '[a] critic who tries to push beyond the limits of community consciousness cannot generate any politically relevant knowledge; only criticism which resonates with the habits and modes of conduct of the intended audiences can do so' (1993: 65, cf. pp. 65–6).[36]

This argument is vulnerable to two objections. First, it assumes that 'disconnected' criticism based on universal principles cannot resonate with members of communities and, as such, cannot inspire people to comply with them. However, it is not clear on what basis this assumption is grounded. Second, and more crucially, the argument presupposes that *if* a principle does not inspire the members of a community *then* it does not apply to them. It assumes that one (conceptual) property of a valid moral scheme is its ability to induce people to comply with it. But this is a highly implausible stipulation. It may be true that the articulation of universal principles does not effect a change in a culture, but why does this invalidate those principles? (C. Jones 1999: 181–2; Kymlicka 1993: 215). Put differently, it is important to bear in mind that moral language often performs a descriptive role. We might want to say that a society is unjust even if those in charge have no inclination to reform it and do not recognize the force of a critique. To deny this and to claim that a principle is valid only if it impels people to change overlooks the descriptive character of much moral language. We may, for example, condemn a society that practises slavery or paedophilia or human sacrifice even if the members of the society in question find the critique of these practices alien. For this reason it is an exaggeration to claim that 'social criticism is *only* relevant if it's an aid to effective practice' (Bell 1993: 65, my emphasis). To rework Marx's famous eleventh thesis on Feuerbach, we might say that philosophers should interpret the world: the point is not simply to change it (although it is that).[37] Even if political philosophy does not induce any change, it is relevant.

# IX

The preceding three conceptual arguments for cultural relativism have proved unpersuasive. There are, nonetheless, other important conceptual arguments against universalism and in favour of a relativist perspective. In *Interpretation and Social Criticism*, Walzer outlines an additional conceptual argument. He distinguishes between three conceptions of moral reasoning. The first maintains that we *discover* moral values; the second maintains that we *invent* them; and the third maintains that we arrive at the appropriate moral values by *interpreting* our social practices (1987). Walzer defends the third, relativistic, conception. One of the main arguments he presents in its favour is that when we reflect on the way in which we make moral decisions we will see that we do so by interpreting our existing social norms: 'moral argument is most often interpretive in character' (1987: 22). As he puts it, '[t]he experience of moral argument is best understood in the interpretive mode. What we do when we argue is to give an account of the actually existing morality' (1987: 21). His claim, then, is that if we examine an argument and 'study its phenomenology, we will see that its real subject is the meaning of the particular moral life shared by the protagonists' (1987: 23). The experience of moral reasoning, thus, fits best with the interpretive (relativist) model.

This argument, note, challenges the claim at the heart of Dworkin and Nussbaum's claim that relativism is self-undermining, namely the claim that the shared norms of communities are anti-relativistic (Section IV). Walzer's claim, by contrast, is that the participants in moral arguments conceive of what they are doing not as following universal principles but rather as adhering to the shared values of their culture. Walzer's position is, however, hard to sustain. As an analysis of the ways in which people hold their ethical beliefs brings out, people do not construe their moral convictions as valid because they conform to their community's way of life. Rather they believe these convictions (e.g. the view that paedophilia is evil) are valid because they are supported by cogent arguments. Amy Gutmann makes the argument persuasively. As she points out, 'the moral claims' made by members of a culture 'are not that their social understandings are *ipso facto* justified because they are dominant, regardless of the content of those understandings' (1993: 176–7). Rather, people adduce arguments for their views on, say, abortion or capital punishment or distribution according to need. It is, thus, inaccurate to claim that we make the decisions on the basis of what we think is the social consensus. Consider a culture that maintains that women should not work but should remain at home. As Gutmann observes

> The cultural relativist claim that this social understanding could be justified by virtue of being the dominant understanding . . . creates a tension with the very content of the understanding itself, that a woman's place is in the home *because* of her natural social function, not because men (or for that matter most men and women) sincerely believe that a woman's place is in the home. (1993: 177)

So, far from fitting in with our moral experience, cultural relativism is actually in conflict with it. And it misdescribes the attitude of those who hold religious or moral beliefs to say that the belief is right because it conforms to the views of the overwhelming majority. One way of putting this point is to say that from *within* a practice persons think of their convictions as being universally valid. The relativist position may work as a third-person account of other people's views (*they* are just following the norms of their culture) but is incompatible with the first person perspective of the participants themselves.[38]

Two further points have to be made in this context. First, it is true that sometimes we make a decision on the basis that something is the convention in our society. The interpretive position may be true of some decisions and, as such, is compatible with universalism, as defined in Section I, which claims only that *some* values have universal form and scope. But it is false as a description of how we think, say, of many key moral values—such as our position on slavery or abortion or genocide or rape or assault. Second, universalists claim that universal norms may be interpreted in different ways depending on the cultural and historical context.[39] They can, then, accept that there is a degree of interpretation without relinquishing their commitment to moral universalism. It is, accordingly, false to construe all moral reasoning as interpretive: interpretation may sometimes be necessary but it is not sufficient.

# X

Universalism has, thus far, managed to deal with the objections levelled against it. For many, however, the most persuasive critiques have yet to be discussed. One common objection levelled against moral universalism is that it presupposes a 'view from nowhere' and the latter, it is argued, is unattainable.[40] The claim is that we all look at moral issues from our point of view: particularity is inescapable and objectivity is a chimera. Our moral judgements and theories are, this argument insists, inextricably shaped by our culture. One cannot transcend one's social environment and thereby secure the 'universal' point of view. Accordingly, we should accept a relativist perspective that is true to our traditions: to ask for more is to ask for the unobtainable. This is, in the terms I am employing, a conceptual argument for it does not object that universalism is morally objectionable. Its complaint, rather, is that universalism requires what is not possible.

This kind of reasoning is commonly adduced. Rorty has long argued 'that there is no standpoint outside the particular historically conditioned and temporary vocabulary we are presently using from which to judge this vocabulary' (1989: 48).[41] Similar claims are advanced by the communitarian political theorist, Daniel Bell. Bell, for example, opines that 'all knowledge is context-bound—the critic cannot extricate herself from her context so as to be true to principles of rational justification independent of any context, even if she tries' (1993: 66: cf. further pp. 66–8). As he adds:

once we recognize that our knowledge is context-bound, that there's no 'objective' standpoint from which to evaluate how we think, act, and judge, this should lead us to abandon this project that aims at finding independent rational justification for morality, an external and universal perspective that's to serve as a critical standard from which to evaluate the morality of actual communities. And if there's no trans-communal ground from which to seek independent vindication for the moral standards of communities, this means that standards of justification emerge from and are part of a community's history and tradition in which they are vindicated.   (1993: 67)[42]

Although frequently invoked, it is not clear how much this argument shows. Its central weakness is that many universalist approaches do not deny that persons' values are shaped from their social perspective. They recognize that we see the world and reach our moral convictions from within our own schemes but observe that this in itself does not establish that there is no correct position.[43] They do not aspire to a 'view from nowhere'. Nussbaum's position is a good case in point. She works from within human experience and posits certain human goods that are presented as being derived from human experience (1992, 1993, 1999, 2000*a*, 2002). Her position, she notes, 'does not derive from any extrahistorical metaphysical conception, or rely on the truth of any form of metaphysical realism' (1992: 223). More generally, the universalist argument sketched in Section V does not posit any view from nowhere but relies rather on the assumption that persons throughout the world possess certain morally relevant properties in common. Furthermore, the method it uses—Rawls's reflective equilibrium—works with persons' moral convictions and moral theories.[44] In other words, a universalist need not adopt a perspective that claims to be outside of history and culture. Perhaps some universalisms do claim to be able to articulate a point free from any societal influences but the crucial point is that not all do.[45]

This last point is unlikely to persuade a relativist fully for underlying the emphasis on the fact that people's identities and beliefs are formed within a cultural context is often a further assumption, namely that *since people come from different cultures they will not agree on any moral values.*

# XI

This leads on to the next argument for cultural relativism. For a sixth conceptual argument draws on the extent of disagreement between members of different cultures and argues, on this basis, that a universalistic ethics is untenable. To present the argument more fully, it makes two claims. First, it claims that there is profound and intractable disagreement across the world on ethical matters. A casual glance at the plurality of different ethical traditions and doctrines makes it apparent that the disagreement is both profound and extensive. To give some highly familiar examples, there is insurmountable disagreement about issues such as abortion, the rights of women in general, the equality of persons, and female genital mutilation/female circumcision. To this we can then add a second claim, namely that the existence of profound disagreement refutes a universalist approach. Universalism, it is claimed, presupposes that people can reach a consensus on ethical matters.

This argument is worth analysing in some depth for two reasons. The first is that it is an extremely popular argument and many find it compelling. The second is that an analysis of the problems that the argument faces provides a positive argument for a version of universalism of justification. Having noted this, let us evaluate this argument. This sixth conceptual defence of relativism is vulnerable to three different types of response.

1. One strategy is to call into question the first premise of this argument—that which asserts the existence of deep and irreconcilable disagreement. It is worth elaborating on this with six comments. First, many maintain that persons from many different cultures converge on some basic moral norms—such as that

persons should not kill innocent people, or rape others, or steal. Such prescriptions can be found in Judaism, Christianity, Islam, Buddhism, and all other religions as well as in secular traditions of thought.[46] Second, this response can be strengthened further if we return to the concept of an 'international overlapping consensus' introduced earlier. As we have seen above, some philosophers have argued that although people affirm different comprehensive doctrines (such as Islam or Buddhism or Daoism) they can and do converge on some specific ethical prescriptions (An-Na'im 1999, esp. pp. 153, 166–8; Bielefeldt 2000: 114–17, esp. p. 116; Dower 1998: 12–13, 43; Pogge 1989: 269, cf. also pp. 227–30; and Taylor 1998, esp. pp. 37–8, 48–53; 1999, esp. pp. 124–6, 133–8, 143–4). There would seem to be some force to this suggestion and it importantly recognizes that disagreement as to which (if any) religion, say, is correct does not preclude convergence on very many moral claims. To these two points we should add a third, namely that cases where societies adopt very different principles might seem to be evidence of a value conflict but often are actually cases where there is no principled disagreement. The members of two different societies may adhere to radically different ideals but do so only because they face different scenarios. This does not constitute a fundamental disagreement. To give an illustration: compare a society faced with a fuel shortage with one that does not and suppose that the former, unlike the latter, restricts people's ability to use up natural resources. The two societies adopt different policies but, and this is the salient point, the difference is not a fundamental one for society 2, let us suppose, would agree to society 1's restrictive policy if it were faced with the same shortage (Brink 1989: 200).[47]

A fourth point should be made. Relativists often suggest that if people follow different principles then this provides support for relativism. As such it is useful to consider alternative universalist responses to the same evidence. A universalist might, for example, adopt the pluralist position defended by Sir Isaiah Berlin. Berlin repudiated relativism; he also rejected a monistic brand of universalism that affirms there to be one universal value. In its stead he argued that there is a plurality of universally valid principles. One is thus faced with a number of incompatible principles and as such some people will inevitably choose to prioritize some principles and others choose others (Berlin 1991*a*, esp. pp. 10–14; 1991*b*: 78–90; Kekes 1994; Perry 1998: 64–5, 70).

What these four points all suggest is that the first premise is more suspect than might first appear. There is far more agreement than it allows. Many, however, are deeply sceptical of such claims, arguing that different cultures are incommensurable and hence unable to resolve disagreements. It is worth then considering whether this is true and its implications for universalism. First, we need to distinguish between two types of incommensurability—conceptual incommensurability and moral incommensurability.[48] Let us consider the first. Conceptual incommensurability obtains when the terms and concepts of some cultures cannot be grasped by the members of other cultures. Moral incommensurability, by contrast, obtains not when members of different cultures cannot grasp the concepts of another culture but when they can but do not see any moral value in them.

With this distinction in mind, let us consider both kinds of incommensurability in turn.

A number of theorists have defended the idea of conceptual incommensurability, arguing that the ethical concepts of one culture cannot be accurately translated into the terms of all other cultures. To give one example, it is often said that some cultures do not have the concept of 'rights' and that the latter cannot be translated into their languages. If this conceptual incommensurability obtains then this would undermine the universalist conception of universal justifiability. However, we have good reason to be suspicious of such claims. First, as both Donald Davidson and Hilary Putnam have argued, there is reason to doubt the coherence of the concept of conceptual incommensurability. Justifications of conceptual incommensurability are prone to undermine themselves for they tend to give an example of a concept that they claim is untranslatable. But in doing so they give a full description of that concept (Davidson 1984, esp. p. 184; Putnam 1981: 114–15).[49] Second, the existence of a common human nature facilitates cross-cultural understanding and communication and thereby undercuts claims of conceptual incommensurability (Berlin 1991*a*: 11).

Let us turn now to what I have termed moral incommensurability. A critic of universalism might argue that members of different cultures often talk past each other, not in the sense that they cannot understand each other, but rather that they have completely different moral priorities. Some western cultures might prioritize rights over community, whereas some African or East Asian cultures may prioritize community over individual rights. Some of these issues will be dealt with in more depth in Chapter 3. In the meantime, however, several points can be made in response to this point. First, we should be wary of any generalizations to the effect that one culture ranks x over y. For example, claims that western cultures prize individuality over community are grossly overstated for they neglect the extent to which very many members of western societies prize friendship, family, workplace solidarity, and their membership of a religious or regional community. Moreover, claims that East Asian traditions are wholly communitarian overlook individualistic strands in Islam, Buddhism, and Confucianism (Inoue 1999: 50–4). Furthermore, any incommensurabilities that obtain are surely likely not to take the form of all the members of one society affirming one value whereas all the members of another society repudiating it. Disagreement will more likely exist within cultures and this undermines, rather than supports, cultural relativism. Finally, this kind of incommensurability is quite consistent with a universalism that affirms a pluralism of values of the kind espoused by Berlin.

2. It may, at this stage, be useful to recap the argument. Thus far we have seen that much of what appears, at first glance, to be ethical disagreement is not in fact disagreement. We have seen, moreover, that anti-universalist arguments that invoke conceptual or moral incommensurability are unconvincing. The points adduced thus far have been directed against the first claim made by the argument under consideration. It is, however, also worth noting that the second

step in the argument is also vulnerable. It suffers, in particular, from two problems.

The first is that the phenomenon of moral disagreement is actually, perhaps surprisingly, problematic for relativism. The point is well made by Nicholas Sturgeon and Bernard Williams. As both observe, when people are parties to a disagreement they both presuppose that there is a correct answer. Without that they are not disagreeing: they simply have different wishes. As Sturgeon writes, '[i]t is at least a superficial oddity in relativism about any topic, not just morality, that a view that typically begins by insisting on the intractability of disagreements that others might hope could be settled, should conclude that the disagreements were never real to begin with' (1994: 81, cf. also Williams 1985: 156–7). Consider, for example, abortion: it is false to all sides in the dispute to take a relativist approach. The point being made returns to the argument given in Section IX to the effect that relativism is in tension with people's understanding of their own moral commitments and principles. This is particularly evident in cases of ethical disagreement. From the point of view of the participants, their view is correct and the view of the other protagonists is false. It would completely misdescribe the situation of people disagreeing about whether women should have the right to vote to say that each is right from their own point of view.

There is a second critical point that can be made against the contention that disagreement entails the falsity of universalism. The latter assertion is frequently made but it requires further support for one might quite consistently hold that (i) 'there is disagreement' and (ii) 'moral universalism is correct' because one also thinks that (iii) 'some disagreement arises because of the fallibility of human reasoning' (Brink 1989: 198; Nagel 1986: 147–8; Scanlon 1998: 354–60, esp. pp. 356–9). Two points are worth making here. The first, and more modest, is that even if one dismisses all the previous objections levelled against the argument, the latter is insufficient. For it to succeed it must not simply establish that there is disagreement but must also discredit universalist attempts to explain such disagreement. Without additional arguments showing that all such attempts are unsuccessful, the argument is insufficient. The second, and more ambitious, point is that, although highly controversial, (iii) has some plausibility. Indeed it would be highly hubristic to claim that one cannot ever be wrong and that our moral reasoning is infallible. A number of everyday phenomena contribute to our fallibility. Inconsistency, factual mistakes, selfishness, manipulation, dogma, laziness, pride and an unwillingness to admit that one is wrong, complacency, and wishful thinking clearly affect people's judgements—*everyone's* judgements—and as such should feature in explanations of ethical disagreement.[50]

3. This section has outlined two critical responses to the defence of relativism under scrutiny. Before proceeding to consider a third set of objections to the argument it is appropriate to pause and note that the last two sets of objections provide some support for a version of universalism of justification. The latter maintains, recall, that there are some moral values that are justifiable to all.

The upshot of the preceding comments is that this is a plausible position. This is borne out by both sets of claims. First, the fact that there is considerable intercultural agreement and that often what appears to be disagreement is not lends support to the idea that some norms could be justifiable to all. The latter gains further support if we adopt the model of an overlapping consensus and if we recognize Berlin's pluralist conception of universalism. In all of these ways we can see ways in which some values can be justified to all. Second, the implication of the second set of points is that some disagreement arises from error, selfishness, indoctrination, and so on. This implies that there would be more agreement among people if their judgements were reached in a situation of full information, equality and with the freedom to make up their own minds. As such, it generates support for a particular version of universalism of justification, namely one that asserts there to be values that can be justified to all persons *when those persons' reasoning is not distorted by self-interest, factual mistakes, complacency, and so on*. Both sets of comments thus support the idea that there are universal norms justifiable to all.

4. Having seen that some of the flaws in the argument under consideration actually provide support for one version of universalism of justification, it is worth returning to a critique of the relativist argument for the latter is vulnerable to a third set of objections. The problem in particular is that the relativist argument being evaluated fails because it overlooks the distinction between the two kinds of universalism distinguished in Section I, named 'universalism of scope' and 'universalism of justification'. Even if one accepts steps one and two of the argument under scrutiny it has force only against the ideal of universal justifiability. It shows that moral norms will not command the assent of all. This, however, does not undermine universalism of scope. One might accept cultural relativism, as defended by this argument, and yet also embrace a morality that has a universal scope (one example of this being Long 2001).

In response to this a relativist might introduce an additional claim. She might argue that moral norms ought to be applied to all people only if they can be justified to all people. This additional premise links universalism of justification and universalism of scope by stipulating that unless universalism of justification is true (i.e. unless moral principles can be justified to all) then universalism of scope is inappropriate (i.e. moral principles should not be applied to all). The argument would then read as follows:

 (i) there is profound disagreement
 (ii) this disagreement invalidates universalism of justification

Therefore:

(iii) universalism of justification is wrong
(iv) if moral norms cannot be justified to all then they ought not to be applied to all (the new premise linking universalism of scope and universalism of justification)

Therefore:

(C) There are no universal moral norms. (cf, further, Wong 1984, 179–90 and Long 2001, esp. 259–71)

Setting aside the truth or falsity of the first and second premises, this argument, and in particular the additional premise, suffer from one critical weakness. This is that the additional premise—premise (iv)—is itself a transcultural normative principle. It affirms a universal principle that it is wrong to impose a principle on a person unless it can be justified to them. The argument is thus self-refuting for it affirms a universalism of scope in order to ground an anti-universalist position. This is not to say that the additional premise is false. It is that if (iv) is true then it subverts the argument for it articulates a universal moral principle.

This section has covered much ground and for this reason it may be useful to draw together its conclusions. What has been seen is that an argument that grounds relativism on the existence of moral disagreement rests on a dubious empirical assumption (point 1) and contains a mistaken inference (disagreement refutes universalism) (point 2). We have also seen that it has no force against a universalism of scope (point 4). Furthermore, the analysis of the first two limitations of the argument have provided support for a universalism of justification (point 3).

# XII

Having considered six conceptual challenges to universalism we may now turn to examine three normative challenges, namely the charge that universalism: (1) represses difference and imposes uniformity, (2) legitimizes power politics, and (3) is illegitimate because a form of external interference.

To take the first charge first, one common complaint against universalist theories is that they stifle diversity and are repressive of plurality and difference. This objection is levelled by some (but not all) postmodernists and post-structuralists.[51] Universal principles are, by their nature, so it is argued, a form of repression: they generate uniformity and sameness and as such are hostile to plurality. A statement of this kind of reasoning can be found in the work of Emmanuel Lévinas who in *Otherwise than Being* objects to 'the subsuming of particular cases under a general rule' (1999 [1974]: 159). The claim is that to invoke universal principles is to subsume all under a general heading and hence to be inattentive to diversity.

This argument against universalism is unconvincing. To see why, it is useful to return to O'Neill's point that universalism is defined in terms of applying the same values (universal form) to all (universal scope). As such, moral universalism, in itself, is not committed to any specific content (O'Neill 1996: 75) and, as we have seen earlier, there is great diversity among universalist approaches from Walzer's 're-iterative universalism' to Nussbaum's Aristotelianism to Habermas's 'discourse ethics'.[52] This point is significant because whilst the argument under scrutiny is applicable against some brands of universalism it lacks force against others. To see this, it is useful to make a distinction between proscriptive and prescriptive principles.[53] The former prohibit some specific activities but do not prescribe any specific ones that everyone must follow. Prescriptive principles, by contrast, do specify some particular activities that everyone must adopt. This distinction is of immense importance because the argument is forceful only against prescriptive universalism and not against proscriptive universalism. Some examples of universalist theories may help to illustrate this point. Stuart Hampshire has defended a procedural form of universalism, according to which all societies should honour certain procedures for resolving conflict. His position is compatible with difference and diversity because these procedures are highly likely to result in different policies in different cultures (1989: 54–5, 63, 72–8, 108–9, 135–46).[54] His brand of universalism does not prescribe any specific policies but permits considerable variation. Furthermore, as we shall see in the following chapter, the same point can be made about individual rights to freedom of association, speech, and belief (Chapter 3, Section X). They permit individuals to choose widely differing personal ideals and hence cannot be accused of being repressive. The challenge thus applies to some tokens but not the type.

Some may concede that some kinds of universalism are less restrictive of cultural diversity than others but, they might argue, all universalisms (whether proscriptive or prescriptive) are insufficiently sensitive to cultural diversity. No matter what the content of one's moral theory, to ascribe the same values to everyone curtails diversity. The argument of the preceding paragraph does not get to the root of the problem because to impose the same rules (universality of form) on everyone (universality of scope) treats everyone identically and subsumes everyone under the same heading. As such universal values cannot show respect for people's particularity and their own distinct cultural identities.[55] Instead, one needs to abandon universal rules and instead grant some exemptions to enable people to practise their way of life.

To this four points should be made. First, a universalist can accept that there should be exceptions to some rules. Their claim is only that there should be *some* universal norms and this is compatible with allowing that some issues should not be governed by universal norms. Second, as Barry has argued, any proposal to exempt some people from general rules must satisfy a number of stringent conditions. It must show that there is a rationale for a rule. It must then show that there is a case for exempting some from that rule. And it must also show that this case applies only to some, and not to all, people for otherwise it would call for the abolition of the rule. As Barry points out, these conditions are hard to meet and consequently many proposed exceptions to rules should be rejected (2001: 32–50, cf. esp. pp. 43, 48, 62).[56] A third point to note is that often exemptions to rules are not required to show respect to different cultural practices. The objective—to have legal arrangements that do not discriminate against cultural minorities—can often be met by new universal rules (Caney 2002*b*: 88–90). Fourth, we should not accept unquestioningly the tacit assumption that cultural diversity should never be restricted and that universal rules should be discarded if they clash with some cultural practices. Two reasons can be given in support of universal rules. First, one standard source of injustice is where like cases are treated in a different way. A framework with universal rules provides a fair environment because, unlike one in which there are differential rules, it treats all persons in an identical fashion. To this it might be added that a situation in which there are no universal rules and some are treated differently to others is a ripe source of discontent and disputes.

A third point to note is that the anti-universalist argument is, itself, actually a form of universalism. The proponents of this argument are opposed to projects that thrust a set of uniform values on everyone else. As such, however, they are themselves articulating a universal principle—namely 'show respect to other persons, allow them the space to practise their way of life'. Their critique can thus be best understood as a critique of some kinds of universalism drawing on an affirmation of another more culturally sensitive universalism. As such, although the argument officially opposes universal rules it is itself inspired by a universal ethic.[57]

# XIII

Given the lack of success of the first normative argument, let us consider a second moral argument against universalism. According to a common line of reasoning, the problem with universalism is that universal moral values are nothing more than a cover for power politics. Imperialists and states with aggressive foreign policies, it is argued, invoke universal moral principles to legitimize their power-driven selfish aims. Universalist projects are inevitably partial and power-motivated and all universalist ideals are suspect because they are used to defend policies of conquest, exploitation, and oppression. Such a line of reasoning is often made by realists. E. H. Carr, for example, levels this accusation against so-called utopians in his celebrated *The Twenty Years' Crisis*. As he writes, 'these supposedly absolute and universal principles were not principles at all, but the unconscious reflexions of national policy based on a particular interpretation of national interest at a particular time' (1995 [1939]: 80). Universal principles are merely 'weapons framed for the furtherance of interests' (1995 [1939]: 65). Scepticism about universal values is also forcefully expressed by Carl Schmitt. He claims that 'a universal concept' like 'humanity' will always be abused by states: '[t]he concept of humanity is an especially useful ideological instrument of imperialist expansion, and in its ethical humanitarian form it is a specific vehicle of economic imperialism. Here one is reminded of a somewhat modified expression of Proudhon's: whoever invokes humanity wants to cheat' (1996 [1932]: 54).

This kind of reasoning is, however, unpersuasive as a critique of moral universalism for a number of reasons. First, the principle underpinning the argument is incorrect. The fact that an ideal is sometimes invoked by some people as a cover for their imperialist designs does not logically imply that the ideal is wrong. It just shows that we should be suspicious of political actors when they invoke moral principles and should not unquestioningly take them at their word. It does not, however, invalidate the (universal) moral norms employed.

A second, and related, problem with the anti-universalist argument is that the argument, if it is a valid one, would also tell against cultural relativism for relativist principles are sometimes used by tyrants to legitimize their oppression. One standard strategy adopted by despots to legitimize practices that outsiders criticize as inhumane is that there are no universal moral values and that their policies are just because they are in conformity with their traditions and history. The argument under examination does not establish that there is anything in particular wrong with universal values.

In addition to this, the argument's empirical claim is, as it stands, far too sweeping to be plausible. Some moral judgements are perhaps nothing more than masked attempts to dominate others but it is incredible to claim of each and every moral judgement made (a) that it is an attempt to exercise power and (b) that it is nothing more than that. A proponent of the argument might address this last point by expanding the notion of power it employs. He or she might draw on the work of Michel Foucault who has argued that all regimes of truth are productions of power. Foucault conceives of 'the exercise of power as a way in which certain actions may structure the field of other possible actions' (2002*b*: 343, cf. also p. 337). On this view, 'power relations' are 'the strategies by which individuals try to direct and control the conduct of others' (1997*b*: 298). To say this is to adopt a very broad definition of power according to which power involves the shaping of people's beliefs. If power is defined in this very broad way then the empirical claim being made becomes much more plausible. Employing this definition Foucault maintains that power is omnipresent. As he writes, '[e]ach society has its regime of truth, its "general politics" of truth—that is, the types of discourse it accepts and makes function as true' (2002*a*: 131). He refers to 'systems of power that produce and sustain' truth (2002*a*: 132).[58]

However, as Foucault himself emphasizes, power thus defined loses its troubling aspect (1997*b*: 298–9; 2002*a*: 120). The idea that power involves affecting others has none of the pejorative connotations that the argument relies on. A philosophical argument can be an exercise of power in this sense but this does not entail either that we cannot evaluate the argument and determine whether it is plausible or that moral argument is somehow repressive. Put succinctly, that moral ideals are exercises of power in Foucault's sense is quite consistent with thinking some sound and some unsound. It is interesting to note in this context that Foucault employs a distinct term, 'domination', to refer to a constant coercive restriction of others' freedom (power as it would normally be defined). And he is emphatic that not all power involves domination (1997*b*: 283, cf. also pp. 292–3, 299). Similarly, he stresses that power is compatible with persons being free (1997*a*: 167; 1997*b*: 292–3; 2002*b*: 342). Broadening the notion of 'power' may thus make the empirical claim more plausible but it does not salvage the argument for the broader concept of power and does not undermine or subvert the legitimacy of universal values.[59]

An additional problem with the argument is that to succeed it has to show that all the techniques that have been proposed to prevent moral argument from being distorted by bias fail. For there are, of course, numerous well-known devices that have been proposed to lessen the probability of moral arguments being employed in the service of one's own ends. One obvious example of a device designed to minimize bias is, of course, Rawls's use of the veil of ignorance in his original position (1999c). Another equally familiar example would be Mill's claim that public debate can help reveal biases and interests (1977a [1859]). The relevant point is, therefore, that the extent to which persons' moral convictions function as a mask for power politics can be scrutinized, contested, and undermined. Therefore, the argument under scrutiny, to be complete, must show why all such techniques for minimizing power politics inevitably fail.

Finally, we should note that this argument actually presupposes rather than entails that universalism is false. For the structure of the argument is that *since* universalism is false, there cannot be anything more to 'universal moral values' than exercises of power. But this, of course, does not establish the falsity of universalism: it is its starting assumption (and an undefended one). This problem is particularly apparent in Waltz's brief statement that '[s]ince justice cannot be objectively defined, the temptation of a powerful nation is to claim that the solution it seeks to impose is a just one' (1979: 201). This begs the question for it assumes, and does not show, that there can be no objective, that is universal, concept of justice.

The preceding points establish that the argument is not a powerful critique of universalism. A final point to make is simply that, as with the previous argument, this critique of moral universalism is itself driven by a moral commitment. Its misgivings about universalism are in part that it is legitimizing oppression and underlying this charge is the conviction that oppression is wrong. Furthermore the conviction driving the argument is most plausibly construed as a *universal* one for its guiding thought is that it is wrong for all persons to thrust their values and interests on others.

# XIV

As we have seen, one fault of the last argument is that it finds no fault with universal principles in particular: its target is really all moral principles. So we need an argument that targets universalism. This leads to the next argument, which like the preceding two arguments is a normative one. According to this third line of reasoning, a relativist position is more plausible because it allows people to pursue their collective ways of life. Universalism, it is argued, is culpable of external interference and does not show respect for different forms of life. This position is articulated very clearly by Walzer. In *Spheres of Justice*, for example, he writes

We are (all of us) culture-producing creatures; we make and inhabit meaningful worlds. Since there is no way to rank and order these worlds with regard to their understanding of social goods, we do justice to actual men and women by respecting their particular creations. . . . Justice is rooted in the distinct understandings of places, honors, jobs, things of all sorts, that constitute a shared way of life. To override those understandings is (always) to act unjustly.   (1983: 314)

He further writes that to disregard the shared understandings of a community is 'an act of disrespect' (1983: 320). A similar argument is made in *Interpretation and Social Criticism*. Moral criticism based on universal criteria—termed 'discon-nected criticism'—invades the life of the community (1987: 64–5). He conjures up 'a universal Office of Social Criticism, where an internationally recruited and specially trained civil service (of professional philosophers? political theorists? theologians?) applied the same moral principles to every country, culture, and religious community in the world' (1994: 48). Cultural relativism shows respect to persons enabling them to live their own way whereas moral universalism is a form of external, colonial, rule. James Tully makes a somewhat similar claim. He objects to what he terms 'modern constitutionalism', an approach which demands identical treatment for all, for overriding the local and particular agreements arrived at by members of historic communities. He thus offers us a bottom-up ideal of negotiated agreements and conventions in contrast to the top-down imposition of universal principles (1995).

This line of reasoning is commonplace but it does run into a number of problems. First, we should immediately record that, as with the preceding two arguments, it is a form of universalism in disguise for it is stating as a universal norm that if people consent to something then it is morally legitimate. Underpinning it is a universalist commitment that stipulates that people, and that includes all people, should not interfere.[60] (Walzer appears later to recognize this for, as has been observed already, in work subsequent to *Spheres of Justice* he embraces what he terms 'reiterative universalism' (1990: 513–15)). We can put this point in another way by consider-ing Bernard Williams's critical discussion of what he terms 'vulgar relativism'. Williams defines the latter as affirming both that a society is just if it conforms to the values shared by its members and also that one country should not impose its values on another country. Williams's point is that the second contention is actually a universalist one. Hence it is incompatible with a relativist repudiation of any universal values (1972: 34–5). So to claim, as Walzer does, that people should not interfere with other communities' ways of ordering their society is to make a universal claim and it requires the rejection of cultural relativism. Put otherwise: consider a culture whose shared values are colonialist and imperialist. If it is true to its shared values, as relativism requires it to be, it must, as a matter of justice, colonize other societies. But if it does this it violates the injunction not to interfere in the affairs of another country.

A second point to note is that this view perhaps gains some intuitive force by being confused with another distinct claim. One might endorse the vision of a society being governed by values it has generated simply because one values the good of solidarity and hence endorses a society in which the principles applied to the society enjoy the common support of the people. But this need not be

a relativist claim but rather a universal claim to the effect that there are some
universal goods like the good of solidarity or social unity.

A further, related, problem with Walzer's defence of cultural relativism is, as
Barry notes, that it rests on a confusion for it suggests that if one accepts universalism one must *ipso facto* endorse intervention (1987: 64, cf. Barry 1995*b*:
76–7). But there is no reason to think that this is so. Two considerations should
be noted here. First, one might argue, as Rawls does, that one can disapprove of
a society and yet also believe that it has the right to be self-governing (1999*b*).
(Rawls's theory is examined in further depth in Chapters 3 and 4). Second, there
is no straightforward inference from the claim that X-ing is wrong to the claim
that it should be prohibited and from the claim that it should be prohibited to the
claim that outsiders are entitled to prohibit it. To be sure, there are cases where
universalists think that the practices observed in some countries are wrong and
that they should be prohibited but then to show why this is wrong requires the
relativist to provide an argument against intervention in all circumstances.
As we shall see later, in Chapter 7, it is difficult to argue that intervention is never
justified.

A fourth problem with the argument is that one of the key themes motivating
the argument being considered is that universalist reasoning is guilty of one
group of people (predominantly, but not exclusively, western) foisting their ideas
on the rest of humanity. It is thus appropriate to ask what the alternative is for
surely, whatever those who are powerful do, they leave their imprint on the lives
of many others. Suppose, for example, that they decide not to implement human
rights but argue that the sovereignty of states should be honoured above all. The
problem here is that the concept of a sovereign state is also a western idea and to
affirm it is to impose one's values on other persons. The core point is that
through our actions and omissions we cannot help but affect the lives of other
persons: it is an inescapable fact of the world. The argument, thus, rests on an illusion (Pogge 1994*b*: 216–17; 1998*b*: 535 fn. 51).

It may be appropriate to sum up here. What we have seen is that none of the
last three arguments invalidates a universalism of scope. Each is vulnerable to
specific objections but they share a common defect, namely that each is reliant
on an alternative universal ethic which insists, respectively, on the value of
'respecting diversity' or 'not using moral language to further one's interests' or
'respecting the rights of communities to be self-determining'.[61] As Kwame
Anthony Appiah has perceptively noted:

it is characteristic of those who pose as antiuniversalists to use the term *universalism* as if
it meant *pseudouniversalism*, and the fact is that their complaint is not with universalism
at all. What they truly object to—and who would not?—is Eurocentric hegemony *posing*
as universalism. Thus, while the debate is couched in terms of the competing claims of
particularism and universalism, the actual ideology of universalism is never interrogated,
and, indeed, is even tacitly accepted. Ironically . . . the attack on something called
"universalism" leads to the occlusion of genuine local difference. (1992: 58)

# XV

It is time to conclude. This chapter has covered much ground. In it we have seen that three common objections to relativism and defences of universalism are un-persuasive. In particular we have seen that

1. the charge that relativism is untenable because it condones unjust practices begs the question;
2. the claim that relativism either aspires to be universally true and is self-contradictory or claims to be relatively true and hence incoherent is too quick; and
3. the contention that relativism is self-undermining is more forceful but that it does not provide support for universalism.

We then

4. turned to a more promising argument for universalism, the General Argument, which argued both that moral principles should apply to all if all persons are similar in morally relevant ways and that persons throughout the world share common morally relevant properties.

Having defended moral universalism, the chapter considered six conceptual counter-arguments. These included the charge that universalism

5. presupposes a common human nature and this is implausible;
6. generates principles that are too abstract and general to be morally relevant;
7. does not chime with people and hence cannot act as effective moral ideals;
8. is false to the way in which we engage in moral argument;
9. fails to recognize the situated nature of moral reflection; and
10. is refuted by the existence of profound moral disagreement.

The chapter argued that none of these arguments is persuasive and also that the criticisms of the last one provide support for a version of universalism of justification. The chapter then turned to consider three normative challenges to universalism, namely the objections that universalism:

11. curtails diversity;
12. is an exercise in power politics; and
13. constitutes interference in the collective life of communities.

Again, it was argued that none of these is persuasive. This chapter has, thus, defended universalism of scope against its critics. It remains to be seen, however, what universal values there are. This task is taken up in Chapters 3 and 4, both of which consider what universal principles of justice there should be.

## NOTES

1. In addressing these topics first, however, this book does not divorce the topics of this chapter from the discussions of civil, political, and economic justice in the next two chapters. Some of the points raised in this chapter will be picked up again in the following chapters.

2. O'Neill writes, '[b]roadly speaking, *universalists* orient ethical reasoning and judgement partly by appeal to certain universal principles that are to hold for all lives and across all situations. The most elementary thought of universalists is formal: there are certain ethical principles or standards which hold for all, and not merely for some cases. This claim about *form* is often closely linked to a second claim about the *scope* of universal principles, which universalists generally think is more-or-less cosmopolitan, at least for some basic principles' (footnote omitted) (1996: 11).

3. The distinction between universalism of scope and universalism of justification is also made by David Wong (1984, p. 189). The term 'universalism of justification' is potentially misleading. Those who reject what I am terming 'universalism of justification' (and who embrace 'universalism of scope') may also seek to justify their principles to everyone in the sense that they can outline the arguments for their principles. What they reject, however, is the view that a principle can apply universally only if all accept the arguments for it. They entertain the possibility that a principle should apply with universal form and scope and that one can give good reasons for it, even though the reasons are ones that not everyone accepts. They may thus be committed to justification but not in the sense employed in the term 'universalism of justification'. (I am grateful to Geoffrey Scarre for raising this issue.)

4. See also Long's invocation and use of this distinction (2001). Long defends a universalism of scope (2001, esp. pp. 233–6) but rejects the idea of universalism of justification (2001: 143–63).

5. Seyla Benhabib, too, makes a similar distinction but employs a wider typology. She distinguishes between four kinds of universalism (1999: 45–7). Universalism, she points out, can have 'a moral meaning' where this states that all persons should be treated as 'moral equals' (1999: 46). This is similar, although not identical, to universalism of scope because it states that one value should be applied to all in the same way. (It is not identical to universalism of scope because it says that *individuals* should be treated with equal respect and universalism is compatible with principles with universal scope and universal form which concern non-individual entities such as nations). A second kind of universalism is what she terms universalism as 'a justification strategy', where this states that norms are universal if justifiable to all (1999: 46). This, then, is equivalent to universalism of justification. A third kind of universalism makes the descriptive claim that all persons share a common human nature (1999: 45–6). Finally, a fourth kind of universalism is a legal universalism that maintains that there should be a universal legal system that treats all in the same way (1999: 46–7). Although Benhabib points out that the four kinds are distinct, she argues that adequate defences of one kind of universalism might rely on one of the other kinds. For example, she holds that legal universalism is plausible only if one embraces moral universalism and, unlike Larmore, she maintains that moral universalism is tenable only if it relies on universal justifiability (1999: 59, fn. 9; cf. also p. 47). I have altered the order in which Benhabib arranges these four kinds of universalism.

6. There is a footnote at the end of this sentence which cites Beitz (1983: 596), cf. Pogge (1989: 270, fn. 37).

7. See, for example, Pogge's statement of moral universalism: (2002*a*, esp. pp. 30–2).
8. The term 'reasonably' is critical here for their claim is that norms must be justified to all who are not exclusively committed to their self-interest and who wish to be able to reach a fair agreement with others.
9. See also Benhabib (1992, 1995, 1999), Forst (2002, esp. pp. 154–229), and Andrew Linklater (1998)—all of whom embrace a universalism of justification as well as a universalism of scope.
10. For other examples: cf. C. Jones (1999: 175) and Hampshire (1983, throughout but esp. pp.126–39). See also Walzer (1987: 23–5).
11. See, more generally, Scanlon's discussion of relativism (1998: 328–61).
12. See Bielefeldt (2000: 114–17, esp. p. 116); Dower (1998: 12–13, 43); Pogge (1989: 269, cf. also pp. 227–30); and Taylor (1998, esp. pp. 37–8, 48–53; 1999, esp. pp. 124–6, 133–8, 143–4). See also Abdullahi An-Na'im (1999, esp. pp. 153, 166–8). For the concept of an overlapping consensus see Rawls (1993*b*: 133–72).
13. For a contemporary analysis see Putnam (1993).
14. For a similar point see Beitz (2001: 279).
15. Some communitarians, of course, do make the meta-ethical claim that valid moral principles are those that map onto the common moral beliefs of a community and, as such, deny moral univeralism. To confuse matters, Walzer explicitly made this claim in *Spheres of Justice* (1983: 313). In his later work, however, he has reconfigured his position, describing it, as noted above, as a kind of univeralism—namely a reiterative universalism.
16. See also Jack Donnelly's distinction between radical, strong, and weak cultural relativism. Radical relativism claims that the only rights people have are those that are derivable from their culture; strong relativism argues that rights are in the main derived from people's culture but should be qualified by some basic human rights; weak relativism maintains that human rights may be abrogated in extreme circumstances. For the definitions see Donnelly (1989: 109–10). Cf. further (1989: 109–24).
17. For examples of this line of reasoning see Alan Gewirth (1994: 29) and Tzvetan Todorov (1993: 389–90).
18. For further germane discussion see Kymlicka's discussion of what interpreting shared values might mean (1993: 211–15).
19. John Kekes explores (but does not endorse) this way of defending relativism: see his discussion of the Dinka practice of burying people alive (1994: 53–9).
20. Hilary Putnam indicts relativism on similar grounds: (1981: 119–24, esp. pp. 119–21).
21. See, relatedly, Habermas's argument that Foucault's genealogical method is defective because it is self-undermining (1987: 279–81, 286).
22. For references to this line of reasoning see Sect. IX.
23. Having said this, this line of reasoning does perhaps generate some support for moral universalism. The thought here is that moral universalism coheres best with people's moral experience and, as such, this gives it prima facie plausibility. For further discussion of this line of reasoning see Caney (1999*b*: 23–4).
24. Some particularists might dispute (P1), arguing that it is inappropriate to think of morality in terms of 'principles'. Space precludes a full discussion of this view. For a convincing critique of such a position see O'Neill (1996: 77–89).
25. On the identification of common human needs see Foot (2002: 33).
26. On people's physiological needs see Keith Graham's penetrating discussion of what he terms 'the material constraint' (1996: 143: cf. further pp. 143–6) and more generally

his discussion of the different kinds of constraint that agents face (1996, esp. pp. 137–43).

27. This point, it is worth stressing, is also recognized by post-structuralist writers such as R. B. J. Walker. Walker writes that 'there does seem to be overwhelming evidence that we all share common vulnerabilities, a common maldevelopment, and a fragile planet. A universalism framed in the arrogance of empires has to be resisted, but the possibilities inherent in connections, in shared vulnerabilities and solidarities, remain to be explored' (1988: 135).

28. For an earlier version of this list cf. Nussbaum (2000a: 78–80). See more generally (2000a: 70–96).

29. Cf. further Nussbaum (1999: 7–8).

30. Rorty, for example, objects to certain kinds of liberals on the grounds that they 'hold onto the Enlightenment notion that there is something called a common human nature, a metaphysical substrate in which things called "rights" are embedded, and that this substrate takes moral precedence over all merely "cultural" superstructures' (1991b: 207). Cf. also (1989: xiii, 59, 195–6; 1991c: 213). See, however, (1991c: 215). For a persuasive critique of Rorty's account of human nature see Geras (1995: 47–70).

31. For good defences of human nature and the morally relevant features of persons': cf. Geras (1983: 95–116), Hurka (1993: 9–51), and Perry (1998: 61–71).

32. In his excellent treatment of the concept, Perry is very clear that whilst there is a common human nature this does not require that people are identical (1998: 61–71, esp. pp. 64–5).

33. We might also note that the denial of human nature opens the way to the worst forms of violence since one common way of legitimizing cruelty to others is to deny that these others are genuinely human (Perry 1998: 59). For example, in 1994 the Hutu dominated radio station branded Tutsis cockroaches (*inyenzi*) that had to be eliminated (Keane 1996: 10).

34. For further discussion see O'Neill's analysis of the objection that moral universalism is guilty of an 'empty formalism' that cannot give guidance (1996: 77: cf. futher pp. 77–89). Her wording recalls, of course, Hegel's critique of Kant's universalist moral philosophy (*moralität*) and his justification of the importance of conventional moral norms (*sittlichkeit*).

35. Cf. also Walzer (1977: xv; 1987: 62). See, further, Norman Daniels's perceptive discussion of Walzer. Daniels argues that Walzer embraces an extreme brand of internalism (1996: 112–13). For his subsequent critique of Walzer's internalism see (1996: 113–17).

36. There's a footnote at the end of this sentence in which Bell refers to Walzer (1988: x, 19, 233–5). See Bell (1993: 82, fn. 22). For a very different approach which also invokes considerations about motivation to defend relativism see Gilbert Harman (1989, esp. pp. 372–3).

37. The original, of course, reads: 'The philosophers have only interpreted the world, in various ways; the point is to change it' (Marx 1988 [1845]: 158).

38. The argument in this paragraph has been made by many. See, for example, Galston (1991: 158); Habermas (1992a: 45–57); Kymlicka (1989: 65–6); Waldron (1989: 575–8; 2000: 234–6). One of the general themes of Nagel's *The Last Word* is that relativist accounts which treat people's views in a sociological fashion as nothing more than the values of their community misconstrue the way in which people regard their own beliefs: see (1997, esp. pp. 13–35, 101–25). See also Dworkin (1996). For further

discussion of how these considerations actually support moral universalism see Caney (1999*b*: 23–4).

39. For pertinent discussion see Brown (1996: 177), McCarthy (1994: 80–1), Walzer (1987: 25; 1994: 1–19).
40. The phrase is, of course, the title of a book by Nagel (1986).
41. See, further, (1991*a*, esp. pp. 29–30; 1991*c*: 212–13).
42. There is a footnote after the word 'communities', which refers to works by Rorty and Tully that advance the same theme: cf. Bell (1993: 82–3, fn. 25).
43. It is interesting, in this context, to consider Alasdair MacIntyre's moral theory. He strongly emphasizes that moral reasoning can only take place within traditions (1988, 1990). But he also denies relativism (1988: 352–69) for he claims that the rational evaluation of traditions is possible (1988, esp. pp. 354–6, 362; 1990: 180–1).
44. A further example of a universalism that is not committed to finding a view from nowhere is Habermas's 'discourse ethics'. As we shall see in Ch. 3 when we examine his defence of universal rights, Habermas defends universalism by analysing the way in which people employ moral language (1992*a*, *b*, 1993). He presents a transcendental argument that derives universal values by exploring the assumptions that underlie our use of moral terms. As such it works from within human experience. For another example see Galston (1991: 49).
45. This argument is also vulnerable to a second objection but since this objection also tells against the next argument it will be discussed in Sect. X.
46. Cf. Harbour (1995: 155–70).
47. For an earlier statement of this last argument see Caney (2000*d*: 57)
48. This distinction is similar, but not identical, to David Wong's distinction between incommensurability of 'translation', 'justification', 'evaluation' (1989: 140–58 esp. p. 140). What I have termed 'conceptual incommensurability' is the same as Wong's 'incommensurability of translation' and what I have termed 'moral incommensurability' combines Wong's last two categories.
49. See also Benhabib's use of Davidson and Putnam in her critique of Lyotard and Rorty (1995: 245).
50. For some of these kinds of consideration see Barry (1995*a*: 195–9, esp. pp. 198–9; 1995*b*: 77–8); Joshua Cohen (1986: 467–8); James Fishkin (1984: 760); James Nickel (1987: 73); and Nagel (1986: 148).
51. It is important to stress that not all postmodernists and post-structuralists make this argument. Some are explicit in their commitment to universal moral principles: Derrida (2000, 2001).
52. O'Neill makes two additional responses against the contention that universalism produces uniformity. She points out, first, that 'universal principles . . . underdetermine action, so must *permit* varied implementation' (1996: 75). Second, she notes that universal principles often apply only to a subgroup of individuals. For instance, a claim that there should be a universal right of parents to financial support would apply only to parents (1996: 75).
53. I borrow this way of putting it from O'Neill. O'Neill seeks to rebut the charge that 'universal principles are *ipso facto* principles that prescribe or proscribe . . . *uniform* treatment for all the cases for which they hold' (1996: 74). My point is that it makes a great difference whether universal principles prescribe conduct, or proscribe it.

54. The same point could be made with reference to Andrew Linklater's brand of universalism. Linklater affirms a universalist approach but, drawing on Habermas, strongly emphasizes the importance of dialogue (1998, esp. pp. 85–108).

55. For an extended argument to the effect that modern liberal thinkers, by treating others on their own liberal terms, assimilate them and disregard their particularity see Tully (1995, esp. pp. 17, 23–5, 31, 34–98). Tully objects strongly to the line of argument—typified by (P3)—to the effect that we should extend rights and duties to others on the basis that they have the same moral properties and standing as everyone else (1995: 97).

56. I believe that Barry somewhat overstates his case and rather more exemptions pass his test than he thinks; cf. Caney (2002*b*).

57. That many critiques of universalism themselves presuppose universal moral principles has often been noted. See, for example, Linklater (1998: 48, 67–73); Thomas McCarthy (1992: xiii, fn. 12); and Stephen White (1992: 134–5).

58. See (2002*a* throughout, esp. pp. 114, 119, 131).

59. Foucault, one might also note, embraces some universal values such as human rights: (2002*c*: 474–5) and (1997*a*: 164). Having said this, he is sceptical of the idea of a universal intellectual (2002*a*: 126–33). Moreover, he is critical of the belief that criticism involves the 'search for formal structures with universal value' (1997*c*: 315).

60. This point is noted by White in his brief but astute comment on Walzer (1992: 134–5).

61. Note, this chapter has concentrated on how well a universalism of scope deals with the anti-universalist arguments since this is the brand of universalism that universalists all affirm. It bears noting that some of the anti-universalist arguments also lack force against a universalism of justification. For example, the claim that moral universalism does not respect cultural diversity would have little force against a universalism of justification for the latter claims that norms are correct only insofar as they can be justified to all. As such it prevents minorities from having the values of a majority imposed on them.

# 3

# Civil and Political Justice

> Three degrees of latitude reverse all jurisprudence, a meridian decides what is
> truth . . . That is droll justice which is bounded by a stream! Truth on this side
> of the Pyrenees, error on that . . . Can there be any thing more absurd than that
> a man should have the right to kill me because he lives across the water.
>
> Blaise Pascal (1885 [1670]: 61)

Having critically examined various objections to moral universalism and indicated
a rationale for universalism, Chapters 3 and 4 consider arguments for two
different types of universal value. This chapter begins this enquiry by analysing
what universal principles of *civil and political justice* (if any) should obtain, where
the phrase *civil and political justice* refers to those principles of justice which
specify what civil and political liberties, if any, people should enjoy.[1] It explores
questions such as: to what civil and political liberties are individuals entitled as
a matter of justice? and, on what grounds are individuals entitled to these liberties?' Does civil and political justice entail a commitment to 'rights' and indeed
'human rights'? Or is the language of rights, as many critics allege, morally unacceptable and a cause of fragmentation and a lack of cohesion? Furthermore,
are attempts to promote human rights to civil and political liberties nothing
more than cultural imperialism?

The following chapter (Chapter 4) then complements this chapter, examining
what universal principles of *distributive justice* should be adopted. These two
chapters thereby link together to provide an analysis of what universal principles
of justice should apply at the global level.[2]

To address the questions that are the focus of this chapter, the chapter begins, in
Section I, with an analysis of human rights since this term plays a central and
important role in a plausible account of civil and political justice. It then puts
forward a general thesis about justifications for civil and political human rights
(Section II). This is followed by an analysis of four cosmopolitan arguments for
human rights that criticizes three of them but defends the fourth (Sections III–VII).
The chapter then considers an alternative non-cosmopolitan approach to defending civil and political human rights, presented by John Rawls in *The Law of
Peoples* (1999*b*) (Section VIII). The remainder of the chapter explores four misgivings about civil and political human rights. These include the objections that
such human rights are a species of imperialism (Section IX), produce homogeneity
(Section X), and generate egoism and destroy community (Section XI). It then

considers realist charges that foreign policy to protect civil and political human rights is in practice selective and partial and a cloak for the pursuit of the national interest (Section XII).

## I

Since this chapter argues that civil and political justice requires that all persons enjoy a set of civil and political human rights, it is necessary to begin with an analysis of human rights, starting with an examination of the concept of a 'right'. In what follows I operate with a fairly general characterization of rights and hope, thereby, to avoid some of the debates concerning the nature of rights. I construe the statement that 'A has a right' as a statement that A is entitled to be treated in certain ways: others are duty bound to treat them in certain ways. These duties are not ones of charity or benevolence or philanthropy: if someone has a right they can claim it as a matter of justice.[3]

This raises the question of *who* has *what* duties. The accounts that follow provide different answers to this question. Two distinctions should be introduced here. First, we should distinguish between those accounts of rights that generate negative duties and those that generate positive duties. Some accounts of rights entail only negative duties, requiring that one abstain from certain actions. Others, by contrast, claim that rights entail positive duties that require not simply that we do not violate someone else's rights but also that we should act to protect the rights of others. A second, separate, distinction has been introduced by Pogge. Pogge distinguishes between interactional and institutional conceptions of rights (1992*a*: 90–101; 1994*a*: 90–8, esp. pp. 90–1; 1995: 113–19; 2000: 51–69). According to an institutional conception, to postulate a right is to say that an institutional scheme should secure this right for its members. The duty to protect a person's rights falls on the fellow members of his or her institutional scheme. According to an interactional view, by contrast, a person's rights generate duties on all other persons and not simply on those who belong to that person's institutional scheme(s). The key difference between the interactional and the institutional approach is that the latter, as its name suggests, attributes moral significance to institutions and the membership of institutions.[4] We are faced then with a variety of different accounts of the relationship between rights and duties—accounts that will be evaluated later.

Having conducted a preliminary analysis of the notion of a right we can turn to the next question: what are 'human' rights? A human right is a right that someone enjoys in virtue of being a human being. To bring out what is distinctive about a human right it is helpful to use H. L. A. Hart's distinction between 'general rights' and 'special rights' (1985: 84–8). Human rights are, in this sense, general rights: all persons have them. Special rights, by contrast, are not rights that a person necessarily has simply by virtue of being a person. Rather someone acquires a special right if there is some special feature about that person that creates a right. One common way of acquiring a special right is, for example, entering a contract with someone else. Hart makes absolutely clear, however, that special rights are not acquired only by consent (1985: 85–7). Someone might have certain rights because they occupy a social role that brings with it certain rights and perhaps also duties even if they did not choose to occupy that social role (1985: 87). We can distinguish between different kinds of special rights. Consider first what one might call *citizenship rights* (or more succinctly *civic rights*), by which I mean those special rights arising from a person's membership of a political community. Civic rights might include, for example, a right to residence or a right to vote in elections in that community or a right to stand for political office. Holders of civic rights may acquire these rights through choice (they have chosen to acquire citizenship and their application has been accepted by the state) or simply because they have been born into that political system. Another category of special rights is what has been termed *cultural rights*, by which is meant those rights that a person has qua member of a cultural community.[5] Recently, for example, many scholars, including most notably Will Kymlicka, have argued that principles of justice should be sensitive to people's cultural identities and that this, in turn, requires that members of some cultures are entitled to special rights in order to protect their cultural identity (1995). On this approach, therefore, some persons (members of minority cultures) possess some special rights (cultural rights) that are ascribable to them because of their membership of their culture. These special rights may include the right to use their own language or the right to educate their children according to the norms of their culture (and thus exempting them from state-level education systems) or the right to wear traditional dress (thus exempting them from state-level rules, like those concerning crash helmets).

Two further points about human rights are in order. First, it may be useful to distinguish between *minimalist* and *maximalist* accounts of civil and political human rights.[6] By the latter I mean an account of human rights that ascribes the traditional liberal democratic set of rights to all persons. This would comprise rights such as the right to freedom of action as long as it does not limit the liberty of others; the rights to freedom of belief, association, and speech; the right to vote; the right to a fair trial; and so on. In other words, a maximalist position ascribes to all persons the conventional set of rights that liberal democratic theory affirms. A minimalist approach, by contrast, ascribes some very fundamental human rights to persons but excludes others (such as, say, the right to vote). As we shall see, many are tempted by minimalist approaches. The analysis that follows calls into question the coherence of this kind of strategy.

Second, and relatedly, when appraising the accounts that follow, we should bear in mind the following three minimal desiderata of a sound theory of human rights. A theory of civil and political human rights must

(1) be able to supply criteria to determine what civil and political human rights persons have (the criterion of *determinacy*);

(2) outline a set of civil and political human rights that is consistent with its account of domestic political theory (the criterion of *domestic-compatibility*);[7] and,

(3) outline a set of civil and political human rights that is internally coherent: that is, it can provide a coherent account both of the rights it affirms and also the proposed rights that it rejects (the criterion of *coherence*).[8]

These three conceptual prerequisites of an adequate theory of human rights are, hopefully, straightforward and uncontroversial. (1) asks only that a theory be able to give guidance on what should be done and (2) and (3) ask only that the overall theory be consistent. Nonetheless, as shall be seen, several common accounts of human rights violate one or more of these conditions. Before proceeding further it may be worth pointing out that (2) does not require that one's account of universal civil and political rights should be *identical* to the civil and political rights that one thinks may apply within the state. (2) is quite consistent with someone affirming one set of rights to apply within the state and another set to apply at the global level *as long as a reason can be given as to why the two contexts are morally disanalogous* and hence the rights that apply in the 'domestic' context should not apply in the 'global' context. To employ the terminology of Chapter 1, to make this argument one would have to engage in level-1 analysis showing how the domestic and global contexts are fundamentally different in morally salient ways.

## II

Having conducted the necessary preliminary analysis, we may now consider the arguments given in defence of civil and political human rights and also the content of these rights. Before analysing the specific arguments, however, I want in this section to present a general claim about arguments for civil and political rights, namely:

the scope$_1$ claim: the standard justifications of rights to civil and political liberties entail that there are *human* rights to these same civil and political liberties.[9]

According to this claim, the conventional rationales for civil and political rights logically imply that everyone has these rights and hence that they are human, as opposed to civic, rights. Lest this statement is misunderstood, it should be stressed that it does not maintain that there can be no special rights. Rather, its contention is that many of the standard arguments for civil and political rights imply that these are human, as opposed to special, rights. It is, thus, not possible to affirm the standard rationales for civil and political rights without ascribing these rights to *all persons* and not just one's fellow citizens.[10] As we shall see later, this point is important when considering some of the popular critiques of civil and political human rights.

Given the importance of this claim, the aim of Sections III–VI is both to evaluate a number of arguments commonly adduced in defence of civil and political human rights and also to provide support for the scope$_1$ claim.

# III

One popular approach is adopted by contractarians such as Brian Barry. Barry maintains that principles are fair if no one could reasonably reject them. He refers to this contractarian account of justice as 'justice as impartiality' and argues that it represents the most plausible account of justice (1995*a*, esp. pp. 67–72).[11] To do this he contrasts it with other theories of justice. Most notably he contrasts it with what he terms 'justice as mutual advantage' where the latter states that principles are fair if self-interested agents accept them (1995*a*: 31–3).[12] Such an approach, argues Barry, is unfair on the weak since it allows the powerful to dictate terms that suit them. If principles do not suit them then they will simply not agree to them and can hold others to ransom (1995*a*: 41–6, 48). His theory of 'justice as impartiality', by contrast, asks what reasonable persons can agree to, maintaining that it is unreasonable to act simply on one's own self-interest and not take into account other people's interests.

Drawing on this theory of justice, Barry then argues that we should accept a set of civil and political human rights granting each person certain traditional liberal freedoms, like freedom of association, belief, expression, and action. His argument for these rights proceeds as follows: persons in all societies are radically divided about the good and hence cannot agree on any perfectionist ideal that promotes certain conceptions of the good (1995*a*: 168–73). This phenomenon may be more pronounced in liberal political regimes but it applies to non-liberal societies as well, and to portray the latter as homogeneous and united in their commitment to a specific conception of the good is simply inaccurate (1995*a*: 4–5). Given this, reasonable persons can reject principles that seek to impose specific conceptions of the good on people. Since principles are fair only if no one can reasonably reject them (1995*a*: 164–8), it follows that political regimes must not impose any conception of the good on their citizens. They should instead be neutral between conceptions of the good and protect the individual freedom of all (1995*a*: 12, 82–5, 143, 160, 172, 177).[13] Barry's contractarianism thus vindicates a traditional set of civil and political human rights and he is adamant that these are rights held by all human beings (1995*a*: 3–7).

Barry's argument is vulnerable to a number of objections. Perhaps the most troubling is the concern that his principle of reasonable rejection assumes a set of rights rather than defends it. The claim that fair principles are ones which no one can reasonably reject is a claim that we have reason to accept only if we accept something fairly close to the conclusion—namely that *all* humans have *equal* rights and hence that a principle is unjust if people withhold their consent from it. Barry's premise assumes the conclusion that it claims to establish since it assumes that a state of affairs is just if *each* reasonable person *consents* to it: this presupposes that they have a *right* to be consulted (Steiner 1996*b*: 311–13). As Barry himself makes clear, his brand of hypothetical contractarianism is a way of explicating an egalitarian perspective according to which each person has an equal moral status (1995a: 7–8, 113; 1998: 146). As such, however, it does not *demonstrate* that all persons have human rights but *assumes* that they do.

This argument does not entail that we should reject Barry's theory of justice as impartiality. Barry accepts that his theory does presuppose some equal moral rights but adds that the contractarian framework is not thereby rendered super-fluous because it provides an instructive way of explicating the idea of equal rights and shedding light on the requirements of justice (1995a: 113, 195–9; Caney 1996b: 282–4). In effect it says that we treat persons with respect and recognize their equal moral rights by constructing principles to which all reasonable persons assent. The evaluation of Barry's argument in the preceding paragraph does not challenge this further claim. What it does, nonetheless, entail is that before we accept Barry's theory as a *justification* of human rights we need to know why we should accept the premise of equal moral human rights in the first place. His argument, thus, fails to provide a defence of civil and political human rights.

Before we examine other attempts to do this, it is worth noting that Barry's claim supports the scope₁ claim. The latter, recall, states that the standard arguments deployed to defend civil and political rights within the state actually often entail that all persons are entitled to the same rights. This is apparent in Barry's argument. Although he himself uses it primarily to defend the idea that the state should be neutral between conceptions of the good when dealing with its own citizens, the logic of his argument entails that all persons enjoy these rights. It holds that these rights are appropriate in any society characterized by pluralism and Barry makes clear that his assumption is that all societies fit this description. The scope₁ claim is thus borne out. Furthermore, we might add, it is borne out because at the heart of Barry's argument is a universalist account of the morally relevant features of persons (what Rawls terms 'moral personality' (1999c: 11, 17, 442–6)). It is a key feature of Barry's argument that principles of justice must secure the consent of *all persons* (not all Americans or all whites or all Swedes) and this makes sense only if we assume a universalist account of moral personality according to which each and every person counts to an equal extent.

## IV

Given the lack of success of the preceding argument, let us move on and consider a second grounding for civil and political human rights. Jürgen Habermas develops what might be called a 'transcendental' argument for such human rights.[14] His argument starts with an analysis of language. He argues that in making moral judgements people hold those moral judgements to be true; they affirm, that is, statements that they claim can be justified to other people. When someone claims, for example, that murder, say, is immoral she is not making an expression of emotion: she is affirming something she holds to be true, something that can be justified to other people. Habermas is thus critical of subjectivist analyses of moral language, for their claim that moral judgements simply express a person's moral view contradicts people's understanding of their moral beliefs (1992*a*: 47–57). Implicit in our moral usage is the belief that principles can be justified to others. But to justify a principle to others precludes getting them to agree by forcing them or misleading them (1992*b*: 134): principles can be legitimate only if all '*freely* accept' them (1992*a*: 93, his emphasis; 1992*b*: 120). Justification, then, presupposes an ideal speech situation in which each person is fully informed and has equal power and in which principles are subjected to real discussion (1986: 25–6; 1992*a*: 66–8; 1993). The justification of principles thus entails a commitment to human rights enabling each to participate in a dialogic process. Human rights are necessary to protect people's ability to take part in dialogue and participate in a process by which principles of justice are negotiated and agreed upon.[15]

Habermas's argument has been criticized in a number of ways. One objection is levelled by Raymond Geuss who denies that one can derive the ideal speech situation from a mere analysis of moral language. As he puts it:

I find it quite hard to burden pre-dynastic Egyptians, ninth century French serfs and early-twentieth-century Yanomamö tribesmen with the view that they are acting correctly if their action is based on a norm on which there would be universal consensus in an ideal speech situation. (1993: 66, cf. pp. 66–7)

And he infers from this that Habermas's argument is doomed.

However, this criticism moves too quickly for Habermas is not claiming that all persons are burdened with 'the view that they are acting correctly if their action is based on a norm on which there would be universal consensus in an ideal speech situation' (Geuss 1993: 66). That is, he is not claiming that all persons do actually accept the validity of the ideal speech situation. His argument, rather, is that all persons (including ninth century French serfs and so on) think that their beliefs about justice are correct. And, he then argues, in a second separate move, that for a principle of justice to be correct it must be justifiable to free and equal persons. Thus construed Habermas's argument is not vulnerable to Geuss's critique.

Whilst Habermas can avoid this first objection his argument faces a second objection. The argument this time is that he has not given us positive reason to accept his claim that principles are correct if they can be justified to free and equal persons. He has not, that is, defended the second step in his argument. Furthermore, we should note that Habermas, like many liberals, distinguishes between judgements about the good life (what he calls ethics) and judgements about justice and the right (what he terms morality). The former refer to judgements about what pursuits are fulfilling and rewarding whereas the latter refer to how to treat people fairly. Habermas's view is that conceptions of the good are historically situated and hence beliefs about the good are correct if they can be justified to *other members of one's cultural community*: one need not be able to justify one's conception of the good to *all persons*.[16] But if he accepts this account of moral justification about the good it raises the question of why he does not also think that ideals of justice are correct if they can be justified to other members of one's community. This objection does not, of course, call into question the validity of Habermas's contention that principles of justice must command the support of persons in an ideal speech situation. This may well be a desirable ideal. Its contention is simply that Habermas's analysis of language does not entail or provide support for this ideal. Hence his commitment to human rights is ungrounded.[17]

Prior to moving on we should again note that this vindication of civil and political human rights also bears out the scope$_1$ claim (Section II). Since this argument focuses on the universal presuppositions of the use of language it cannot coherently be used to support civil and political rights in some countries only. Its premises and its reasoning, if they are valid, show that all users of language (and hence all persons across the world) enjoy civil and political rights.[18] Anyone who used Habermas's argument to defend civil and political rights but only for one country or a group of countries is misunderstanding its logic. Moreover, as in the preceding argument, the explanation for this is that at the argument's heart is a commitment to a universalist account of the morally relevant attributes of persons. It assumes that arguments about justice can be valid only if they are defensible to *all* free and equal *persons*. Its account of justification thus assumes the moral irrelevance of people's ethnicity and class: what is morally relevant is a person's common humanity.

## V

Given the failure of the two preceding arguments, let us now consider a third cosmopolitan defence of (or approach to defending) civil and political human rights, namely deontological approaches. By the latter I mean those that defend civil and political human rights on the grounds that this is what is required if we are to treat persons with respect. An evocative account of the deontological perspective is developed by Frances Kamm. Kamm argues that a deontological perspective gives expression to the fact that persons have an equal moral 'status' (1992, esp. pp. 385–9). The deontological perspective is also given eloquent expression by Thomas Nagel who argues that humans possess a distinct moral dignity that demands respect. One fails to treat persons with respect by using them to pursue social goals (1995).[19] Like Kamm, Nagel too uses the idea of 'moral status' to capture this (1995: 85–93, 96–107).[20]

Having presented the deontological approach, it is worth making a number of observations about this line of reasoning. First, we should be careful to record that this line of reasoning generates *negative* duties on others, enjoining them not to do certain things, but does not generate *positive* duties on others to protect rights and prevent rights-violations. Nagel, for example, is explicit about this. As he reasons, if there were positive duties to protect rights then one might be required to violate one person's right if that were the best way to prevent other more serious or more numerous rights-violations. A system of positive duties would, thereby, result in people treating others as a means to an end and this is a violation of the key deontological claim (1995: 87–93). Positive duties result in what Robert Nozick has termed 'a utilitarianism of rights' (1974: 28) and should accordingly be rejected.

Second, the deontological approach does not, in general, rest on complicated moral reasoning or protracted moral argument. Rather, it simply seeks to capture a deep moral conviction. A good example of this is Nozick's affirmation of rights (1974: 29–33) but similar points can be made about Nagel. What he seeks to do is to articulate a basic moral intuition about the respect owed to individuals.

A third, and related, point is that, whilst the intuitions to which deontologists appeal have resonance among many in western liberal societies, they may not have the same appeal to some members of non-western traditions. Accordingly, if someone does not share that intuition it is difficult to do much to persuade them. It is, of course, widely recognized that members of some cultures do not share these convictions. To give an example, some Buddhists would regard as untenable the emphasis on the inviolability of the person that characterizes a deontological perspective (Inada 1998).[21] Furthermore, there are other non-western interpretations of human dignity which eschew the concept of rights (Donnelly 1989: 49–55). Recognizing people's moral status does not therefore straightforwardly entail accepting rights.

The deontological approach suffers from two weaknesses. First, it is insensitive to outcomes and its refusal to posit positive duties is hard to sustain. This problem is explored more fully in Chapter 6, when discussing the ethics of waging war, but in the meantime it is worth recording the worry that there is something perverse about a political morality that contains negative duties only. The most powerful challenge to such a conception is articulated by Amartya Sen, who points out that deontologists forbid someone from violating one right (even a very minor right) to prevent a large number of very grave rights violations. To illustrate and give force to his argument he gives the example of someone called Ali, who is the target of a racist gang that plans to beat him up. One does not know where Ali is going but can find out by breaking into Charles's office and looking on his desk for there is a piece of paper there revealing Ali's whereabouts (1988: 191–6). Now, deontologists would maintain that one should not violate someone's right to privacy and would condemn breaking into Charles's office. But this position is hard to defend and surely there is a case for breaking in (a minor rights violation) to prevent serious bodily injury to Ali. A system of purely negative duties, then, is counterintuitive because of its indifference to outcomes (1988, esp. pp. 190–1, 195–6).

Second, the deontological claim is open to the charge of indeterminacy and, thereby, violates the first of the three desiderata of an adequate theory of human rights listed in Section I. Which particular rights do humans possess if we accept the ideal of respect for persons? A common answer to this question is that respect for persons requires granting people freedom of choice. But this does not solve the problem for the question, then, is which particular freedoms should be secured (Bellamy 1992, esp. pp. 89–90, 92, 95)? Such problems do not invalidate a deontological approach but they do suggest that reference to treating persons with respect needs to be supplemented with an account of the morally relevant features of persons that merit respect. As James Griffin rightly notes, '[w]e cannot begin to work out a substantive theory of rights—what rights there actually are—without a substantive theory of goods. We need to know what is at the centre of a valuable human life and so requires special protection' (1986: 64; chapter XI in general).

It is important to emphasize that neither of these two objections establishes that a political theory based on the idea of respect for persons should be rejected. Rather they entail, first, that this compelling ideal should be explicated in such a way that it allows positive duties and overcomes Sen's objection and, second, that it gives an account of the morally relevant interests of persons that should be respected. The next type of argument analysed seeks to address both of these concerns.

However, before we examine this, it should be recorded that deontological arguments for civil and political human rights also add further support to the scope$_1$ claim. Deontological arguments are often used by members of western societies to defend their own rights but the core moral claim they are articulating generates general, or human, rights as opposed to special rights. It would, for example, be very odd to think that deontologists are right to emphasize the inviolability of *persons* but to conclude from this that it grounds only civic rights: the moral rationale for it invokes universal properties and thus generates (if it generates anything) human rights. As with the two previous arguments, the deontological arguments considered show how the sorts of reasoning standardly deployed to defend civil and political rights within one's own state actually entail that all persons (and not just one's fellow citizens) should enjoy these rights. Moreover, they do so because they employ a universalist conception of moral personality: the argument affirms that (at least some of) persons' civil and political rights are owed to them in virtue of their humanity (and their nationality or civic identity or race or class or skin colour are not morally relevant).

## VI

At this point it is worth turning our attention to what I have termed 'well-being-based' justifications of civil and political human rights. These defend civil and political human rights on the grounds that they are necessary if human beings are to flourish. Such arguments make four claims. First, they start with the claim, articulated in the preceding section, that any adequate account of justice must recognize persons' equal moral standing. Persons have a certain status as human beings and justice requires that they be treated with respect. As we have seen, however, this insight on its own is insufficient because it does not explain what specific rights persons have. It needs to be supplemented with an account of what aspects of persons should be treated with respect.

Second, what I am terming 'well-being' based arguments maintain that to treat persons with respect we must respect their interests. Human rights must be informed by an account of persons' human interests.[22] As Raz puts it in his statement of the 'interest' theory of rights: ' "X has a right" if and only if X can have rights, and, other things being equal, an aspect of X's well-being (his interest) is a sufficient reason for holding some other person(s) to be under a duty' (1986: 166).[23]

The third step in the argument is the claim that one primary interest is a person's interest in well-being. That is, persons have an interest in leading a fulfilling and rewarding life (Dworkin 2000, ch. 6, esp. pp. 242–76; Kymlicka 1989: 10–12; 1995: 80–2; 2002: 13–20, 214–17). One might distinguish here between basic and expansive accounts of this interest. Basic accounts might stress people's interest in not being tortured, killed, imprisoned without trial. More expansive accounts, by contrast, might include a fuller account of the human good. Nussbaum, for example, affirms a thick but flexible theory of the good. As has been seen in Chapter 2, Nussbaum outlines ten human goods. These include: (1) 'life'; (2) 'bodily health'; (3) 'bodily integrity'; (4) 'senses, imagination, and thought'; (5) 'emotions'; (6) 'practical reason'; (7) 'affiliation' where this comprises 'friendship' and 'respect'; (8) 'other species'; (9) 'play'; and finally (10) 'control over one's environment', where this includes control over both the 'political' and the 'material' environment (2002: 129–30).[24] These elements of the good—what Nussbaum terms capabilities—constitute her account of the good life.[25]

Finally, the argument claims that persons' interest in well-being is best served by a set of liberal civil and political human rights. To see this, and the specific rights supported, we should consider a number of standard and very familiar 'well-being' based arguments:

1. First, persons have an interest in physical safety and this issues straightforwardly in a right not to be killed or physically harmed since these actions violate that interest. This argument thus moves in a fairly uncontroversial manner directly from a core interest to an important right and does not require any additional premises. To put this in practical terms, human rights to physical safety are justified because they protect people from actions such as setting someone alight because they are of a different race to you or physically beating someone who is of the 'wrong' religion or attaching electrodes to someone's genitalia to extract information or shooting someone because he is a Serb or a Tutsi. One common objection to this argument is that it presupposes a universal account of harm but that there are no such universal bads. Often allegedly universal bads are deemed good by some (Horton 1985). The supposition that pain is a universal bad is, for example, vulnerable to the objection that some people sometimes choose painful activities. However, as Martha Nussbaum has pointed out. This kind of argument can be met by maintaining that people have a human right not to suffer the *involuntary* infliction of physical damage.[26] The latter right prohibits all of the vile acts described above but also permits someone to choose to inflict pain on himself. Furthermore, one might add, those who

engage in painful activities do not think that the latter should be imposed involuntarily on people. They want to have the opportunity to engage in such activities and also the right not to have pain inflicted on them without any consent, and this the right to physical integrity protects. The first argument thus stands.

2. A second argument maintains simply that agency is an important human good. There is value in being in charge of one's own life and making one's own decisions (Griffin 1986: 67, 225–6). This is not necessarily the only or the most important good but it is, many would argue, a significant one. Clearly, however, this value is served only if each individual has a right over his or her own life and can thereby exercise choice and act on her own judgement. In criticism of this argument it is sometimes claimed that agency is only a parochial western concern. However, such sweeping assertions are misplaced for the contention that persons flourish by making their own decisions can be found in non-western cultures such as Buddhism. Buddhists strongly emphasize the need for individuals to seek their own perfection (Caney 2000d: 67–8; Taylor 1999: 134). A central tenet is that one can only acquire independence from cravings and illusions through one's own reflection and action. Furthermore the idea that individuality is peculiar only to western cultures is refuted by Ghanaian philosophers, such as Kwame Gyeke and Kwasi Wiredu, both of whom argue that some African traditions of thought, such as the Akan, stress the value of individuality and independence (Gyeke 1997: 40–1, 63; Wiredu 1996: 157–71).[27]

3. The case for civil and political human rights receives further support from a third consideration. For Mill's claim that individuals are often best at discerning what it is their own interest (1977a [1859]: 277) also supports the contention that civil and political human rights enable people to flourish. The claim, note, is not that individuals are perfect judges nor that they are always better judges of their good than others.[28] It is more modestly that, although there are exceptions, it nonetheless applies in a great number of cases.

4. An additional reason why those concerned with promoting people's well-being should accept liberal civil and political rights is again provided by Mill. Whereas the last argument appealed to the ability of people to know their interests better than others, this fourth consideration points out that individuals tend to be more motivated to look after their own interests than others are. So even if an outside body knows a person's interests better than he himself does, Mill argues that '[h]e is the person most interested in his own well-being' (1977a [1859]: 277) and others should therefore not be in charge of his life. Again, then, a system of individual civil and political human rights is best suited to producing a state of affairs in which each individual flourishes and leads a fulfilling life.[29]

5. A further consideration that can be adduced in defence of civil and political human rights is that coercion is too blunt an instrument to improve people's lives. Illiberal policies intended to suppress some undesirable practices are therefore likely also to suppress some desirable practices (Raz 1986: 418–19). Coercion then is a 'clumsy tool' and attempts by political authorities to prohibit activities

deemed 'unworthy' almost always prevent people from rich and fulfilling activities. Given this a commitment to enabling human flourishing requires a commitment to extensive civil and political human rights.[30]

These five well-being based considerations suggest that civil and political human rights can be defended on the grounds that they enable human beings to flourish and lead fulfilling lives. All of the above provide support for the contention that persons have a human right to freedom of action as long as they do not restrict the rights of others. So this would justify rights to freedom of belief, association, expression, and non-harmful conduct in general.[31] The above analysis does not, note, exhaust all the possibilities. One might supplement it, for example, with an analysis of the right to democratic government for this too can plausibly be defended on grounds similar to those developed above. To take one (again very common) claim, one might argue that this right is justified because democratic authorities have an incentive to produce just policies and citizens have the opportunity to render it accountable. Amartya Sen has famously defended a specific version of this argument, arguing that democratic governments do not ever result in famines (1999*a*: 90–3; 1999*b*: 4–5, 10–11, 16, 51–3, 147–54, 157–8, 178–88).

The above arguments, thus, provide strong support for a set of civil and political human rights. Four additional points should be made in support of the above lines of reasoning. First, it should be stressed that the preceding analysis aims simply to suggest the ways in which civil and political human rights are justified because they enable people to live fulfilling lives. They could, no doubt, be explored more fully, with due qualifications and nuances added; and, clearly, each of the individual arguments requires much more elaboration. The above, however, are intended simply to lay out the broad structure of several powerful well-being based lines of argument.

Second, it should also be observed that whilst each of the above arguments, when considered individually, faces exceptions, the whole presents a powerful case. It is artificial to consider each in isolation and when we consider all five in unison we get a strong composite case. To give an example: even if someone is not best at ascertaining her interests that does not justify paternalism for she might be the best guardian of her own interests. Or even if neither of those arguments apply in a particular case it might be the case that coercion is too blunt. And so on. In other words, paternalism on any one issue can be justified only if none of the five considerations adduced apply. This establishes a very strong case against paternalism.

Third, the well-being based position is strengthened further when we bear in mind that it overcomes one of the limitations of the previous arguments, namely indeterminacy (Griffin 1986: 64), and, as such, does not fall foul of the first prerequisite of an adequate account of human rights. Accounts of well-being enable us to arbitrate between different claims to have rights and those liberties which best protect central human interests will be selected. Moreover, unlike the preceding deontological argument, this approach is, obviously, not indifferent to outcomes and is therefore not vulnerable to Sen's critique.

Finally, we might also note that an additional advantage of the well-being approach is that it can explain why people care more about some liberties and rights (like the right to physical security or the right to freedom of expression) than they do about others (like the right, say, to eat banana flavoured ice-cream). Whereas people are strongly committed to the former, and may even fight for them, they are not to the latter. The well-being approach easily explains why, pointing out that the former rights clearly contribute more to human well-being than does the latter.

These virtues notwithstanding, someone might resist the well-being approach on the grounds that the argument's reliance on an account of human interests is unacceptable because any account we draw up of human interests will inevitably only be a partial one, reflecting our specific concerns. A properly universalist account of human goods is, the objection maintains, unobtainable. This objection contains within it an important insight: many accounts of people's universal interests have historically been partial and have foisted on humanity at large the preconceptions and ideals held by a minority. Some human rights movements no doubt are predicated on culturally specific western ideals of what is fitting for human beings.

An objection that emphasizes related concerns to this will be explored in much greater depth later in this chapter (Section IX). In the meantime, however, we can nonetheless make two counter-arguments. First, whilst some human rights policies have been predicated on a partial vision of human interests this in no way entails that all such policies are doomed to a similar parochialism. What it implies rather is the need for a more ecumenical view that genuinely encompasses the perspectives of all and the objection has given us no reason to think such a project unattainable. It does not then imply the abandonment of human rights but rather enjoins us to be ever vigilant in our ascription of human interests.[32] Second, and building on this first response, the claim under scrutiny in fact provides further support for civil and political human rights. For surely one instructive way of minimising the likelihood of foisting a partial vision of human interests on all human beings is to protect each person's human interest in freedom of belief and expression. The latter enables everyone to articulate their views and beliefs about their essential interests and thereby minimizes the probability of constructing a partial and selective account of people's interests. These rights provide people with the opportunity to contest and dispute any account of human interests that does not resonate with them. In short, then, the objection entails, not the abandonment of civil and political human rights, but the need for a more extensive commitment to such rights.

At this stage we may return to the scope$_1$ claim. Its claim that the arguments that underpin our commitment to civil and political rights establish that these are human rights is also illustrated by our analysis of well-being based arguments. Consider again the premises: the appeal is to utility (for utilitarians) or human flourishing (for perfectionists) and thus rights are ascribed to all capable of utility or flourishing and that means all persons (unless one can show that only some can enjoy utility or flourish). To put the point another way: the logic of the above arguments is that it would be incoherent to defend the civil and political rights of one's fellow citizens on the above well-being based considerations but deny the same rights to foreigners.[33] And, as with the earlier arguments, the explanation for this is that underlying all the well-being based arguments for civil and political human rights is a universalist moral personality which denies the moral relevance of people's cultural identity to (some of) their entitlements. The premises of well-being based arguments refer thus to the interests of all persons, not the interests or well-being of Christians or Jews or blacks or women or one's fellow nationals.

# VII

This concludes the consideration of cosmopolitan arguments for universal civil and political rights. At this point it is worth taking stock. Several points should be noted.

First, as we have seen, the preceding four types of argument have all borne out the scope$_1$ claim. This is significant—and this is why it has been stressed—for it shows that in order to argue that there are universal rights one need not subscribe to any one (of the four) particular theories. One of the implications of the scope$_1$ claim is that *many* of the standard arguments for civil and political rights rely on universalist premises and hence necessarily establish that those rights have a universal scope.[34]

Further to this, we have seen that the scope$_1$ claim holds because the standard arguments for civil and political rights invoke a universalist 'moral personality'. That is, the morally relevant aspect of persons is the right to be subject to principles to which they can reasonably consent (for contractarians), or their use of moral language (for Habermas), or their humanity and status as persons (for deontologists), or their ability to lead a fulfilling life (for perfectionists). As such, it would be incoherent to adopt any of these lines of reasoning for a particular right and then ascribe that right only to other members of one's community.[35]

A third point worth noting is a corollary of the first two. This is that the arguments for cosmopolitan principles of civil and political justice analysed above conform to the logical structure of the General Argument for universalism canvassed in Chapter 2, Section V. The latter, recall, maintains that the moral values that apply to some persons must apply to all persons if all persons are similar in a morally relevant way. Now what each of the preceding arguments has done is to conform exactly to this pattern. Each identifies and defends a value that applies to some (e.g. that freedom of action is justified because each is the best judge of her own interests). Each then argues that all persons are in a relevantly similar situation (e.g. all persons are the best judges of their own interests)[36] and hence concludes that the value in question applies to everyone. Given that all persons are similar *in a morally relevant way* (i.e. (P3) holds) the reasoning underpinning the value logically implies that the value applies to all. Put otherwise: the use of a universal moral personality fits the pattern required by the general universalist argument given in Chapter 2. It performs the role of (P3) for it identifies a way in which all persons are similar in a morally relevant way. Some further examples illustrate the point. For deontologists the first move is to defend civil and political rights in terms of showing respect for a person's capacity for autonomy. The second move is then to note that the morally relevant property that justified the value—the capacity to be autonomous—is a universal property: (P3) is, thereby, met. Hence deontological arguments must apply to all persons and not just one's fellow citizens. The defences of universal civil and political rights thus conform to the template specified by the General Argument.

Two further points should, however, be made about the scope$_1$ claim. First, the implications of the claim should not be exaggerated. If valid, it shows that there are universal civil and political rights but it does not say what their precise content is. Nor does it say who is duty-bound to protect these rights. To answer these questions one needs more than it supplies and must draw on a particular political theory of rights. Second, the scope$_1$ claim does not, note, claim that there are no special rights and that all rights are universal rights. Its claim is that the rationale underpinning many (but not all) civil and political rights entails that these rights must be held universally. However, it is quite compatible with this to add that by exercising their universal civil and political rights, individuals may create special rights. Individuals who hold the right to freedom of speech, action, association, and so on can make contracts with each other, in which case the contracting parties, but not others, have certain special rights. The key point, though, is that these special rights arise in a background in which persons have universal civil and political rights and that the rationale for those universal civil and political rights embodies the scope$_1$ claim.

# VIII

Having examined a number of prominent cosmopolitan vindications of universal civil and political rights, it is appropriate to consider alternative justifications of universal civil and political rights. Some explicitly adopt a different approach, eschewing egalitarian and individualist assumptions and avoiding cosmopolitan tenets. The most notable example of such an approach is John Rawls's *The Law of Peoples* (1999*b*) and this section will accordingly focus on his arguments in this work. The latter is not Rawls's only discussion of international justice. There was a very brief discussion in *A Theory of Justice* and in 1993 he published an Amnesty Lecture on 'The Law of Peoples' (1993*a*). It is, however, his fullest and most sophisticated treatment. For our purposes there are two important aspects of Rawls's perspective on human rights, namely, his critique of cosmopolitan arguments for human rights (the negative component) and his defence of some human rights (the positive component).

Rawls's argument is complex and requires some preliminary clarification. We can, I think, comprehend his argument best if we consider it in several stages. First, we need to understand some technical terms that he deploys in his argument. Rawls's argument rests on a typology of five different types of society. There are, first, liberal societies: these are committed to individual rights, they prioritize these over the public good, and they ensure that all have some economic resources (1999*b*: 14–15).[37] In addition to this: they have a specific political constitution; their members share a common political culture; and they have a 'moral nature', by which is meant that they respect the autonomy of other political communities (1999*b*: 23–5). A second type of society is what Rawls terms 'decent peoples' (1999*b*: 4). He concentrates on one particular type of decent society which he refers to as a 'decent hierarchical society' (1999*b*: 63–78). These are not aggressive (1999*b*: 64). Furthermore, they affirm some human rights; their members are conceived of as capable of bearing duties; and their legal officials believe that the law embodies a commitment to a 'common good idea of justice' (1999*b*: 66, cf. pp. 65–7). As a corollary of these last three features, Rawls says that such societies may be said to have a 'decent consultation hierarchy' (1999*b*: 71, cf. pp. 71–5).[38] Third, there are what Rawls terms 'outlaw states', which are aggressive toward other political communities and treat their own members despotically (1999*b*: 4). Fourth, there are 'societies burdened by unfavorable conditions': these are societies that are prevented from being decent by unpropitious cultural and/or economic conditions (1999*b*: 4, cf. pp. 4–5, 105–13). Finally, there are 'benevolent absolutisms' (1999*b*: 4). These comply with some fundamental rights. Unlike decent hierarchical societies, however, the political structure contains no procedures for consulting the people.

Employing this typology, Rawls argues that fair principles of international justice are those that liberal and decent peoples can both accept. He thus affirms a kind of people-centred contractarianism. Unlike the individualistic brands of contractarianism affirmed by Barry and Beitz the contracting parties for Rawls's international contract are certain kinds of peoples—liberal and decent peoples. Note, however, that other kinds of regime—outlaw states, benevolent absolutisms, and societies with unfavourable socio-economic conditions—are not party to the contract.

This raises the question of why we should accept Rawls's method. Rawls defends his approach on the grounds that it shows tolerance to decent non-liberal societies. He maintains that liberals would be acting intolerantly, and therefore wrongly, if they sought to apply their egalitarian liberal ideals at the global level: hence egalitarian liberal cosmopolitanism is illegitimate.[39] Rather liberal societies should show respect to societies, such as 'decent societies', that observe minimal moral constraints even if they are not liberal (1999*b*: 59–60, 67–80, 82–4). To demand that they all accept liberal norms would be to act in an illegitimate manner. By adopting his people-centred contractarianism, then, Rawls articulates this idea of toleration for he disallows liberals from imposing their values on everyone else (1999*b*: 18–19, 59–60, 68, 82–5, 121–3).

The next, and final, question to be addressed, then, is what principles would be agreed to by these liberal and decent societies. Rawls argues that both liberal and decent hierarchical societies would consent to the following eight principles:

'1. Peoples are free and independent, and their freedom and independence are to be respected by other peoples.
2. Peoples are to observe treaties and undertakings.
3. Peoples are equal and are parties to the agreements that bind them.
4. Peoples are to observe a duty of non-intervention.
5. Peoples have the right of self-defence but no right to instigate war for reasons other than self-defence.
6. Peoples are to honour human rights.
7. Peoples are to observe certain specified restrictions in the conduct of war.
8. Peoples have a duty to assist other peoples living under unfavourable conditions that prevent their having a just or decent political and social regime' (1999b: 37).[40]

From our point of view, what is most important here is that both liberal and hierarchical societies consent to human rights—principle 6. Elsewhere in *The Law of Peoples*, Rawls elaborates on which rights he takes to be human rights:

Among the human rights are the right to life (to the means of subsistence and security); to liberty (to freedom from slavery, serfdom, and forced occupation, and to a sufficient measure of liberty of conscience to ensure freedom of religion and thought); to property (personal property); and to formal equality as expressed by the rules of natural justice (that is, that similar cases be treated similarly). (1999b: 65)[41]

Rawls's account of human rights and his repudiation of cosmopolitanism is vulnerable to (at least) six objections. Before exploring them it is important to note that Rawls's account is an account of how *peoples* should behave in the international realm.[42] His contention is that it would be intolerant for liberal peoples, for example, to foist their political ideals on decent non-liberal regimes. It is, however, silent on how individuals or social movements can act. This is significant for someone can accept Rawls's arguments about the conduct of peoples and yet also accept a cosmopolitan account on how individuals (and social movements) should act. Such a person would adopt the slogan 'cosmopolitanism for persons and Rawlsianism for peoples'. This is not a trivial point for much campaigning about human rights is undertaken by social movements, including Amnesty International and feminist associations, and such institutions (and even private individuals) can potentially play a large role. So although they would, presumably, be disallowed from coercive imposition there is little, on Rawls's people-centred approach, to say what would be objectionable with non-state actors from non-coercively promoting human rights (Caney 2001a: 128).

1. Let us turn now to an evaluation of Rawls's argument. One problem with Rawls's argument stems from the specific brand of contractarianism it affirms— one in which fair principles of international conduct are those which are affirmed by liberal and hierarchical peoples. Its reliance on collective units, such as peoples, as the contracting parties is problematic because peoples often, if not always, contain different communities and individuals who adhere to very different beliefs and values. Rawls's aim is to create a tolerant international order but by allowing peoples to construct the international law it sanctions outcomes in which a collective can impose its values on the minority groups and individuals in its society. In that sense, it does not articulate its guiding value— the ideal of toleration (Buchanan 2000: 697–8 and also 716–20; Caney 2002*a*: 99–104; Kuper 2000: 644, 648–52; Kok-Chor Tan 2000: 28–45; Tesón 1998: 113–14). Given the pluralistic nature of all communities it is surely better to ask what political principles individuals will agree to.

2. Even if we accept a contract comprised by peoples, a second problem with Rawls's defence of his preferred human rights is that these societies are *defined* as ones committed to human rights: in effect, then, Rawls's argument claims that human rights should apply globally because some societies (those committed to human rights) can agree on such a principle (Beitz 2000: 685–6; Caney 2001*a*: 131; Jones 1996: 193–5; Mason 2000: 186). The conclusion is thus contained within the premise and societies who reject principles of human rights are omitted from the contract. The problem with Rawls's people-based contract is thus similar to the problem with Barry's individualist contract: the contractual frame- work assumes the answers it is supposed to yield. To put this point another way, it is worth returning to the point that Rawls's two international contracts comprise only liberal peoples and decent non-liberal peoples. The other three types of regime are thereby disallowed from participation in any of the contracts. This presupposes that they are illegitimate but this is what is at stake (Beitz 2000: 686; Jones 1996: 195).[43]

3. Third, and related to this, Rawls's account is rather ad hoc. Why, a critic might ask, are some rights protected (such as the right not to be enslaved) but others are not? On what basis can one draw the line between those we think essential and those that we value for ourselves but do not think should be regarded as essential (Beitz 2000: 686–7; Caney 2001*a*: 131; McCarthy 1997: 212; Moellendorf 2002*a*: 10–14, 18, 28–9)? Without an answer to these questions Rawls's theory of human rights would violate the first of the three conditions of an adequate theory of human rights—the criterion of *determinacy*.

Rawls does address this issue. He argues that a society can be 'decent' only if it can accurately be described as a 'system of social cooperation' and he argues further that '[w]hat have come to be called human rights are recognized as necessary conditions of any system of social cooperation. When they are regu- larly violated, we have command by force, a slave system, and no cooperation of any kind' (1999*b*: 68). The rights that decent societies honour are, thus, not random or arbitrary: rather they value those rights necessary for the scheme to be describable as cooperative.

Whilst this does supply a criterion, it runs into two problems. The first is that it is not clear why the ideal of cooperation should play this role. Why is decency defined in terms of cooperation as opposed to some other ideal? The second problem is that the concept is too thin and meagre in its content to play the role that Rawls wants it to. 'Cooperation' is not what Bernard Williams calls a thick ethical concept (1985: 129, 140, 143–5, 163, 200) and is too indeterminate to provide precise instructions as to which rights are mandatory and which not. Someone can, for example, plausibly argue that equal political rights are necessary for a regime to be truly or fully cooperative and that no regime with entrenched power inequalities can accurately be described as cooperative. My point is not necessarily that this is so but that it has as good a claim to be an interpretation of the cooperative ideal as Rawls's more parsimonious account. The charge thus remains: Rawls's account of minimal rights is ad hoc.

4. One can go further than this, however, and argue not just that we lack good reason to accept Rawls's minimum but also that we have good reason to reject it. This point is pressed by the next three arguments. The first argument to do so argues that Rawls's position is vulnerable to an internal critique. In particular, the charge is that Rawls's global minimum is incompatible with his views about domestic justice. It, thereby, fails to meet the second condition of a theory of human rights—the criterion of *domestic-compatibility*. If one thinks, as he does, that persons' civil and political liberties should not depend on their class or their ethnicity how can one attribute such importance to their nationality? And if one grounds, as he does, his domestic theory by invoking persons' moral powers and interests in pursuing a conception of the good and in rationally forming and revising it (2001: 18–24), how can one hold firmly to it when making domestic principles of justice but disregard it altogether when dealing with foreign persons?[44] The relevance of the scope$_1$ claim can be seen here. The reason the latter has been repeatedly stressed in the discussion of cosmopolitan arguments for civil and political human rights is, in part, that it shows what is so problematic with accounts that, like Rawls's, seek to ground civil and political rights in persons' moral powers and interests but which deny that all persons enjoy these very same civil and political rights. The force of the scope$_1$ claim is that one cannot, as it were, apply these universalist arguments for citizens and not apply them to foreigners when the very terms of the arguments (the moral powers and interests of persons) do not justify this kind of domestic/international split. One cannot coherently affirm Rawls's domestic theory and adhere to his international theory. It thereby fails the criterion of *domestic-compatibility*.[45]

5. Having considered one internal critique of Rawls's minimal rights, we can now consider a second. This second internal critique maintains that one cannot coherently both embrace the rights that Rawls does embrace and also reject

some of the rights that Rawls rejects. The claim is that they stand or fall as a package. Thus, whereas the first drew attention to a contradiction between Rawls's account of minimum rights and his domestic theory, this second internal critique draws attention to a contradiction between his account of minimum rights and his rejection of other proposed human rights. The charge is that his theory fails the criterion of *coherence*.

To develop this criticism it is worth considering what one might term *rights holism*. As I define this term, it maintains that the acceptance of some specific rights implies the acceptance of some other specific rights. It claims that certain rights are interconnected. It might be contrasted with an atomistic approach where this argues that the case for each individual right can be judged in isolation of the case for other rights. Rights might be interconnected for at least four reasons. Two of these are noted by Cécile Fabre. As she observes, there might be a 'logical' relationship between two rights such that one right may entail another. To give Fabre's example, the right to privacy might entail the right to housing. Second, one might make an 'empirical' link, arguing that the best way to protect right P is to attribute to people right Q (2000: 123–4).[46] To Fabre's analysis one might add a third possibility, arguing that there is a 'normative' relationship between two rights, where a normative relationship obtains when the rationale grounding one right also grounds another distinct right. If this is true then one cannot coherently affirm the former and deny the latter. Fourth, one might make what could be called an 'incompleteness' argument for linking two rights. What I mean by this is that there might be a good argument for a specific right but that that right requires for its valid implementation another right.

Now using this analysis we can see that implicit in Rawls's position is the assumption that there is no *logical-* or *empirical-* or *normative-* or *incompleteness-*derived interconnections between his preferred set of human rights and those rights that he rejects. Some critics have, however, forcefully challenged this assumption. Perhaps the strongest version emphasizes *empirical* interconnections. Andrew Kuper, for example, makes such a case against Rawls's rejection of the right to democratic government. Invoking research by Sen, Kuper points out that democratic government has been empirically proven to be necessary for the protection of Rawls's other commitments, such as the right to freedom of expression (2000: 663–4). As such one cannot, as Rawls seeks to do, affirm the latter rights but reject democratic government.

This point should not be misconstrued. The claim is not that Rawls rejects a holistic approach for he may well accept one and think his set of rights hang well together. The objection rather is that they do not and hence it is mistaken to build some rights into *The Law of Peoples* and to reject others that are corollaries of the former rights. Rawls himself considers the particular issue at stake and says that if it turned out that the basic human rights he affirms could not be protected in the absence of democratic institutions, and hence would not be honoured in a decent hierarchical society, *then* 'the case for liberal democracy is made' (1999*b*: 79). But this is a very curious position. Why does Rawls not actually explore the evidence on democratization and human rights and base his theory on that? Why not take into account all relevant empirical data to see if his view is tenable? Elsewhere in *The Law of Peoples* Rawls draws on the relevant empirical literature: for instance, he supports his Society of Peoples by drawing on the empirical claim that democracies do not war with other democracies (1999*b*: 44–54, 125). It is then somewhat peculiar to outline a position that depends on certain empirical conditions being met and to affirm its value without examining the extensive empirical material available to see whether the empirical conditions obtain.[47]

**6.** Thus far we have seen that Rawls's account of minimum rights suffers from two internal critiques. The final objection is an external critique. The objection is simply that his account of rights is unduly minimal and acquiesces in injustice.[48] To see this consider what it would prohibit and what it would allow. Rawls's basic rights include a right to subsistence, a right not to be enslaved, and a right not to be a serf (1999*b*: 65, 79). As long as states observe these minimal standards they satisfy Rawls's account of rights. This, however, would allow the deprivation of the right to vote (UDHR Article 21) to people because they are women or black or from a lower caste[49]; the payment of miserable, and unequal, levels of pay to some because of their ethnicity; the deprivation of health care to some because of their conception of the good (they are homosexual, say); the denial of the right to education to members of some castes (contra UDHR Article 26); the rejection of the right to assembly (UDHR Article 20). Rawls's sense is that a society can be decent and yet allow any of these. My query is whether this is in fact so. When answering this we should also refer back again to the scope₁ claim. For if we think that it is wrong to deprive persons in our society of the right to vote because we think that 'all persons have a right to determine the law of their country' or that 'inclusive democracies produce better decisions' then we must abandon Rawls's account of human rights. Similarly, if we think that persons have a right to engage in sexual acts with other consenting adults and we do so for deontological reasons (such as that all persons are ends in themselves) or for consequentialist reasons (such as that each person knows best what is in her own interests) then, again, we must reject Rawls's account of basic rights for being too low.

Both Rawls's critique of cosmopolitan accounts of civil and political rights and his justification of his own set of civil and political human rights are therefore unsuccessful.[50] As was noted earlier, Rawls's theory is what was termed a minimalist account of human rights and before moving on to consider objections to civil and political human rights it may be useful to note that some of the problems Rawls faces are problems that any minimalist account may encounter. Consider again the three desiderata specified in Section I. Minimalist accounts encounter problems meeting each of these criteria.[51]

First, there is the problem of *indeterminacy*: if one claims that members of one's own society enjoy a certain set of rights and that other human beings enjoy some but not all of these rights one has to explain why one draws the line between human rights and other rights where one does. As we saw, Rawls does not give a convincing answer to this question and it is difficult to see on what basis a minimalist can draw the line. A cosmopolitan, drawing on the scope$_1$ claim, can deal with this question for their answer is that we should look to the rationale underpinning our rights. In some cases, the rationale for some holding these rights implies that all do. However, where the vindication of our rights does not draw on universalist premises it will not have this implication. In other words, there is no arbitrary or ad hoc drawing of the line; rather a reasoned theoretical account can be given.

A second general problem faced by minimalist accounts concerns their fit or lack of fit with their domestic political theory (*domestic-compatibility*). This brings us back to the scope$_1$ claim for the problem with a minimal account is that the rationales for some people (members of liberal democratic societies) enjoying the full liberal package of rights entail that all other persons enjoy them. For this reason, it is incoherent to affirm these rights for some but to deny them to others.

Finally, if we turn to the third criterion, the holistic and interconnected nature of many rights undermines the prospects of a minimal approach. A minimal approach could succeed if both the proposed minimal rights hung together in a coherent way and *they did not entail any more-than-minimal rights*. But the discussion of rights-holism has shown that very basic rights tend to entail more extensive liberal rights. Accordingly, a minimalist position becomes hard to maintain.[52]

# IX

Having considered five justifications of civil and political human rights, the rest of this chapter now considers four challenges to these ideals. Some of these are presented by those who affirm a realist perspective; others from those who think that human rights are insufficiently sensitive to people's national identities and are, more generally, culturally insensitive. Others come from those sympathetic to the society of states. I shall begin the examination of critiques with several arguments examined in the last chapter which object to universalism in general. It is important to consider these for whilst we saw in the last chapter that they do not undermine all universalist approaches, it is thought by many that they do undermine the kind of universalism that affirms civil and political human rights. Having considered these arguments, the chapter then considers some entirely new objections, all of which are directed specifically at civil and political human rights (and not at universalism in general). None of them takes a relativist approach because that has been discussed in Chapter 2 above.

Let us begin then by returning to one of the normative arguments against universalism introduced in the last chapter—that which complains that universal principles are imperialistic and violate the right of cultures to be self-determining

(Chapter 2, Section XIV). As was argued there, this does not entail the rejection of universalism per se and it is, indeed, itself a universal principle. It affirms the universal principle that *it is wrong to foist alien ideals on other cultures*. Let us term this the *universal principle of cultural respect*. That this is a universal principle, however, does not show that it poses no challenge to human rights. On the contrary, many appeal to this universal principle and, relying on it, criticize the idea of universal civil and political rights. They argue that the latter are alien to many non-western cultures and thus an ethic of respect for other cultures demands that people do not impose universal civil and political rights in those cultures whose members reject them. They invoke one universalism in order to reject another.[53]

When broken down into its constituent parts, this makes two claims. First it holds that

(1) human rights thinking is peculiar to western thinking and does not command the consent of all cultures.

This does possess a great deal of plausibility. Many cite Islam in this context and in particular its attribution of different rights to Muslims, 'People of the Book', and 'Unbelievers'. Male members of the former are attributed the fullest set of rights. Members of the second category hold some rights (such as the right to property and to follow their faith) but not others (such as the right to take part in politics and the right to try and convert others). Finally, members of the third group may only have a temporary right to pass through the Islamic land.[54] Another example of a culture said to be at odds with the ethos of a human rights regime is Confucianism. The latter places a strong emphasis on filial piety, enjoining people to act in a harmonious fashion rather than assert their rights.[55] Human rights also run contrary to some African perspectives on morality. Consider, for example, the practice of *trokosi* which is practised by the Ewe people (in the south-east of Ghana, Togo, and Benin Republics) and Ga Adangbes (in south Ghana) (Quashigah 1998: 194). *Trokosi* refers to the practice whereby a virgin is handed over to a priest to be a slave in recompense for a wrong committed by her family. As the priest's slave she may be required to have sex with him and/or cook and look after his house (Quashigah 1998: 193–215).[56]

To this, the argument then adds the following claim:

(2) one should not impose values on people that they do not endorse (the universal principle of cultural respect).

Therefore, it concludes:

(C) one should not impose human rights on people who do not endorse them and universal principles of civil and political human rights are illegitimate.

The argument under scrutiny, thus, affirms a kind of universalism but, it is claimed, a superior kind to the universalisms that embrace universal human rights. Before evaluating this argument, it is useful to compare it with the argument that Rawls develops in *The Law of Peoples* for in some ways it is simply a more sweeping version of Rawls's minimalism. Whereas Rawls maintains that it would be intolerant for liberals to thrust their conceptions of human rights on non-liberal regimes but does nonetheless endorse some civil and political human rights, this argument also invokes an ideal of toleration but adopts a more minimal position, tending even to reject any civil and political human rights.

How persuasive is this reasoning? It is worth considering it at length because it is frequently invoked, not only by academics but also by politicians. One line of defence against this argument focuses on premise (1). Consider three such counter-arguments. First, many make much of the historical pedigree of the concept of human rights, stressing its origin in western political thought. The promotion of human rights is criticized on the grounds that it is applying a western concept to non-western cultures. Such reasoning is, however, highly dubious. It is a non sequitur to suggest that since a moral concept first occurs in one place (say the west) it should therefore not be adopted elsewhere (Donnelly 1989: 60). The geographical location of the invention of an idea does not determine its later applicability.

Second, it is important to observe that we need a more nuanced account of the possible relationship between human rights, on the one hand, and non-western cultures, on the other hand, than the critics of humans rights employ. According to the argument being considered the relationship between rights and non-western traditions is one of incompatibility and conflict.[57] It assumes, moreover, that since non-western cultures tend to lack the concept of rights *therefore* rights are incompatible with that culture. This, however, does not follow and we should note that many ethical traditions which do not employ the concept of rights nonetheless prescribe actions which coincide with rights policies. Those who affirm a duty-based ethic, for example, enjoin rulers not to be cruel and not to be tyrannical. They may not deploy the term 'rights' but their ethical injunctions result in the same policies as human rights. In other cases, human rights theorists can argue for the possibility of an 'overlapping consensus' on human rights (An Na'im 1999, esp. pp. 153, 166–8; Bielefeldt 2000: 114–17, esp. p. 116; Chan 1999: 212; Dower 1998: 12–13, 43; Taylor 1998, esp. pp. 37–8, 48–53; Taylor 1999, esp. pp. 124–6, 133–8, 143–4). As Sen points out, it is inaccurate to think that 'asian values' are hostile to liberty since thinkers like Confucius and Kautilya and religions like Islam contain tolerant aspects to their political thought (1999b: 234–40). A case in point is the Buddhist emperor Aśoka who declared in his *Rock Edict VII* that he 'wishes members of all faiths to live everywhere in his kingdom' (1978: 51). Aśoka insisted that '[t]he faiths of others all deserve to be honored' (1978: 51). Further, he insists, in *Rock Edict XII*, that 'concord alone is commendable, for through concord men may learn and respect the conception of Dharma accepted by others' (1978: 52).[58]

Third, it is important to note the context in which people criticize attempts to promote human rights. The need to promote human rights is often made by former colonial powers or currently powerful states. Given this, it is hardly surprising that members of some countries resent being given high-handed lectures on rights by powerful states with poor contemporary or historical records.[59] In the light of this it is reasonable to suggest that some of the animus directed against human rights is explicable as hostility to being lectured at by those with poor records themselves (Yasuaki 1999: 104–6). To put the point more positively: global norms affirming basic human rights are likely to enjoy greater legitimacy if those who campaign for them recognize the flaws in their historical record and apply the norms as consistently to their own country as they do to foreigners. In this light, the United States's decision not to support the International Criminal Court (whilst also sanctioning ad hoc war crimes tribunals for the former Yugoslavia and Rwanda) undermines its claims to be committed to universal civil and political rights. Without this equal handed treatment, it is hardly surprising that human rights norms will be perceived as the imposition of alien ideals.

The above considerations suggest various ways in which the conflict between human rights, on the one hand, and various cultures, on the other, tends to be exaggerated. The point, nonetheless, remains that there will be cases where human rights clash with the values affirmed by non-western (and indeed, western) cultures. There will, that is, be cases of incompatibility. Does this, then, imply that human rights to civil and political liberties should be rejected? Not necessarily. This depends on whether we accept the universal principle of cultural respect. The latter faces a number of problems.

One important point to bear in mind when considering whether to reject human rights because others disagree with them is *who* it is that is rejecting the human rights in question (Caney 2001*a*: 129–30; Tan 2000: 36). Many of those critical of human rights are, for example, political leaders of non-western political regimes. Prominent examples include Lee Kwan Yew of Singapore, Mahhathir Mohammed of Malaysia, and Deng Xiao Peng of China. Each of the above have stated that human rights are incompatible with the traditions of non-western countries like their own. We should not, however, infer from this that the peoples of those countries are necessarily similarly hostile to human rights, that these political elites are representative of their peoples. And it is open to us to question whether they are making a principled rejection of human rights or whether, as has been argued of some East Asian political elites, they wish simply to preserve their power base (Christie 1995: 204, 213–18). We should, in addition to this, distinguish between cases where X rejects the claim that they have rights, on the one hand, and cases where X claims those rights for himself but denies them to others. The latter does not represent a credible point against principles of human rights. Put differently: if someone thinks that they themselves do not have human rights then this principled good-faith rejection is worth taking seriously. But where the rejection occurs simply because one person wishes to control others and so augment his power this does not amount to a powerful counter-argument against human rights. We should consider the practice of *trokosi* in this light. That the male priests—who benefit from this system—affirm this does not in any way sanctify the tradition.

The argument is also vulnerable to an immanent critique. At its heart is the claim that we show respect to people by respecting their cultures. For this to be true, however, these cultures must be genuinely theirs rather than, say, imposed on them by powerful political elites. But then, for these cultural practices to be genuinely theirs the members of the culture must have both the chance to contribute to the shaping of cultural norms and also the chance to leave. Thus the logic underlying the universal principle of cultural respect actually requires us to accept certain human rights such as the right of freedom of expression and belief as well as the right to emigrate. Without these rights what one is respecting is not people's genuine commitment to their culture but the political creations of an elite which has manipulated ways of life to serve its interests (Caney 2000c: 544–5).[60] Judith Shklar puts the point forcefully:

For an inquiry into the preferences of the oppressed to mean anything at all, one would have to conduct it under conditions that make it possible for the most deprived members of society to speak without fear and with adequate information. How else can one know whether they really share the values of the masters? Historians indeed know that they have not, but that is retrospection. Here and now there is no substitute for consent under conditions that make it genuine. (1990: 115; cf. also 1990: 116)

(2) is thus untenable for the intuition that underlies the argument, when considered more closely, entails support for civil and political human rights (Jones 1994: 216).

Third we should consider *what* it is that is to be respected as well as *who* is claiming it should be respected. The claim that we should not affirm human rights that clash with cultural practices gains force by employing vague phrases and eschewing concrete examples. Many who criticize civil and political human rights for being incompatible with some cultural practices employ highly abstract terms, asserting that the rights contradict 'cultural traditions' or do not respect the 'other'. Presented in the abstract this sounds attractive but if the critique of these rights is to have force the cultural traditions must have a specific content. Consider, in this context, some fairly standard examples of practices that clash with civil and political human rights—practices such as the enslavement of those deemed to be inferior or subhuman; the stoning to death of a woman who commits adultery; the killing of a woman who dishonours her family by leaving a violent husband; and the persecution of homosexuals. Or consider the practice whereby a human being (often a child) is sacrificed and his or her organs are used to engage in witchcraft. This takes place in some African communities, such as the Yoruba in Nigeria, and a case also occurred in the UK in September 2001. For the critique of human rights to go through the critic has to show not just that civil and political rights conflict with someone else's culture but that we have reason to accord primacy to the latter and to reject the former. Moreover he or she has to do this, not in general terms, but with reference to specific practices such as those cited above. Terms like 'culture' and 'cultural identity' tend to obscure this for they sound attractive and benign but, as the above examples illustrate, cultures can be cruel, oppressive, exclusionary, and violent.[61]

Fourth, and relatedly, the claim that there is a universal injunction not to further values that people reject should surely take into account the validity of those values. We should thus raise the question of whether the cultural practice that disavows civil and political human rights is *justified* and whether the beliefs on which it rests are sound.[62] We have no a priori reason to assume that the practice is in all cases justified and that its beliefs are well-borne out.[63] Perhaps, in cases of incompatibility, the human rights should take precedence. To illustrate this point, let us examine several challenges to civil and political human rights. Consider, for example, the argument that such rights cause crime and drug use. Since this argument makes statements that purport to be objectively valid, it is appropriate to evaluate their cogency rather than assume that they are necessarily correct and beyond any kind of scrutiny whatsoever. Or consider Thabo Mbeki's policies towards AIDS which are predicated on his belief that there is no link between AIDS and HIV (McGreal 2002: 42–7). The universal principle of cultural respect enjoins us to respect his practices but surely whether we should do so ought to depend in part on the soundness of his assumptions.[64] Given the momentous importance of these policies (it affects whether people live or die) and given the dubiousness of Mbeki's assumptions, it is hard to see why we should be required to respect the practice.[65]

Finally, it is appropriate, when assessing the argument in question, to return to the scope$_1$ claim. As we saw earlier in Sections II–VI, the sorts of considerations often invoked in defence of civil and political rights entail that these rights should be held by all. This puts some proponents of the argument under scrutiny in a problematic position. Many, for example, are committed to their own liberal rights but, persuaded by the argument being considered, conclude that members of non-western societies do not possess these rights. The scope$_1$ claim undermines this position, however, in the same way that it undermines Rawls's unduly minimal set of basic rights. The reason is that the arguments for thinking that westerners have rights also show that non-westerners too have these rights. The position thus does not meet the condition of *domestic-compatibility*. The argument being examined does not invalidate the cosmopolitan reasoning for civil and political human rights. All it says is that some peope reject its conclusion. That they do should not be ignored but it is not, in itself, reason to show that one should abandon one's commitment to such human rights.

In conclusion, then, the claim that civil and political human rights should be abandoned because they are incompatible with cultural practices is found wanting. On a conciliatory note, cosmopolitans can plausibly argue (i) that the extent of incompatibility is exaggerated. In a more combative vein they can, however, also argue (ii) that where there is conflict this does not entail the falsity of the human rights perspective for the principle of the unconditional respect for cultural practices is untenable.

## X

Having considered one challenge, let us now consider a second universalist objection to civil and political human rights which, like the preceding argument, draws on an argument considered in the last chapter (Chapter 2 Section XII).

As we saw there, one argument against universalism accuses it of resulting in uniformity and we saw that this has force against some conceptions of universalism but not against others. It thus remains to be seen whether civil and political human rights fall into the first category or the second. Some maintain, for example, that civil and political human rights do generate uniformity. They charge that such rights would result in the spread of a westernized culture everywhere. They would eliminate diversity and traditional ways of life and engender a homogenized, bland world of stultifying uniformity.

This critique of civil and political human rights is, however, deeply flawed. In the first place, it overlooks the fact that human rights comprise only one aspect of morality. A system of human rights specifies only some common basic standards. They thus allow that there are other moral ideals that vary from one culture to another and, as such, they will not engender commonality (Booth 1999: 55; Caney 1997*a*: 34).

Indeed, to think that human rights result in homogeneity rests on an impoverished conception of human nature for it fails to recognize the human faculty for imagination, creativity, and diversity. We can go further. Human rights do not simply not generate uniformity: they positively facilitate pluralism. To take an obvious example: possessing the right not to be killed or tortured allows people to engage in their very different forms of life. Consider, moreover, the claim that individuals have a right to participate in the political process of their society. By exercising this right, the members of a society are enabled to promote their ideals, and those favoured by members of one political system may very well differ radically from those of another. In other words, the exercise of a common right is very likely to issue in diverse outcomes. Similarly, civil and political human rights allow individuals with different values to practise their different ways of life (Jones 1999: 175).

One further consideration that should be borne in mind is that those who defend civil and political human rights allow that such rights may sometimes be interpreted differently in different contexts. Sen provides a good example of this in a discussion of shame and self-respect where he points out that notions of shame are culturally constructed (1999*b*: 73–4). This is not to say that there can be unlimited discretion on how we interpret human rights: it is just to say that the core general values affirmed by human rights permit different cultural instantiations. As such it further weakens the claim that civil and political human rights issue in uniformity.

# XI

For some critics of civil and political human rights the latter are undesirable, not because they are incompatible with other cultures, but for the different reason that they undermine one specific value, namely community. Rights, many communitarians object, corrode communal relations and result in fragmentation.[66] Related concerns are expressed by non-western philosophies. Some members of

East Asian cultures object to individualism and egoism and charge rights with inculcating these kinds of character traits. Confucianism, for example, places a strong emphasis on filial piety and duties to one's close attachments. More generally, Confucianism is hostile to adversarial concepts such as rights and Confucius counsels those who disagree 'not to resort to litigation in the first place' (1979: bk. XII, paragraph 13, p. 115).

Prior to examining this argument we should make two observations. First, it overcomes a shortcoming of the argument discussed in Section IX because it claims not just that human rights destroy some ways of life; it claims, rather, that they destroy a deep and important value—namely community. Human rights are undesirable because they undermine something of great value. The second, and related, important point to record is that the argument at stake is a universalist argument. It is not dependent on a commitment to moral relativism and is more naturally read as claiming that community is an important human (that is universal) good that is threatened by rights.

The most significant problem with this argument is that it overlooks the very many ways in which civil and political rights provide the background within which communities can flourish. This point has been made particularly clearly by Allen Buchanan (1989: 858, 861–5) and Joseph Raz (1986: 251–5). As they rightly point out, individual rights can protect and promote communal activities. The right to freedom of association, for example, enables religious communities to practise their way of life with their own communal traditions and norms. Freedom of action enables individuals to club together, form a commune, or live in their traditional community. Rights provide people with options, including the option to practise communitarian conceptions of the good. Likewise, the right to freedom of belief enables members of religious communities to perpetuate their community. Moreover, as Mill emphasized, extending the right to vote to all members of a political system helps engender a common sense of public spirit (1977b [1861]: 400–1, 412). Democratic rights can, thereby, help foster a political *community*. As such, then, individual civil and political rights do not of necessity lead to an aggressive or adversarial or litigious culture.

A human rights theorist can, perhaps, acknowledge that some rights are guilty of the charge made. Some cultures are, perhaps, obsessed with rights and think only or primarily in terms of what people owe them. This consideration, however, does not give us a reason to abandon rights per se but it might give us reason to abandon some specific liberties claimed to be rights. The communitarian argument, for example, does not give us any reason to reject the right to a fair trial but does raise a question mark over other proposed rights (such as, for example, the claim that children born using artificial insemination have the right to know who the donors are). A wholesale condemnation of rights is thus misjudged.

This leads on to a third point, namely that it is unhelpful to examine the claim that human rights are wrong because they erode communal relations in the abstract. The reason for this is that whether eroding communal relations is a vice or a virtue depends on the specific nature of the 'community'. We have no reason to assume that each and every established social structure is valuable. Some, for example, repress individuals. Others involve the subjugation of subgroups, like women, homosexuals, or members of an ethnic minority. It is imperative then when addressing the claim that rights are malign because they undermine communal patterns to examine the specific concrete forms of life that rights undermine (if any) and evaluate their moral characteristics.

For these three reasons the claim that civil and political human rights are undesirable because destructive of human communities is untenable. Rights liberate people: they relieve them from oppressive communities and provide the framework within which communal lives can be lived.

# XII

Let us now consider a series of closely related objections commonly levelled against the promotion of civil and political human rights from a realist perspective. Many realists are sceptical of policies designed to promote civil and political human rights. Three distinct reasons are proffered.

1. First, realists object that human rights policies inevitably tend to be selective and biased. States, the objection runs, will emphasize the importance of human rights when dealing with some states but not with others with whom they may have trade or other types of link. The motives of those who intervened in Yugoslavia in 1999, for instance, are often impugned on the grounds that if they were genuinely committed to human rights they would also have intervened in Russia to protect Chechnya. States, it is asserted, inevitably take a partial approach and this shows that they are not really ever concerned with human rights at all. If they were, they would take an across-the-board approach and intervene equally everywhere. This realist argument claims then to unmask foreign policy that purports to be committed to human rights as being nothing of the sort.[67]

These considerations do not undermine the proposition that states should pursue civil and political human rights. In the first place, someone committed to these rights might just accept the factual claims made, agreeing that states are often selective in their human rights foreign policy, *but* respond that it does not follow from this that states (and other institutions) should abjure the pursuit of these rights. Rather what they should do is take an impartial response and defend civil and political human rights on an equal basis. In other words, the response would be a greater commitment to human rights rather an abandonment of that ideal.

Second, the argument falsely assumes that if one accepts civil and political human rights one is thereby committed to calling for states to adopt an identical response in all circumstances. One might quite reasonably call for different policies in different contexts consistent with their commitment to human rights.

Indeed the latter may *require* different responses to human rights violations in different circumstances. For example, those who favoured military intervention against Yugoslavia in 1999 were not thereby necessarily contradicting themselves if they did not call for the same response to Russia's treatment of the Chechens. The degree of rights violations may differ. In addition, the chances of success may be quite different and an intervention to protect human rights is not justified if it will be unsuccessful. A selective, or rather discriminating, approach can therefore be justified. Identical treatment is inappropriate in non-identical cirumstances.

To this we should add that often a state that seeks to protect human rights abroad adopts policies that look, at least at first glance, not too dissimilar to traditional realist policy. As we have just seen, a human rights policy that seeks to be effective will take into account the probability that any action it adopts will work. And it is reasonable to think that human rights policy has more chance of working against weak states than strong states. Hence a state committed to human rights has good reason to pressurize weak states and not take on the powerful. But, and this is the point that is crucial here, such a policy looks quite similar to a state that acts on realist grounds for it too will not take on powerful states. Realist scepticism about humanitarianism thus gains plausibility because any human rights policy that seeks to be effective looks, superficially, like a state operating on realist lines.

A further point a human rights theorist might make is that *even* if states do not and will not adopt an impartial approach it is better that they do something rather than nothing. At least, then, some people's rights would be protected and some rights violations averted. Against this a realist might respond that such half-hearted protection of civil and political human rights discredits the whole idea of human rights for it appears partial and selective and therefore not humanitarian. This, though, is rather perverse for it would imply that it is better not to perform one good deed because one cannot or will not perform all good deeds. This call for inaction thus condemns us to accepting worse outcomes than is necessary and it forbids any kind of improvement.

2. Given the failure of the first line of reasoning, let us consider a second, distinct, realist argument. This claims that it would be quite wrong for a state consistently to promote human rights for such a policy sometimes conflicts with more important goals. As Morgenthau writes, 'the principle of the defense of human rights cannot be consistently applied in foreign policy because it can and it must come in conflict with other interests that may be more important than the defense of human rights in a particular instance' (1979: 7). He then adds that 'once you fail to defend human rights in a particular instance, you have given up the defense of human rights and you have accepted another principle to guide your actions. And this is indeed what has happened and is bound to happen if you are not a Don Quixote who foolishly but consistently follows a disastrous path of action' (1979: 7).

But this line of reasoning contains a non sequitur. Even if we grant Morgenthau's assumption that it is sometimes more important to pursue the national interest than to protect the civil and political human rights of others, it is simply incorrect to claim that one has abandoned the notion of human rights. I may have a duty to comfort a friend if he is distressed but I may also have a duty (say to give first aid to a crash victim) that happens to clash with this and that trumps it. In complying with the latter it does not follow that one has abandoned the principle of comforting friends. Likewise to claim that civil and political human rights are not the sole determinant of our actions does not entail that they should not be a determinant at all.

3. The previous two claims have been negative. A third, more positive, claim is that the most effective way of furthering civil and political rights in the world is to set a good example by having an internally just regime. The suggestion here is that members of other societies will be encouraged by this vision of a fair society and thus work within their own societies to bring about a just and fair political framework that respects people's civil and political liberties (Morgenthau 1979: 5–6).

This view is hard to sustain. It combines an extreme scepticism about the efficacy of external pressure with an extreme optimism about the power of example. A fuller treatment of the former—that is the effectiveness of external intervention and pressure—will have to await Chapter 7, which discusses the ethical issues surrounding intervention. In the meantime we can observe two problems with its emphasis on the power of example. First, those who live in a despotical regime (even if inspired by the example set) may not be *able* to secure their human rights. So even if internally liberal societies create a desire in others to emulate their system this gives us no reason to think that they will succeed in doing so. Second, the existence of an internally just regime may not induce those living in unjust regimes to want to reform their society. Rather it may simply induce in them a *desire* to immigrate to the fair society rather than struggle at home. To use Albert Hirschman's terminology, one might say that the existence of fair societies is likely to generate in members of unjust societies a desire to 'exit' their society and move to a fairer society rather than a desire to stay and 'voice' their views and thereby reform their own society (1970). Moreover, this is an entirely reasonable and rational response.

# XIII

This chapter has sought to evaluate competing conceptions of civil and political justice and, given that it has explored a large number of competing arguments, it may be useful to recap some of the points that have been made. The chapter has explored four cosmopolitan arguments, arguing in particular that

(1) the contractarian vindication of civil and political human rights begs the question;

(2) the transcendental argument also does not ground civil and political human rights.

We have moreover seen that

(3) deontological accounts have more force but are indeterminate and issue in paradoxical conclusions; and
(4) these flaws are remedied by a number of well-being based arguments for civil and political human rights.

We have also noted that

(5) the logic underlying many domestic theories of civil and political justice entails that there are global civil and political liberties (the $scope_1$ claim); and,
(6) the cosmopolitan arguments conform to the logical structure specified by the General Argument.

Turning now to non-cosmopolitan approaches, the chapter argued that

(7) Rawls's defence of a minimal set of civil and political human rights encountered a number of serious problems.

Finally, we have seen that none of the critiques of civil and political human rights have force and that

(8) the objection that they do not accord sufficient respect to cultural practices is untenable;
(9) the fears about uniformity are ill-founded;
(10) the concerns that rights engender selfishness are unpersuasive; and
(11) realist concerns about bias and selectivity are misplaced.

This concludes the examination of civil and political justice. Some have criticized liberal accounts of human rights for focusing exclusively on civil and political liberties and being silent on economic rights. Chapter 4 takes up this issue, focusing on global principles of distributive justice.

## NOTES

1. As the title of this book states, this work is focused on universal principles of *justice*. In concentrating on such universal principles, I am not assuming that they are the only universal principles. There may be, for example, universal principles of compassion or mercy or generosity (all of them plausible candidates for being universal principles and none of them principles of justice). It is, however, worth focusing on principles of justice because most of those who do affirm universal principles construe them as principles of justice and also ascribe very great moral worth to justice. Furthermore, the existence and importance of other types of universal moral values is recognized, and indeed stressed, at various stages in the argument (Ch. 3, Sect. XI).

2. At this point, someone might argue that there are types of justice other than civil and political justice and distributive justice. Some argue, for example, in defence of 'cultural justice'. (For the concept see Fraser (1997, esp. pp. 13–15).) These types of claims are not, however, omitted by my typology: some of the issues raised under the heading of 'cultural justice' are examined in this chapter, Sect. IX, and in Ch. 5, Sects XII–XVI.
3. For an excellent analysis of rights see Jones (1994).
4. Pogge defends negative (institutional) duties: see, for example, Pogge (1989: 276–8; 1994a: 92–3).
5. For this term see Kukathas (1992: 105–39).
6. I borrow the terms 'maximalism' and 'minimalism' from Walzer (1994). See also Beitz's similar distinction between 'the nonpartisan or restricted conception of human rights' and 'the liberal or full conception of human rights' (2001: 270). Beitz makes a powerful case for the universal application of the full liberal package and asks why one should not apply the full conception (2001: 270).
7. A similar, but distinct, criterion is defended by the international lawyer Lea Brilmayer in her *Justifying International Acts* (1989). She affirms what she terms a 'vertical perspective', where this states that 'a state's actions outside its territory, and against noncitizens, must be evaluated in terms of the political justification that grants that state the right to operate domestically' (1989: 2). See further her affirmation of a 'consistency requirement between domestic and international norms' (1989: 28, cf. pp. 23, 24, 28–9, 48, 81, 161). Her criterion is, however, importantly different to that employed in this book. First, her consistency requirement is one that applies to states: it requires states to be consistent in the way that they treat members and non-members. The criterion of 'domestic-compatibility', by contrast, makes no reference to states and does not presuppose that there should be states (cf. Ch. 5). Second, even assuming that there are states, 'domestic-compatibility' does not restrict the consistency requirement to states alone: as I define it, the criterion of domestic-compatibility applies to principles of justice and includes as duty-bearers individuals, international institutions, and so on. So, unlike Brilmayer's vertical thesis, it is not framed in terms of the *state* being consistent. It is directed toward individuals, NGOs, economic corporations, churches, and so on and enjoins them to be consistent in their treatment of citizens and non-citizens. A third difference is that Brilmayer's vertical thesis applies when a state exerts 'power' (1989: 2, 16, 87) or 'influence' (1989: 144, 158, 159) or 'coercion' (1989: 11, 12, 17, 22, 24, 43, 44, 118, 135, 137, 159, 160) over non-members. It then stipulates that if it exerts power/influence/coercion over non-citizens then it must treat them in a way that is consistent with the way that it treats its own citizens. The criterion of domestic-compatibility, by contrast, applies even in the absence of power or coercion. A fourth difference is that the criterion of domestic-compatibility is not a 'vertical' claim for it does not put the hierarchical relationship between a polity and its treatment of persons under its coercion at its heart. It has a horizontal character: insisting that all agents (including individuals, associations, states, and international institutions) ascribe rights and duties to non-citizens in a way consistent with the way in which they ascribe rights and duties to the citizens of their own country. It is not 'vertical' in nature, starting from a state–citizen relationship and generalizing it. More generally, then, the criterion of domestic-compatibility is wider in its remit than, and different in its focus to, Brilmayer's vertical thesis.

8. For further pertinent discussion see Nickel (1987: 101–5).

9. I refer to this as a scope$_1$ claim because the following chapter advances a structurally similar claim about the arguments for economic rights (which I term the scope$_2$ claim).

10. I refer to the 'standard' rationales because what follows does not demonstrate that there are absolutely no theories that do not support universal civil political rights. The claim is that the conventional approaches employed to defend civil and political rights (and four types of them are considered) conform to the scope$_1$ claim.

11. Barry's theory is indebted to the work of Thomas Scanlon (1982). For Scanlon's most recent statement of this contractualist theory see Scanlon (1998).

12. He also contrasts it with a second theory that he dubs 'justice as reciprocity'. This theory is not discussed further and so shall not be outlined at great length here. Briefly stated, this theory makes two claims. First, it argues that principles are fair if they are mutually advantageous. It adds, however, second, that people should comply with these rules out of a sense of fairness (1995*a*: 46–8).

13. Since it is common to claim that defences of liberal rights depend on western assumptions it is worth noting that the key claims affirmed by Barry—that the state should eschew controversial assumptions and be neutral between conceptions of the good to enjoy public support—can also be found in Indian political discourse. According to Sunil Khilnani, Nehru embraced 'public, secular arguments' (1997: 177) for the same reason. See further (1997: 173–8, esp. pp. 177–8). In addition, the Japanese scholar Inoue Tatsuo employs an argument on similar lines to Barry's to show that liberal civil and political rights are applicable to Asian countries (1999: 42–9).

14. Habermas refers to his argument as a 'transcendental-pragmatic justification of discourse ethics' (1992*a*: 94; cf. also 1992*b*: 116).

15. For this line of reasoning see (1992*a*: throughout, esp. pp. 58–109; 1992*b*). For a recent statement on the derivation of rights see (1997*a*: ch. 3, and 454–7). For his derivation of five specific rights see his discussion in *Between Facts and Norms* (1997*a*: 122–31). For his general theoretical background see (1986: 1–141, esp. pp. 15–19, 22–6, 37–40, 42, 75).

16. For Habermas's distinction between the good and the right, his contention that beliefs about the good cannot be justified to all, and his claim that political institutions should be neutral between conceptions of the good, see (1992*a*: 104, 108; 1992*b*: 178, 180–1).

17. I am indebted to Graham Long for discussions on these issues; for his critique of Habermas, cf. Long (2001: 116–32).

18. For Habermas's universalism see (1986: 42; 1992*a*: 76–9; 1992*b*: 116–17, 121, 129–30).

19. Note that Nagel also accepts that rights have value in virtue of their consequences (1995: 86–7).

20. Nagel cites Kamm in this context: cf. (1995: 89–90, fn. 3). For another exponent of a deontological perspective see Hillel Steiner's affirmation of self-ownership (1994: 231–3) and the right to equal freedom (1994: 188–228).

21. See, further, Keown, Prebish, and Husted (1998).

22. See, for example, Nussbaum (2002: 136, 138–9).

23. The word 'duty' is followed by a footnote in which Raz cites works by Dworkin, MacCormick, and K. Campbell (1986: 166, fn. 2).

24. For an earlier statement of the list see Nussbaum (1992: 222).

25. My argument thus far is indebted to the work of Dworkin and Kymlicka. They too affirm the ideal of equal respect for persons (step 1) and they explicate this in terms

of people's interests (step 2). See, for example, Dworkin (2000) and Kymlicka (2002: esp. pp. 3–5; cf. also 1989) for their affirmation of the ideal of treating persons as equals and their explication of this in terms of respecting persons' interests. As noted in the text, they also affirm step (3). They have not, to my knowledge, explicitly invoked this to defend human rights or applied it internationally. My argument also has much in common with Allen Buchanan's defence of human rights in his recent *Justice, Legitimacy, and Self-Determination.* He also invokes the 'moral equality of persons' (2003: 82), claims that this entails respecting persons' interests in well-being, and deduces from this certain rights (2003: 82–5). There are differences between my account and Buchanan's concerning the fourth and final step of the argument: he too affirms consideration 1 (concerning physical safety) but does not rely on considerations 2, 3, 4, and 5. For an additional account which also invokes persons' interests (and considerations 1 and 2 below) see Nickel's discussion of 'prudential' arguments for human rights (1987: 84–90). By contrast with the argument given here, such prudential arguments do not aim to treat persons as equals and are grounded in what self-interested people could agree on.

26. My response here follows Nussbaum (2002: 131–2). When considering the contention that food is not a good because some choose to fast she replies that what matters is granting persons the capability to have food. In such circumstances '[t]he person with plenty of food may always choose to fast, but there is a great difference between fasting and starving, and it is this difference that we wish to capture' (2002: 131).

27. See further Gyeke's defence of a brand of communitarianism that affirms the central importance of rights: (1997: 35–76).

28. In a trenchant analysis, Robert Goodin persuasively shows that many of the claims about the individual's ability to know his interests best are exception-ridden (1990: 181–95, esp. pp. 188–91).

29. I am indebted to Peter Jones for this point: cf. Jones (1983: 167).

30. The term 'clumsy tool' was coined by Donald Regan (1989: 1082–3).

31. There are, of course, also specific arguments for specific liberties. For one example: Mill defends freedom of expression on the grounds that, although it does not guarantee it, it provides a propitious environment for the discovery of truth (1977*a* [1859]: ch. II, pp. 228–59).

32. See, in this connection, Onuma Yasuaki's discussion of an 'intercivilizational' approach to human rights: (1999).

33. Mill, of course, did make this claim, claiming that 'barbarians' were not fit to make up their own minds (1977*a* [1859]: 224).

34. This is well brought out by Tesón (1998: 111).

35. For a robust statement of the universalist implications of liberalism see Barry (2001: 138–40, 283–4).

36. I set aside exceptions such as the mentally handicapped, children, and the senile.

37. See, further, (1999*b*: 49–51).

38. Rawls describes an imaginary society, Kazanistan, to illustrate this type of society (1999*b*: 75–8).

39. For his repudiation of cosmopolitanism see (1999*b*: 82–3, 119–20).

40. The word 'regime' is followed by a footnote that refers to (1999*b*: sects. 15 and 16). See (1999*b*: 37, fn. 43). For the consent of hierarchical societies to these eight principles see (1999*b*: 69, 85).

41. After the word 'security', there is a footnote which refers to Shue (1996*a*: 23) and Vincent (1986): (1999*b*: 65, fn. 1). After the word 'thought', there is a footnote

which states that 'this liberty of conscience may not be as extensive nor as equal for all members of society: for instance, one religion may legally predominate in the state government, while other religions, though tolerated, may be denied the right to hold certain positions' (1999*b*: 65, fn. 2). There is a third footnote, after the word 'similarly', which refers to Hart's *The Concept of Law* (1997: 156ff) (1999*b*: 65, fn. 3). For further pronouncements on the content of human rights cf. also Rawls's (1999*b*: 79, 80 fn. 23).

42. See Ch. 1, Sect. III for a discussion of the concept of a 'people'.

43. It is perhaps interesting to contrast Rawls's international contracts with his domestic one. In the latter, all citizens of a state are party to the contract. There is no suggestion that (setting aside children and the insane) some adults should not be allowed in. Given this, one might ask, why should not all types of regime be admitted into the international contract? Alternatively, one might ask whether some normal adult citizens should be excluded from the domestic contract?

44. For this line of argument see Beitz (1983: 596), Caney (2002*a*: 106–7), Kuper (2000: 649–52, esp. pp. 651–2), Pogge (2001*b*: 247), Tan (2000: 28–32, cf. also pp. 32–3), and Téson (1998: 111).

45. Put otherwise, Rawls has failed to justify his level-1 assumption that the global and domestic domains are subject to fundamentally different moral values.

46. See too James Nickel's similar distinction between 'logical' and 'practical' interconnections between rights (1987: 101). See, more generally, (1987: 101–5).

47. The above has focused on empirical interconnections between rights. Others have criticized Rawls by emphasizing what I have termed *incompleteness*-derived interconnections. Focusing again on Rawls's repudiation of democracy, Thomas McCarthy has argued that if we accept Rawls's basic rights we must also accept the right to democratic government (1999: 200–1). His argument draws on Habermas and makes the claim that fundamental liberal rights need to be legitimized to be valid. Hence a commitment to individual human rights is incomplete unless it is also combined with a commitment to legitimizing these rights through democratic deliberation and decision-making. One cannot, therefore, consistently affirm Rawls's basic rights and reject democracy. For Habermas's most sustained defence of this claim see Habermas (1997*a*).

48. The charge that Rawls's theory concedes too much to non-liberal perspectives and tolerates the intolerable is made by many: cf. Ackerman (1994: 381–3); Beitz (2000: 681); Buchanan (2000: 697–8, cf. further 716–20); Caney (2002*a*: 98–104, 111–12); Kuper (2000: 645, 648–53); McCarthy (1997: 211–13, 215–16); Moellendorf (2002*a*: 28); Pogge (1994*b*: 216–18); Tan (2000: 28–45, 79–89); Téson (1998: 109–22).

49. For criticism of Rawls for his exclusion of democratic rights see Téson (1998: 115–17).

50. For additional criticism of Rawls's argument here cf. Caney (2002*a*: 99–114).

51. For a good critical discussion of minimalism see Beitz (2001).

52. Note: an ultra-minimal position, which eschews any civil and political human rights, would avoid some of these problems. First, it does not violate the criterion of *determinacy* (the first criterion): since it rejects all candidates for civil and political rights there is no problem about where to draw the line. Second, it is not guilty of affirming some rights but rejecting others that are entailed by the former set and thereby failing the criterion of *coherence* (the third criterion). However, it would, of course, violate the second criterion—*domestic-compatibility*.

53. For one example, see Zolo (1997: 118–19). See also Bilahari Kausikan's discussion. Kausikan thinks there are some common values (such as prohibitions of 'genocide, murder, torture, or slavery' (1996: 216)), but that there is cross cultural disagreement on other practices (such as 'capital punishment, detention without trial, or curbs on press freedoms' (1996: 217)). Accordingly, human rights theorists who argue that the death penalty, detention without trial, and restrictions on press freedom are unjust are guilty of cultural imposition.

54. This account is heavily indebted to Abdullahi An-Na'im (1987: 11).

55. For a good discussion of the relationship between Confucianism and human rights see Chan (1999: 212–37).

56. On the relationship between human rights and African morality see, more generally, Tiyanjana Maluwa (1997: 55–71).

57. On the possible logical relations between human rights and cultures, see Caney (2000d: 52–8).

58. See also Sen's brief discussion of Aśoka (1999b: 235–6). More generally on the extent to which Buddhism is compatible with, and supportive of, human rights see Caney (2000d: 66–70).

59. For an example of this kind of response to western politicians stressing the importance of human rights see Kausikan (1996: 211).

60. See, further, Barry (1995a: 198–9; 1995b: 77–8); Joshua Cohen (1986: 462–3); and James Fishkin (1984: 760). See also Walzer's interesting recognition of this kind of point (1994: 27).

61. On the value-laden nature of the concept of culture see Jones (1994: 218).

62. This point picks up and illustrates a point made in Ch. 2, Sect. XI.

63. The argument here is indebted to Jones (1999: 81–3).

64. Consider, in this light, other beliefs held about AIDS and HIV. McGreal reports that in South Africa there have been a number of instances of HIV-positive adults raping babies in the belief that doing so will cure them of HIV. He also reports that 25% of young South Africans believe that one can heal oneself of HIV by having sexual intercourse with a virgin (2002: 44). Such cases bring out the importance of noting that where a practice is based on false beliefs, and has such enormous effects on others, there is no case for deferring to that culturally entrenched belief.

65. For another example of this, consider the belief that democratic government impedes economic growth. Surely whether this belief should be respected depends in part on how well-grounded it is. Many have argued that it is dubious. Sen's version of this claim has already been mentioned in this chapter (Sect. VI). See, further, Donnelly (1989: 184–202), Goodin (1979: 31–42). For an earlier use of this example to make the same point see Caney (2002a: 107–8) and Buchanan (2003: 104 and more generally pp. 104–6).

66. For contemporary communitarian concerns see Bell (1993). Bell argues that rights may legitimately be restricted to protect community (1993: 140–3, 183). See also Michael Sandel (1982: 34–5).

67. On this see also Kausikan's statement that 'the Western promotion of human rights was shaped by and deployed as an ideological instrument of the East–West struggle' (1996: 203, cf. further p. 207). This argument, of course, draws on and develops the kind of anti-universalist reasoning examined in Ch. 2, Sect. XIII.

# 4

## Distributive Justice

Our normal attitude to foreigners is a complete negation of that absence of discrimination on irrelevant grounds which we have recognized as the principle of equality.

E. H. Carr (1995 [1939]: 149)

I believe in the right of every living human being, without distinction of colour, race, sex or professed belief or opinion, to liberty, life and subsistence, to complete protection from ill-treatment, equality of opportunity in the pursuit of happiness and an equal voice in the collective government of mankind.

H. G. Wells (1940: 101)

One of the striking features of much traditional political philosophy until recently was that it assumed that principles of distributive justice should operate at the state level. That is, the conventional wisdom was, and to some extent still is, that if there are any legitimate principles of distributive justice (and some deny that there are) they should be implemented within states. Duties of distributive justice thus apply within states or nations but do not apply globally. Accordingly, those who affirmed human rights tended to affirm civil and political human rights but deny economic human rights. This chapter aims to explore whether there are global principles of distributive justice. Are there cosmopolitan principles of distributive justice and, if so, what do they prescribe? Or, does justice apply between co-nationals or between co-citizens?[1]

To answer these questions, the chapter begins by examining the notion of distributive justice (Section I) and then outlining several cosmopolitan perspectives on distributive justice (Sections II–VI). The remainder of the chapter considers three alternatives to these cosmopolitan conceptions, beginning with Rawls's account of international justice, focusing on his critique of cosmopolitan conceptions and his defence of an account centred on the ideal of a Society of well-ordered Peoples (VII–VIII). The chapter then examines three claims about the nature of distributive justice, all of which emphasize the moral relevance of persons' membership in nations (IX–XI). It concludes by examining two realist claims about distributive justice (XII–XIII). What the chapter seeks to do is: to motivate some support for four particular cosmopolitan principles of distributive justice; to suggest that cosmopolitan accounts, in general, can meet the objections leveled against them by their critics; and to provide a critical analysis of competing approaches.

# I

Let us begin, therefore, with an analysis of the notion of distributive justice. What does a theory of distributive justice require? Any comprehensive analysis of distributive justice must speak to the following questions:

1. What sorts of entities are included within systems of distributive justice (humans, all sentient creatures, collective entities such as states or nations)?
2. Who are the rightful recipients of goods, and who is obligated to distribute these goods?
3. What should people have fair shares of (income, happiness)?
4. According to what criterion of distributive justice should goods be distributed (equality, according to desert, or the market)?[2]

It may be helpful to consider each of these in turn. (1) and (2) concern what is widely referred to as the scope of justice (Jones 1999: 5–7; O'Neill 1994: 79–84; Welch 1993: 200*ff*). The question they both address is: who is included within the scope of distributive justice? (1) addresses the more basic question of what sort of entities count as potential members of a scheme of distributive justice. Some, for example, argue that individual human beings are the legitimate recipients of goods. Others, by contrast, might argue that in international affairs rights and duties are possessed by collective entities, such as states or nations, and that justice is owed to them (and not to individuals). Much discussion by state officials and international lawyers conceives of international justice in terms of what is owed to the state. Furthermore, they do not mean by this that goods should be transferred to states as the most efficacious way of allocating goods to individuals. They mean rather that the ultimate possessor of the right is the collective entity that is the state.

Once a theory of distributive justice has identified which sort of entities are potential rights-holders and duty-bearers, it has to address a further question. To see this consider someone who gives an individualist answer to (1). This, in itself, does not tell us which individuals are entitled to receive goods from which other human beings (i.e. question (2)). We need then to know which groups of individuals comprise the scope of distributive justice. A variety of different answers is possible. One might, for example, take the cosmopolitan position that principles of distributive justice include everyone in the world within their scope. Alternatively, one might adopt an individualist answer to (1) but think that schemes of distributive justice apply within nations. Hence persons owe duties of distributive justice, not to all persons, but only to those persons who are members of their own nation. In short, a theory of distributive justice needs to provide an account of *who* is governed by a theory of distributive justice. Note also that someone might affirm a statist position on (1) but also accept that there should be world-level principles of distributive justice. According to such a position, states may be required to distribute resources to other states. Such a position, we might say, affirms *global* principles of distributive justice but since it denies that resources should be distributed to persons it rejects *cosmopolitan* principles of distributive justice.

An additional question that a theory of distributive justice must address is: 'what should there be fair amounts of?' Much has been written on this question (question (3)). Many of these discussions have not been specifically addressed to matters of global justice but they may, nonetheless, be applicable to the global realm. To give some examples: one possibility might be that a theory of justice should ensure that each person has a fair share of 'resources' (Dworkin 2000: 65–119). Alternatively, one might think that principles of distributive justice should be concerned with human happiness and seek to promote welfare. A third position is canvassed by Martha Nussbaum and Amartya Sen, both of whom think that distributive principles should be concerned with peoples' capability to function in certain ways (Nussbaum 2000*a*: 70–110; Sen 1993).[3] I shall simply employ the term 'goods' to cover any of these possibilities.

A fourth question remains, namely: 'how should goods be distributed?' Should they, for example, be distributed equally? Or in a way that maximizes total happiness? Or according to merit? Or according to who is most needy? It is an obvious point to note that there is little consensus as to which specific criterion of distributive justice should be adopted. On the other hand, it is also clear that almost everyone agrees that if principles of distributive justice apply to a group of people then they should not allow extreme poverty or starvation among the members of that group. (There are notable counter-examples, such as Nozick (1974), but they are exceptionally rare.) Utilitarians, egalitarians, and those who believe in distribution according to need, for example, may agree on some basic principles of distributive justice.

A further point remains to be made about the nature of distributive justice, namely that it differs from other types of moral relationship. What is distinctive about principles of distributive justice is that they refer to that to which people are *entitled*. We should thus recognize that there are arguments for the global redistribution of wealth which appeal not to what people can demand as a matter of justice but instead to duties of benevolence, or humanity, or charity.[4]

One final point: as in Chapter 3, this chapter notes that any defensible account of global rights must meet the three criteria of *determinacy*, *domestic-compatibility*, and *coherence* (cf. Chapter 3, Section I). The package of global economic rights defended must be determinate, compatible with 'domestic' theory, and internally coherent.

## II

Having provided a conceptual analysis of the nature of distributive justice, this section and Sections III–VI explore several cosmopolitan perspectives on distributive justice. It will not be possible to address all such perspectives for the last twenty-five years have seen the publication of an enormous number of writings on global distributive justice. This chapter shall thus focus on what I take to be some of the most influential and important theories. However, before examining these theories, it is important to make a number of preliminary points about the nature of cosmopolitan accounts of distributive justice and about the general nature of the reasoning underpinning cosmopolitan principles of distributive justice.

First, it is necessary to make some clarificatory points about the nature of cosmopolitan approaches to distributive justice. Five points in particular should be made. The first concerns *who* is entitled to the goods transferred. Here it is clear that most contemporary cosmopolitans affirm that the duties are owed to individuals (and not states). This, for example, is made clear by Beitz (1999*c*: 152–3) and Pogge (1994*b*: 202). An alternative view has been taken by Barry, who once argued that states were entitled to receive resources (1991*c*: 203–8; 1991*d*: 239–40). In recent publications, however, he rejects this position. And indeed, given cosmopolitanism's individualist assumptions, his later position is most in keeping with cosmopolitan tenets (1998: 159–60; 1999: 36–40).

Second, we should distinguish between fundamental principles and derivative principles. The former refer to the most basic moral principles whereas the latter refer to principles that are entailed by the fundamental principles (Barry 1995*a*: part III; Jones 1999: 117–18, 121–8). The cosmopolitans' central claim is that, at the fundamental level, all persons should be included within the scope of distributive justice. Cosmopolitans recognize, however, that these principles may sometimes best be realized if people comply with special duties to some. In other words, they recognize the possibility that although justice is fundamentally impartial between persons it may in some cases sanction policies in which people are partial to some people (their friends, say, or family members). The clearest example of this would be a form of global utilitarianism which is obviously cosmopolitan at the fundamental level (each person's utility is included and treated equally) but would sanction people having special duties to some if that best promotes total utility (Goodin 1988: sec. V; Singer 1979: 172).[5] As we shall see in later sections of this chapter, this point has significance and some positions that appear to reject cosmopolitanism in fact do not dispute its fundamental claims.

A third important distinction is that between what one might term modest and ambitious cosmopolitanism. The former simply makes the positive claim that there should be principles of distributive justice with a global scope. Ambitious cosmopolitanism, by contrast, makes both this positive claim and also the negative claim that persons do not have any obligations of distributive justice to fellow-nationals or fellow-citizens.[6] Many cosmopolitans simply make the modest claim (Nussbaum 1996: 9, 13; Sen 1996: 112–15). Barry, for example, affirms cosmopolitan principles of distributive justice but also accepts special duties of distributive justice to co-citizens (1996: 431; 1999: 59).[7] Others, however, do appear to make the stronger claim (Beitz 1988*a*: 192; 1999*c*: 182; Singer 1972).[8]

Fourth, it is important to bear in mind the distinction, invoked by Pogge and introduced in the Chapter 3, between 'institutional' and 'interactional' approaches. An institutional approach, recall, maintains that principles of justice apply to 'institutions', where Pogge employs this to refer to schemes of trade, communication, and interdependence generally. An interactional approach, by contrast, maintains that principles of justice apply even in the absence of a common institutional background.[9] Thus if we lived in a world without extensive global interdependence, the institutional approach would deny that there are any cosmopolitan principles of distributive justice whereas the interactional approach would state that there are. Although he has constructed this distinction, Pogge maintains that in our world such is the extent of global interdependence that the institutional view generates global principles of distributive justice (1994a: 91–8; 1998b: 504–10, esp. pp. 504–7): thus the philosophical distinction does not make any practical difference.[10] Even if this is true and institutional and interactional views happen in our world to converge, it is still important to base one's conclusions on a sound theory and not to hold a view based on faulty theoretical assumptions. For this reason, this chapter will evaluate the plausibility of institutionalism and interactionalism (in Section III).

A final point worth making about cosmopolitan theories of distributive justice concerns the principles they affirm and the policies they prescribe. The conclusions reached will be examined later but it may be useful to present them briefly here simply to give a foretaste of the policies at stake. These are many and various. To give some examples: Pogge has defended what he terms a 'global resource dividend', where this requires that people should be taxed for using the resources in their territory and the proceeds spent on improving the poor throughout the world (1998b: 501–36; 2002b: 196–215).[11] Shue (1996a) and C. Jones (1999) have argued that there is a human right to subsistence. Another, more radical, proposal, put forward by Hillel Steiner, is that all persons have a natural right to an equal portion of the Earth's natural resources (1994: 235–6, 262–5, 270; 1999: 173–7).[12] One of the most important contributions has been made by Beitz: he maintains that Rawls's 'difference principle' (which stipulates that inequalities should be arranged to maximize the condition of the least advantaged) should be adopted at the global level (1999c: 150–3).[13] That is, inequalities can be justified only if they maximize the condition of the least well-off person(s) in the world. Stepping away from suggestions made by political philosophers, a number of proposals of international distributive justice have been put forward by social movements and have been discussed in the public realm. Some, for example, have campaigned for the cancellation of Third World debt. Others have proposed principles of fair trade (including, for example, demands for equal pay for equal work). A third proposal that has been mooted is James Tobin's proposed tax on international money markets. Tobin himself suggested that these should be taxed in order to discourage volatility in international financial markets but it has subsequently been adopted by others who argue that its proceeds can and should be spent on alleviating poverty (Tobin 1982: 488–94; Eichengreen, Tobin, and Wyplosz 1995). Some have argued that allowing individuals the freedom to migrate would ameliorate the severe deprivation that marks the world. A standard economics textbook, for instance, maintains that '[t]he quickest way to equalize world income distribution would be to permit free migration between countries'

(Begg, Fischer, and Dornbusch 1991: 644).[14] Finally, we might note a number of proposals mooted by the Commission on Global Governance (1995: 217–21). It floats the idea of taxing multinational corporations, arguing that a global tax regime is required given the number of companies not exclusively based in one country (1995: 220). It also proposes a number of '[c]harges for use of the global commons' such as charging people for: the use of flight paths, the use of the oceans, the right to dump waste (which is not so toxic that dumping should be banned), the right to fish, and the right to engage in undertakings in Antarctica (1995: 220, cf. also pp. 220–1). This multiplicity of proposals gives us some flavour of the sort of principles of distributive justice and the policy proposals that cosmopolitans have advocated.

Having elaborated further on some general aspects of the cosmopolitan approach to questions of distributive justice, I now want to introduce a general claim about the character of the arguments employed to defend cosmopolitan principles of distributive justice. Chapter 3, recall, argued, in particular, that

the scope$_1$ claim: the standard justifications of rights to civil and political liberties entail that there are *human* rights to these same civil and political liberties.

An analogous point can be made about distributive justice. In what follows, then, I shall be suggesting that

the scope$_2$ claim: the standard justifications of principles of distributive justice entail that there are cosmopolitan principles of distributive justice.

The latter maintains that the very logic that underpins most domestic theories of justice actually implies that these theories of distributive justice should be enacted at the global, and not (or not simply) the domestic, level. It has been defended very persuasively by Samuel Black in a penetrating analysis (1991, esp. pp. 355–7).[15] In the latter Black refers to what he terms 'the fallacy of *restricted universalism*' where this states that '[a] distributive theory, that ascribes rights and claims on the basis of certain universal attributes of persons, cannot at the same time restrict the grounds for those claims to a person's membership or status within a given society' (1991: 357). His point is that the arguments for distribution within the state actually justify global distribution. What follows seeks, in part, to illustrate and lend support to Black's contention.

Having presented this general claim let us now consider several prominent defences of cosmopolitan principles of distributive justice. In doing so, my aim is, following the pattern of the Chapter 3, to evaluate these arguments and, in doing so, to provide some support for the scope$_2$ claim.[16]

## III

It is appropriate to begin with Beitz's work. His work *Political Theory and International Relations*, first published in 1979 and republished in 1999, is the first, and remains one of the most sophisticated, cosmopolitan analyses of distributive justice (1999c). Broadly speaking, Beitz adopts Rawls's theory of distributive justice (as developed in *A Theory of Justice*) and seeks to show that, contrary to Rawls's own claims, the logic of his theory implies that there should be cosmopolitan principles of distributive justice. Given this it is necessary to give a brief résumé of Rawls's theory of distributive justice. Rawls argues that fair principles of distributive justice are those that individuals would choose in a hypothetical contract (the 'original position') in which they are denied knowledge of their abilities and conception of the good (these are hidden behind the 'veil of ignorance'). This contract, he claims, produces fair principles of justice because people are unable to choose principles that simply suit their interests. They are forced to consider the position of each and everyone and therefore the principles they choose will be impartial ones. Rawls also argues that principles of distributive justice operate solely within systems of cooperation. Norms of justice, that is, should determine the distribution of those goods resulting from cooperation and they apply only to those who are part of that process of cooperation. This is, to use Pogge's terms, an 'institutionalist' position. Rawls then further maintains that states are reasonably self-contained systems of cooperation and so distribution should take place within states. He thus produces a domestic, rather than a global, theory of distributive justice. Rawls did, however, argue in *A Theory of Justice* that there are some appropriate global principles (though not principles of distributive justice) and to construct these he again employs the idea of a hypothetical contract. In this international hypothetical contract, representatives of (internally just) states are asked to consider what rules they would choose if they did not know what state they represented. But such parties, Rawls claims, would not choose principles of international *distributive* justice (1999*c*: 331–3). They would, instead, simply choose rights to self-determination and to defend themselves, the principle that states should honour any agreements they make, and some rules of 'jus in bello' (1999*c*: 332–3).

*Version A.* Beitz starts from this theory. However, unlike Rawls who thinks that distributive justice applies within states, Beitz maintains that this theoretical framework supports cosmopolitan principles of distributive justice. Why? Beitz gives two arguments.

The first concerns natural resources. Beitz argues that the distribution of these is utterly arbitrary. Those who live in Kuwait, for example, cannot claim to be entitled to the oil reserves lying under the land. Similarly, those who live on land that has coal or iron or other valued resources have no special moral claim to them. States and nations cannot, then, claim that they ought to be the exclusive beneficiaries of the natural resources in their territory. Now if we combine this point with Rawls's international contract, we will arrive, Beitz argues, at a global principle of distributive justice specifying the distribution of natural resources. As he writes, '[n]ot knowing the resource endowments of their own societies, the parties would agree on a resource redistribution principle that would give each society a fair chance to develop just political institutions and an economy capable of satisfying its members' basic needs' (1999*c*: 141). Thus, the parties in Rawls's international contract would reject Rawls's own suggested principles and would choose a global principle of distributive justice concerning natural resources (1999*c*: 136–43).

Beitz's second argument starts again from Rawls's institutionalist framework but argues, against Rawls, that there is a global system of cooperation. Beitz backs up this claim by drawing on a considerable amount of empirical research (1999*c*: 144–52). He concludes that 'international economic interdependence constitutes a scheme of social cooperation like those to which requirements of distributive justice have often been thought to apply' (1999*c*: 154). As a consequence, there should not be a contract at the domestic level at which participants decide how goods should be distributed within society followed by an international contract between states. Rather, there should be a single global hypothetical contract in which people are asked what principles of distributive justice they would choose if they did not know their talents or conception of the good or what society they came from. Furthermore, following Rawls, Beitz claims that individuals would choose the difference principle. So whereas Rawls's domestic contract delivers a difference principle with a domestic scope, Beitz's global contract delivers a global difference principle. The same line of reasoning, we might note, has also been employed against Rawls by Pogge in *Realizing Rawls* (1989: part III) and Thomas Scanlon (1985: 202).[17]

Having presented Beitz's two arguments it is important to be clear on the relationship between them. Beitz is *not* proposing both a principle of international justice concerning natural resources, on the one hand, and also a global difference principle, on the other. His position, rather, is that the second contract supersedes the first. Since there is global interdependence the approach employed in his first argument (a contract within the state followed by a contract between states) is inappropriate. The aim of his first argument is not to defend a particular principle that he thinks should be applied in the world as we know it: it is, rather, to show that, contrary to what Rawls himself claims, Rawls's own state-centric theoretical framework yields a global principle of distributive justice. Put otherwise: Beitz's first argument is primarily a critique of Rawls. His second, however, also expresses his positive view as to what principles of distributive justice should be implemented at the global level (as well as also being a critique of Rawls for failing to recognize that his theory, once conjoined with facts about the modern world, entails a global difference principle).

Beitz's view has been much criticized, especially his second argument. I shall consider two major challenges to his argument before then drawing attention to two other objections. One forceful criticism came from Barry who argued, against Beitz, that there is no global interdependence of the appropriate type. Barry argues that whilst there is international trade it is not accurate to refer to it as a scheme of mutually advantageous cooperation and since distributive justice (for Rawls) applies to schemes of mutually advantageous cooperation there are no global principles of distributive justice (1991*c*: 194). The key point, then, is that on Rawls's theory distributive principles apply to cooperative arrangements and, Barry maintained, that the international economy is not cooperative in this way.[18]

This criticism is, however, rather too swift. It is important to be clear, when appraising Beitz's (and Pogge's) argument, what the core moral claim is. Beitz escapes Barry's critique because his claim is that principles of distributive justice apply to groups of people who are interconnected in some way, even if that interconnection is not mutually beneficial or cooperative. As he writes in *Political Theory and International Relations*: 'the requirements of justice apply to institutions and practices (whether or not they are genuinely cooperative) in which social activity produces relative or absolute benefits or burdens that would not exist if the social activity did not take place' (1999*c*: 131). And again:

It has been argued that some poor countries' relations with the rich have actually worsened economic conditions among the poor countries' worst-off groups. This raises the question of whether interdependence must actually benefit everyone involved to give rise to questions of justice. I think the answer is clearly negative; countries A and B are involved in social cooperation even if A (a rich country) could get along without B (a poor country), but instead exploits it, while B gets nothing out of its 'cooperation' but exacerbated class divisions and Coca-Cola factories.   (1999*c*: 150, fn. 52)

He makes explicit, then, that 'everyone need not be advantaged by the cooperative scheme in order for requirements of justice to apply' (1999*c*: 150, fn. 52). Beitz cannot thus be accused of assuming that global interaction is of mutual benefit to all (1999*c*: 152). Pogge, too, makes clear that his institutionalist position does not assume that interconnection is mutually beneficial: the claim is that distributive justice operates among those who are interconnected.[19] Thus construed the claim escapes Barry's objection. Its contention is simply that, given interdependence, the standard of living of people is profoundly affected by the actions of people living in other countries. There is an international economy that has deep effects on people's lives. The role of principles of distributive justice is to govern the shared framework within which interaction takes place. Beitz's (and Pogge's) claim thus still stands and Barry's critique of it is unpersuasive.

A second major objection to the argument targets the moral claim that principles of distributive justice (such as the difference principle) apply within schemes of cooperation. As was noted above, this is an 'institutionalist' claim. Here it is worth contrasting Beitz's position with that of Pogge. Pogge is what we might term an unrestricted institutionalist: he works on the assumption that *all* principles of justice apply only within systems of cooperation. Beitz, by contrast, is what we might term a restricted institutionalist: *some* principles of justice (such as the difference principle) apply only within systems of cooperation but other principles (such as his principle concerning the distribution of resources) apply even among persons who are not members of the same system of cooperation. This difference notwithstanding, both have maintained that the difference principle applies only among those who are interconnected. It is this moral premise that is most vulnerable in Beitz's and Pogge's argument against Rawls, and in what follows we shall note three reasons why an 'institutionalist' position (whether it is unrestricted or restricted) is problematic. Setting Beitz aside for a moment, we have two good reasons to dwell on the plausibility of an institutionalist approach. First, it is relevant not only for economic rights but also for civil and political rights. An institutionalist position claims that persons have duties to protect the civil and political rights of those who are part of the same scheme (and not of those who are disconnected from them). Second, in addition to Beitz, many others ground a cosmopolitan approach to distributive justice on the assumption that distributive justice pertains only among those interconnected (and on the assumption that the world is an integrated system of interconnection). As has been seen, institutionalism is an integral feature of Pogge's conception of global justice. Furthermore, Darrel Moellendorf also argues in this way in his recent *Cosmopolitan Justice*. There, like Beitz and Pogge, he maintains both that justice applies within systems of cooperation (2002*a*: 30–6, 39–40, 43, 48, 53, 62, 72) and that there is a global system (2002*a*: 36–8).[20] Much rests, then, on whether we think that (some or all or no) principles of justice apply only among persons who are interconnected. There are a number of reasons why institutionalism is questionable.

1. One problem is that it is hard to see why economic interaction has any moral relevance from the point of view of distributive justice.[21] We can look at principles of distributive justice from two directions—from an 'entitlement' perspective (which considers the reasons why people are entitled to certain goods) and a 'duty-bearer' perspective (which considers the reasons why people are obligated to others).[22] If we consider the sorts of reasons given to explain why one person is entitled to certain goods it is difficult to see how and why the fact that one group of people is linked together by interaction should impact on their entitlements. Consider a world with two separate systems of interaction that have no contact but are aware of each other and suppose that one of them is prosperous whereas the other is extremely impoverished. Compare, now, two individuals—one from the prosperous system and the other from the impoverished system—who are identical in their abilities and needs. The member of the prosperous system receives more. But it is difficult to see why—concentrating on any possible and reasonable criteria for entitlement—this is fair. *Ex hypothesi*, she is not more hard-working or more gifted or more needy. In all respects they are identical (bar one, namely that one is lucky to live in the prosperous society and one is not) and yet an institutionalist approach confers on one many more benefits. Moreover, it does so wholly arbitrarily because there is no ground on which the member of the prosperous society can claim to be entitled to more (Barry 1989: 239). Institutional schemes do not track any properties that would generate entitlements and as such they treat people unfairly, denying some their entitlements.[23]

This point can be strengthened further by considering a point commonly made by institutionalists themselves about what constitute morally arbitrary influences on people's entitlements. Moellendorf, for example, writes that '[s]ince one's place of birth is morally arbitrary, it should not affect one's life prospects or one's access to opportunities' (2002*a*: 55, cf. also p. 79).[24] But, if we accept this (and it is a powerful line of reasoning), it causes problems for an institutionalist perspective. Can someone not equally persuasively argue that 'one's life prospects or one's access to opportunities' should not depend on 'morally arbitrary' considerations such as which associational scheme one is born into? Moellendorf's own institutionalist approach contradicts its own guiding principle by penalizing some on the basis of their 'place of birth'. If someone is born into an impoverished system that has no links with the rest of the world, Moellendorf must maintain that members of the latter have no duties of justice to the former—thereby penalizing them simply because of their 'place of birth'. Put otherwise: if it is arbitrary for some to face worse options because they come from a particular nation, is it not equally arbitrary to penalize someone for coming from a particular institutional scheme? The logic of the intuition underpinning cosmopolitanism thus subverts an institutional perspective. The first problem with an institutionalist approach, then, is that we have no reason to think that membership of an institutional scheme has moral relevance for it does not track any entitlement-creating properties.

2. The first point issues a challenge to institutionalists, asking them to provide an explanation as to why membership of institutional systems is of moral relevance and querying the possibility of there being a satisfactory explanation. Given this it is worth considering two arguments adduced in defence of institutionalism. The first, and most common, defence of institutionalism runs as follows: institutional frameworks have moral significance because they have an enormous impact on people and on their fundamental interests and options. Their moral importance stems, then, from the extent to which they affect people's ability to further their interests and to exercise their abilities and pursue their conception of the good (Rawls 1999*c*: 7; 2001: 55–7). Membership of global systems, then, is morally significant because of the outcomes the latter produce (C. Jones 1999: 7–8; Moellendorf 2002*a*: 32–3, 37–8). Let us call this the 'impact argument'.

This defence of the moral significance of institutionalism is, however, problematic because persons external to an economic–political system may also have an effect on people's interests. If one values institutions because, and to the extent that, they foster or thwart people's interests that presupposes that what matters is fostering and not thwarting people's interests. And that, in turn, shows that agents external to an institutional system may also have moral significance and responsibility if they are able to have an effect on people's interests. The impact argument then cannot vindicate institutionalism; rather it entails ascribing duties to all who can make a difference. And that constitutes an interactional position.

In addition, this line of reasoning fails to justify Beitz's claim that some principles apply without economic interdependence (an international contract containing states resulting in his natural resources principle) whereas others only apply with it (a global original position resulting in his global difference principle). The problem is this: to assert that all states should have an equal portion of the Earth's natural resources presupposes that states can contact each other. This is necessary so that states that are over-endowed with natural resources can redistribute their resources to those that are under-endowed with natural resources. But if states can contact each other then, obviously, they can exert an effect on each other. But if this is the case then, according to the impact argument given above, there should be a global original position. And in the global original position, according to Beitz, parties will choose a global difference principle and not adopt any natural resource principle. In short, then, the necessary preconditions of the natural resource principle when combined with the above outcome-oriented argument as to why interdependence matters entail both that there should not be an international contract comprising states and also, following from this, that there is no case for Beitz's natural resources principle. The impact argument cannot then sustain Beitz's particular version of institutionalism.[25]

3. Given the failure of the first argument, let us consider a second argument for the claim that distributive justice applies to those linked by interaction—that given by Pogge. Pogge's argument focuses on the 'duty bearer' rather than on the 'entitlement-bearer'. He begins by invoking the distinction between positive and negative duties. He then argues that, as a matter of justice, persons have a negative duty not to sustain an unjust socio-economic structure. As he puts the point, persons have a '*negative* duty not to uphold injustice, not to contribute to or profit from the unjust impoverishment of others' (2002*b*: 197; cf. also 1994*a*: 92–3; 2002*b*: 197–8). Membership of institutions is important then because as a member one is subject to a negative duty not to 'uphold' unjust institutions: this is, moreover, a duty that one can only have as a member of an institution. So by construing justice as requiring a negative duty not to support unjust institutional frameworks to which one belongs we arrive at the conclusion that obligations of justice apply to, and among, members of institutions. And if we add the contention that there are global institutional frameworks we arrive at the conclusion that persons are under a negative duty not to impose unjust global institutional frameworks on the rest of the world (1989: 276–8; 1994*a*: 92–3; 2002*b*: 197–8, 201, 203, 204, 210, 211).

Pogge's argument is powerful and merits more attention than I can give it here.[26] Here I wish only to note that it vindicates neither an unrestricted institutionalism nor Beitz's particular version. Consider the first point first. Pogge's argument cannot entail an unrestricted institutionalism for one critical reason. What it shows at most is that membership in an institutional scheme has some moral relevance because one has a negative duty not to participate in any unjust social order. However, the fact that one has a negative duty not to participate in unjust social schemes obviously does not entail that these are the only duties of justice that one has. It does not, that is, refute the proposition that persons have positive duties to all persons one can affect regardless of whether one has causal links with them. As such, it does not vindicate an unrestricted institutionalist position.[27]

We might, further, note in this context that an unrestricted institutionalist position issues in some very severe conclusions. For where deprivation arises not because of people's violation of a negative duty not to sustain an unjust institutional framework but because of other variables, an unrestricted institutionalist position would offer the deprived in question no protection. So if people face deprivation, even death, because of a lack of natural resources or disease or isolation an unrestricted institutionalist cannot ensure adequate protection of these essential interests. To restrict our duties of justice to the negative duty of our not imposing unjust global economic frameworks on others, as Pogge suggests, would then allow there to be poverty, malnutrition, and misery stemming from these other variables. It would also mean that we have no duty of justice to assist those whose deprivation stems not from our imposition on them of an unfair global economic system but from the oppression and injustice of their own government. These considerations, in themselves, do not, of course, demonstrate that there are positive duties of justice to assist all who suffer because of these other variables but they do accentuate the need for there to be an argument *against* positive duties.[28] We might, then, say that an unrestricted institutionalist position pays too much attention to 'duty-bearers' and not enough to 'entitlement-bearers'—to the needy, the hungry, and the sick.[29]

What of Beitz's position? As has been emphasized above, he does not affirm unrestricted institutionalism so the last two points do not undermine his position. As we have also seen, he maintains that if there were no global interdependence then there should be a contract between states (and an interactional principle concerning natural resources) and if there were interdependence then there should be a global contract containing persons (and consequently a global difference principle). Can Pogge's argument provide support for this brand of restricted institutionalism? I do not think so. His 'negative duty' argument can establish that some (negative) duties of distributive justice apply only in circumstances of interdependence but it does not indicate why the global original position (and the global duties arising from the global difference principle) fall into this institutionalist category. It does not, that is, establish that there should be a global original position (and a global difference principle) *only if there is interdependence*. For aught that it shows there might be a global original position containing all independently of whether all participate in a global economic system. It does not, then, give us any reason to reject a position which claims, first, that there should be a global original position (and consequently a global difference principle) even if there is no interdependence and also, second, that there should be other principles of distributive justice that pertain only among members of institutional frameworks (where this second component is justified by Pogge's 'negative duty' argument). It, therefore, gives no support to the way that Beitz distinguishes between institutional principles (which apply with interdependence) and interactional ones (which apply without it). It does not, we might say, justify Beitz's cut.

*Version B.* Given the above three objections to (restricted or unrestricted) 'institutionalism', Beitz and Pogge's argument for globalizing Rawls's difference principle is unconvincing. The moral premise on which their argument depends is implausible. This, though, does not entail the rejection of the idea of a global original position and/or a global difference principle. One might defend an original position including all persons in the world *not* on the grounds considered above but simply on the grounds that persons are entitled to be included in the contract in virtue of their rights and interests as human beings. This is, indeed, precisely the position adopted by David A. J. Richards. He maintains that fair principles are ones that would be accepted in a contract containing all persons and in which people are behind a veil of ignorance (1982, esp. pp. 278–82, 289–93). He justifies the use of such a global hypothetical contract on the grounds that 'one's membership in one nation as opposed to another and the natural inequality among nations may be as morally fortuitous as any other natural fact' (1982: 290).[30] All persons, qua persons, are entitled to be included in the hypothetical contract. Whether everyone is a member of a common institutional scheme is simply not relevant. The same position is also defended by Beitz himself in an article published four years after *Political Theory and International Relations* which criticizes the latter's reliance on interdependence but defends the use of a global original position and the global difference principle (1983, esp. p. 595). Beitz accepts Richards's criticism of his earlier views on the moral significance of interdependence (1983: 595, fn. 8, which cites Richards (1982: 287–93)). Accordingly he reformulates his position. He claims that the morally relevant aspects of persons are the 'two essential powers of moral personality—a capacity for an effective sense of justice and a capacity to form, revise, and pursue a conception of the good' (1983: 595, cf. also pp. 593, 596).[31] In virtue of these universal properties all who have these properties are entitled to be represented in a global original position.[32]

Thus far we have considered two objections to Beitz's arguments. The first relied on a misconception. The second was more persuasive but, as we have seen, Beitz can, and does, reformulate his theory to recognize that institutionalism is implausible. Even if someone accepts this, however, it does not follow that we must agree with all of Beitz's claims. Even if his use of a global original position and a global difference principle can meet the first two objections a critic might reject his theory on at least two further grounds. The first is that, as we saw in Chapter 3, there is good reason to be sceptical of the claim that a hypothetical contract can provide independent support for principles of justice. Second, even if we accept the validity of the hypothetical contract, a critic may always question whether the parties would choose the difference principle. We should be clear, however, that such an argument is not a critique of a cosmopolitan approach for it does not deny that there would be any cosmopolitan principles of distributive justice: its denial is rather that they would choose one specific cosmopolitan principle. In other words the challenge is not to Beitz's cosmopolitanism per se.[33]

Having evaluated two contractarian arguments (Beitz's original argument and the later version affirmed by himself and Richards), it is worth observing that both support and illustrate the scope$_2$ claim. Consider Version A. Its central thesis is that the logic of Rawls's domestic theory of distributive justice (principles of distributive justice should apply to persons who participate in the same economic scheme) impels us to apply this theory globally. The cosmopolitan principles are not tacked on in an ad hoc way: rather they flow directly from the rationale underlying a 'domestic' theory of justice. The same is, again, true of Version B. Beitz and Richards's point is that if one grounds distribution within the state on the principle that persons have moral significance in virtue of their possession of the two moral powers one is inexorably drawn to a global application of that theory. The reason for this is that the account of 'moral personality' on which the argument rests is a universalist one, citing universal properties, and so it will necessarily yield cosmopolitan principles of justice.[34] To argue that what is relevant is persons' capacity for forming, revising, and pursuing conceptions of the good and having a sense of justice and yet restrict resources only to those in one's society would be to be guilty of what Black has termed 'the fallacy of *restricted universalism*' (1991: 357).

# IV

Having considered several contractarian theories of global justice, let us now consider a second approach. This section outlines a number of different theories, all of which are outcome-centred and all of which maintain that there are cosmopolitan principles of distributive justice.

A useful place to start is Singer's article entitled 'Famine, Affluence and Morality' (1972: 229–43).[35] In the latter Singer begins with the assumption that poverty is clearly a bad (1972: 231). He then argues that persons have a duty to prevent bad things from happening. Singer distinguishes here between two versions of this claim. According to one, 'if it is in our power to prevent something bad from happening, without thereby sacrificing anything of *comparable moral importance*, we ought, morally, to do it' (1972: 231, my emphasis). Lest we find this too strong, Singer argues that we could accept a weaker claim, namely, 'if it is in our power to prevent something very bad from happening, without thereby sacrificing *anything morally significant*, we ought, morally, to do it' (1972: 231, my emphasis). The difference between the two versions is that a person A is excused of aiding someone according to the second version if that imposes a significant moral cost on her: for A to be excused according to the first version that moral cost must be 'comparable' to the cost to the poor person that A would otherwise help. On the basis of these premises, Singer maintains, we are driven to the conclusion that affluent persons have obligations to aid the impoverished, wherever they live and whatever their nationality. There is a demanding duty of aid.[36]

One criticism that might be made of Singer's argument is that it equates actions with omissions. Someone might protest that not saving a person's life is not the same as killing them. Whether this is so is open to question. But we do not have to settle this question for one may argue that even if not saving a life is not as bad as killing them it is nonetheless deeply morally wrong. To take an example that Singer uses (1972: 231), one *might* say that walking by a puddle while a child drowns in it is not as morally wrong as pushing a baby into the puddle but that walking by is seriously morally wrong. It is very hard to think of any credible reason to dispute this. So someone may still argue, along lines indebted to Singer, that we are under a duty to distribute resources to the impoverished.

A second response to Singer is that his moral scheme is extremely arduous. Two kinds of reply might be made to this objection. First, one might reply that that does not show that he is wrong. Perhaps morality is highly demanding. Moreover, one might add that a moral system which does not sanction aid is highly onerous for the weak and defenceless (Caney 1996a: 136, fn. 16; Jones 1999: 34–5).[37] But suppose one accepts that moral systems should not be demanding. Here one might draw on Samuel Scheffler's argument that persons have an 'agent-centred prerogative' not to promote desirable states of affairs. They have, so he argues, permission to pursue their own projects.[38] Drawing on this, one can revise a broadly consequentialist perspective to overcome the objection that consequentialism is too strenuous.

With this in mind, it is appropriate to draw attention to other consequentialist discussions of cosmopolitan distributive justice which do not make the same demanding claims that Singer does. A more modest conception—which does not require the sacrifice of people's own commitments—is articulated by Robert Goodin. He maintains that we have a duty to aid the vulnerable (1985: 33–144) and he argues, moreover, that this principle mandates international aid (1985: 161–9). In his view this is required by justice (1985: 159–61), although it should also be noted that he thinks it is best couched in terms of humanity (1985: 161–9, esp. pp. 161–4). The central point, though, is that he articulates a consequentialist principle that is to be adopted globally and which condemns the current world order but does not commit itself to Singer's extremism.[39]

Consequentialist approaches to global distributive justice can thus combat or accommodate many of the misgivings that people have about them. Moreover, on a more positive note, an important advantage of a consequentialist theory of justice is simply that it would seem extremely implausible to claim that principles of distributive justice should be utterly indifferent to the outcomes they generate. Any theory of distributive justice that ignores consequences, that is indifferent to our most important interests, is surely implausible. If, however, we do accept a modified version of consequentialism, such as Goodin's, we are thereby committed to extensive cosmopolitan principles of distributive justice.

A modified version of consequentialism is, however, not without its own difficulties. Two problems arise which derive from the modifications made to combat common concerns about maximizing brands of consequentialism. These may rescue consequentialism from some criticisms but they come at a cost for they make the resulting theory both *incomplete* and also highly *indeterminate*.

Consider the charge of incompleteness first. One common fear about a maximizing consequentialism is that it issues in deeply troubling outcomes which deny some their basic rights. This is of course a staple criticism of maximizing consequentialism. If it is a powerful concern, however, this entails that consequentialism is acceptable as long as it is modified in such a way as to disallow violations of core and basic rights.[40] This is an entirely plausible move but, and this is the crucial point, if this is the strategy adopted it requires a theory of rights to specify what outcomes are not allowed. Consequentialism on its own is incomplete.[41]

Second, non-maximizing consequentialisms such as Scheffler's tend to be highly *indeterminate* and, as such, fail the first desiderata of a sound theory of global economic justice.[42] Nussbaum's Aristotelian approach is a case in point. She persuasively defends global principles of distributive justice that protect persons' capacity to flourish and lead fulfilling lives. Her claim is that principles of justice should be sensitive to what matters in life and that what we value is an ability to lead a decent and fulfilling life (2000*a*). But it is far from clear what distributive principle should be adopted. Nussbaum herself states that we should aspire to a state of affairs where everyone is above a certain 'threshold' (2000*a*: 12). Given the parlous state of the world this seems a sensible objective for the here and now but it does not answer the theoretical question of whether we should ideally be concerned only with ensuring all are above this minimum acceptable level. So, whilst it is right to emphasize that justice should be concerned with people's interests, it does not satisfactorily address the *distributive* question of how we should distribute 'goods' and 'bads'. One can accept that 'capabilities' matter and think that they should be maximized. Or that people should have equal amounts of them. Or some other distributive criterion. Consequentialist accounts, thus, fail to provide a convincing answer to the question of how burdens and benefits should be divided, even if they provide a good answer to the question of what we judge to be a benefit and what a burden. For these two reasons, consequentialist accounts need to be supplemented.

This leads naturally to a third distinct approach to global justice—namely those centred around the notion of rights. Before we explore the latter we should note that the scope$_2$ claim is again confirmed. The latter, recall, states that the logic underpinning most theories of distributive justice generates the conclusion that there are cosmopolitan principles of distributive justice. The point here is that the rationales underlying consequentialist theories—such as 'protecting the vulnerable'—entail a universalist or cosmopolitan conclusion (Goodin 1985: throughout but esp. pp. 11, 154). If this is true one cannot accept a consequentialist perspective without also embracing cosmopolitan principles. Furthermore, the reason why the scope$_2$ claim applies is that consequentialist theories all rely on a universalist moral personality.[43] What matters is a person's capacity for utility (for utilitarians) or their neediness (for need-based theories of justice) or their vulnerability (for Goodin) or their capacity to flourish (for perfectionists). In each case, the criteria invoked are capacities all persons possess and they deny the relevance of people's ethnicity, race, class, or nationality for their entitlements: as such they each entail a theory with a cosmopolitan character. This point is indeed stressed by Goodin, Nussbaum, and Singer who emphasize that given the above criteria we can attach no fundamental moral importance to someone's nationality or citizenship (Goodin 1985: 11, 154; Nussbaum 1996: 14; Singer 1977: 42–3; Singer 1979: 171–2).

## V

Let us now consider a third cosmopolitan perspective on global justice, namely rights-based approaches. As we saw in Chapter 3, many have defended human rights to civil and political liberties. In this section I wish to examine the arguments of those who claim that persons also have a human right to certain economic resources. A number of theorists have adopted a rights-based approach. Jones (1999: ch. 3) and Shue (1996*a*), for example, defend the human right to subsistence. Pogge also adopts a rights-based approach and defends Articles 25 and 28 of the Universal Declaration of Human Rights (1998*b*: 501).[44] Article 25 states that 'Everyone has the right to a standard of living adequate for the health and well-being of himself and of his family, including food, clothing, housing and medical care and necessary social services . . .' (Article 25 (1)). Moreover, as we saw earlier in this chapter and in the preceding chapter, Pogge defends an institutional conception of rights: in his view a just world order is one that secures people's enjoyment of their human rights and this includes economic rights. Thus he supports Article 28 which states that 'Everyone is entitled to a social and international order in which the rights and freedoms set forth in this Declaration can be fully realised'. In his *Democracy and the Global Order* David Held adopts a more expansive set of human rights. He invokes an ideal of autonomy and from it derives seven types of human right, three of which concern economic entitlements and hence are relevant here.[45] The three types of rights in question are: 'health' rights, where this includes the right to good health and a non-harmful environment (1995: 192, 194–5); 'social' rights, where this includes rights to child support and education (1995: 192, 195); and 'economic' rights, where this includes the right to a minimum wage and the opportunity to be economically independent (1995: 193, 197–8).[46] There is, thus, a considerable variety among rights-based accounts of global distributive justice.

1. On what basis can one defend a right to economic goods? And what goods are thus defended? To answer this question, let us start with the arguments developed by Shue. In his book *Basic Rights*, Shue defends the human right to subsistence (1996*a*: 22–7). He makes a conditional argument, arguing that the right to subsistence is necessary for persons to enjoy other rights. As such it is a basic right.[47] His key point is that one cannot possibly enjoy other rights—like the right to freedom of association, say, or free speech—unless one has enough to subsist. To use his terminology, subsistence is one of several 'inherent necessities' for the exercise of any right (1996*a*: 26–7). His claim is not that subsistence is

valuable as a 'mere means to an end': it is that the right to subsistence is a logically necessary component of other rights (1996*a*: 27). Hence it is not possible to affirm rights to free speech, conscience, and association and yet also deny the right to subsistence. To use the terminology of Chapter 3, Shue defends a logical version of *rights holism* (Chapter 3, Section VIII).

Shue's claim is an attractive one but it is open to the charge that he tries to squeeze too much content out of his argument. According to Shue, his argument shows that persons have a basic right to 'minimum economic security, or subsistence' where this comprises 'unpolluted air, unpolluted water, adequate food, adequate clothing, adequate shelter, and minimal preventive public health care' (1996*a*: 23). Is it, however, true that one needs not to be malnourished to exercise free speech? Or, consider diseases like rickets: can one not exercise freedom of conscience even though one is suffering from rickets? Or consider the right to a fair trial: can one not exercise this right even if one is suffering from emphysema? None of these are intended to question, in any way, the badness of emphysema or rickets but they do call into question that the right to subsistence is a logical prerequisite of other rights.[48]

2. Given this, one might consider a much more straightforward derivation of the right to subsistence. The argument proceeds as follows. Rights, as we saw in the preceding chapter when vindicating civil and political rights, should protect important human interests (Chapter 3, Section VI). They should, that is, not be indifferent to what people care about but should protect fundamental interests. One uncontroversial human interest is a person's interest in good health and avoiding malnutrition, starvation, and disease. Thus, given both of these assumptions, persons have a right to subsistence. This line of reasoning—given by, among others, Jones (1999: 61–2)—has much to be said for it.[49] That persons have an interest in avoiding starvation or malnutrition is, surely, relatively uncontroversial. Its claim about the nature of rights is also plausible. When we think about the rights people treasure most—like the right not to be tortured or the right to freedom of belief— we can see that these rights protect interests people value highly. Any credible account of people's rights reflects what is important to persons—their fundamental interests. Given then that subsistence is a fundamental interest and given this account of rights, it follows that persons have a right to subsistence.

One counter-argument against this argument, and against rights-centred accounts more generally, is that it fails to provide an adequate account of persons' duties. According to this objection, any complete account of distributive justice must explain who is duty bound to ensure that people receive their entitlements. But, the argument continues, cosmopolitan theories based on persons' rights do not, and maybe cannot, provide such an account.[50] If an inhabitant of Bihar, say, has a right to food whose duty is it to ensure that she receives her due?

This objection is right to emphasize that proclaiming a set of human rights but not dealing with the question of duties is inadequate. Nonetheless rights-based accounts have a reasonable response for they may reply along the following lines. For people to receive their entitlements it is important that there be political institutions in place whose role it is to protect peoples's rights. We can, then, infer from this what our duties are, namely we have duties to support those institutional arrangements that would best protect people's rights.[51] A rights-centred account can thus provide a compelling response to this objection.

Before we move on, it is worth noting again that the scope$_2$ claim is borne out. That is to say, the logic of Shue's argument, by invoking the logical presuppositions of other human rights, entails that all persons have such subsistence rights. The value to which it appeals—persons' civil and political human rights—is by its very nature a universal value. Similarly, the logic of Jones's argument—grounding economic rights on people's fundamental interests—necessarily entails a theory of distributive justice that ascribes economic rights to all persons.[52] To put the point another way, one cannot coherently employ Shue's or Jones's argument and conclude that members of nation X alone have a right to subsistence.[53] Moreover, as in the two preceding arguments, we can again see that the reason the scope$_2$ claim obtains is that the arguments considered all invoke a universalist moral personality. Shue and Jones's arguments rest on the moral personality of all persons as rights bearers and attribute no moral relevance to persons' nationality or ethnicity or civic identity.[54]

# VI

This concludes the analysis of arguments for cosmopolitan principles of distributive justice. It is worth reiterating the point that there are numerous other interesting and important cosmopolitan accounts of distributive justice. Space, however, precludes an examination of these.[55]

As in Chapter 3, it is worth reflecting on the general nature of the cosmopolitan arguments before proceeding further. Several conclusions have emerged. First, as in Chapter 3, the scope claim, in this chapter the scope$_2$ claim, has been borne out. The internal logic of the standard theories of distributive justice generates cosmopolitan principles of distributive justice. The rationale underlying contractarian, consequentialist, and rights-based theories entails that there are cosmopolitan principles of distributive justice. This conclusion is important (and has therefore been emphasized in the preceding Sections III, IV, and V) for it establishes that to show that there are cosmopolitan principles of distributive justice one need not rely on any one specific theory of distributive justice. One need not choose between them to show that there should be principles of distributive justice with a global scope. In the same way that all roads are said to lead to Rome, so many (including most, if not all, standard) theories of distributive justice lead to a cosmopolitan account of the scope of distributive justice. The scope$_2$ claim is, moreover, highly significant because if true it constitutes a contradiction in everyday moral thinking which is committed to the above lines of reasoning and yet also repudiates cosmopolitan principles of distributive justice. If the scope$_2$ claim is true then this is incoherent and cosmopolitan arguments are supplying an immanent critique of common-sense morality.

We have also seen, second, that the scope$_2$ claim obtains because (as in Chapter 3) common to all arguments for cosmopolitan principles of distributive justice is a universalist conception of moral personality according to which persons' entitlements should not be determined by their nationality or citizenship.[56] The latter is an integral component in the justifications of cosmopolitan principles of distributive justice developed by contractarians (Beitz, Richards),[57] consequentialists (Goodin, Nussbaum, Singer), and rights-based theorists (Shue, Jones, Held, Pogge).[58] The point can be put in more colloquial terms: in recent years the term 'postcode lottery' has been employed in Britain to criticize the situation in which people who lived in the jurisdictions of different councils have very unequal access to health and education. This, it was said, was unfair for it is wrong that someone should get less simply because he or she lives in one place rather than another. The cosmopolitan point is simply to radicalize this and to see through its logic to the global level.[59]

This last point about moral personality brings out another point, namely that the arguments for cosmopolitan principles of distributive justice have all taken the form laid out by the *General Argument* for moral universalism outlined in Chapter 2, Section V. That is, all have defended a value (such as the right to subsistence) and they have, then, argued that the rationale for this applying to some (they need food) applies to all for all persons share the morally relevant property that justifies the value (in this case, needing food). To use the terms of the General Argument, the arguments above have been seeking to make good (P3): they have sought to show why the morally relevant properties that ground redistribution are properties held by all persons.

Whilst important, the significance of the scope$_2$ claim should not be overstated. In the first place, as we shall see, there are a number of arguments that dispute it. Furthermore, even if correct, the scope$_2$ claim shows that conventional theories of distributive justice generate a cosmopolitan answer to the question of the *scope* of distributive justice. But in doing so, they do not provide answers to other crucial questions, including, most obviously, 'what distributive principle should be adopted?' To answer such questions, one must appraise the specific theories of distributive justice on offer.

In what follows I want tentatively to put forward a number of candidates that might be worth considering. Drawing on some of the theories of distributive justice analysed, I want to suggest four principles that we might consider adopting. First, as we have seen above, there is a persuasive argument, presented by Charles Jones, to the effect that:

Principle 1: persons have a human right to subsistence.

To this we might consider adding a *second* principle, namely global equality of opportunity. This states that:

Principle 2: persons of different nations should enjoy equal opportunities: no one should face worse opportunities because of their nationality.

The reasoning for this draws straightforwardly from the reasoning for domestic equality of opportunity. If one thinks, as egalitarian liberals do, that it is unjust if persons fare worse because of their class or ethnic identity one should surely also think that it is unjust if persons fare worse because of their nationality. The logic underpinning equality of opportunity entails that it should be globalized.[60] Consider a world in which people's basic rights are secured but in which people of different nations face radically unequal opportunities. This world does not include starvation but it does consign some to misery and poverty and others to great wealth for no reason other than that some are Namibian, say, and that others are American. It is difficult to see why such arbitrary facts about people should determine their prospects in life. Given that it is an injustice that some face worse opportunities because of their class or their ethnicity, is it not an injustice that some face worse opportunities because of their nationality?

One might think, however, that these first two principles, although necessary, are insufficient for they are compatible with some people being paid much worse for no reason other than that they are foreign. Surely, however, how much one owes to someone else for performing a task should not vary with their race or nationality. If, however, we accept this then we should accept the following:

> Principle 3: 'Everyone, without any discrimination, has the right to equal pay for equal work' (Article 23(2) of the Universal Declaration of Human Rights).

My suggestion then is that at the very minimum we should accept that people should not receive unequal remuneration for equal work. What is relevant when determining someone's pay is the quality of their work or the demand for the product but their nationality is surely simply not germane. Such a principle would no doubt condemn much international trade. Of course, in suggesting such a principle we should be aware that there are difficulties in specifying what constitutes 'equal pay'.[61] It may, for example, not be appropriate to provide people with the same amount of money in two different countries without examining what uses that money could be put to. For this reason it is better to talk about equal remuneration for equal work where remuneration refers to the benefits received.

One final point: even if people have a right to subsistence and equality of opportunity and equal pay, this might not be enough. It sanctions, for example, grossly unequal outcomes in which some live at just above the subsistence level. They are perhaps not naturally gifted and so while they are not denied equal opportunities and while they are paid for the work done they are, because of their lack of talent, extremely poor. For this reason one might countenance an additional principle, namely:

> Principle 4: '[b]enefiting people matters more the worse off these people are' (Parfit 1998: 12: cf. further pp. 11–15).

I should stress yet again the tentative nature of these proposals. There are, however, three considerations in their favour. The first concerns the demandingness of the principles in question. Some proposed principles of cosmopolitan justice are extremely onerous, a good case in point being Singer's global utilitarianism. The above four principles, however, are not vulnerable to this charge. At the same time, the four principles also avoid the undue minimalism of a global principle of subsistence rights which is compatible with some individuals facing poorer opportunities and with some being paid less for no reason other than their nationality. The principles in question thus strike a balance between the undue laxness of a basic rights view and the undue strenuousness of a maximizing consequentialist view (Caney 2001*a*: 116).

A second point in their favour is that the four principles canvassed above enjoy ecumenical appeal. That is, a variety of different ethical perspectives can agree on these principles, especially the first three. The claim that persons should receive equal remuneration for equal work, for example, is not tied to any specific controversial theory (unlike, say, the idea of a global difference principle) and is accepted by a number of different theories, ranging from desert-based to Rawlsian to consequentialist approaches. Similarly, the ideal of equality of opportunity is accepted by people adopting vastly different theoretical perspectives (Boxill 1987: 143–4).

A third point should also be made, namely that *if* the scope$_2$ claim is true then there is, in a sense, no option but to accept these principles. That is, *if* we accept these values in the domestic realm, then, *if* the scope$_2$ claim is true, we are inexorably driven to accepting them at the global level whether we want to or not. We have no choice in the matter. The principles listed above, then, are an inescapable implication of our domestic commitments. As such they, of course, meet the condition of *domestic-compatibility*. They also, we should observe, satisfy the two other criteria. They are *determinate* and internally *coherent*.

Having examined various cosmopolitan theories of distributive justice, the rest of this chapter considers alternative perspectives on the nature of distributive justice. Prior to doing so it is worth noting that to dispute a cosmopolitan perspective, and the scope$_2$ claim it affirms, critics must show that there is some fundamental difference between the domestic realm (where such principles of justice may apply) and the global realm (where they may not). To use the terminology introduced in Chapter 1, critics must engage in level-1 analysis and challenge cosmopolitanism's level-1 assumptions about the relationship between domestic and global political theory. As we have seen above, the cosmopolitan claim is that the principles of distributive justice that are standardly employed in the domestic realm should inform the global realm. This is precisely what critics of cosmopolitanism, such as Miller, challenge (2000*c*: 174). And to ground this challenge, critics must be able to identify ways in which the global domain is fundamentally different in character to the domestic domain and hence that we cannot simply apply domestic theories of distributive justice to the world at large.[62] By undermining cosmopolitanism's level-1 analysis and presuppositions, a critic could then, if he were successful, establish that the scope$_2$ claim is false. In doing so, the critic would, note, meet the condition of *domestic-compatibility*. That is, he would be explaining why his 'domestic' principles and his 'global' principles are consistent even though they are different because his point is that the two realms are disanalagous in an ethically significant way.[63]

# VII

This chapter has, thus far, considered the case for cosmopolitan principles of distributive justice. There are, however, many counter-arguments and alternative conceptions of distributive justice. As was noted earlier, Rawls did very briefly outline some principles of international justice in *A Theory of Justice*. Having derived justice within the state he employs a second hypothetical contract at which representatives of states choose, from behind a veil of ignorance, principles to govern international politics. Furthermore, as was stressed earlier, Rawls argues that such representatives would not choose any principles of international distribution (1999*c*: 331–3). Rawls's most sophisticated treatment of distributive matter is, however, in *The Law of Peoples* and so in Sections VIII and IX, I want to examine two critiques of cosmopolitan distributive justice developed in this work.[64]

Since Rawls's theory was described at length in Chapter 3, it is both unnecessary and undesirable to expound his approach to international justice at great length. Rather this section shall restate the key features of his theory and relay their application to questions of *distributive justice*. As we saw in the preceding chapter there are four key features of Rawls's argument. First: his typology of societies. Rawls distinguishes between five kinds of regime—liberal peoples, decent hierarchical peoples, outlaw states, societies with unfavourable conditions, and benevolent absolutisms (1999*b*: 4). A second aspect of his theory is its method. Rawls maintains that just principles are those that liberal and decent societies will endorse. A third feature of his approach is its fundamental normative idea: Rawls adopts the method he does to model the idea of toleration. Toleration, he argues, requires that egalitarian liberals do not foist their values on non-liberal peoples (1999*b*: 18–19, 59–60, 68, 82–5, 121–3). There are some societies that, although not liberal, are morally adequate and should be respected (1999*b*: 59–60, 67–80, 82–4). Finally, there are Rawls's principles of international justice. Using his contractarian method, Rawls derives eight principles of international justice (1999*b*: 37) (listed in Chapter 3, Section VIII).

What bearing does this have for distributive justice? Rawls makes three claims. First, he makes the negative claim that cosmopolitan principles of distributive justice are inappropriate because they exhibit intolerance toward non-liberal societies. Rawls thus rejects the account of cosmopolitan distributive justice advanced in Sections II–VI. He would also, note, reject some of the economic proposals contained in the Millennium Development Goals agreed at the United Nations Millennium Summit in September 2000. He would, for instance, reject the third Millennium Goal where this aims to 'promote gender equality and empower women'. Its aspiration to 'eliminate gender disparity in primary and secondary education' (www.un.org/millenniumgoals/index.shtml) would, in virtue of its commitment to sexual equality, be deemed unacceptably liberal. Second, on a positive level: all persons have some basic economic rights and Rawls accepts Shue's account of basic rights. Rawls's sixth principle of international justice, thus, affirms that '[p]eoples are to honor human rights' (1999*b*: 37). Elsewhere he elaborates on the content of these human rights arguing that persons have a human right 'to the means of subsistence' and to 'freedom from slavery, serfdom, and forced occupation' (1999*b*: 65).[65] Third, Rawls argues that the parties would accept a duty of assistance to burdened societies. His eighth principle of international justice affirms that '[p]eoples have a duty to assist other peoples living under unfavourable conditions that prevent their having a just or decent political and social regime' (1999*b*: 37).[66] This requires a little more elaboration. The thought underlying Rawls's reasoning here is that there are some societies that would be well ordered were it not for adverse conditions. Thus liberal and decent hierarchical societies have a duty to enable them to become well-ordered. This duty generates three guidelines. First, Rawls says that wealth is not an important variable (1999*b*: 106–7). Rather, and this is his second guideline, what matters for attaining a decent regime is having an appropriate culture (1999*b*: 108–11). Third, he adds that the aim of the duty of assistance is to enable burdened societies 'to become members of the Society of well-ordered Peoples' (1999*b*: 111–12).

Prior to evaluating Rawls's argument we should note that, as with other challenges to cosmopolitan theories of distributive justice, Rawls's argument provides an account and explanation of how the domestic realm (which in liberal societies can be regulated by liberal principles) differs in morally significant ways from the global realm (which may not). It thereby constitutes a critique of cosmopolitans' level-1 analysis of the relationship between domestic and global political theory. The guiding principle is that where there is a shared commitment to egalitarian liberal ideals (as there is in some societies) then they may apply but that where there is no such shared commitment (as is the case in the global realm) such ideals may not apply (Caney 2001*a*: 128). The scope$_2$ claim can thus be rebutted because the domestic realm is morally disanalogous to the global realm: as such, principles that should be applied in the former should not be applied in the latter and cosmopolitanism's level-1 analysis is flawed.

How satisfactory is Rawls's treatment of distributive justice?[67] Does it represent a more compelling vision than the cosmopolitan ideal developed by thinkers like Beitz and Pogge? I think not. Several questions about the plausibility of a people-based contractarian theory have been raised in Chapter 3, and it is worth noting briefly that they also undermine his analysis of global distributive justice. The objections leveled, recall, include the following:

1. Rawls's use of peoples is morally questionable because peoples are never homogeneous and hence what peoples may agree to may include policies that are unfair to individuals and minorities (Buchanan 2000: 697–8 and also 716–20; Caney 2002*a*: 99–104; Kuper 2000: 644, 648–52; Tan 2000: 28–45; Tesón 1998: 113–14).

2. Rawls's argument fails to derive human rights because the two societies he endorses are pre-programmed to endorse human rights (Beitz 2000: 685–6; Caney 2001*a*: 131; P. Jones 1996: 193–5; Mason 2000: 186).
3. Rawls's position is ad hoc: he accepts some basic rights but not others and it is not clear on what basis he does so. His theory thus violates the criterion of *determinacy* (Beitz 2000: 686–7; Caney 2001*a*: 131; McCarthy 1997: 212; Moellendorf 2002*a*: 10–14, 18, 28–9).
4. There is an incoherence in his thought for the arguments he gives for civil and political liberties entail that there should be global civil and political liberties. His theory thus violates the criterion of *domestic-compatibility* (Beitz 1983: 596; Caney 2002*a*: 106–7; Kuper 2000: 649–52, esp. pp. 651–2; Pogge 2001*b*: 247; Tan 2000: 28–32, cf. also pp. 32–3; Tesón 1998: 111).
5. There is an additional incoherence in his thought for he rejects some proposed human rights that are a precondition of other human rights that he affirms (Kuper 2000: 663–4). His theory thus violates the criterion of *coherence*.

These points (or variants of them) also vitiate his treatment of international distributive justice. (1) targets Rawls's method and hence, of course, is as forceful a critique of Rawls's treatment of international distributive justice as it is of his treatment of international civil and political justice. If we turn to (2) and (3) we can see that analogous criticisms can be made of Rawls's treatment of distributive justice. Along the lines of (2), we may note that Rawls stipulates that decent societies are committed to certain economic rights including the right of subsistence: hence it is no surprise that they accept the sixth principle affirming precisely these rights. His argument for the basic economic rights he affirms thus presupposes the answers that it is supposed to yield.

A variant on (3) can also be levelled against Rawls's treatment of economic rights. Rawls rejects some international principles (such as equality of opportunity) but affirms others (such as the right to subsistence) without persuasively explaining where he draws the line and why. Furthermore, the idea which he appeals to in order to derive the contents of these basic rights—the notion of a 'system of social cooperation' (1999*b*: 68)—is no more helpful in telling us what economic human rights we have than it is in telling us what civil and political human rights we have. Can one not argue that a truly cooperative system would grant each and every member equal opportunities and would preclude the massive inequalities that Rawls's scheme would permit?

If we turn now to (4) we can see that an analogous point can be made against Rawls's package of economic rights. This, indeed, is, in part, the point made earlier in Sections II–VI. The ideas that motivate Rawls's theory of justice as fairness entail the global application of his ideas. The idea that persons should not fare worse in life because of their social identity (such as their ethnic or class identity) is, of course, an idea central to Rawls's domestic political theory. But, then, as we have seen (and as many of Rawls's cosmopolitan critics have argued), if this is right then it is equally objectionable that persons fare worse in life because of their national or civic identity[68] and yet this is exactly what Rawls's Society of well-ordered Peoples would entail. This, of course, is the point made by the scope$_2$ claim.

Consider, finally, objection (5). A version of this also surfaces in Rawls's economic principles. The problem takes the form of a trilemma. Rawls affirms a human right to subsistence; he also rejects the notion of there being a human right to democratic government. And yet there is good reason to think that the former right can be realized only if there is democratic government. Rawls's position on this is somewhat curious for he refers directly to Sen's well-known work on how democracies prevent famines (Rawls 1999*b*: 109). He explicitly refers to 'the success of *democratic regimes* in coping with poverty and hunger' (1999*b*: 109, fn. 35, emphasis added). But this gives us no reason to think, as he appears to, that decent well-ordered societies will also for Sen-like reasons prevent famine because he is quite emphatic that decent peoples may be thoroughly undemocratic in their decision-making processes.

Suppose, however, we set these problems to one side. There are two further problems with Rawls's theory, problems that are particular to his account of distributive justice and which do not concern his theory as a whole. The first concerns his rejection of more expansive forms of global redistribution. Why would peoples not agree to more global redistribution? One reason is that Rawls defines peoples in such a way that they will not (1999*b*: 29, 32, 34, 44–5). But to this we might ask, as Pogge has done, why we should assume that liberal and decent societies have no interest whatsoever in having more resources rather than less (1994*b*: 208–11)? Why, in particular, would members of liberal societies want more primary goods in the domestic contract but not want more primary goods in the international contract (Pogge 1994*b*: 210–11; Wenar 2001: 88)? Furthermore, even if one works within the motivations that Rawls specifies, there are three reasons why the societies in a Rawlsian international contract would choose greater international redistribution.[69] First, Rawls says that the parties wish to preserve their equal standing (1999*b*: 115): however, as Beitz and Buchanan argue, given that genuine independence requires material wealth the parties can argue that political equality and independence require redistribution (Beitz 2000: 693–4; Buchanan 2000: 708–10, 711–15). Second, Rawls says that the parties wish to protect their self-respect (1999*b*: 114): again, however, this can justify global redistribution for, as Beitz, Buchanan, and Wenar argue, international inequalities can corrode self-respect (Beitz 2000: 693; Buchanan 2000: 708–9; Wenar 2001: 88). Consider, finally, Rawls's account of stability. He maintains that the parties will be concerned about stability and that this will be secured only if the societies in the Society of Peoples each enjoy 'success' where success includes 'the decent economic well-being of all its people' (1999*b*: 45). Again, however, given this, the parties will ensure that distributive principles are in place so that no society is disaffected with the Society of Peoples because of its low (absolute or relative) standard of living. In short, then, Rawls's argument is vulnerable to an immanent critique for even operating within his parameters there are cogent (Rawlsian) arguments for embracing much more egalitarian principles of global justice than the meagre ones that he countenances. Using a terminology introduced earlier in this Chapter (Section I), one might say that Rawls's own theory should lead him to accept *global* principles of distributive justice even if it does not lead him to accept *cosmopolitan* principles of distributive justice.

A second vulnerable aspect of Rawls's treatment of international distributive justice concerns his account of the nature of the duties to burdened societies. Rawls, as we have seen, thinks that wealth is not of critical importance and hence wealthy liberal and decent societies are not required to redistribute it. Rawls's analysis is, however, problematic in a number of respects. First, while his empirical claim about the insignificance of natural resources may be true, it is a bold and sweeping claim and we do need more empirical confirmation for his contention than he supplies. Rawls cites one book in support of his claim, namely David Landes (1998) *The Wealth and Poverty of Nations* (Rawls 1999*b*: 117, fn. 51). However, for all his emphasis on culture, even Landes explicitly disavows any 'monocausal explanations' of growth, stating that 'culture does not stand alone' (1998: 517).[70] Second, Rawls's claim that domestic factors and not international factors are the prime cause of a society's development can be correct only if the former are unaffected by the latter. But as both Beitz and Pogge observe, a society's political structure and culture may be greatly affected by international factors (Beitz 1999*a*: 279, and more generally, pp. 279–80; Beitz 1999*b*: 525, and more generally, pp. 524–6; Pogge 1994*b*: 213–14). To argue that the political structure of a society is the prime determinant of economic growth is therefore highly questionable. Third, and relatedly, in his analysis of the factors influencing a people's standard of living, Rawls concentrates almost exclusively on domestic factors (like the culture of a country) or physical factors (like a country's natural resources). Accordingly, as almost all commentators on *The Law of Peoples* observe, he fails to recognize the tremendous role played by transnational phenomena.[71]

# VIII

Having considered one Rawlsian challenge to cosmopolitan accounts of distributive justice, it is worth considering a second. According to this second argument, cosmopolitan principles of the sort discussed earlier are mistaken because they fail to recognize the implications of the moral significance of a people's having autonomy. The thought here is that where a people is self-governing then it, and not external bodies, is responsible for ensuring that its members receive their just entitlements. This argument is developed by Rawls in *The Law of Peoples* where he gives two examples to illustrate his contention. In one example, there are two regimes: one opts to industrialize thereby augmenting its wealth and the other decides not to, preferring to stay in a pastoral state. The second example also comprises two regimes: one enacts a restrictive population programme, limiting population growth markedly, and one does not. The suggestion in both cases is that the society which industrialized, and which therefore has more wealth, and the society that adopted a prudent population policy, and which therefore also has more wealth per person, should not have to bale out those who pursued alternative policies (1999*b*: 117–18). Cosmopolitan principles of justice would, however, demand that the wealthy always redistribute their wealth in this way and hence should be rejected. Much the same argument, we should note, has been given by David Miller who similarly argues that societies (in his case nations) should take responsibility for their choices (1995: 108; 1999: 193–7).[72]

This critique is, however, unpersuasive. In the first place, it is extremely unjust toward individuals. Why should a member of a Third World country be economically disadvantaged because of a decision that the political elite in that country made and with which they disagreed? The intuition doing the work in Rawls's and Miller's argument is surely that we think that individuals should be responsible for the choices they make and that others are not duty bound to assist someone who has chosen poorly. But this applies to individuals and it would seem highly unjust to disadvantage an individual because of a decision that he or she did not take but that some, possibly unelected, politicians took.[73] It is worth emphasizing here that Rawls applies this example to decent hierarchical societies, that is societies that are not democratic, and hence those who suffer the penalty can in no sense be said to have brought it upon themselves or be responsible for their condition.

A second point worth noting is that the intuition underlying the argument—namely that with the right of self-determination comes the responsibility—applies only in certain contexts and to certain principles.[74] Suppose we ignore the first objection and treat nations/peoples/states as akin to individuals. We believe that they should take responsibility within a just *basic structure*. Indeed Rawls forcefully makes this point (1993*b*: 189–90).[75] It follows that the critique of cosmopolitanism under scrutiny is incomplete for it is silent on the question of what constitutes a fair world basic structure (Caney 2000*a*: 143–4; 2002*a*: 116–17; Pogge 2001*a*: 16–17; 2001*b*: 250–3). And it therefore fails to show what is wrong with cosmopolitan accounts of the world basic structure.

A third problem with the argument in question concerns the nature of the position it is criticizing. Both Rawls and Miller maintain that this argument subverts egalitarian conceptions of cosmopolitanism and both also affirm some minimal economic rights (such as the right to subsistence). The puzzling feature about their position is their belief that their argument tells against the former (egalitarian principles) but not against the latter (some basic rights). Consider the society that does not adopt a population policy and suppose that there is, as a result, such a growth in population that the regime cannot afford to feed its own citizens. Now, on the one hand, Rawls affirms a human right to subsistence and this would imply that outside agencies should assist (1999*b*: 65). On the other hand, the force of his argument against egalitarian conceptions applies just as much here: where peoples are responsible they must be accountable for the actions they take and hence no external support is justified.[76] Exactly the same point may be made against Miller for he too criticizes egalitarian cosmopolitans and he too embraces the basic right to subsistence (1999: 198–200; for further pertinent discussion cf. pp. 198–204). Miller and Rawls must thus: *either* abandon their argument against egalitarian conceptions of cosmopolitan distributive justice, *or* abandon their commitment to any economic human rights, *or* provide some explanation as to why their economic human rights are immune to their argument whereas other proposed economic human rights should be rejected.[77]

# IX

Section VIII examined one challenge to a cosmopolitan approach that arose if one took seriously the autonomy of nations. In this section I want to consider a second misgiving that one might have about cosmopolitan principles of distributive justice that also faults them by appealing to nationalist theory. The argument runs as follows: principles of distributive justice, if they are to be put into practice, must be able to motivate people to comply with them. But, the argument continues, people are not and cannot be motivated to act on cosmopolitan principles of distributive justice. They are willing to be taxed so that those with whom they identify, their fellow-nationals, may benefit but they are not willing to be taxed for the benefit of foreigners. Before appraising this argument it is worth noting that it can take two slightly different versions. On one version (hereafter the *individualistic* version) it is a claim about the obligations of individuals. Individuals, it is claimed, will not be swayed to act on cosmopolitan lines and hence lack an obligation to do so. Ethical obligations, it is argued, should follow our sentiments and inclinations and these are local in character.[78] On a second version of the argument (hereafter the *societal* version) it is a claim about the necessary preconditions of a scheme of distributive justice. The thought here is that a system of justice, to be successfully implemented, must be one with which the participants identify. Without social support a distributive scheme will collapse. It then adds that people bond with fellow nationals and can identify with them: the requisite identification exists at the national level but does not exist at the supra-national level. Given this, the argument continues, supra-national schemes of distributive justice (whether at the global level or at the level of regions like the European community) cannot work. Since cosmopolitan schemes cannot command the requisite social support they are not feasible and should be abandoned.[79] To sum up then: the first version maintains that an individual's obligations are only to those with whom he or she identifies and that persons identify only with fellow nationals; and the second version makes a sociological claim about the feasibility of schemes of distributive justice, arguing that these cannot be applied at the supra-national level because the necessary level of identification does not exist.

Both variants of the argument, note, have the right structure to challenge a wholly cosmopolitan approach (and its level-1 assumptions about the relationship between domestic and global political theory). For both identify a property (social identification) that, they claim, must be present for principles to apply and both, moreover, claim that this property exists at the national level (hence

there can be principles of distributive justice within the nation) but is absent at
the global level (hence there can be no cosmopolitan principles of distributive
justice). As such, the arguments are of the right type to undermine cosmopolitanism's level-1 analysis and to refute the scope$_2$ claim. If they can show that the
domestic realm is different from the global in a morally significant way then they
can show that it is inappropriate to argue, as the scope$_2$ claim does, that the principles we think pertain at the domestic level should be applied globally. By doing
so they can also meet the criterion of *domestic-compatibility* because they can
explain how one can consistently adopt certain principles at the domestic level
and yet not adopt them at the global level.

How plausible are these related lines of reasoning? Let us consider the
*individualistic* version first. This is the weaker of the two versions. It rests on the
pivotal assumption that one has obligations only if one is motivated to comply
with them but this is a highly dubious assumption. It entails the implausible
conclusion that one can escape one's obligations to others if one lacks any inclination to perform them and this is hard to accept.[80] This point undermines the
*individualistic* version but does not refute the *societal* version.

However, three points might be made against the *societal* version. First, it might
be argued that it overstates the necessity of 'national' sentiments. There are, for
example, instances of multinational states that appear quite workable. The members can be united by factors other than a common national identity. A common
citizenship may, for example, unite people to support a system of distributive justice. If this is so, then the claim that schemes of distributive justice must be under-
pinned by a common sense of national unity is questionable. The key point is that
there are forms of social unity other than national identity (Mason 1995: 243–52;
1999: 261–86; 2000: ch. 5, esp. pp. 116, 118–20, 127–42). Furthermore, as
Daniel Weinstock has pointed out, restricting distribution to fellow-nationals is
invidious in a multinational society for it means excluding co-citizens who are not
co-nationals (1996: 92). Moreover, people (such as immigrants) may identify
more with co-nationals back home rather than fellow citizens (1996: 93).[81]

Second, one might note, on an *ad hominem* level, that one of the leading protagonists of this argument, namely Miller himself, advances some principles of
international distributive justice. Miller defends three principles of international
justice. These include: first, a principle of basic human rights that follows Shue's
account of basic rights; second, a principle of non-exploitation that prohibits
people from exploiting foreigners; and, third, a principle requiring that each
national community has the opportunity to acquire the resources necessary for
it to be self-determining (2000c: 174–8).[82] If he is to fault the cosmopolitan
approach Miller must thus either abandon any international principles or he must
explain why compliance with his three principles is possible whereas compliance
with other cosmopolitan inspired programmes is not.

These two responses, however, do not meet the objection leveled against cosmopolitan schemes of distributive justice. The first point shows that people may
be motivated by a common civic identity but this does not show the viability of

a cosmopolitan system of distribution and the second point shows, if true, that some adherents of the argument perhaps contradict themselves. Neither helps vindicate the cosmopolitan approach. To do the latter, cosmopolitans might adopt a third response. They might, for example, quite reasonably dispute the model of human motivation this argument employs. The argument in question presupposes an ahistorical and unchanging account of human nature, assuming that we are necessarily only willing to make sacrifices for fellow-nationals. As Goodin and others have pointed out, however, such an account is too static and neglects the fact that people's willingness to adhere to principles depends considerably on political institutions, the behaviour of others, and prevalent social norms.[83] After all, in earlier periods in history the idea that people would identify with and be willing to make sacrifices for a group of 58 million would have seemed quite fantastic.[84] It would therefore be erroneous simply to make the a priori assumption that the motivations people currently have are invariant. Relatedly, the argument in question relies on an impoverished moral psychology, assuming that people are motivated solely by loyalties and attachments to members of their community. It thereby underestimates peoples' ability to be motivated by their moral values.[85] People might, for example, seek to combat something (like apartheid or landmines or cruelty to animals or child abuse) not because they necessarily share the same identity as the oppressed (or feel themselves to be part of the same community) but because of their commitment to principles of universal rights. Given this, however, it seems reasonable to suggest, against Miller (1995: 57–8), that people may be motivated by cosmopolitan distributive ideals. Consider, in this light, Falk's claim that the current world order is a form of 'global apartheid' and is analogous in morally relevant respects to South African apartheid (1995: 49–55). It does not seem far fetched to me to think that showing that this analogy holds may affect people's behaviour. By employing analogies like this, cosmopolitan ideals can harness already existing powerful motivations.[86]

## X

Sections VIII and IX have examined two nationalist points. This section considers a third claim advanced by nationalists in criticism of cosmopolitan schemes of distributive justice. The claim in question maintains that what was termed above ambitious cosmopolitanism (Section II) is incorrect for persons have special obligations of distributive justice to their fellow nationals. This position is consistent with thinking that persons have some obligations of distributive justice to all but what it insists on is that persons have special duties to the other members of their nation. A wholly cosmopolitan outlook, it charges, is faulty because it allows only agent-neutral values in and overlooks the ties that come with social roles and membership in communities. Furthermore, it should be stressed, these are ties of distributive justice. The claim is that membership of a nation generates duties to one's fellow nationals and also entitlements one can claim of them.[87] Why should one accept this claim? Consider two lines of reasoning.

1. *The intuitive argument.* One argument for this claim draws directly on people's moral convictions. It makes two claims. First, it makes the claim that correct moral principles are those that cohere with people's intuitions. Second, it then claims that people have a strong intuition that one should favour one's fellow nationals over foreigners. It would, so the argument runs, be counter-intuitive to adopt a purely agent-neutral approach that treats foreigners and nationals identically. One has a duty to prioritize the interests of fellow nationals (Miller 2000a: 25–6, 39–40; Tamir 1993: 99–102).

This argument is vulnerable to a number of objections. First, one can call into question its method. Why should one take people's intuitions as authoritative (Freeman 1994: 82–3; C. Jones 1996: 76–7)? In particular, why should one take them as authoritative given that they are profoundly shaped by a nationalist political scheme (Weinstock 1999: 519–24)?

Furthermore, even if we rely on intuitions for our moral conclusions, it is not straightforwardly obvious that people do think that persons have special duties to their fellow nationals. What is plausible is the claim that persons have special ties to morally valuable communities. In other words not any kind of social organization generates special obligations and a more plausible view is that membership of a social body entails obligations to fellow members only if it possesses moral value and is not unjust (Caney 1996a). Accordingly, membership of a nation can entail special duties to fellow nationals only if that nation is a morally satisfactory form of human association.[88]

Third, and finally, even if we think that persons have special obligations to fellow nationals we cannot infer from this that they are obligations of distributive justice.[89] The latter are one specific kind of obligation. The intuitive argument thus has to explain why these obligations are ones that people can claim as a matter of justice. Furthermore, this is a difficult task for as we saw earlier (and as the scope$_2$ claim shows) the logic of most theories of distributive justice ascribe no role to people's social identities. They hold that resources should be distributed according to universal properties such as need or desert but claims like 'she is British' are not good reasons.

In the light of this, what we need if we are to accept the claim that persons have special obligations of justice to fellow nationals is an argument that can show not just that persons have obligations to fellow nationals but that these are obligations of distributive justice.

2. *The reciprocity argument.* The next argument to be considered is better able to meet these criteria. What I have termed the 'reciprocity' argument maintains that persons who engage in a system of cooperation acquire special rights to the goods produced by that cooperation and have entitlements to these goods that non-participants lack (Rawls 1999c: 96–8, 301–8). The argument then adds, on an empirical level, that nations constitute systems of social cooperation. Hence fellow nationals have special rights and special duties acquired because of their membership of a nation. This line of reasoning is given by Jeff McMahan (1997: 129) and

Miller (1995: 65–7). This mode of argument, note, meets the condition specified at the end of Section VI: it identifies a property that exists within nations (social cooperation) that does not exist at the global level. Furthermore, it relies on a common conception of distributive justice and hence meets the condition that undermined the last argument.

One critical response to this argument maintains that it gains force by eliding the distinction between nations and states (Barry 1996: 431). The suggestion here is that this argument is more plausible as a defence of the claim that citizens have special obligations to fellow citizens because as members of the same political regime they participate in a system of cooperation. Richard Dagger similarly defends special obligations to fellow citizens along these lines. In his discussion and justification of what he terms 'the *argument from reciprocity*' he defends special obligations to fellow citizens on the grounds that a *state* is a cooperative system (1997: 46–60, esp. pp. 46–8, 59–60).

Whilst this might be a more plausible argument, the claim that persons have special obligations to fellow nationals (or fellow citizens) because the nation (or state) is a system of cooperation encounters a number of problems. The first problem is an empirical one, namely that the claim that either nations or states comprise schemes of reciprocity is hard to sustain. In the modern world, members of nations are scattered throughout the world: they cooperate and interact with members of other nations and often have no links with their own co-nationals. British nationals for example often work abroad and foreigners often work in Britain. It is thus not credible to claim that the British economy is a system of social cooperation between the members of one nation (Mason 1997: 433–4; 2000: 104).

To this we should add, second, that this argument has no force when a social institution is not cooperative. As Dagger rightly points out, this argument cannot ground special duties in societies that are coercive or exploitative (1997: 59–60).

Finally, as a number of critics have noted, this argument denies rights to those unable to take part in systems of cooperation. This has two implications. First, it cannot ground obligations to those fellow nationals (or fellow citizens) who are mentally or physically disabled or indeed to future generations so it does not show that persons have obligations of distributive justice to *all* fellow nationals (or *all* fellow citizens). It does not then support the nationalist claim under scrutiny (nor the statist revision offered by Dagger). Second, by claiming that persons do not owe obligations of distributive justice to the handicapped it loses credibility as a theory of distributive justice (Goodin 1988: sec. IV, p. 678; Tamir 1993: 120).

Neither of the two arguments is, therefore, persuasive.

# XI

Having examined three nationalist theses about international distributive justice, let us now consider a fourth. This fourth thesis does not deny the cosmopolitan contention that people have entitlements as specified by a global theory of justice.

But it does take exception to the claim that everyone has the same duties to ensure that people receive their just entitlements. It makes the following claim:

the *allocation of duty* thesis: nations have special duties to ensure that their members receive their just entitlements as defined by a cosmopolitan theory of distributive justice.

Miller, for example, defends this claim in *On Nationality*. He agrees with Shue's (cosmopolitan) claim that individuals have a human right to liberty, security, and subsistence but he maintains that the duty to ensure that people receive their entitlements belongs mainly to fellow nationals (1995: 75–7; cf. also 1999: 200, 202). Again this illustrates the point that the contrast between cosmopolitanism and nationalism is more complex than is normally imagined since Miller's claim does not challenge the cosmopolitan affirmation of rights. Furthermore, the claim that not everyone has a duty to ensure that other people receive their cosmopolitan entitlements is also made by cosmopolitans like Shue—although he would not claim that nations have special duties to protect their own members' rights (1988: 687–704).

Miller's claim that the duties to ensure that people receive their just entitlements should not be borne equally by everyone is plausible. His argument for the 'allocation of duty' thesis is, however, unpersuasive. He defends his claim that individuals should promote the basic rights of their fellow nationals on the following grounds: (P1) human beings have certain basic rights. (P2) Individuals are under special obligations to their fellow nationals. Therefore, (C) individuals are under a special obligation to ensure that their fellow nationals' basic rights are observed. Thus he writes: '*Who* has the obligation to protect these basic rights? Given what has been said so far about the role of shared identities in generating obligations, we must suppose that it falls in the first place on the national and smaller local communities to which the rights-bearer belongs' (1995: 75).

This argument, however, fails for two reasons. First, (P1) and (P2) do not imply (C).[90] One can, for example, accept both premises and deny (C). Just because X has a right to alpha and I have a duty to X, does not show that I have a duty to provide X with alpha. Suppose, for example, that a married man, A, has a right to a job. A's spouse, we believe, has special duties to A. These two claims do not, however, imply that the central responsibility for ensuring that A's right is observed should be borne by his wife. A second problem with this argument is that it succeeds only if we also accept that individuals bear special obligations of distributive justice to co-nationals and, as has been argued above, this thesis is implausible.[91]

# XII

This chapter has concentrated, thus far, on cosmopolitan accounts of distributive justice and the alternative conceptions of justice that have been advanced by Rawls and nationalist thinkers like Miller and Tamir. The remaining sections of the chapter turn to realist perspectives on global principles of distributive justice. One powerful and frequently expressed line of reasoning objects that cosmopolitan analyses of distributive justice are utopian and unworkable. The next

two sections explore two distinct arguments, both of which challenge cosmopolitan principles of distributive justice from a realist point of view.[92]

First is what might be termed 'the systemic argument'. One commonly adduced
critique of the cosmopolitan programme (including, but not restricted to, the
cosmopolitan approach to distributive justice) argues that the international system is such that states cannot act in the way required to bring about cosmopolitan
justice. The realist challenge makes a clear contrast between the domestic realm
(where the state can, normally, enforce compliance with a distributive programme)
and the global realm (where no equivalent coercive agency exists). As such it disputes the cosmopolitan contention that our domestic commitments imply global
principles of distributive justice (the scope$_2$ claim) by arguing that there is a fundamental morally significant contrast between the two domains. It disputes, that is,
cosmopolitanism's level-1 analysis. Since there is this morally significant difference
(namely, the lack of a coercive agent) one cannot simply conclude, as the scope$_2$
claim maintains, that the principles fit for the domestic realm should be applied
in the global realm. One can, that is, consistently *both* affirm certain principles for
the domestic level *and* deny that these principles should apply at the global level
and thereby meet the criterion of *domestic-compatibility*.

Consider, for example, the famous account of international politics provided
by Kenneth Waltz (1979)—an account which many others, broadly speaking,
also accept (Mearsheimer 1990: 5–56; 1995: 5–49). According to Waltz, the
international system is a 'self-help' system in which the unit members (i.e. states)
have no choice but to pursue their own interests. If they do not they will lose out.
The dynamics of the system are thus such that unless one looks out for one's own
interests one will go to the wall. There is therefore no possibility for the pursuit of
moralistic ideals like eliminating poverty (Art and Waltz 1983: 1–32, esp. p. 6;
Mearsheimer 1995: 48, fn. 182; Zolo 1997: p. 69). To apply justice at the global
level thus shows a failure to understand the dynamics of the international system.

This argument depends fundamentally on its account of the character of the
international system. It assumes, first, that the international system will always
have a statist character and, second, that under a system of states, the states
are unable to act on cosmopolitan grounds. The first assumption is subjected to
criticism in Chapter 5, and so will not be discussed further here, save to say that
it ignores the historical evidence and takes an excessively deterministic view
(Linklater 1998: ch. 1, esp. pp. 18–22, 215–16).

Even if we accept this first assumption, the anti-cosmopolitan conclusions do
not follow because the second assumption is flawed for two reasons. One problem arises because this very formal and abstract account of the workings of the
international system is implausible. For example, as Beitz pointed out in his
critique of realism, published in the same year as Waltz's *Theory of International
Politics*, some states are a good deal more powerful and wealthy than others
(1999c: 40–2; cf. also Brilmayer 1994). Accordingly they are able to comply
with cosmopolitan principles without them being unable to resist domination by
others. Consider, for example, the specific example of debt cancellation. Writing

in 1999, the Harvard economist Jeffrey Sachs wrote that 'if the US were to write down the debts in their entirety, the budgetary costs would be just $600 million, or around 0.000075 per cent of US Gross National Product' (1999: 8). Such a policy can have a dramatic effect on those living in debtor countries: money can be spent on education and health rather than repaying debts that previous, often corrupt, governments took out. But while such an action makes a large difference to the beneficiaries, it represents a minor cost to the United States. Put another way, the dynamics of the international system are not such that they prevent a state from acting on cosmopolitan lines.

A second flaw in the realist argument is more important yet, for it targets the assumption that there cannot be cooperation to pursue cosmopolitan ideals of distributive justice. It may be useful to illustrate this point by considering a concrete issue. Many affirm this realist claim in connection with the proposal to tax international currency speculation (the Tobin tax mentioned in Section I). Against the latter proposal, the critics argue that if a state, or group of states, decides to tax currency speculation in its jurisdiction, speculators will simply move elsewhere. Unilateral action is insufficient but collective action is unattainable. Hence the idea of international taxation is doomed.[93] This line of reasoning, though common, is misplaced. A Tobin tax can overcome the problems in three ways. First, international institutions can stipulate that no one can be a member of their institution and thereby enjoy the benefits it brings without signing up to the tax (Raffer 1998: 535). Furthermore, it has been noted that financial speculation is heavily concentrated in a small number of places: 'at present nine countries account for 84 per cent of foreign exchange transactions' (Arestis and Sawyer 1999: 162). Given this, one need only secure their agreement for the tax to be implemented. This, of course, raises the question of whether speculators will simply set up elsewhere. This is where two further responses to the objection become relevant. For the second reply to the objection is that one can discourage dealers from setting up outside the zones being taxed by a Tobin tax by levying 'a punitive tax' on those speculators trading with those in a tax-free zone (Kenen 1996: 119, 119–20; cf. also Arestis and Sawyer 1999: 162). Moreover, the third and final point to make is that there are ways of levying the tax which make it much more difficult to evade. One can tax a financial transaction either at the market where two dealers make the transaction (the dealing site) or at the place where the deals are booked and registered (the booking site). As Kenen notes, if one adopts the second policy, then it is easy to evade the tax: the brokers can simply book their deals on computers based in a tax free zone. However, as he also points out, if the source of taxation is the dealing site then it becomes much more difficult to evade the tax for the company has to move its dealing offices and dealers to another country not applying the Tobin tax. And this is costly and inefficient (Kenen 1996: 111–12; cf. also Arestis and Sawyer 1999: 162).[94] In these ways the appropriate level of cooperation is attainable (Wachtel 2000: 340–1).

The point of the above brief excursus is not to defend the Tobin tax but rather to illustrate the ways in which cooperation to achieve a cosmopolitan goal can be reached. It also serves both to bring out that universal cooperation may not be required, and also to point out that a simple realist model fails to recognize ways of securing cooperation.

In short then the systemic argument fails even if we accept a statist framework, because first the furtherance of some cosmopolitan ideals does not necessarily depend on cooperation and second because, to the extent that it does, some cooperation is possible.

Before moving on to consider a positive realist argument it bears noting that there are other realist arguments against cosmopolitan principles of distributive justice which charge that cosmopolitan attempts to alleviate the needs of the global poor inevitably fail. For example, many object that foreign aid

(1) goes to corrupt third world dictators rather than the needy;
(2) is frequently badly organized and inefficient (Krasner 1992: 49–50); and
(3) increases population in poor countries which in turn prolongs the problem of poverty (Hardin 1996: 5–15).

Space precludes an examination of these but two points are worth making. First, many dispute the three empirical claims cited above, claiming that, although aid has sometimes been guilty of the above faults, they do not pose insurmountable obstacles to the pursuit of a fair world (Cassen 1994). Second, none of the three claims challenge the fundamental moral claims given by cosmopolitans. They are directed against specific policies and programmes but not against the moral principles. There is, then, *in this sense* not necessarily a value-conflict between these realist points and cosmopolitan principles of justice.[95] This bears out the point made in Section I of the utility of differentiating between different levels of philosophical analysis and distinguishing between claims about what fundamentally matters and claims about what particular policies should be adopted.

# XIII

As well as the critique just considered, realists also defend a positive thesis arguing that the state has a duty to pursue the national interest. The next argument considered seeks to show both that states do not have any duty to comply with cosmopolitan justice and that states have special duties to their citizens. States, that is, should pursue the national interest. The argument in question draws on the strong intuition that states have a special relationship with their citizens. One might, for example, argue that states are bound by a contractual duty to their people. According to this argument, states should not seek to improve the quality of life of people overseas but should rather seek to protect their own interest. Isn't this a datum of common sense? Intuitively speaking, it would seem bizarre to claim that state A has no more duties to one of its citizens than does state B. Drawing on such intuitions, then, it is argued that a state has special duties to its own citizens that other states or external institutions do not have and that it should eschew cosmopolitan ideals (Kennan 1985/86: 206).[96] This argument, note, points to a morally significant difference between the domestic and the global domains, namely that the latter contains bodies (namely states) which have duties to their people and there is no analogue within states.

Certainly this argument does articulate a very powerful intuition but we need to explore in closer detail exactly what it establishes. As many have pointed out, it fails to show that states should not comply with cosmopolitan principles of distributive justice. It does not, that is, establish that there are no global principles of justice which bind states and other actors. The reason for this is that whilst we think that institutions (like states or trade unions or churches or social movements) are entitled to represent the ends of their members (and may even be duty-bound to do so) it does not follow that they can do whatever they want. They can, we think, pursue their ends *within the context of a fair overall framework* (Barry 1991*b*: 165–6; Pogge 1994*b*: 221–2; Pogge 1998*a*: 474–6). So whilst leaders of social institutions (like trade unions or churches) have a duty to further the interests of their members this does not entitle them to take what is not theirs or to kill people if that furthers their members' interests. Their duty to their citizens applies within a set of parameters defined by a theory of justice. Accordingly to rebut the cosmopolitan, the realist must challenge the cosmopolitan account of these parameters and this the argument does not do. Accordingly the argument under question fails to undermine cosmopolitan principles of distributive justice.[97]

# XIV

It is time to conclude. This chapter has covered a considerable amount of ground and it may be appropriate to sum up the findings. It has argued that:

1. contractarian accounts of cosmopolitan justice can overcome two challenges but prove ultimately unconvincing;
2. consequentialist accounts of cosmopolitan justice can also overcome some common objections but are incomplete and indeterminate;
3. existing rights-based approaches are plausible but insufficient;
4. the rationale underlying traditional domestic theories of distributive justice actually justifies the global application of their theories (the scope$_2$ claim) and this is because they rely on a universalist conception of moral personality;
5. the cosmopolitan arguments conform to the logical structure specified by the General Argument;
6. we may identify four plausible principles of cosmopolitan distributive justice.

The chapter then analysed two Rawlsian arguments, finding that

7. Rawls's appeal to toleration fails to invalidate cosmopolitan principles of distributive justice;
8. Rawls's (and Miller's) responsibility argument is incomplete and rests on a dubious analogy.

The chapter then turned to three nationalist claims, arguing that

9. arguments that cosmopolitan schemes of distributive justice are unfeasible are unpersuasive;
10. both arguments to the effect that persons have special obligations of distributive justice to fellow nationals are unconvincing; and
11. the claim that persons have cosmopolitan rights but that the duty to uphold them falls on fellow nationals is unpersuasive.

The chapter finally discussed two realist claims:

12. the negative claim that global schemes of distributive justice are unworkable and utopian;
13. the claim that the only distributive duty states have is a contractual duty to maximize the condition of their members.

Having considered now universal principles of civil and political justice and universal principles of distributive justice, a natural question to ask is what political institutions are most appropriate in the light of these ideals. This is the subject of Chapter 5.

## NOTES

1. For some good surveys of the competing perspectives on global distributive justice see Brown (1992: 155–92; 1997*b*: 273–97), O'Neill (2000: 115–42), and Jones (1999).
2. For an instructive discussion of the questions that follow see Jones (1999: 2–8).
3. For further discussion of these possibilities and a defence of a fourth perspective see G. A. Cohen (1989: 906–44).
4. See, for example, Barry (1991*c*: 182–7). Barry's discussion focuses on a famous argument given by Peter Singer (1972: 229–43). He suggests that it is best construed not as a claim about 'justice' but about 'humanity'. Singer's argument is discussed in Sect. IV of this chapter.
5. More generally, a commitment to cosmopolitan fundamental principles can justify special obligations to fellow nationals where there is a correlation between the reasons that cosmopolitans think can justify redistribution, on the one hand, and nationality, on the other. See Goodin (1988: esp. pp. 663–4 and also pp. 678–86), Barry (1996: 431), Jones (1999: 130–1, 133–4).
6. For a similar distinction see Miller (1998: 166–7).
7. As does Moellendorf (2002*a*: 39–43, 48–50, 72, 129).
8. See also Caney (1999*a*) for a critique of the claim that persons have special obligations of distributive justice to fellow nationals.
9. See Pogge (1992*a*: 90–101; 1994*a*: 90–8, esp. pp. 90–91; 1995: 113–19).
10. A similar point also applies to O'Neill's account of justice. She argues that people are bound by duties of justice to other people only if they are connected in some way (1994: 81–3; 1996: 105–6, 112–13). She then argues that, given the high levels of global interconnectedness, the scope of justice in our world is global or pretty much so (1996: 113–21, esp. p. 121).

11. For earlier discussions see Pogge (1992*a*: 96–7; 1994*b*: 199–205).

12. Barry also once argued that there should be global equality of resources (1991*d*: 237–9; 1991*c*: 196–203).

13. David Richards has also defended a global difference principle (1982: 287–93, esp. pp. 292–3). He also defends a principle of 'mutual aid' where this requires that people come to the aid of needy people (1982: 282–7).

14. See, further, Bader (1997), Barry and Goodin (1992), and Black (1991, esp. pp. 360–2, 373–7). Some defenders of global capitalism maintain, of course, that open markets (for commodities, factors of production, and finance, as well as labour) are the best means for furthering the condition, of the most disadvantaged.

15. The same point is made by P. Jones (1994: 167) and Téson (1998: 111). See also C. Jones (1999: 8).

16. A question: if this hypothesis was confirmed in the case of civil and political justice would it not perhaps be surprising if it did not also apply to distributive justice?

17. For Pogge's defence of a global original position see (1989: 246–59). Pogge also defends a global difference principle (see, for example, (1989: 250–3)). The condition of the globally worse off has very great weight even if it does not have absolute priority (1989: 274–5).

18. For this criticism see also Brown (1992: 176, 180; 1993: 521–2; 1997*b*: 289–90; 2002*b*: 173).

19. Pogge's institutionalism runs throughout all his work on distributive justice: for clear examples see (1989: 262–3, 273–80). For his critical discussion of, and reply to Barry's critique of, Beitz see (1989: 263–5).

20. Moellendorf, like Beitz, Pogge, and Scanlon, also defends a global difference principle (2002*a*: 80–1).

21. Compare Murphy (1998: 273).

22. Shue also makes this distinction in his illuminating discussion of institutional and interactional accounts (1996*a*: 164–6).

23. Beitz makes a similar point in an article published four years after the first edition of *Political Theory and International Relations* (1983: 595). Cf. also Buchanan (1999*b*: 72).

24. See also Pogge (1989: 247; 1994*b*: 198).

25. See also Pogge's rejection of Beitz's non-institutional component (1989: 241) and also his criticism of Beitz's resource principle (1989: 251–2).

26. For a fuller analysis see Caney (forthcoming *a*).

27. Pogge, I should emphasize, does not reject positive duties of justice. He wishes to stay agnostic on this issue. His main aim is to argue that we have negative duties of justice not to uphold unjust institutional schemes and to show that compliance with this would prevent a great deal of the poverty and suffering that exists. At most his strategy is to argue that we do not need positive duties for we can achieve all that is necessary through the notion of a negative duty not to impose unjust institutions on people.

28. For a more comprehensive analysis of these considerations see Caney (forthcoming *a*) where I argue that there are positive duties of justice to ensure that persons do not suffer deprivation.

29. For pertinent discussion see Shue (1996*a*: 164–6; 1996*b*, esp. pp. 117, 119, 126).

30. For Richards's position see also (1971: 138–40).

31. There is a footnote after the word 'good' which refers to Rawls's 1980 lectures on Kantian Constructivism in Moral Theory (1983: 595, fn. 6).

32. It should, however, be noted that in his more recent writings Beitz appears to maintain, in a similar way to the book, the moral relevance of economic interdependence: Beitz (1999*b*: 516–18, 521–4, esp. pp. 523–4). See also (1999*c*: 200–5).

33. This section has focused exclusively on cosmopolitan reworkings of Rawls's theory. We should, of course, note that there are other contractarian theories of global distributive justice. For example, Barry employs his contractarian theory to defend four principles of cosmopolitan distributive justice (1998: 147–9). Since the theoretical method Barry employs was criticized at length in Ch. 3, this chapter will not explore his defence.

34. For Beitz's explicit affirmation of a universalist moral personality and affirmation of the irrelevance of a person's nationality or citizenship for their entitlements see Beitz (1979: 417–20; 1983: 593, 595–6; 1988*a*: 191–3; 1994: 124–5).

35. For Singer's most recent views see (2002: 150–95).

36. Singer, it should be noted, thinks that his argument makes a claim about justice (Singer 1979: 166, 173–4).

37. Cf. also Waldron (1990: 267–71). See, more generally, Jones's discussion of demandingess (1999: 33–9).

38. For Scheffler's discussion of the nature of an 'agent-centred prerogative' see (1982: 14–26) and for his discussion of its rationale see (1982: 41–70, esp. pp. 56–70).

39. On the consequentialist character of his principle of 'protecting the vulnerable' see Goodin (1985: 109–14). Goodin does, though, point out that this principle is compatible with, and might be accepted by, nonconsequentialist perspectives (1985: 115–17).

40. See Scheffler's argument that consequentialism should be distribution sensitive. It should not necessarily maximize good outcomes and may instead seek to ensure a fair distribution of desirable outcomes (1982: 26–32, 70–9). Scheffler terms his theory, which combines the agent-centred prerogative with a sensitivity to how well-being is distributed, 'the distributive hybrid' (1982: 32, cf. pp. 32–40).

41. This coheres with the account of civil and political rights adumbrated in Ch. 3. The latter, recall, draws on the ideal of respecting persons and, arguing that respecting persons involves respecting their interests equally, defends universal civil and political rights on the basis that these best further the equal interests of all. It is thus concerned with outcomes but, it is crucial to note, unlike the consequentialist theory criticized in the text, it embeds it in a theory based on the ideal of treating persons with respect. So although it is concerned with outcomes, it is not consequentialist in the sense criticized here. It is not committed to maximization; it does not need to be supplemented by a theory of rights because it is based on the right to be treated equally; and it is not indeterminate.

42. Scheffler recognises this (1982: 39–40, cf. also p. 31).

43. The principle which underlies Singer's utilitarianism also bears this out. He appeals to persons' equal moral standing (1979: 14–23, esp. p. 23). Such a principle will, of course, generate universal principles.

44. For Pogge's analysis of the concept of human rights see Pogge (1992*a*: 89–101; 1995: 103–20; 2000: 45–69). As we saw in Sect. III of this chapter, in his earlier work, Pogge worked within Rawls's contractarian theory of justice, seeking to apply it globally (1989: part III). He has subsequently shifted his position.

45. For his statement of the seven types of rights that should be protected in the name of autonomy see (1995: 192–4).

46. For another rights-based account of cosmopolitan principles of distributive justice see Beetham (1995: 41–60).

47. For Shue's concept of a basic right see (1996*a*: 18–20).
48. For likeminded criticism see also Nickel (1987: 103–4).
49. Jones also subscribes to Shue's defence of a human right to subsistence: see (1999: 59–61).
50. O'Neill argues that rights theorists' account of who bears the obligations for welfare rights is unsatisfactory and an obligation-based approach is preferable (1996: 129–35).
51. For this line of reasoning: see C. Jones (1999: 66–72, esp. pp. 68–9), Shue (1988, esp. pp. 695–8, 702–4; 1996*a*: 17, 59–60, 159–61, 164–6, 168–9, 173–80). Shue's position should be compared with Pogge's. Unlike Shue, Pogge stipulates, as we have seen, that duties of distributive justice fall only on fellow members of institutional set ups (1994*a*: 91–3). Since he accepts globalization, he thinks, however, that this duty (to create and support institutions to protect human rights) extends universally (1994*a*: 91–8). That is, affluent persons have a duty to create and support institutions that protect the human rights of all persons.
52. For a recognition, and endorsement of this point, see C. Jones (1999: 6, 8).
53. This conclusion is also true of other rights-based defences of theory of cosmopolitan principles of distributive justice. Consider two other rights-based theories. For example, Hillel Steiner defends each person's right to an equal portion of natural resources (1994: 262–5, 270). He makes clear that the reasoning grounding people's rights does not depend on arbitrary aspects like someone's nationality and that the logic for these rights generates global rights. This is true whether the right is a civil and political right, like the right not to be shot (1994: 262), or an economic right, like person's right to material resources (1994: 265). The same is also true of Philippe van Parijs's defence of an unconditional basic income. Van Parijs argues that persons have a right to an unconditional income if they are to enjoy real freedom. He recognizes, moreover, that the logic of his argument shows that *all persons* have this right: see van Parijs (1995: 227–8). His book thus defends real freedom 'for all' (1995).
54. The same, note, is true of Pogge. See Pogge (1989: 247; 1994*b*: 198). For a particularly interesting development of this point see Pogge (1992*b*: throughout but esp. pp. 88–90, pp. 92–95).
55. For one important perspective omitted from the above analysis see O'Neill (1986, 1996).
56. This point applies also to other arguments for cosmopolitan principles of distributive justice not examined above. It is, for example, an explicit feature of Veit Bader's justification of a cosmopolitan account of distributive justice: this both affirms a universalist moral personality and argues for the irrelevance of nationality (Bader 1997: esp. pp. 32–3). See also Carens (1987: 252, 256).
57. See, in addition, Barry (1991*d*: 226; 1998: 146).
58. O'Neill might appear to be a counter-example to this claim for she criticizes attempts to defend cosmopolitanism which are predicated upon an account of persons' 'moral standing' or 'moral considerability' (1996: 94) on the grounds that these metaphysical concepts are mired in controversy (1996: 91–6).
59. For a contrasting view to that defended in this paragraph, see Molly Cochran's interesting analysis of the role that conceptions of 'moral personality' play in arguments for cosmopolitanism: Cochran (1999: ch. 1). By contrast with the view defended here, Cochran argues that a universalist account of moral personality is present in only some vindications of cosmopolitanism (like Beitz's) and not in others (like Pogge's) (1999: 30, 40–1, 44–9).

60. The ideal of global equality of opportunity has been defended by a number of philosophers: Barry (1991*d*: 226, 237–9) and Pogge (1994*b*: 196). For my own defence of this principle see Caney (2000*a*; 2001*a*). For a different conception of global equality of opportunity and a different rationale for this principle see Buchanan (2000: 711, 714). Buchanan clearly distances himself from the one I endorse (2000: 712, fn. 14). Moellendorf also defends the idea of global equality of opportunity (2002*a*: 48–50, 79–80). Note, though, that by contrast with the position defended in the text, he adopts an 'institutionalist' perspective and his argument for it relies on there being global interdependence. See Sect. III of this chapter. For criticism of the idea of global equality of opportunity see Boxill (1987).

61. For further discussion and criticism of the equal pay principle along these grounds see Shue (1983: 274–83, esp. pp. 274–8) and Lehman (1986: 155–62).

62. For an illuminating discussion of various ways in which one might argue that the global realm is fundamentally different to the domestic realm (and a cosmopolitan response to each of them) see Beitz (1999*c*: 154–61 but also 13–66; 1999*b*: 521–4).

63. This brings out the point noted above (Ch. 3, Sect. I) that the criterion of domestic compatibility does not require that the same principles apply in domestic and global realms (à la scope claim). Different ones can apply if one can give a good reason as to why the two realms are disanalogous.

64. For a somewhat similar approach to Rawls's see Nardin's important work *Law, Morality, and the Relations of States* (1983). As I noted in Chapter 1, Section III, Nardin distinguishes between two conceptions of international morality. According to the 'practical' conception, states are duty bound to respect the equality and independence of other states. According to the 'purposive' conception, states have a duty to promote some ideal (whether it is a religion like Christianity or an ideology like communism or a cosmopolitan programme) (1983: ch. 1). Nardin argues for the former and against the latter in part on the grounds that a society of states acting on the practical conception protects diversity (1983: 5, 12, 22, 24, 229–30, 231–2, 305, 322–4; 1992: 23–4).

65. Rawls refers to Shue (1996*a*: 23) and Vincent (1986) on the right to subsistence (1999*b*: 65, fn. 1).

66. There is a footnote after the word 'regime' in which Rawls refers to secs. 15 and 16 of (1999*b*): see (1999*b*: 37, fn. 43).

67. There are a number of illuminating discussions of *The Law of Peoples*. These include, among others, Beitz (2000: 669–96), Brown (2000: 125–32; 2002*a*), Buchanan (2000: 697–721), Kuper (2000: 640–74), and Pogge (2001*b*: 246–53).

68. This point is made, against Rawls, by many cosmopolitans: see, for example, Beitz (1983: 593, 595–6), Pogge (1989: 247), Singer (2002: 176–7).

69. For an additional consideration see Pogge (1994*b*: 213–14).

70. For a comprehensive review of the literature on this empirical issue see Michael L. Ross (1999: 297–322). Curiously Rawls himself inadvertently concedes that societies are sometimes burdened because they 'lack . . . the material and technological resources needed to be well-ordered' (1999*b*: 106).

71. For some examples, see Brown (2000: 130–1), Buchanan (2000: esp. pp. 703–12), Hurrell (2001: 48), and Pogge (2001*b*: 251–3). See also Caney (2002*a*: secs. IV and V).

72. For further discussion of this argument see Elfstrom (1983: 712–14, 722); Jones (1990: 48–9; 1994: 166–7).

73. This point is made by many: see, for example, Beitz (1999*b*: 527–8; 2000: 692), Caney (2000*a*: 142–3; 2002*a*: 116), Green (1996: 200), and Jones (1990: 49).

74. Miller, it should be noted, does recognize that there can be a variety of reasons why a state fails to secure people's economic entitlements. He considers four possible explanations and their implications for outsiders' duties in Miller (1999: 201–4). For a critique of his discussion see Caney (2003: 304–7).

75. As Barry points out, we accept redistribution within the state even though we accord families considerable independence (1999: 51). That an institution has autonomy does not imply that it forfeits any distributive entitlements.

76. I have developed this argument more fully elsewhere: cf. Caney (2003: 303–5).

77. For further discussion see Caney (2000*a*: 139–44: 2002*a*: 114–17).

78. For this kind of reasoning see MacIntyre (1984: 17), Miller (1988: 650–1; 1995: 57–8), and Rorty (1989: 190–1, 198).

79. This line of argument is stressed by Margaret Canovan (1996*a*: 3, 28, 30–2, 34–5; 1996*b*: 73–5, 78), Miller (1988: 661; 1989, esp. pp. 59–60, 68; 1995: 93–6; 1997: 70; 2000*a*: 31–2), and Tamir (1993: 118).

80. For a persuasive, related point, see Goodin (1992*a*: 249; cf. more generally, 1992*a*: 248–9, 252–4).

81. For further sceptical comments on the extent to which a sense of nationality enables the effective functioning of schemes of justice see Arthur Ripstein (1997: 214–16).

82. For Miller's most comprehensive statement to date see Miller (2000*c*). For earlier statements of his preferred principles of international distributive justice see Miller (1995: 104–8, esp. pp. 104–5; 1999: 198–209).

83. See Goodin (1985: 167). Goodin also cites Beitz (1999*c*: 155–6) and Singer. The relevant passage from Singer is (1972: 237). See also Beitz (2000: 683) on this point.

84. For an illuminating discussion see Geras (1995: 78–81, esp. p. 78).

85. See, further, Andreas Føllesdal (forthcoming, sec III.1.5) and C. Jones (1999: 137–47). For illuminating discussions of moral psychology see, more generally, Barry's account of the desire to act in a reasonable and justifiable manner (1989: 284–5, 363–4) and Rawls's discussion of principle-dependent and conception-dependent desires (1993*b*: 83–6).

86. For further discussion see Caney (1999*a*: 130–2).

87. Such claims are advanced by Miller (1995: ch. 3 and in ch. 4, pp. 83–5, 98); Tamir (1993: 104–11). Some question whether the obligations that come with one's social identity are best thought of as obligations of justice. See, for example, Sandel's eloquent discussion (1982: 179).

88. See further Buchanan (1989: 874–6, esp. p. 874), Dworkin (1986*a*: ch. 6, esp. pp. 199–204), Friedman (1991, esp. pp. 819–21, p. 835), C. Jones (1999: 127–30), Mason (1997, esp. pp. 439–46), Nathanson (1989: 551–2), Raz (1989: 18–21), Scheffler (1995; 1997: 189–209, esp. pp. 197–200), and A. John Simmons (1996, esp. pp. 264, 266–7, 269–70). Daniel Weinstock also argues persuasively that our intuitions do not clearly show that persons have obligations to fellow nationals (1999: 528–33).

89. For this point see Caney (1999*a*: 128–33). Moellendorf makes the same point: see (2002*a*: 52–3).

90. See also Freeman (2000: 72).

91. Miller does give another argument for the 'allocation of duty' thesis. He maintains that it would be inappropriate to ascribe duties to all human beings because to require outside agents to implement cosmopolitan principles of justice justifies external

interference and a violation of the right of nations to be self-governing (Miller 1995: 77–8; cf. also Brown 1992: 168–9, 171; 1993: 522). Duties to protect cosmopolitan rights thus fall on fellow nationals. Space precludes a fuller discussion of this argument. Two points however should be borne in mind. First, its claim that outsiders do not have obligations rests on the assumption that intervention is required and this is disputable. There are surely ways of assisting a nation that do not compromise its independence (Barry 1996: 432–3; Green 1996: 200). Its empirical presuppositions are thus questionable. So too are its normative presuppositions and this is the second problem with the argument. For its critique of universal duties to succeed it has to show that national self-government has value even where it results in calamitous decisions. The value of self-government and the virtues and vices of intervention are discussed later (in Chs. 5 and 7). In the meantime, however, one can argue that the argument under scrutiny deifies the nation (or nation-state) for it ascribes it value independently of how it impacts on human lives. What, one might ask, is valuable about self-determination if it leads to a state of affairs in which people lack their entitlements? If a national government is producing policies that deny people their basic rights and entitlements then what is so valuable about non-intervention? For a fuller critique see Caney (2000*a*: 135–9).

92. For good critical analyses of realism see Barry (1991*b*: 159–81), Brilmayer (1994), Donnelly (1992: 85–111), Goodin (1992*a*: 248–64), and Thompson (1992: 27–43).

93. For such scepticism see the UK HM Treasury's critical analysis of the tax (2001: pp. xii–xiii). The UK's International Development Committee is more sympathetic but it too is unconvinced of the feasibility of the tax (2002: 25–7). For more general criticism of the Tobin tax see Garber and Taylor (1995).

94. For the last two points see also Jetin and Brunhoff (2000: 208, and also pp. 207–10 more generally).

95. As a number of writers have pointed out, much realist argument claims in effect that the best way to promote the well-being of all is for states to advance their own national interest. Such arguments provide a cosmopolitan critique of international aid (it benefits no one) and a cosmopolitan justification of the pursuit of the national interest (this best promotes the standard of living of all). For this convergence between realism and cosmopolitanism see also: Mapel and Nardin (1992: 300), Mason and Wheeler (1996, esp. pp. 100–6), and Thompson (1992: 28).

96. See also Goldman (1982: 450).

97. For further discussion of this argument see Beitz (1999*c*: 24), Cohen (1984: 300), Dower (1998: 31, 37–8). See here Buchanan's illuminating discussion of the duties of states. See, in particular, his critique of what he terms the 'discretionary association' view, which is the view that the prime duty of states is to protect their members' interests (1999*a*: 74–82) and, in particular, his discussion of the realist maxim of promoting national interests (1999*a*: 78–9). He defends instead the view that the state has a duty to further just institutions (1999*a*: 82–7). For further discussion of the legitimate role of democratically elected authorities and the limitations on their duties to be partial, see Pogge's excellent discussion (1998*a*: 464–96, esp. pp. 474–6).

# 5

# Political Structures

> Political Science, and to hardly a less extent political economy, have been taught hitherto with a nationalist bias, with an excessive emphasis on the State and its problems ... Both political science and political economy stand, therefore, in great need of widening their horizon. They need to be rewritten with the world as their stage and the welfare of humanity as their theme ... It is still possible, of course, that we may even then conclude that the State, as we know it, is the best available instrument for social progress. But it is no less possible that we may come to the contrary conclusion, and decide that in its present form the State is rather an obstacle in the path of our civilized ideals.
>
> David Mitrany (1933: 97–8)

Any complete account of global political theory must address the question of what *political institutions* are appropriate. How should the world be structured? Is there a case for global political institutions? If so, what form should they take and should they complement or replace a framework of states? Indeed, should there be a states system? If so, what place, if any, should be granted to nations? Is there a case for national self-determination, either as nation-states or as sub-state political authorities? These are some of the questions this chapter aims to address. Any answer to these questions must consider the two following questions.

First: where should political borders fall? Should they be territorially defined? Or should the persons to be governed by a specific political unit be determined by other criteria? If there are territorially defined borders should they map onto the contours of national communities? Or around systems of economic interdependence? Or where people themselves choose them to fall?

Second: how much moral importance should be attached to political borders (Pogge 1992a: 93–5)? Do borders allow units complete control over their citizens or is it conditional? Should political authority be undivided? Or may there be different levels of authority performing different functions, each with different borders and with none being superior to the others?

To answer these questions, this chapter will start with a conceptual analysis of some possible political frameworks (Section I). It then considers three cosmopolitan approaches to the question of how political power should be institutionalized (Sections II–VI). This is followed by an analysis of the misgivings about cosmopolitan political proposals voiced by statists (including both realists and those who affirm the 'society of states') and by those sympathetic to the idea of a global civil society (Sections VII–XI). The remainder of this chapter then evaluates nationalist claims that any defensible account of political institutions should grant autonomy to nations (Sections XII–XVI). Its aim is to defend a cosmopolitan political programme—one in which there are democratic supra-state institutions charged with protecting people's civil, political, and economic rights—and to rebut the challenges of statists and nationalists or to show that they can be accommodated by cosmopolitans.

# I

Prior to examining these normative arguments it is important to have a clear idea about the possibilities available. And to do this it is worth beginning by analysing the concept at the heart of many contemporary political approaches—namely the concept of state sovereignty—before then noting alternative political frameworks. To start here does not reflect a prejudice in favour of sovereign states. (Indeed, as will become clear, there is a strong case against a statist-order). Rather, it represents a good starting point because the commitment to sovereign states is so deeply entrenched in much international relations theory and political theory that it is worth bringing out the defining features of state sovereignty and making explicit what is taken for granted. This enables us to see the possibility of other arrangements and not mistake what exists now for an essential feature of the world. In addition, identifying the specific characteristics of a state-based order better enables us to evaluate each of them.

What then is 'state sovereignty'? A useful starting point is provided by Daniel Philpott who defines sovereignty as 'supreme authority within a territory' (1999: 570).[1] Three features of this definition are worth noting. First, the concept of sovereignty is a 'juridical' one (Jackson 1999: 432; James 1986: 39–45). As Beitz puts the point: 'it refers to the state's authority, not its actual capacity, to coerce. As classically conceived, sovereignty is a juridical idea' (1991: 238, see also p. 241). It should not thus be confused with economic strength or political power. I shall refer to this property as *legality*.[2]

Second, a political unit is sovereign if it is the 'supreme authority' (Philpott 1999: 570). County councils, thus, have some authority but they are not states because they are not the supreme authority over their area: ultimate authority rests with another entity. This feature of sovereignty—which I shall call *supremacy*—is universally stressed. F. H. Hinsley, for example, characterizes sovereignty as follows: 'the idea of sovereignty was the idea that there is a final and absolute political authority in the political community; and everything that needs to be added to complete the definition is added if this statement is continued in the following words: "*and no final and absolute authority exists elsewhere*"' (1986: 26). This feature of sovereignty is often unpacked into two further features——namely 'internal' and 'external' sovereignty (Beitz 1991: 237–44, esp. p. 238; Jackson 1999: 433; Philpott 1999: 570–1). The former refers to the fact that there is no person or institution within the state which has

variety of earlier political systems. Indeed, as is widely stressed, the current statist framework dates, very roughly, from the Peace of Westphalia in 1650. As Hedley Bull notes, in the middle ages no political institutions enjoyed *supremacy*: 'no ruler or state was sovereign in the sense of being supreme over a given territory and a given segment of the Christian population; each had to share authority with vassals beneath, and with the Pope and (in Germany and Italy) the Holy Roman Emperor above' (1977: 254, cf. also pp. 254–5). These points remind us of the important but often neglected fact that there could be, and have been, alternatives to a statist framework. But should we call for non-statist political frameworks? Or is a statist order the most defensible global order? These questions will be explored in the rest of this chapter.

## II

Let us begin then with cosmopolitan perspectives. It is important to observe that, as we noted in Chapter 1, cosmopolitans affirm certain moral tenets and are not thereby logically compelled to accept global political institutions. Beitz, for example, clearly distinguishes between *moral cosmopolitanism* (which affirms a set of universal ethical claims) and *institutional cosmopolitanism* (which affirms a world state) (1994: 124–6).[6] Acceptance of cosmopolitan ideals, like civil and political rights and global economic justice, thus does not, in itself, entail acceptance of legal or institutional cosmopolitanism. What, then, is the cosmopolitan position on political institutions? Within cosmopolitan writings, we can find three distinct types of approach to this question, namely what I shall term *intrinsic, right-based*, and *instrumental* approaches.[7] These are defined as follows.

The *intrinsic* approach maintains that any plausible cosmopolitanism must include as one of its central moral tenets a commitment to the rights of self-government. As a corollary, it then argues, the appropriate political structures are those that people themselves choose. People have the right to decide who governs them, where the boundaries fall, with whom they are to be governed, and what type of political authority should govern them.

The *right-based* approach, as its name suggests, also starts with the claim that a credible cosmopolitan commitment must refer to people's right to be self-governing. However, it interprets this right differently and its claim is not that people have the right to choose where the borders fall. It maintains, rather, that people have a right to exercise control over the social, economic, and political forces that govern what they are able to do: the appropriate political institutions are those that allow people to govern the forces that structure what they can do in life.

The *instrumental* approach maintains that appropriate political institutions are those that best further cosmopolitan moral ideals (like, for example, human rights or international distributive justice or the protection of the environment). This third approach thus adopts a consequentialist perspective, although the goals by which institutions are to be judged are the promotion of cosmopolitan ideals of justice rather than utilitarian objectives like the satisfaction of wants or preferences. The normative criterion here is 'what political system best advances the rights of individual men and women throughout the world'.[8]

One can, of course, combine these approaches. One might think, for example, that *instrumental* considerations are relevant but that the *right-based* view also attests to an important value that should be accommodated. According to such a mixed view, unless these two approaches imply exactly the same institutions, we would have to take both considerations into account and seek to balance the competing considerations where they conflict. How persuasive are these approaches, and what do they justify? They will be examined in Sections III, IV, and V.

# III

Let us begin by examining the *intrinsic* approach. This can be subdivided into two approaches—an individualist and a collectivist version. Let us consider the individualist version first. According to philosophers like Harry Beran, David Gauthier, and Hillel Steiner, individuals possess certain rights and liberties. We recognize, they maintain, the value of freedom and one important right is the right of freedom of association. This, however, bears directly on the question of what sort of political institutions there should be. It follows from the right of freedom of association that people may choose by whom they are to be governed. As Beran writes: 'Because of liberalism's commitment to freedom as an ultimate value, liberals see the ideal society as one that comes "as close as a society can to being a voluntary scheme." This . . . mean[s] that all relationships among sane adults in such a society should be voluntary' (1984: 24, see also 24–6).[9] They may, for example, secede from a state and form their own political community with others who also so choose. The same position is expressed by Gauthier (1994) and Steiner (1996a: 143–4). As free agents, people should be free to choose who is to be part of the political system (who are their fellow citizens) and they may choose the type of political authority (state or otherwise) who is to rule them. The principle of individual choice is thus the fundamental principle and the correct political institutions are those that result from people's free choices.

This radically individualistic position suffers from two serious problems. First, it is not clear why a commitment to liberty *does* imply that a political institution is legitimate only if it is one to which individuals consent. One could—without contradiction—argue that individuals should be free and that a political institution (like a state) that protects their liberty is legitimate regardless of whether the individuals consent to that institution.[10] In other words, one could argue that what follows from the worth of liberty is simply that the state has a duty to maintain its citizens' liberty (and not violate other people's liberty). On this alternative (*instrumental*) approach, the appropriate response to the claim that freedom is valuable is that we should adopt whichever political system best protects it. Indeed, Rawls, whom Beran quotes in the passage reproduced above, does not argue that accepting the ideal of liberty entails that a political regime has authority only if its citizens consent. Expressed in another way, one can distinguish between the questions 'who should rule?' and 'how should the rulers govern?' and argue that a commitment to liberty provides an answer to the second question.[11]

Second, there is the obvious but very important point that a purely individualistic approach would be highly impractical. Many important objectives can be attained only if people comply or are made to comply with them. By allowing individuals to opt out, any form of concerted action (to prevent pollution, say) would often be difficult and costly. In other words, one of the standard objections to the market—its susceptibility to collective action problems and its failure to secure public goods—can also be made against this position. In addition to this, the resulting outcome may well be highly inimical to freedom (Wellman 1995: 156). The decisions made legitimately by some individuals may result in states of affairs where others' freedom is greatly impeded. Imagine, for example, an individual cut off from the rest of the world because those around him have chosen to form a political community and will not let him out. We, thus, have no reason to accept the individualistic version and good reason to reject it.

Given this, let us consider the collectivist version of the *intrinsic* approach. This too argues that people should be free to choose who is to be part of the political system (who are their fellow citizens) and they may choose the type of political authority (state or otherwise) who is to rule them. By contrast with the individualistic approach, however, the collectivist position argues not that individuals have the right to choose their political authority but rather that peoples/communities have this right. This is commonly expressed as the right of a people to democratic government. One version of this argument has been clearly set out by Daniel Philpott who maintains that 'any group of individuals within a defined territory which desires to govern itself more independently enjoys a prima facie right to self-determination—a legal arrangement which gives it independent statehood or greater autonomy within a federal state. The form of self-determination I leave open' (1995: 353).[12] Philpott adds that 'a group's right to self-determination is qualified by the injustices it inflicts on the larger state' (1995: 363, see generally pp. 363–4). As long as this condition is met, peoples have a right to decide with whom and by whom they are governed.

Pogge also affirms some support for the collectivist version of the *intrinsic* approach (although, as we shall see later, he also invokes *instrumental* considerations). In particular, he affirms two principles. First, a people may democratically decide to join with another people as long as the latter also democratically agree to it and as long as any people left over can form their own unit or join with someone of their choice (1994*a*: 112). Second, a people may democratically decide 'to form themselves into a political unit of a level commensurate with their number' (1994*a*: 112) as long as (a) minorities can join up with another system, (b) they can form their own self-governing system, and (c) the people left over can form a viable unit or join up with someone of their choice (1994*a*: 112–13).[13] In short, the global political system should, in part, reflect the choices of peoples.[14]

Now why should we accept this approach? Philpott provides the fullest discussion so I shall focus on his reasoning. His argument rests on the following moral premise:

1. Autonomy is valuable where autonomy entails: (a) the protection of traditional liberties (1995: 356); (b) democratic government, that is, people 'participating and holding representatives accountable' (1995: 357); and, (c) 'distributive justice' (1995: 358).

He then argues that

2. Democratic government entails allowing people to chose to which political system they belong and by whom they are governed (1995: 358–61).

Thus autonomy leads to democracy and democracy leads to people choosing where the borders fall and by which political system they are governed.

This argument is, however, also unconvincing. First, it is far from clear why valuing individual freedom requires valuing democracy. There is certainly no logical link between valuing autonomy and valuing democracy and, as I argued above, one might infer from the claim that autonomy is valuable that we should design a political framework that best protects it (Buchanan 1998*b*: 17–18). Furthermore, democracy may often result in limitations of people's freedom if the demos so decides. Accordingly, valuing autonomy not only does not commit one to valuing democracy: it may lead one to wish to circumscribe democratic government. Premise (1) is therefore inaccurate.

This point notwithstanding, Philpott's claim that democratic government is valuable is a plausible one that most people would happily accept. Accepting this, however, does not deliver his conclusions because premise (2) is highly questionable. In particular, thinking that democracy is valuable does not commit one to the conclusion that democratic majorities should decide where the borders fall and the political structure of the institutions that govern them. Someone persuaded of the value of democracy might just think that the states we currently have should be democratic ones. To value democracy, one might claim, just shows that one should have a democratic state: it does not show that people can choose to secede (George 1993: 512). (Yet another account of the implications of a commitment to democracy is explored in Section IV.) Endorsing the value of democracy thus does not uniquely select Philpott's preferred solution.[15]

Finally, even if we accept that, in principle, democracy requires allowing groups to choose the nature and borders of the polity to govern them, it is often highly impractical. The problem here is twofold: first, the collectivist version of the *intrinsic* argument presupposes one can identify a group who choose to be governed together. Groups, however, rarely have the clearly demarcated boundaries which are needed if we are to draw political borders around them. Sir Ivor Jenning's famous statement is entirely apposite: 'On the surface it seemed reasonable: let the people decide. It was in fact ridiculous because the people cannot decide until someone decides who are the people' (cited in

Buchheit 1978: 9).[16] Second, even if we could discern precisely who is to be a member of a group, groups are frequently not geographically concentrated in such a way that all the relevant members are in the same territory. Since, however, the most convenient way of arranging borders is, often if not always, to do it on territorial grounds (including all the people in territory X under the same form of governance), the fact that groups are intermingled with people from other groups causes serious problems.

Neither the *individualistic* nor the *collectivist* version of the *intrinsic* argument, therefore, represent plausible approaches to the questions which are the focus of this chapter.

# IV

Let us therefore consider an alternative perspective—what I have termed the *right-based* approach. This view has enjoyed support recently. Both David Held in *Democracy and the Global Order* (1995) and Andrew Linklater in *The Transformation of Political Community* (1998) outline this argument and maintain that it provides support for a reform of the current statist international system towards a system of cosmopolitan democracy which is more inclusive.[17]

Their argument makes two claims. First: they make the *moral* claim that

(1) persons have a democratic right to be able to affect the social–economic–political system in which they live and which determines what they are able to do.

In other words, political institutions should be so structured that people are able to exercise control over the social–economic–political processes that define the environment in which they live and determine the kind of choices available to them (Held 1995: 145–56; Linklater 1996*a*: 85–8; Linklater 1996*b*, esp. pp. 286, 294–6; Linklater 1998: 7, 91, 101).[18] Democratic political structures should, therefore, map onto economic systems and include all who are affected within their scope. In this way people have a right to hold accountable—through democratic bodies—the social and economic institutions that exert an impact on what they are able to do. This claim, it is important to note, is distinct from the moral tenet contained in the preceding argument: the claim is not that people have a right to decide where the borders fall. Rather, it is that democratic political structures should map onto systems of economic and political interdependence.

Held and Linklater then make an additional claim, namely the *empirical* claim that

(2) the social–economic–political system in which people live (and which determines what they are able to do) is, in part, global in nature.

Held provides the most extensive analysis of the ways in which this is the case and so I shall concentrate on his analysis. Held argues that there are five 'disjunctures' between the notion of self-governing states and the profoundly interdependent character of the modern world—five ways in which the factors which determine what people can do in life extend beyond states (1995: chs. 5 and 6). First, international law has developed and expanded considerably (examples including the UN Declaration of Human Rights, UN Convenants of Rights, and the European Convention for the Protection of Human Rights and Fundamental Freedoms) (1995: 101–7). Second, there has been an increase in the role of international institutions. International 'regimes', the International Monetary Fund, the World Bank, the UN, the European Union, and UNESCO exercise power and influence over people's lives (1995: 107–13). To this list one can add also the World Trade Organization which was born in 1995. Third, influence extends beyond states because of supra-national military institutions. Institutions like NATO and the Western European Union and Conference on Security and Cooperation in Europe clearly have a considerable impact on people's lives (1995: 113–20). The fourth 'disjuncture' is the way that cultures are increasingly influenced by other cultures, a process furthered by the increase in transnational media and communications networks (1995: 121–7). Finally, and perhaps most importantly, there is economic globalization (1995: 127–34) and in particular the increasingly global nature of financial markets and production (1995: 127). These five phenomena, so argues Held, undermine the conventional belief that democracy is served simply by having states which elect governments. Any purely statist framework is undemocratic because people's lives are profoundly influenced by powers that transcend their state's boundaries.

What framework should we adopt? Linklater recommends creating 'institutional frameworks which widen the boundaries of the dialogic community' (1998: 7). He favours more inclusive political systems and is sympathetic to international institutions like the European Union (1996a: 95–9; 1998: 7–8, 44–5, 193–204). More detailed proposals are given by Held who proposes the following long-run measures:

'1. Entrenchment of cosmopolitan democratic law: new Charter of Rights and Obligations locked into different domains of political, social, and economic power
2. Global Parliament (with limited revenue-raising capacity) connected to regions, nations and localities. Creation of a public issue Boundary Court
3. Separation of political and economic interests; public funding of deliberative assemblies and electoral processes
4. Interconnected global legal system, embracing elements of criminal and civil law. Establishment of an International Criminal Court
5. Establishment of the accountability of international and transnational economic agencies to parliaments and assemblies at regional and global levels
6. Permanent shift of a growing proportion of a nation state's coercive capability to regional and global institutions, with the ultimate aim of demilitarization and the transcendence of the war system (1995: 279)[19]'

How persuasive are Held and Linklater's arguments?[20] Three objections might be made. First, some have challenged the factual claim and dispute the claim that we live in a globalized world (Hirst and Thompson 1996). Nonetheless, Held and others have made a persuasive case for the existence of globalization and, whilst there may be disagreements about the extent to which this is unprecedented, it is hard to disagree with the claim that people's lives are profoundly affected by forces outside their own state and which they are unable to influence (Held et al. 1999).

A second objection targets the *moral* claim. This, recall, states that people are entitled to exercise control over the institutions and processes that affect them and what they can do. Whilst this does seem intuitively appealing it is vulnerable to a powerful objection. The problem is that there are many instances where people are profoundly affected by the actions of others but in which we do not think that the former have a democratic right to govern the behaviour of the latter. That A is affected by the decision of B does not entail that A may vote on whether and how B may act. This point has been famously made by Nozick in a quite different context. Consider four men who wish to marry a woman. It does not follow from the fact that their lives will be deeply and profoundly affected by her decision which if any to marry that they have a democratic right to determine her behaviour (1974: 268–70)! She has a right to make her own decision freely.[21]

Premise (1) can, however, be reformulated in such a way as to avoid this objection. Consider the following principle:

(1a) persons have a democratic right to be able to affect those aspects of the social–economic–political system in which they live that impact on *their ability to exercise their rights*.

This avoids the objection leveled against (1): we do not think that the four would-be suitors have any rights at stake. If the woman chooses not to marry them she has not infringed any of their rights. (1a) thus does not issue in the counter-intuitive outcomes that (1) does.[22] And (1a) does seem to capture a powerful intuition: part of the appeal of democratic institutions is that they enable people to exercise control over the institutions and practices that affect their use of their rights.[23] Furthermore, when conjoined with the *empirical* premise, the revised version of the *moral* premise does support Held and Linklater's ideal of cosmopolitan democracy. Given the extent of globalization, people's ability to exercise their rights is affected by forces beyond their own state. Their right to physical security is affected by global phenomena like international law, transnational political structures, and transnational security frameworks (Held's first, second, and third factors). Furthermore, their right to economic well-being is affected by supra-state political bodies (like the IMF and World Bank) and the global economy (Held's second and fifth factors). The second objection can thus be met.

The *right-based* argument is, however, incomplete. Before we accept its conclusions we need to know (a) whether the democratic principle represented by 'cosmopolitan democracy' conflicts with other moral values. For example, would democratic global institutions be illiberal and intolerant? Or, would cosmopolitan democracy prove incompatible with honouring other values like the self-determination of communities? In addition, (b) we need to know whether cosmopolitan global institutions would be stable. Would they enjoy the public support required for democratic institutions to flourish? Those who favour cosmopolitan institutions must provide answers to these serious questions. Since, however, they are standardly raised by statists and nationalists when defending their own preferred political frameworks, I shall postpone discussion of them until later sections. In the meantime, we can conclude that the *right-based* argument has some force but remains incomplete and in need of further normative argument.[24]

Before proceeding further, it is worth noting that the logical structure of the *right-based* argument takes the same form as the scope$_1$ and scope$_2$ claims defended earlier in Chapters 3 and 4. There, recall, it was argued that the rationales for, respectively, the 'civil and political rights' and the 'principles of distributive justice' that are normally thought to apply within the state show that there should be universal 'civil and political rights' and 'universal principles of distributive justice'. The *right-based* argument just considered conforms exactly to this pattern and it accordingly supports the following,

the scope$_3$ claim: the rationale for the democratic right to exercise control over the institutions and processes that affect persons' ability to exercise their rights entails (given globalization) that there should be a global democratic political framework.[25]

## V

Having analysed two cosmopolitan approaches to the issue of what political institutions are most appropriate, let us now consider the third—what I have termed the *instrumental* approach.[26] The latter, recall, makes the following *moral* claim

(1) Appropriate political institutions are those that best further cosmopolitan ideals (i.e. the protection of human rights, the securing of a healthy environment, and the observance of cosmopolitan ideals of distributive justice).

This seems an intuitively plausible approach: it would be peculiar when assessing which political institutions are most desirable not to take into account their impact on people's lives, and, in particular, their impact on people's ability to exercise their rights. Accordingly, many cosmopolitans adopt an instrumental approach.[27] Furthermore, many of these argue that a state-based order is not effective at securing cosmopolitan ideals and should therefore be supplemented with, or replaced by, global political institutions. In other words, they make the following *empirical* claim

(2) Supra-state political institutions are required to further cosmopolitan ideals.

Why should we accept this claim? Such institutions might be justified for the following reasons.

*Ensuring compliance.* The first consideration draws on the claim (defended in Chapter 4) that there are some global principles of distributive justice that require the redistribution of wealth from the affluent to the impoverished of this world. It then points out that under any purely state-based system, there is no global political authority to ensure that people will adhere to these principles. Compliance is optional and there are no sanctions or costs to secure adherence to norms of international justice. Those who are obligated are, under a statist system, given the choice of whether they will in fact perform their duties. Of course, it is possible that people will fulfil their cosmopolitan duties but there is no assurance that this will be the case and accordingly very little is transferred. We should consider in this context the domestic case. Proponents of distributive justice do not think that the wealthy should be given a choice as to whether to adhere to their duties. If we accept this, though, does not the same logic apply to global principles of justice?[28]

*Collective action problems.* A second consideration in support of supra-state political institutions is that, under a purely statist international system, states do not cooperate to produce public goods like a healthy environment (Falk 1995: 74–8; Goodin 1992*b*: 157–68; Pogge 1994*a*: 105) or the absence of war (Pogge 1994*a*: 103).[29] The argument is the same as that given in defence of the state: individuals left to their own devices will not cooperate to produce goods that everyone wants. The cosmopolitan argument simply applies this reasoning which we find valid in the domestic case to global 'public goods'.

*Institutional considerations.* A third reason in support of a cosmopolitan political framework is that supra-state political authorities can check the power of states and are more protective of liberty than a purely statist framework. This argument invokes the principle that liberty is best protected when power is not monopolized by one institution or group of people and hence maintains that a system which divides power between global authorities and states protects people's liberty better than a purely statist framework in which states can persecute their citizens at will.[30]

These, I believe, are powerful arguments for creating supra-state global institutions to ensure that states treat outsiders fairly (and comply with principles of international distributive justice) and also respect the rights of insiders (and not persecute individuals or minorities in their own state). They do not necessarily call for the abolition of states but they do provide support for the creation and empowerment of supra-state political authorities. There are, however, powerful challenges to this line of argument, and Sections VII–X will consider some objections to this *instrumental* defence of cosmopolitan political structures issued by those who favour a state-based order.

# VI

Prior to doing so, however, four points should be made about the nature of the political framework being defended.

1. First, we need to analyse the relationship between the *right-based* approach and the *instrumental* approach since both have some force (a point noted

by Pogge 1994*a*: 103–11). This raises the possibility that they issue in conflicting outcomes. Three points should be made here. First, where such a conflict does arise, it does not represent a problem with cosmopolitanism in particular but is a general problem that applies in any context when we are considering the legitimacy of democratic decision-making. It applies to domestic questions as much as to global ones. This, of course, does not help us to address the question of how the two ideals relate. Second, and more constructively, under normal circumstances it is highly likely that the *right-based* and *instrumental* approaches will converge on the same political framework. The two approaches would result in conflicting outcomes when the people whose rights are affected by an institution or set of institutions are less competent at making decisions that secure their rights and entitlements than a non-democratic body. In such a scenario, the *right-based* approach would recommend that people have a right to regulate the agents and institutions that affect the exercise of their rights and the *instrumental* approach, by contrast, would favour the non-democratic framework since that system would best secure people's rights. In practice, however, such a conflict is highly improbable because it is difficult to see why non-democratic bodies would have both the knowledge and the inclination to further economic, civil, and political rights (although cf. Caney forthcoming *b*). Third, the right-based approach and instrumental approach can be reconciled in an additional way. For it is widely recognized that people cannot genuinely exercise their democratic voting rights unless they possess a measure of economic resources. If this is true (and it is hard to dispute) then it has the implication that the rights-based ideal requires economic distribution (including meeting subsistence needs. This, in turn, entails that global political authorities be instituted which (instrumentally) ensure that this distribution takes place. The realization of the right-based approach thus requires the instrumental protection of economic rights.[31]

2. If we return now to the question 'What is the nature of the political framework being defended?', the analysis of Sections IV and V strongly suggests that the most plausible account is that given by Held and described in Section IV. This, recall, calls for democratically elected global and regional supra-state political authorities standing over and above 'states' (1995: 279). To put matters more concretely, the right-based considerations considered earlier provide support for the suggestions of those like Daniele Archibugi that there should be a directly elected second assembly at the United Nations (Archibugi 1995: 137–43). In this way, people can hold to account the powerful economic and social forces that determine their rights and fundamental interests. Rights-based considerations also point to the need for a reform of the membership and voting rules of the UN Security Council, which at the moment is governed by statist principles and which arbitrarily privileges powerful states which can prevent action through vetos (Archibugi 1995: 149–55).[32] In addition they highlight the need for influential institutions such as the World Bank and the International

Monetary Fund to be far more accountable than they currently are.[33] They also make a case for democratizing the World Trade Organization and ensuring that its decisions are accountable either to directly elected individuals (McGrew 1999: 197–216) or to a democratic second assembly of the United Nations and not, as is currently the case, the representatives of states.[34] These kinds of institutional reforms would enable people to hold to account the social and economic institutions that determine their use of their rights: they can, therefore, be defended on right-based grounds.[35]

Furthermore, as was also argued above, there is good reason to think that such a democratic framework—complemented by the other proposals Held favours (a strengthened system of international law and international judicial system) (1995: 279)—would also be the most effective way of protecting people's civil, political, and economic rights, enabling people to defend their rights. Effective and accountable international institutions are needed to implement cosmopolitan principles of justice. Again, to focus on specific proposals, the instrumental considerations adduced above would generate support for a number of proposals. First, there is a strong instrumental case for the creation of a new economic institution with an overview for all economic matters that can coordinate the IMF, WTO, and the World Bank in the pursuit of global norms of distributive justice. Such an institution is needed to further compliance and to overcome collective action problems (reasons 1 and 2 above). Given this one might endorse the proposal made in the report by the Commission for Global Governance for a global 'Economic Security Council' (1995: 153–62). Second, one might argue on instrumental grounds that there should be a permanent UN volunteer force—a suggestion made by two previous Under-Secretaries-General at the United Nations, namely Brian Urquhart and James Jonah (Franck 1997: 315) and also by the Commission on Global Governance (1995: 110–12). This would have two advantages over the current ways of dealing with severe human rights abuses in other countries. First, it would enable swift action rather than the delayed responses that currently occur; and, second, a volunteer force would be capable of more coherent and organized action than the alternative approach, which is to assemble a multi-national force that has never worked together before and which lacks a well thought-out chain of command. Such functional considerations (both concerning collective action problems) thus support a UN volunteer force. Third, as several note, we have strong instrumental reasons for strengthening the importance and role of the International Court of Justice. At present its jurisdiction is not mandatory and it deals only with inter-state disputes. However, as Archibugi points out, there is a case for making its jurisdiction compulsory and for broadening its remit to uphold and protect individual human rights (1995: 143–9; cf. also Franck 1997: 316–47). Finally, there is, as Kevin Jackson argues, a compelling case for a 'cosmopolitan court for transnational corporate wrongdoing' to arbitrate on issues concerning corporate wrongdoing. Many countries are often too poor to take on the corporations that violate acceptable norms of economic conduct and they cannot ensure compliance.

Furthermore, many economic enterprises straddle many different jurisdictions and there is need therefore for a Court with universal jurisdiction to take an overarching view (Jackson 1998). In short: cosmopolitan political institutions are supported on both *right-based* and *instrumental* grounds.

3. Before proceeding further it may be useful to relate the institutional framework sketched above to the conceptual analysis of Section I and in doing so to note how the proposed political order departs from the concept of (sovereign) statehood. It is in particular worth noting that the framework being defended is not a global state. It rejects not simply a global system of states but also the utility of relying on sovereign statehood itself. Rather what is being envisioned is a political order in which the units may lack the properties of sovereign statehood like *comprehensiveness* and *supremacy*.[36] Let us examine the first two properties. Consider, first, comprehensiveness: both instrumental and right-based cosmopolitan arguments support institutions that may not be *comprehensive*. Take, for example, the claim that people have a democratic right to exercise control over the factors that affect their rights. Some of these factors are likely to be global in nature (say, the global economy impacting on their right to subsistence) whereas other factors (say, people in their vicinity affecting their right not to be assaulted) are more local. Given this, there is a case for different institutions operating at different levels and addressing different policy issues. Consider also an instrumental perspective on comprehensiveness. Whereas, some matters like cultural issues are best dealt with by local—i.e. 'sub-state'—authorities, others which cover a wider range of issues (like protecting the environment or administering cosmopolitan principles of fair trade) may be more effectively dealt with by 'supra-state' authorities (O'Neill 1994: 72; 2000: 172, 179).

If we turn now from *comprehensiveness* to *supremacy* it follows, given the earlier reasoning, that since it is in practice impossible to keep policy areas utterly separate, a system in which no institution has comprehensiveness also lacks supremacy. There may be no one political institution that has final authority. Supra-state, regional, state-level, and sub-state levels would have no privileged status over each other. This is often said to be a problem but, from an instrumental cosmopolitan perspective, it is an advantage since it prevents the centralization of coercive power. It forces people and different institutions to negotiate and cooperate with each other.

In these ways, then, it is important to record that what is being envisioned is not simply a move from a society of states to a world state. Rather, by proposing a framework in which some of the units may lack *supremacy* and *comprehensiveness*, what is envisioned is a move away from sovereign statehood.

4. One further point should be made about the case for global political institutions. The arguments given above favour one specific supra-state political order (or variants on it). They do not entail that *any* supra-state political arrangement is superior to *any* statist framework. The claim is not that non-statist frameworks as a type are superior to each and every token from the statist

type. It is, thus, unhelpful to ask whether a system of states is better than a system including global political institutions. What is being defended is only a specific version of the latter (a token or number of tokens) not the type itself. It is a corollary of this that some statist frameworks may be better (on instrumental and intrinsic considerations) than some supra-state frameworks (say, a global tyranny). The claim, then, is that the global schema outlined above is better than the current system of states (and also any likely reformulation of that system).

## VII

Having considered three types of cosmopolitan approach, I now want to consider the challenges to the cosmopolitan political framework defended above. Many have deep misgivings about cosmopolitan political institutions and argue the merits of a state-based world order. Realists, for example, have been highly critical of global institutions, as have proponents of a 'society of states' like Bull (1977) and Frost (1996). Of course, realists and 'society of states' theorists do disagree extensively on many issues: nonetheless they do share some common concerns about legal/institutional cosmopolitanism. Sections VIII, IX, X, and XI will explore four defences of a statist international order (one of them given by both statist traditions whereas the other three are more likely to come only from a 'society of states' approach). All four, we should record, are *instrumental* arguments. That is, they maintain that a state-centric framework results in better outcomes than global political institutions. The arguments given can be divided into four categories: (a) a liberty-based argument to the effect that global political institutions would prove to be tyrannical; (b) arguments to the effect that the advantages claimed for global political institutions can be provided by states; (c) arguments to the effect that one can attain cosmopolitan objectives without global institutions by reforming the internal structure of states; and (d) Frost's Hegelian argument for 'a society of states'.

Let us start with the liberty-based argument. This is, perhaps, the most frequently adduced argument against global political institutions. Its charge is simply that global political institutions—most notably a world government—involve a centralization of power and this is inimical to freedom.[37] Freedom requires the fragmentation of power and a system of checks and balances (which is provided by a society of states), not the untrammeled power afforded by a world government (Nardin 1983: 238–9). An additional consideration sometimes adduced is that under a system of states people may always emigrate if they dislike their current political authority but under a world state this source of escape is not available (barring space travel!) (Boxill 1987: 160–6; Bull 1977: 253–4; Walzer 1980: 228). Similar concerns are expressed by realists like Danilo Zolo who, in his critique of cosmopolitanism, charges that transnational institutions tend to be partial to the interests of major powers. Global government, he writes, 'would end in the creation of an absolutely "sovereign" and uncontrollable institution and would consequently make both the international protection of rights and the search for peace even more precarious' (1997: 121). It would result in 'a hierarchical institutional model which superimposes the hegemonic tactics and aspirations of a narrow elite of superpowers on the sovereignty of all other countries' (1995: 164).[38]

This critique of global political institutions is, however, unpersuasive. First, it is too undiscriminating. It has force against a world state in which all power is concentrated in one global executive. But, as we have seen above, there are many other options available to the cosmopolitan and most cosmopolitans have explicitly rejected the ideal of global government (Falk 1995: 6–8; Pogge 1988: 284–304).[39] Furthermore, those who endorse supra-state political institutions can accept the principle (on which the critique rests) that what causes oppression is the concentration of power. They can argue, however, that this does not require the states system. There are, as O'Neill points out, other ways of dividing power (Jones 1999: 229; O'Neill 1994: 71–2).[40] The liberty-based argument is, therefore, unpersuasive as a critique of cosmopolitan proposals to wrest power from states and allocate them to supra-state bodies for such proposals are built on the principle of dividing power to render political institutions accountable. As we have seen in the preceding section, one of the virtues of creating supra-state authorities is precisely that they represent a system of checks and balances.

A second, and related, flaw in the liberty argument for a purely statist order is that it ignores the ways in which the states system can, and frequently does, systematically restrict individual liberty. The central defect—the absolute concentration of power—is one that can be found in a statist framework precisely because the latter grants to states untrammeled power to persecute their peoples. Unlike a multi-level system of cosmopolitan governance, the rights and interests of a people are entirely dependent on the conduct of their state.

Finally, it is important to address the claim that a states system, unlike a world state (or system of cosmopolitan governance), provides people with a right to emigrate. Two points are worth making here: first, there is no reason why a multi-level system of governance should lack the right to emigrate. It simply supplements states with supra-state bodies, coordinating action and ensuring that people receive their entitlements and that their rights are secured. Second, it is not true that the states system guarantees people a right to emigrate. Frequently they are unable to because their state prevents it; or where it allows it, they are too poor to move.

For these three reasons, then, the liberty-based argument does not justify a purely statist framework. In addition, it does not undermine the case for the multi-level cosmopolitan political institutions defended earlier in Sections IV, V, and VI.

## VIII

Realists and 'society of states' theorists do, however, give other arguments against global political institutions and in defence of a framework of states. This section discusses a second type of argument mounted: namely the contention that a statist framework can provide the alleged advantages of a cosmopolitan political order. There is therefore no need to abolish the current system. This argument is developed at greatest length by Hedley Bull in *The Anarchical Society*. He considers three important objectives—achieving stability, promoting economic justice, and protecting the environment—and argues in each case that the states system represents the optimal way of attaining these objectives (1977: 283–95). His arguments thus represent a direct challenge to the *instrumental* arguments presented in Section V.

Bull adopts several strategies. First, he argues that many of the problems that afflict global politics have their roots in factors other than the existence of states. Hence, reforming the state-order or abolishing it do not address the real problems. He makes this point, for example, about economic justice, arguing that 'economic and social injustice in human society have deeper causes than the existence of the states system, and these causes would be operative also in any alternative universal political order' (1977: 291). He makes the same point about protecting the environment (1977: 293–4).

This, however, does not undermine the case for cosmopolitan political structures. It may be true (and seems quite plausible) that some problems are affected, perhaps greatly, by factors other than whether there are states or not. But this does not establish that the international political system has no impact on economic justice, say, or the protection of the environment. That X (the states system) is not the sole cause of the deterioration of the environment or the lack of global justice does not mean that it has no causal impact. And once we recognize that, it is open to ask which political structures have the most desirable effects (and thus, whether cosmopolitan political structures are needed to supplement or replace states). Bull's point about the non-political causes of global problems, thus, gives us no reason to ignore political causes. Accordingly it gives us no reason to prefer a statist order and reject cosmopolitan political frameworks. Furthermore, it is hard to see why political factors do not play a large role in the degree to which the environment is protected and in the extent of global injustice. The collective action problems involved in getting states to cooperate to protect the environment, for example, are surely one important reason why environmental protection is not attained. Bull's first strategy is, therefore, unpersuasive.

A second strategy Bull adopts in his attempt to establish that a state-based order is as good, if not better, at securing important goals like stability, justice, and environmental protection is to claim that in a statist order, the units (states) may cooperate to provide the goods in question. Cosmopolitan political structures are therefore not needed because states on their own are able to cooperate to bring about order (1977: 287–8), justice (1977: 292), and a healthy environment (1977: 294–5). Someone might seek to supplement Bull's argument by drawing on 'regime theory' where the latter maintains that states can and do develop patterns of cooperation (Krasner 1983*b*; Ritterberger 1993).[41]

The appropriate rejoinder to this argument is that Bull's premise is true: it is possible that states will cooperate to achieve goals cosmopolitans invoke. But this does not undermine the case for global political institutions for three reasons. First, we should recognize, as we do at the domestic level, that making compliance optional rarely results in compliance. From an *instrumental* point of view, it is insufficient to claim in defence of a political framework that it is *possible* that individuals under it might contribute to certain important objectives: one needs to know rather whether those objectives are more likely to be attained under this system rather than under an alternative. Second, as has been pointed out before, states may simply not want to secure these cosmopolitan goals so even if there is cooperation it may not be cooperation that furthers justice. Indeed, we should not simply assume that cooperation is always a good: sometimes states cooperate in unjust selfish projects which are of benefit to themselves and their partners and detrimental to the rights of others.[42] Third, even if they did want to secure cosmopolitan goals, they face enormous problems posed by transaction costs, assurance dilemmas, and prisoner's dilemmas. Bull's point thus provides little support for preferring his society of states to a cosmopolitan order and it is disingenuous to point out the *possibility* of something happening under a system without examining its *probability* given the underlying pressures and incentive structures. We should look at what outcomes the states system is inclined to produce rather than what it might produce if states happened to adopt one course of action.[43]

Bull's *instrumental* considerations, thus, give us no reason to adopt a purely statist framework or to reject cosmopolitan political institutions.

# IX

Having analysed two statist arguments, let us now examine a third. This third argument, like the preceding argument, maintains that global political institutions are unnecessary. The reasons it gives for this are, however, distinct from the preceding argument for, unlike the latter, it argues thus: the best way to ensure that people receive their just entitlements is to focus on the internal structure of states. This line of argument provides what one might, following Waltz, term a 'second image' argument (1959). That is, the solution lies not with human nature (first image) or the international system (third image) but with the nature of the units. If we reform states we can achieve cosmopolitan goals.

To make this claim less abstract consider three lines of reasoning all of which fit under this heading. First, as has been noted in Chapter 2, Sen has argued that democratic institutions prevent the occurrence of famine (1999*a*: 90–3; 1999*b*: 4–5, 10–11, 51–3, 147–54, 157–8, 178–88). Drawing on this, someone might argue that there is no need for global institutions to meet the cosmopolitan goal of universal access to subsistence: rather a system of states, each of which is democratic, would be sufficient. The internal constitution of states, thus, furthers the attainment of the cosmopolitan goals. A second line of reasoning similarly invokes the ideal of democracy. This time the claim is that the best way to ensure peace—surely an ideal all cosmopolitans value—is to have a world order of democratic states. This claim is associated with Kant's essay on 'Perpetual Peace' (1989 [1795]). An important contemporary version of this argument has been defended by Michael Doyle. He has provided a systematic empirical discussion of this claim and concurs that democracies do not go to war with each other, although they do war against non-democratic states.[44] Accordingly, a defender of a statist order might draw on this claim to maintain that cosmopolitan values do not require cosmopolitan institutions but can be yielded by a world populated by democratic states. For a third related strategy one might consider an argument associated with Jeremy Bentham. In his 'A Plan For An Universal and Perpetual Peace' (1962 [1786–9]), Bentham argued that in their foreign policy states should adopt a principle of publicity. His thought is that if they do so, peace is much more likely to obtain and the open glare of publicity discourages unfair action. If states are forced to be transparent they have to justify their action and it is accordingly more difficult (although not impossible) to act in a blatantly unjust fashion.[45] Thus pulling these together, someone might maintain that the best solution to solve the ills of the world is to work within a system of states and that a world of democratic states that respected the principle of publicity would ensure peace, subsistence for all, and non-aggression.[46]

How forceful is this argument? The first point we should note is that the three versions of the 'second image' argument outlined above do not, in themselves, give one a reason to reject cosmopolitan political institutions for a proponent of the latter can integrate their insights and argue that what we should have is democratic transparent global institutions. If democracy and publicity engender fair outcomes, then an advocate of strengthened international institutions can simply accommodate these points by arguing that since this is so then 'democratic' supra-state institutions whose decision-making procedures are transparent and open to public scrutiny would also ensure peace and subsistence. The 'second image' argument, *on its own*, does not therefore show that global institutions are wrong: if correct, it shows just that they are unnecessary.

This does not, however, show that the 'second image' argument can be disregarded. It can be used in a number of ways. First, someone might argue that it is easier to ensure that states are democratic and transparent than it would be to ensure that there are transparent democratic international institutions. Hence, given that transparent democratic states serve cosmopolitan ideals and given that it is more difficult to set up transparent democratic global institutions, we have prima facie reason to seek to foster the former. The cosmopolitan institutions described earlier are thus *less desirable*. Second, someone might even argue that transparent democratic international institutions are not possible (cf. Section XIII of this chapter) or have undesirable side-effects and hence should be rejected (cf. Section VII of this chapter) but that this is not as much of a problem as might be thought since transparent democratic states would serve cosmopolitan ideals as much as is required. Thus while the 'second image' argument on its own does not show that there is anything wrong with strengthened international institutions it can, when supplemented with other claims, form part of a critique of such institutions.

With this in mind, let us consider the 'second image' argument. How persuasive is it? This line of reasoning does have some force. For instance, the claim that democracy prevents famine has been well-substantiated by Sen; and Doyle's analysis of the claim that democracies do not war with each other is comprehensive and meticulous. Nonetheless, the above 'second image' argument is unpersuasive and suffers from three problems. First, its aims (such as peace and the avoidance of famine) are unduly modest from a cosmopolitan point of view for, as we saw in Chapter 4, global distributive justice requires more than that people have access to food. A system of democratic states is quite compatible with massive global inequalities (including inequalities of opportunity) and is consistent with a world in which some are consigned to lives of gruelling poverty.

Second, a wholly 'second image' approach is theoretically implausible. Democratic states may show *some* consideration for foreigners but it is difficult to accept that this statist institutional structure is the most likely to deliver cosmopolitan outcomes. Consider the incentives facing democratically elected officials in a world of states. Their incentive is to win elections and to do so to cater for the wishes and beliefs of their own citizens. They will therefore serve cosmopolitan ideals only if their citizens happen to have strong cosmopolitan beliefs. Since foreigners do not have an input into the decision-making process, we can have little confidence that the decisions will regularly and systematically respect their rights. The most likely institutional structure to do that would be one in which all those whose rights are affected have a vote in the decision-making process and, as we have seen earlier, that requires democratic supra-state institutions. A system of democratic states is, thus, not the most effective institutional system if we are to further cosmopolitan goals. This point about the theoretical limitations of the 'second image' arguments is further borne out if we consider the foreign policy record of transparent democratic states. None of these states gives anything like 0.7 per cent of its GNP on overseas aid (the UN target). Moreover, many liberal democracies have highly restrictive immigration laws, even though this would be one way of assisting disadvantaged foreigners. These results should not surprise us if we consider the existing electoral incentives facing politicians and they suggest that extending the suffrage is the most appropriate institutional set-up for enabling persons to protect their entitlements.

A third problem with the argument is that in prescribing a system of democratic states it ignores the effects of the international order on the ability of states to be democratic. As Pogge points out, accounts of global poverty that explain it in terms of 'domestic' factors such as whether a state is democratic or not are radically incomplete for they overlook the international factors influencing whether or not a state is democratic (2001*d*: throughout but esp. pp. 330–8, 341–3).[47] One illustration of this point concerns corruption. Pogge points out that where states lack economic wealth they are vulnerable to corruption from external bodies. Democratic institutions cannot persist and function effectively because officials and politicians can be bribed by foreign companies and politicians (2001*d*: 333–4). Whether a state functions democratically or not thus depends on international factors. Pogge illustrates his case further by drawing attention to what he terms the 'international borrowing privilege' (2001*d*: 334–5) and the 'international resource privilege' (2001*d*: 335–7). The former refers to the international practice according to which a state is entitled to take out a loan, whether or not it is democratic, and successor governments can be required to pay it back. The latter refers to the practice whereby a state is regarded by other states and by foreign companies as owning all the territory in its jurisdiction and thus having the right to sell it off for the profit of the politicians. Both practices—international practices—profoundly affect the ability of a state to be democratic and are examples of how the 'international' structures the 'domestic' (2001*d*: 337–8).[48]

This undermines the second image argument for the latter presuppose *either* that global factors do not affect domestic ones *or* that a fair global order exists. The former is, as we have seen, false.[49] Moreover, the latter cannot be presupposed because this state of affairs (a just world order) is what the second image proposals are designed to achieve: they cannot then simply assume it.

The three second order considerations (Sen's claim about famines, Doyle's about war, and Bentham's about publicity) are thus not sufficient to show us that cosmopolitan ideals can be attained without global institutions. Internally democratic states are not enough.[50]

# X

Having considered three unsuccessful defences of a state system and critiques of the proposal to create global political institutions, let us now consider a fourth argument—one put forward by Mervyn Frost in *Ethics in International Relations*. Frost provides an interesting and sophisticated argument for the 'society of states' which appeals to Hegel's political philosophy (Frost 1996, esp. ch. 5). Like the two preceding arguments, Frost's argument is *instrumental* in the sense that I am using that term: it maintains that the value of political institutions is a function of the effect they have on humans. His central claim is that individuals need to be members of a state in a society of states if they are to flourish: 'sovereign states and the system of sovereign states are necessary to the flourishing of individuality' (1996: 155). Why should we accept this claim? Frost answers this by first defending the importance of the state and then the importance of the state being a member of the 'society of states'.

Why should we value the state? Frost's argument starts with an analysis of other institutions like the 'family' and 'civil society' and, like Hegel, he argues that whilst they serve important functions they both have their limitations. (See (1996: 143–5) for the analysis of the family and (1996: 145–7) for the analysis of civil society.) The state is needed to overcome an atomized society and to provide political unity and recognition. Frost writes that, without the state, people 'feel alienated' (1996: 148). Membership of a state provides an acknowledgement of one's status by others and a reconciliation with the political system and laws. It has value because of its contribution to well-being (1996: 147–50).

The next step in the argument is Frost's emphasis on the state's membership of a 'society of sovereign states' (1996: 150). Why does this matter? Frost's argument is that members of a state derive benefit from their membership only if their state is accorded respect by other states. Persons cannot flourish if their state is denied political recognition by other states (1996: 150–8). The 'society of states' therefore has value because and to the extent that it contributes to well-being.

How persuasive is this defence of the 'society of states'? And does it undermine the case for global political institutions? I think that defenders of global political institutions can respond to Frost's argument. One can agree with Frost that the family and civil society are insufficient. Human beings, one can agree, require membership of a political regime. What is questionable is whether this good—the good of membership in autonomous political units—requires sovereign states. What matters from a Hegelian point of view is being reconciled with a political unit and being recognized by other members of that unit. This, however, does not require that the political unit be a territorial unit (an essential feature of a state). Nor does it require that the political regime in question have unlimited authority (another essential feature of a state). Two central features of the state—territoriality and sovereignty—are, therefore, not required for this good. Surely what is needed is membership of political units with considerable autonomy which are recognized by other units to have worth and autonomy. And such institutions are quite compatible with the cosmopolitan framework defended earlier (i.e. one in which supra-state political institutions regulate and monitor the conduct of political communities). This framework, to recall, simply denies states absolute power and calls for supra-state bodies to regulate their conduct and promote compliance with global norms.[51] In short, then: Frost identifies an important value but it is one that can be accommodated by a cosmopolitan political order. A society of sovereign states is not required.

# XI

The preceding sections have examined four types of statist critique of global institutions. This section considers another perspective which is also critical of such global institutions but which, unlike the preceding four arguments, stresses the importance of what is often referred to as global civil society (where this includes NGOs, social movements, and other non-state actors). The claim is that non-political bodies (like Amnesty, Oxfam, CAFOD, Greenpeace, and CND) should raise issues and seek to cajole states, citizens, and economic enterprises to act on cosmopolitan grounds. According to this approach, it is important that people deliberate with people from other countries to challenge and contest the prevailing ideologies, like global capitalism, that dominate the world. It rejects global institutions and calls instead for a global civil society (Dryzek 2000: 115–39). Two points can be made in defence of this approach. First, on a theoretical level, social movements can exercise influence over existing international institutions such as the World Bank. As some have noted, they can supply relevant information and assist in the implementation of policies. They can also threaten to thwart policies unless some concessions are made. And they can pressurize states not to be corrupt (O'Brien et al. 2000: 19). For all these reasons they can exercise some leverage over existing international institutions. Second, on an empirical level, advocates of the role of civil society can point out that non-state actors have had some success. One notable example is their ability to prevent the enactment of the OECD's Plans for Multilateral Agreement on Investment (Sklair 2002: 287–91).[52] Global civil society, it might thus be argued, is an effective mechanism for attaining cosmopolitan goals.

These considerations, however, do not show that democratic global institutions are unnecessary. Following the arguments given in Sections IV and V, it is clear that civil society alone is not enough. First, on instrumental grounds, we have seen that a statist order possesses certain deep structural features that frustrate cosmopolitan ideals. In addition to this, the relative power of the existing social movements will reflect the prevailing (unjust) distribution of wealth and resources. As the report of the Commission on Global Governance notes, '[f]ewer than 15 per cent of NGOs registered with the UN Economic and Social Council (ECOSOC) are from developing countries' (1995: 153). Similarly, a recent United Nations Development Programme Report found that '[o]f the 738 NGOs accredited to the WTO's 1999 ministerial conference in Seattle Washington, 87% were from industrial countries' (UNDP 2002: 8). The most disadvantaged groups will then be least able to make their voice heard. Third, the case for an active civil society gives us no reason to abandon the right-based case for supra-state political institutions for it cannot ensure that all are able to exercise control over the institutions that impact on their rights. Fourth, an active civil society would surely require the political frameworks defended earlier since these facilitate discussion, argument, and debate.

The claim that cosmopolitan political institutions are unnecessary because global civil society is sufficient is, therefore, implausible. The arguments in the previous paragraph should not, however, lead us to overlook the importance of doing more than calling for new supra-state institutions. Institutions on their own are not guaranteed to produce benign policies and what is needed are certain character traits and a certain culture as well. This is brought out by David Campbell who commends a certain ethos—what he terms 'the ethos of democracy' (1998: 196)—by which he means a culture in which people call into question established identities, entrenched understandings about the way things ought to be, and ways of framing questions about what we ought to do and who 'we' are (1998: 195–208, 219). Campbell does not, however, reject the cosmopolitan institutional schemes proposed by writers like Held. Indeed he expresses some sympathy with them but he emphasizes that they alone are insufficient (1998: 194–5, 202).[53] Without a democratic culture, cosmopolitan institutional frameworks are likely to stagnate and are less likely to be able to challenge and contest prevalent attitudes (towards, among other issues, duties to those overseas). Global political institutions should thus be complemented with, rather than replaced by, a transnational democratic culture.

In conclusion, then, the strong claim that global institutions are *unnecessary* because a global civil society is sufficient is implausible.[54] However, the weak claim that global political institutions are *insufficient* and that there should be a renovated civil society to complement new political institutions is much more credible. According to this weaker version cosmopolitans should both affirm new political institutions and also call for action from non-political actors.

# XII

Having analysed cosmopolitan, realist, and 'society of states' perspectives on which political structures and institutions are most appropriate, the remainder of this chapter examines nationalist perspectives on these issues. Before considering the arguments they adduce, we should present the ideal they defend, namely that of national self-determination.

National self-determination can be understood in a strong or a weak sense. In the strong sense, it insists that a nation be given statehood, whereas in the weak sense it requires only that a nation be given some form of self-government. Weak national self-determination is thus compatible with global political institutions or states in which nations are granted some political autonomy. It can, for example, take the form of confederations, federations, consociational democracies, unitary states with sub-state autonomy (that is, regional parliaments, local governments, and so on), or supra-state institutions that grant nations some role (like a Europe of the regions) (Buchanan 1991: 49–50; Buchanan 1993: 587–9; MacCormick 1996: 34–52; Tamir 1991: 586–90; Tamir 1993: 9, 74–5, 142–67). Many who defend national self-determination advocate giving nations statehood but some are explicit that, if this is not possible, nations should be given self-government in this weak form (Barry 1987: 352–3).

Why, however, should national communities have any sort of political authority? Why should political borders map onto nations? Nationalists have given (at least) four answers to this question: what might be termed the 'distributive justice' argument, the 'trust' argument, the 'Kantian' argument, and the 'well-being' argument. I shall therefore examine each of these in turn.

The first defence argues that national self-determination is desirable because it best furthers ideals of distributive justice. This argument is given by Miller in *On Nationality*. As we saw in Chapter 4, Section X, he maintains that, as a matter of justice, members of nations have special obligations to fellow-nationals. He then argues that we can best fulfil our obligations to fellow nationals if nations are granted political power. It is, he argues, much more difficult for members of a nation to fulfil their national obligations unless nations have political power to compel people to comply (1995: 83–5, 98).[55]

This argument suffers from a number of problems. First, as has been argued earlier, it is questionable whether people have special duties to fellow nationals and, even if they do, it is implausible to claim that these are obligations of distributive justice (Chapter 4, Section X; Caney 1996a, 1999a).

Second, even if there are obligations of distributive justice to fellow nationals, Miller's argument succeeds only if we assume that these obligations are enforceable. The argument, as it stands, is therefore incomplete. Moreover, we do not think that friends should be compelled to care for their friends. Nor do we think that someone should be forced to put the interests of his sister or brother above those of complete strangers. Given this, why should we accept Miller's contention that a political system should be created to compel us to devote more of our money to fellow nationals than to foreigners? If these other special obligations are non-enforceable then why should national obligations be enforceable?[56]

Finally, even if we have special obligations (of distributive justice) to fellow-nationals *and* those obligations are prima facie enforceable, the argument still does not entail its conclusion. Before we accept the latter we must also consider if there are other prima facie enforceable obligations and if national self-determination hinders the enforcement of those obligations. As we have seen earlier, we have obligations to the impoverished on this earth (Chapter 4, Sections II–VI). Granting power to nations and thereby compelling people to distribute resources to fellow nationals is, however, likely to make it more difficult to ensure that people comply with these cosmopolitan duties.

# XIII

Miller gives a second defence of national self-determination, arguing that states need nations if they are to perform some important roles because nations provide 'trust' (1995: 90–8). In particular, Miller argues that 'the provision of public goods such as a clean and healthy environment' requires a society in which people are willing to cooperate with others (1995: 91). Since one very strong adhesive is a sense of nationality, political units (like states) will be able to perform their roles when the people are united by national ties. In addition, he argues that democratic states require a commitment to the common good and a willingness on the part of all to cooperate with others and to treat others with respect. Such attitudes, again, are provided by nations (1995: 96–8).[57] Thus, members of political systems must trust one another and this trust is supplied by nations. This conclusion has two implications: the positive implication is that nations should be granted self-determination, and the negative implication is that supra-state institutions of the sort discussed earlier will be unfeasible.[58]

Let us discuss the positive claim first. The trust-based defence of national self-determination runs into two problems. First, it is questionable whether either democratic institutions or the overcoming of collective action problems require nationality. Miller is right to emphasize the significance of 'trust' in overcoming collective action problems but we have no reason to accept his assumption that nationality is the only or best form of trust. Collective action problems can be overcome at a sub-national level by giving regions some political autonomy. As Robert Putnam has pointed out in his study of Italian democracy, citizens in the northern regions have been able to draw on long-standing civic traditions to cooperate to provide public goods (1993, esp. ch. 6). It is also possible that sufficient trust can exist between citizens in multinational political regimes. The important point is that a common nationality is not the only source of cohesion (Mason 1999: 261–86; 2000: ch. 5, esp. pp. 116, 118–19, 127–42). Can citizenship not also induce a sense of reciprocity?

Secondly, overcoming some collective action problems may well exacerbate the difficulties of overcoming other collective action problems. Some of the most pressing collective action problems arise with global problems such as environmental pollution. Now giving nations statehood or enhanced political autonomy will clearly produce more political players (either as states or sub-state bodies) and the more actors there are the more difficult it will be to secure international agreement. Consequently, allowing nations rights of self-government would worsen the prospects of solving some collective action problems.

Let us now consider the negative claim—namely the thesis that bodies larger than nations will be unable to operate successfully because they cannot draw on the requisite political culture and reserves of trust. If true, this constitutes a serious and powerful criticism of the types of political institutions favoured by Held, Linklater, and Pogge. However, we have good reason to question the notion of human nature assumed by the trust argument. The latter is predicated on a static unvarying concept of human nature. Consequently, it ignores the ways in which people's inclinations are influenced by their social environment and the prevailing norms and political and social institutions.[59] They are, that is, not fixed in stone and inflexible but are, at least in part, endogenous. To think that people can only trust fellow nationals is then to mistake a feature of the contemporary world as an unchanging feature of the world for all time. A salutary and fascinating illustration of this point is Eugen Weber's celebrated work *Peasants into Frenchmen* (1977) which chronicles how in the early twentieth century, many French men and women spoke languages other than French as their first language, regarded anyone from outside their village as complete foreigners, and did not in anyway regard themselves as French. Accordingly, it would be unwarranted to assume that people's current motivations are fixed and unchanging. To this we should also note that persons throughout the world are in any case already bound by an extensive range of global norms—such as those established by the WTO—and these institutional frameworks are complied with.

The 'trust' argument thus fails to establish either (a) the positive point that states require nations and hence that we should map states onto national communities or (b) the negative point that transnational political institutions (like the European Union or global institutions) cannot flourish because they lack the requisite civic culture.[60]

Before proceeding further it is worth considering a variation on the negative argument propounded by Kymlicka. Kymlicka argues against the proposals for democratized supra-state institutions on the grounds that democratic institutions should, in the main, take place within national communities because democratic deliberation and communication can take place only when people speak the same language (2001*a*: 213–15; 2001*b*: 226–7; 2001*c*: 324–6). Kymlicka's argument is, however, overstated. Whilst it may be ideal for all members of a democratic system to speak the same language, it is not essential. What *is* necessary is that members of the same political system can understand the point of view of others but this does not presuppose that they speak the same language. They can find out the views of their fellow citizens through translation on the radio, television, Internet, and so on. One can understand others when their views and arguments are relayed via television and newspapers in one's own tongue. Furthermore, such limitations that exist because of the lack of a common language are surely worth accepting given the overwhelming need for supra-state institutions.

# XIV

How else might we justify national self-determination. Neil MacCormick has advanced a 'Kantian' argument for national self-determination that is grounded in Kant's principle of respect for persons. MacCormick advances the following three claims:

(1) Persons should be treated with respect.
(2) Respect for persons entails respecting integral features of their personality, such as their membership of a nation.
(3) Respect for a person's membership of a nation requires that their nation be given some political autonomy.[61]

He is, we should note here, keen to emphasize that his arguments 'certainly do not support the facile assumption that sovereign statehood is the only acceptable status fitted to the essence of nationhood' (1982: 264).

How persuasive is this argument? (1) is relatively uncontroversial but both (2) and (3) are questionable. Some critics challenge (3) and question whether respect for a person's nationality requires that this person's nation be given political power (Graham 1986: 138–9; A. Vincent 1997: 290). As David George argues, '[r]espect for nations (as for families and religious communities) out of respect for persons who are their members minimally requires that the state protect them from attacks as it protects the persons of their individual members' (1994: 76) but it does not require anything more than this like giving families or nations or religious communities political power. George assumes that MacCormick is defending the creation of nation-states (a position MacCormick explicitly rejects) and directs his criticism against that. But his criticism can be directed against weak as well as strong national self-determination. Why should respecting someone's cultural identity imply granting that culture political power? This is an important challenge and it is one that MacCormick does not address. It can, however, be met and a reply to this objection will be outlined in Section XV.

Prior to this, we should record that even if the first objection is met, MacCormick's argument faces other problems. In particular, it is unclear why one should respect the features of a person's character by which he or she defines themselves. What if a person's anti-semitism or chauvinism is an integral part of who they are? To claim here that this feature of their personality should be respected is, of course, utterly unacceptable. So, to establish that one should respect someone's nationality, one must show that nationality is not obnoxious in the same way that racism and sexism are (George 1994: 76–7; Graham 1986: 139–40; A. Vincent 1997: 290). Indeed surely one needs to show not just that nations are not obnoxious: one must establish that nations are worthy of respect.

# XV

The three nationalist arguments considered so far have proved unsuccessful at showing that nations should be granted political power. Let us therefore consider a fourth argument—namely what I have termed the 'well-being' argument—an argument which I think is more persuasive than the preceding ones (but which is also compatible with cosmopolitanism). According to this argument, national self-determination is justifiable because, and to the extent that, it furthers people's well-being (Margalit and Raz 1990; Miller 1995: 85–8; Nielsen 1993; Tamir 1993: 72–7). The argument makes three claims:

(1) Political institutions should be designed to further people's well-being.
(2) An individual's membership of a nation furthers his or her well-being.
(3) Granting nations some political power can best further a nation's culture.

Therefore

(C) National self-determination is, ceteris paribus, valuable.

Let us consider each of the steps. (1) is surely a plausible assumption: that a political arrangement furthers people's well-being is a reason in favour of that political arrangement. People clearly care about their well-being and quality of life generally and on this basis it would be implausible to devise a political system that fails to promote this important concern.[62] (1), it is also worth recording, is an *instrumentalist* claim that cosmopolitans can quite happily accept (assuming that they think that well-being matters).

(2) is more controversial. The claim that a person's membership of a nation furthers their well-being is, however, supported by two considerations (Buchanan 1991: 53–4). First, as Kymlicka has emphasized in much of his work, individual freedom requires that individuals have a choice of different conceptions of the good to pursue and this, in turn, requires a culture which instantiates an array of

conceptions of the good. Individual choice thus requires the existence of a rich and varied culture. Furthermore, for most people this role is played by their *national* culture (Kymlicka 1989: 135–205; 1995, esp. pp. 82–90, 105). As Avishai Margalit and Joseph Raz argue, members of a nation draw on their culture to select ways of life instantiated in that culture. A national culture is therefore an important source of conceptions of the good (1990: 449). Second, one can plausibly argue that belonging to a community is one element of a fulfilling life. We all value being a part of a community and for many membership of a nation is an important source of well-being. They take pride in the achievements of their nation and wish to see their nation flourish, where this might involve anything from supporting their nation's music, literature, poetry, sport, and pastimes, and/or protecting their historic monuments and countryside. For both these reasons, then, national cultures further people's well-being.

The next step in the argument—that is, (3)'s claim that nations with some political autonomy are best suited to promoting national cultures—is also supported by two arguments. First, as Margalit and Raz point out, national self-determination is defensible on instrumental grounds as the institutional framework most likely to promote the interests people have in their national culture (Margalit and Raz 1990: 450–1, 457; Miller 1995: 88; Nielsen 1993: 32–3). The reasoning underlying this claim is simply that self-determining nations (where this includes both weak and strong forms of self-determination) have both the incentive and the ability to foster their nation's culture and heritage. Members of nations are more concerned than outsiders to further their own culture and consequently politicians in such a system will have a greater incentive to promote their nation's culture than they would in another system. In addition, because they have political autonomy they can implement political measures to protect their national cultures: they can use public subsidies to support their national heritage.

Premise (3) is also supported by a second consideration—namely the value many find in the embodiment of a national identity in political institutions. National self-determination has symbolic importance for a national culture and, as Berlin and Tamir argue, members of a nation want to be governed by institutions and people that are 'theirs' (Berlin 1982*b*: 156–61; Tamir 1993: 71–5). The importance people attribute to the political *recognition* of their identity can be considerable and this lends further support to (3) (Taylor 1992).[63]

To sum up: the 'well-being' argument maintains that a person's membership of a nation furthers their well-being (providing a menu of choices and being a component in many people's well-being) and it also maintains that national self-determination is required in order to promote national cultures. Hence national self-determination is, ceteris paribus, valuable. It is important to note, here, that the character of the argument is one that moral cosmopolitans can quite readily accept.[64] It invokes a value (well-being through membership of a nation) and argues, along instrumental lines, that political institutions should bear this in mind (Beitz, 1994: 129–32, 134; Jones 1996: 83–4).

## XVI

How persuasive is this argument? The reasoning underlying the argument is, I believe, cogent (nationality matters and institutions can protect national cultures) but it does need to be heavily qualified and once that is done it has a considerably restricted place in institutional design. Five factors severely limit its applicability—two of them factual assumptions on which the argument rests, the remaining three being countervailing normative considerations. Let us begin with the factual assumptions on which this argument is predicated. The 'well-being' argument assumes, first, that one can easily pick out national communities, thereby discerning who belongs and who does not, and can accordingly map political institutions onto national communities. Such a precise and uncontroversial conception of who belongs to which nation is, however, often rare. Edges are frequently blurred and different people may deploy different criteria of nationality resulting in different accounts of the membership of a nation (French and Gutmann 1974: 139–40; George 1994: 78–80; P. Jones 1994: 185; Kedourie 1996: 65, 115–20; O'Neill 1994: 77–8). In some instances national identity as such is relatively uncontested—consider the Scottish and Welsh in the United Kingdom—but these certainly should not be assumed to be the norm.

Second, the argument in question assumes a rather static concept of nationality. Accordingly, it fails to recognize that national sentiments may alter with the creation of new political structures (like a new state or devolved powers within a state). It is therefore not simply a question of granting a nation powers of representation and thereby satisfying the demands of its members: the very character of the nation may then change. As Donald Horowitz points out, '[s]ecession or partition usually makes ethnic relations worse, because it simplifies intergroup confrontations' (1998: 191, 191–2 on the dynamic character of ethnicity). The same point is made by John McGarry who records that 'the process of new-state formation can exacerbate intergroup conflict. The new state's dominant group, concerned about the loyalty of minorities, especially if the state's borders are contested, is often in no mood to accommodate them' (1998: 221). His point, then, is that the nature of national sentiments is in part a function of prevailing institutional arrangements and institutional restructuring may meet some nationalist interests only to create others. These then provide support for Rogers Brubaker's critique of what he terms 'the "architectonic illusion" ' where '[t]his is the belief that if one gets the 'grand architecture' right—if one discovers and establishes the proper territorial and institutional framework—then one can conclusively satisfy legitimate nationalist demands and thereby resolve national conflicts' (1998: 235, and in general pp. 235–41). The fluid and reactive nature of nationality often (if not always) means that this is a chimera.

Suppose, however, that these first two problems do not apply: even then the 'well-being' argument needs to be qualified further. It is important to reiterate here that the upshot of the 'well-being' argument is that national self-determination is valuable *other things being equal*. This qualifying clause is, however, tremendously important. The 'well-being' argument does not imply that other values (like interests other than people's interest in their national culture) should be ignored. It articulates one important *instrumental* consideration that should be combined with others—like the pursuit of human rights and global principles of distributive justice. Accordingly, we cannot conclude on its basis alone that a nation can form its own political unit until we take into account *other values* and the moral claims of *other people* (Beitz 1994: 131–4). Three normative considerations in particular should be incorporated into the assessment of national self-determination.

The first is that (as adherents to this argument emphasize) national self-determination is defensible only if it does not result in violations of people's rights (Margalit and Raz 1990: 449, 451, 459–60). In practice, however, nationalist movements have often been repressive and intolerant. Unfortunately the examples of this are all too familiar: the anti-semitic character of German nationalism during the third Reich; Serbian nationalism during the 1990s and the resultant treatment of Kosovan Albanians; Hutu nationalism resulting in genocide in 1994 (Keane 1996). These are, of course, the most extreme and horrific examples of illiberal nationalism. They should not lead us to ignore less dramatic but nonetheless unacceptable forms of nationalism which are much more common. These include, for example, the nationalist policies pursued in Slovakia towards the Hungarian minority living in the south of the country (Leff 1997: 163–8). Similarly, they include the citizenship laws adopted by Baltic states like Latvia which, on the basis of the 1994 citizenship law, denied citizenship to 30 per cent of the population (most of whom were Russians) (G. Smith 1996: 163). This meant, incidentally, that they were denied voting rights and rights to buy 'companies, land and housing' (G. Smith 1996: 165, cf. pp. 165–6). The general point is simply that 'national self-determination' will never result in a political unit in which all the members belong to the nation in question. National minorities will always exist and this leaves them vulnerable to the policies of the majority.

Against this we should note that not all nationalist movements are illiberal (Kohn 1967: 329–31, 574; Plamentatz 1976). Anthony Smith has argued that nationalist movements took a liberal form in the 'Ivory Coast, Zambia, Ghana after Nkrumah, Tunisia, Egypt since Nasser' (1995: 151). And, one might add, nationalist movements in Scotland and Wales represent fundamentally liberal forms of nationalism. The point, however, still remains: national self-determination is frequently open to the risk of intolerance and rights violations.

It also often engenders instability and this is a second normative concern that should be factored in. This instability arises, in part, because of the two factual points made earlier—(a) the disagreement surrounding the membership of specific nations and (b) the dynamic character of nationalism. The destabilizing effects of the former are obvious—if there is no clear uncontroversial account of who belongs to a given nation and who does not then unrest and instability are likely to arise (P. Jones 1994: 185; Kedourie 1996: xvi, 63–4, 73, 110–11, 133–4). In addition, as we have seen above, the allocation of political power to a nation may alter the existing sentiments and cultural affiliations, engendering more nationalist demands. In general, then, granting nations political power can generate instability (see further Brubaker 1998: 4–7, 55–76). Again this will not always be the case—where identities are relatively uncontroversial and where national self-determination does not result in new vulnerable minorities—but it is often the case and should always be borne in mind.

There is one final normative qualification to the 'well-being' argument. As was pointed out before, this argument appeals to one value (well-being) and we have seen so far that that should be weighed against other *values* (rights and disorder) and the rights and interests of other *people*. We should also record other sources of well-being than nationality. Premise (2) of the 'well-being' argument is incomplete because people have attachments other than their nation and these may be more important from the point of view of their well-being. As Buchanan points out, we need to know 'what is so special about nations?' (1998*a*). People's religion, for example, may be an important source of their personal fulfilment and flourishing. This is important because furthering their well-being may require furthering these other factors and doing so may conflict with national self-determination (Buchanan 1998*a*: 293–9, 302–3; George 1994: 77–8; A. Vincent 1997: 285–8). More generally, some may find fulfilment not through membership of a fixed community but by leading a hybrid way of life. They might, that is, subscribe to *cultural cosmopolitanism* (Chapter 1, Section I; Waldron 1992: 751–92).

Now drawing these points together, then, we may conclude that the well-being argument has some force but only where five strict assumptions are met: namely, there are clearly defined nations; the new political institutions meet nationalist demands; national self-determination does not result in injustice, or instability; and it does not counteract other important attachments and interests. Thus qualified, the nationalist measures defended by the well-being argument are consistent with the cosmopolitan conception of democracy outlined in Section VI. The conclusions it supports—granting nations some political autonomy—are compatible with the cosmopolitan framework defended earlier since the latter affirms the importance of promoting people's well-being and it calls for the existence of sub-state political authorities. In addition, the 'well-being' argument recognizes the value of rights (values which, for intrinsic and instrumental reasons, support cosmopolitan democracy). Respecting people's interests in local cultures is thus compatible with the ideal of cosmopolitan democracy.[65]

# XVII

It is time to conclude. This chapter has examined three perspectives on how political institutions should be designed—cosmopolitan, statist and, nationalist approaches—and, in particular, has sought to examine the institutional commitments of those who embrace cosmopolitan ideals. Furthermore, it has argued that

1. the *intrinsic* cosmopolitan approach is unconvincing;
2. the *right-based* and *instrumental* cosmopolitan approaches are persuasive and provide support for a multi-level system of governance in which supra-state authorities monitor the conduct of states (and powerful economic and social institutions) and seek to ensure their compliance with cosmopolitan ideals of justice.

It has, in addition, argued that

3. none of the four statist arguments nor the 'global civil society' argument undermine the cosmopolitan argument.

We have also seen that

4. the 'distributive justice', 'trust', and 'Kantian' arguments for national self-determination are unconvincing; but
5. the 'well-being' argument articulates a value which can and should be accommodated by cosmopolitans but only when heavily qualified: the construction of political institutions should bear in mind their effect on people's cultures including their national cultures.

Global political institutions should, therefore, be constructed to reflect three important values: the protection of civil and political human rights and the pursuit of cosmopolitan distributive principles (an *instrumental* consideration); the ability of people to affirm their cultural and national commitments (an *instrumental* consideration); and the ability of people to hold accountable the institutions and agents that affect the exercise of their rights (a *right-based* consideration). Finally, this chapter has argued that these values support a system of multi-level governance in which power is removed from states to both supra-state and sub-state political authorities.

## NOTES

1. Philpott follows this definition with a footnote citing a large number of writers who subscribe to similar conceptions of sovereignty (1999: 570, fn. 10). For a fairly similar definition see Biersteker and Weber, who write: 'we provisionally define the "territorial state" as a geographically-contained structure whose agents claim ultimate political authority within their domain' (1996: 2). They are however, keen to stress the provisional nature of their definition, arguing that no final definition is possible because of the disputed character of sovereignty, and they stress the socially constructed nature of sovereignty (1996: 3–18). A good analysis of sovereignty is provided by Beitz (1991: 237–44).

2. This can be contrasted with Moellendorf's conception of 'sovereignty'. He defines sovereignty in terms of authority but, by contrast with the position in the text, defines whether an institution is sovereign in terms of whether it enjoys 'moral authority' (rather than legal sovereignty) (2002*a*: 105, 106, cf. also p. 103). This is a puzzling conception of sovereignty and has the counter-intuitive implication that it is logically impossible to have a morally evil sovereign state.

3. The territorial dimensions are often overlooked. One important exception to this is Baldwin (1992) which combines both historical and philosophical analysis of the role of territoriality. See also Ruggie (1993, esp. pp. 149–52).

4. It is noticeable that the notion of world government has attracted the attention of some novelists in addition to H. G. Wells. Thomas Mann has two characters (Herr Settembrini and Herr Naphta) discuss it in *The Magic Mountain* (1985 [1924]: ch. VI, sections on 'A New-Comer' (esp. pp. 380–6) and 'Of the City of God, and Deliverance by Evil' (esp. p. 402)). Similarly in *The Brothers Karamazov* Fyodor Dostoyevsky writes '[t]he great conquerors, the Timurs and Ghenghis-Khans, swept like a whirlwind over the earth, striving to conquer the world, but, though unconsciously, they expressed the same great need of mankind for a universal and world-wide union. By accepting the world and Caesar's purple, you would have founded the world state and given universal peace' (1988 [1880]: 302).

5. For an instructive analysis of the nature of the European Union see Bellamy and Castiglione (1997).

6. Cf. also Pogge's distinction between 'moral cosmopolitanism' and 'legal cosmopolitanism' (1994*a*: 90). What Beitz terms 'institutional cosmopolitanism' should not be confused with what Pogge means by 'institutional cosmopolitanism' (where the latter was examined in Ch. 4, Sect. III, and is contrasted with what Pogge terms 'interactional cosmopolitanism'). As we have just seen, Beitz employs the term 'institutional cosmopolitanism' to denote the view that there should be global political institutions. What Pogge terms an 'institutional cosmopolitanism', by contrast, makes no claim about how the world should be organized: its claim is that the scope of principles of justice is determined by the extent of social, economic, and political interdependence and maintains that since there is global interdependence there are global duties. It is a thesis about who has obligations to whom; it is not a thesis about what political institutions are best. Cf. Pogge (1994*a*: 90–8, esp. pp. 90–1) and the discussion in Ch. 4, Sect. III.

7. This typology expands on one given by Beitz, who distinguishes between 'intrinsic' and 'instrumental' approaches (1994: 131–4).

8. To use concepts invoked in another context by Nozick: the intrinsic approach is a 'historical' theory (legitimate institutions are those that are chosen). The instrumental and right-based approaches, on the other hand, are 'end-state' theories since they both prescribe a certain structure. See Nozick (1974: 153–5).

9. The internal quotation in Beran's passage is from Rawls (1999*c*: 12). In this footnote, Beran also cites Pateman (1979). For further affirmations of this argument see Beran (1987: 26–36) on consent theory and (1987: 37–42) on how this justifies secession. See also Beran (1994: 56–62).

10. See, for example, Raz's 'service' conception of authority (1986: part 1).

11. For a related distinction see Berlin (1982*a*: xliii; 1982*b*: 121–2) and Margalit and Raz (1990: 454–5).

12. Philpott explicitly criticizes the individualistic approach (1995: 368–9).

13. See generally Pogge (1994*a*: 112–17).
14. See also Baldwin (1992, esp. pp. 222–9).
15. Buchanan goes further, arguing that allowing secession can in fact subvert democratic government. He does not reject the right to secede but does point out ways in which, unless several conditions are specified, secession can allow parties to undermine democratic decision-making by threatening to secede unless they get their way (1998*b*: 21–4).
16. The quotation is from Jenning's book, *The Approach to Self-Government* (Cambridge: Cambridge University Press, 1956), p. 56. For Philpott's response to this objection see (1995: 364–5).
17. See also Pogge (1989: 249–50; 1994*a*: 107–9). A considerable literature has now grown up around the idea of 'cosmopolitan democracy': see Archibugi and Held (1995) and Archibugi, Held, and Köhler (1998).
18. (1) is also endorsed by Tony McGrew (1997: 231–7, 249–53, 262). Thomas McCarthy also appears to endorse 'the general principle that people should have a say in the political decisions that significantly affect their lives' (1999: 209). This passage is followed by a footnote that attributes this view to Held (1995) (McCarthy 1999: 213, fn. 26). It is interesting to note that (1) is also affirmed by the United Nations Development Programme: (UNDP 2002: 7–8, 51, 102, 112–21).
19. Held also outlines six less radical (but still ambitious) short-term proposals, which include reforming the United Nations and making it more democratic (1995: 279). Note, one of the proposals—that there should be an International Criminal Court— has already occurred. The latter came into existence on 1 July 2002.
20. As well as affirming the right-based argument (cf. 1995: 145, 147, 153, 155, 226, 228, 231–2, 235–6, 237, fn. 6), Held also appears, at times, to defend cosmopolitan institutions on instrumental grounds. That is, on some occasions, he defends global institutions on the grounds that they are the best way to defend individual rights. See, for example, (1995: 155–6, 223; 1998: 21, 25). One complication to this is that Held tends to value these individual rights on the grounds that they enable people to participate in the democratic process (1995: 187, 190, 199–200, 208, 210–12, 223–4).
21. For another critical discussion of a principle like (1) and its implications for institutional design, cf. Saward (2000: 32–46). Saward makes some criticisms of (1), arguing that it should not be the fundamental principle determining the structure of political institutions but that it should nonetheless play a significant (albeit subordinate) role (2000, esp. pp. 37–8).
22. Pogge is also aware of the problems with principles like (1). He writes that 'persons have a right to an institutional order under which those significantly and *legitimately* affected by a political decision have a roughly equal opportunity to influence the making of this decision' (1994*a*: 105, my emphasis). The word 'legitimately' is included to exclude certain ways in which one is affected by something (such as that I am upset that a relative is not awarded a pay increase). My being affected in this way does not entitle me to have a vote on whether they should receive a pay increase. After the word 'legitimately' there is a footnote in which Pogge elaborates on what 'legitimately' means in this context (1994*a*: 120, fn. 28).
23. Held can easily accommodate this revision for he has a full and rich account of person's rights: cf. (1995: 191–200) for his account of the seven types of rights he endorses.

24. For further criticism see Whelan (1983: 19). Whelan points out that the group of people affected by the same economic forces, say, might not be affected by the same environmental forces. Accordingly, principles like (1) and (1a) would result in multiple borders, where the group of people voting on issues x, y, and z are not the same people who vote on issues a, b, and c. He fails, however, to say why this is a defect. In addition, this is a phenomenon that we cope with fairly easily. Someone might vote with one group of people to decide their local MP but with another group of people to decide their MEP and with a third distinct group of people to decide their union representative and with yet another group of people to decide the policies of a social movement to which they belong (like CND).

25. There are, in fact, two distinct ways in which I would argue that democracy should be globalized. The first way contends that the justification of democratic government relies on universal considerations and hence entails that all persons have a right to democratic government (where that is possible). The second way is that defended in the text. It contends that given that the democratic ideal entails that persons should be able to exercise control over the institutions that structure their ability to exercise their rights, and given globalization, there should be democratic global institutions. The second view presupposes the first but is clearly distinct from it for the first is not necessarily committed to any global institutions.

26. Others, like Wellman, refer to this as a 'teleological' approach (1995: 156–60).

27. For examples see Barry (1998: 153–6; 1999: sec. IV, esp. pp. 36–40); Beitz (1994: throughout but esp. pp. 125–6, 129–35); Falk (1995), Charles Jones (1999: 206–10, 214–15, 217), Kuper (2000: 657, 658), O'Neill (1996: 166–83, esp. 172–4; 2000: 139–42, 170–2, 179–85, 199–201), Pogge (1994a: 103–5), van Parijs (1995: 228–33), Young (2000: 5–6, 17, 26–36, 209). Habermas also adopts a fairly instrumental perspective and presents a measured and cautious defence of supra-state institutions (1997b: 127–35; 2001a: 53–7; 2001b: 104–12). Instrumental approaches are also employed by earlier writers. See, for example, David Mitrany's 'functionalist' approach (1933). Friedrich Hayek also defends international institutions on instrumental grounds in *The Road to Serfdom* (1976 [1944]: ch. XV). He argues for an international federation to impose rules of laissez-faire, arbitrate, implement, and uphold international law, protect individual rights, and thereby secure peace (1976 [1944]: 169, 172–6).

28. See further Pogge (1994a: 104–5). Of course, someone might challenge this argument, arguing that the international case is relevantly different from the domestic case. Two such arguments are considered later in this chapter: cf. Sect. VII and XIII.

29. The claim that international institutions are required to prevent war has been pressed by many. Albert Einstein and Sigmund Freud both argued along these lines. Einstein calls for 'a legislative and judicial body to settle every conflict arising between nations' (1991 [1933]: 346). Freud opines that '[w]ars will only be prevented with certainty if mankind unites in setting up a central authority to which the right of giving judgement upon all conflicts of interest shall be handed over. There are clearly two separate requirements involved in this: the creation of a supreme agency and its endowment with the necessary power. One without the other would be useless' (1991 [1933]: 354).

30. See, again, Pogge (1994a: 103–4). For a fuller analysis of the reasons supporting (2) see Caney (forthcoming b).

31. The last two points return us to the notion of 'rights-holism' discussed in Ch. 3 Sect. VIII.

32. Thomas Franck also suggests both a directly elected second assembly (with representation mirroring population size) and a reform of the voting procedure (1997: 483–4, cf. more generally pp. 481–4).

33. On the unaccountable nature of the World Bank, cf. Woods (2001: 83–100).

34. Cf. also Iris Marion Young's discussion (2000: 270, 274). She also emphasizes the need to reform the United Nations (2000: 271–4).

35. For similar, but more modest, proposals to reform the IMF, World Bank, United Nations, and the WTO, see UNDP (2002: 113–21).

36. I shall not consider whether there should be a non-territorial component to institutional design. It is conceptually possible to have non-territorial political institutions (say a parliament for members of a nation wherever they may be or a parliament for members of a religion wherever they may be) but I think that the right-based and instrumental considerations adduced earlier (plus considerations of feasibility) will generally (if not always) tend to favour territorial forms of political representation. For further discussion see Kuper (2000: 657–8).

37. For these concerns see Kant's essay on 'Perpetual Peace' esp. (1989 [1795]: 113–14). Hannah Arendt also predicts that world government would be 'a forbidding nightmare of tyranny' (1957: 539).

38. See also Zolo (1995: 3–15, 121, 165, 166).

39. Kai Nielsen, who endorses a world state, seeks to meet the objection that this would be tyrannical by arguing that it should be a federation (1988: 263–82).

40. See also, in this context, Jones's defence of what he terms 'qualified sovereigntism' (1999: 214), Cf. (1999: ch. 8, esp. pp. 214–19 and p. 230).

41. On Stephen Krasner's well-known definition, '[i]nternational regimes are defined as principles, norms, rules, and decision-making procedures around which actor expectations converge in a given issue-area' (1983*a*: 1).

42. For a discussion of the value of regimes as judged by cosmopolitan criteria see Keohane (1984: 249–57, esp. pp. 255–7).

43. Bull does make other points. First, in his discussion of peace, he points out that although states have warred we should not reject a state order until we have also considered the disadvantages of other systems (1977: 284–5). This is undeniably true and any *instrumental* appraisal of a statist order should take this factor into account. It does not, however, give us any reason to think that the disadvantages of a cosmopolitan order will outweigh the advantages. It is a sensible methodological point rather than a reason against global political structures. Second, in his discussion of peace, Bull makes the point that by parcelling people who disagree into different states, a statist order prevents some conflict from arising (1977: 286–7). The point is that people throughout the world disagree quite profoundly on many issues and one way of avoiding conflict is to design a system where those who conflict do not have to try to live with each other and are partitioned into different political communities. Again this is a relevant consideration. The flaw is that all states contain many conflicting ethnic groups, nations, cultures, and religious communities and hence a state order does not keep those who disagree apart (cf. the number of civil wars).

44. For Doyle's discussion of the empirical evidence supporting the claim see (1997: 258–65, 284–98). For his discussion of the reasons why liberal democracies do not wage war against other liberal democracies cf. (1997: 280–4); and for the claim that

liberal democracies attack non-democracies cf. (1997: 265–75). Doyle, it should be noted, treats Kant's argument as a 'third image' argument, rather than a 'second image' one (1997: 252, 301).

45. Cf. Proposition XIV of Bentham's tract which states '[t]hat secresy in the operations of the foreign department in England ought not to be endured, being altogether useless, and equally repugnant to the interests of liberty and peace' (1962 [1786–9]: 554, cf. pp.554–60). For a good discussion of the role that publicity can play see John Macmillan (1998: 643–67).

It should be stressed that Bentham is not endorsing a wholly 'second image' approach for he also endorses global institutions. He recommends that there should be 'a common court of judicature, for the decision of differences between the several nations' (1962 [1786–9]: 552, cf. pp. 552–4). This role would be performed by 'a Congress or Diet' comprising two representatives from each country. He writes that '[i]ts power would consist—1. In reporting its opinion; 2. In causing that opinion to be circulated in the dominions of each state . . . ; 3. After a certain time, in putting the refractory state under the ban of Europe' (1962 [1786–9]: 554).

46. The three 'second image' arguments given are not exhaustive. For example, a fourth relevant 'second image' argument contends that states with an extensive domestic distributive programme are inclined to spend more on overseas development aid than are other states. This claim is fequently made and has some support. For a thorough analysis of the claimed connection see Noël and Thérien (1995: 523–53).

47. Since I have referred to Sen's argument that democracies prevent famines to illustrate the 'second image' approach it is worth noting that Pogge mentions Sen as one of his targets (2001*d*, esp. p. 329).

48. Pogge proposes that members of the international order (such as states, MNCs, international institutions) should ascribe these rights (the resource privilege and the borrowing privilege) only to democratic states (2001*d*: 338–41). For more on the two privileges see also (2001*c*: 10–23).

49. For another illustration of the fact that democracy within the state presupposes certain international preconditions consider the role and impact of international institutions such as the IMF and World Bank. Frequently, the latter have granted loans only on condition that the assisted state comply with rules specified by the lender (conditionality). Such restraints clearly limit its democratic autonomy. This, however, again constitutes an illustration of the international presuppositions of democratic government.

50. One early sceptic of second image arguments is Jean-Jacques Rousseau who, in his 'Discourse on Political Economy', remarks that 'it is not impossible that a well-governed republic could wage an unjust war' (1991*a* [1755]: 4).

51. Frost, I should note, does not address this form of cosmopolitan proposal. He does consider world government arguing that such a state 'would be justified if it came about through the voluntary action of all sovereign states' (1996: 157, more generally pp. 157–8). For further criticism of Frost's argument see Jones (1999: 219–21, 223–5).

52. See also Sklair's discussion of the role played by social movements during and after the 1999 WTO meeting in Seattle (2002: 291–3). For further studies of the role of 'global civil society' see Keck and Sikkink (1998), Lipschutz (1996), and Wapner (1996).

53. The case for 'a democratic ethos' is also powerfully articulated by William Connolly (1991: 476, see more generally pp. 476–81). He, however, does not make any reference to the need to create new institutional frameworks and appears simply to accept the 'territorial state' (1991: 476).

54. It should be stressed that the alternatives to Held's proposals that have been considered in Sect. VIII, IX, and XI do not exhaust all the possibilities. There are other institutional proposals designed to ensure 'democratic' and 'accountable' governance in a globalizing world which reject the type of global institutions favoured by Held. Cf, for example, Saward's outline of five non-permanent mechanisms for making decisions more accountable without accepting Held's institutional proposals (2000: 40–5). For an analysis of alternatives see Caney (forthcoming *b*).

55. See also Barry (1991*a*: 174–5).

56. For further criticism see Caney (1999*a*: 133–5).

57. For further discussion see Barry (1991*a*: 174–5, 177–8).

58. The negative implication is made by a number of others from a variety of different traditions: see, for example, Kymlicka (2001*b*: 238–40), Morgenthau (1985: 534–7), Sandel (1996: 339–41, 344–6). Finally, cf. more generally Miller's argument that the ideal of citizenship, with its attendant notions of a commitment to the common good and to participation in the polity, cannot be realized at the supra-national level (2000*b*: esp. 81–9).

59. A similar point was made in Ch. 4, Sect. IX. For references to those who have made likeminded points see the sources cited in Ch. 4, fns. 83 and 84.

60. Iris Marion Young also notes that political identities supportive of cosmopolitan justice may be fostered (2000: 242–3).

61. For this argument see MacCormick (1982: 261–4; 1991: 16–18; 1996: 35–51).

62. The most persuasive argument for civil and political human rights, recall, drew on people's interest in well-being: Ch. 3, Sect. VI.

63. For criticism of this see Margalit and Raz (1990: 451–3).

64. Of course, this is not true of those who subscribe to what I have termed *cultural cosmopolitanism* especially the strong version of that position (Ch. 1, Sect. I).

65. See, further on this, Bellamy and Castiglione (1997). See also Young's discussion in *Inclusion and Democracy* (2000). She defends both national self-determination (2000: 251–65) and cosmopolitan democracy (2000: 265–75). For her dual vision see (2000: 237, 265–71, 275). Interestingly some earlier proponents of international institutions are also sympathetic to devolving powers to cultural communities. Mitrany, for instance, writes 'human progress might be served best by a combination of the two lines of political organization which hitherto have been applied rather in opposition to each other. A functional integration of technical services upon the largest possible international scale would seem to be as indispensable, as a more liberal devolution of cultural activities, which should free the individual genius of each regional or national group, would seem to be desirable as a more rational approach to the ideal ends of political society' (1933: 102).

# 6

# Just War

Examining Magistrate Ivanov to Rubashov: 'I don't approve of mixing ideologies', Ivanov continued. 'There are only two conceptions of human ethics, and they are at opposite poles. One of them is Christian and humane, declares the individual to be sacrosanct, and asserts that the rules of arithmetic are not to be applied to human units. The other starts from the basic principle that a collective aim justifies all means, and not only allows, but demands, that the individual should in every way be subordinated and sacrificed to the community—which may dispose of it as an experimentation rabbit or a sacrificial lamb. The first conception could be called anti-vivisection morality, the second, vivisection morality. Humbugs and dilettantes have always tried to mix the two conceptions; in practice, it is impossible. Whoever is burdened with power and responsibility finds out on the first occasion that he has to choose; and he is fatally driven to the second alternative. Do you know, since the establishment of Christianity as a state religion, a single example of a state which really followed a Christian policy? You can't point out one. In times of need—and politics are chronically in a time of need—the rulers were always able to evoke 'exceptional circumstances,' which demanded exceptional measures of defence. Since the existence of nations and classes, they live in a permanent state of mutual self-defense, which forces them eternally to defer to another time the putting into practice of humanism . . .

*Darkness at Noon* (Koestler 1987 [1940]: 128)

Thus far, this book has focused on ideal theory. Chapter 3 sought to identify what civil and political universal principles, if any, should be adopted at the global level. In a similar vein, Chapter 4 sought to identify what principles of distributive justice, if any, should apply globally. And Chapter 5 has examined what political institutions are ideal. Together, these present an account of the ideal to which we should aspire. In Chapters 6 and 7, I want to move from ideal theory to non-ideal theory.[1] A complete analysis must address what principles should apply when injustices have been committed (or, perhaps, are about to be committed). We might distinguish between two separate types of injustice. First, there are situations where a political regime and its members are attacked by an external agent. Let us call these *external wrongs*. In such circumstances may a regime wage war in self-defence? May it wage war to recover resources wrongly taken from it and may it wage war to punish an aggressor? Furthermore, are other political regimes permitted, or even required, to wage war to defend a regime that has been wronged? These questions—questions concerning *just war*—are examined in this chapter. Chapter 7 addresses a second kind of scenario in which injustice is taking place. It addresses situations in which wrongs are being committed within a political regime and focuses on the question of whether outside political regimes are ever morally permitted, or required, to intervene to prevent such wrongs. Chapter 7 deals, then, with what one might term *internal wrongs* and analyses whether *humanitarian intervention* is justified to address internal wrongs.

Both chapters seek to provide principles that should apply when some people have violated (or are about to violate) the entitlements of others. They are required only because people fail to live up to the standards specified by principles of justice. The theories of just warfare and intervention may be described as outlining what Michael Sandel terms 'remedial virtues' (1982: 32) for we need only advert to such theories because we are living in a less than ideal world.

Broadly speaking, the aim of this chapter is to analyse a number of prominent views concerning the nature of a just war and, having criticized them, to outline the account of a just war that follows from a cosmopolitan perspective. It explores different philosophical approaches at a general level, analysing their accounts of when war may be waged (*jus ad bellum*) and how it may be waged (*jus in bello*). To do this it begins, in Section I, with some methodological observations. The chapter then examines several leading perspectives on the nature of just war. Sections II and III, thus, examine Michael Walzer's influential treatment of this subject in *Just and Unjust Wars* (1977), criticizing in particular his account of *jus ad bellum* and his derivation of rules of *jus in bello*. Section IV analyses Terry Nardin's state-centric account of just war in *Law, Morality and the Relations of States* (1983). The following four sections turn to more cosmopolitan perspectives. Section V outlines the general structure of a cosmopolitan theory of just war. Sections VI and VII then examine particular cosmopolitan accounts of some aspects of just war, analysing utilitarian and deontological approaches.[2] Having criticized these accounts, it then outlines an alternative cosmopolitan rights-based approach which avoids the objections levelled against the preceding two theories (Section VIII). The remainder of the chapter analyses realist misgivings about both traditional and cosmopolitan conceptions of *jus ad bellum* and *jus in bello* (Sections IX and X).

# I

Let me begin then with four preliminary points. First, although this chapter examines just war theory throughout it does not seek to provide a comprehensive account of when and how war should be waged. Two types of war are excluded. First, it does not examine the ethical issues surrounding war that takes place within a political regime (civil war). The latter is a concern for a domestic, as opposed to a global, political theory.[3] Second, this chapter does not examine whether a political regime may wage war to protect human rights within another regime. This question is examined in Chapter 7. This chapter's fundamental concern is with the courses of action that political regimes may adopt when a regime is wronged by an external agent. This is its primary focus and it analyses just war theory at length only because it is thought by many that political regimes may respond to external wrongs by waging war.

Second, it is worth stressing that this chapter focuses on how *political regimes* can respond to wrongs perpetrated by *external agents*. Both italicized phrases require elaboration. The term 'political regimes' has been chosen rather than 'states' so that it can accommodate the issues that would arise between non-sovereign political systems of the kind discussed in Chapter 5. In this way it has greater flexibility and wider applicability. The term 'external agents' has been chosen rather than states because political regimes can be wronged by actors including, but not restricted to, states. Again, the rationale for this usage is that it increases the relevance and applicability of the discussion. To restrict the focus to wrongs committed by other *states* would prevent the chapter from being able to address how political regimes may respond to attacks such as those made by Al-Qa'ida on 11 September 2001.

Third, although this chapter focuses on the *just* responses to external wrongs, it is not assumed that justice is the only relevant value. On the contrary, it is entirely reasonable to argue that values such as compassion, forgiveness, and mercy, for example, should inform how regimes respond to external wrongs. The focus on justice is justified, however, on the grounds that it should define the environment within which people act. Within this fair background, other virtues may be entirely appropriate.

Fourth, and finally, it is worth perhaps observing that, in comparison with other topics in global political theory (such as 'what principles of distributive justice, if any, should govern international affairs?' and 'how defensible is the project of creating democratic supra-state institutions?'), there is a considerable degree of consensus both among philosophers writing on the subject but also among people of different cultures. This point should not be overstated. Clearly, pacifists and realists both disagree profoundly and intractably with the traditional just war approach. Clearly, also, Muslims, Jews, Christians, atheists, and Buddhists will not speak with one voice on all aspects to do with when and how war may be waged. My point is simply that *in comparison to* other topics there is a greater degree of commonality, where this should not be confused with homogeneity. The very idea of a 'just war' tradition bears this out. There is, for example, no comparable 'international distributive justice' tradition. Just war theory is traditionally defined in terms of certain rules of *jus ad bellum* and certain rules of *jus in bello*. Standard accounts of *jus ad bellum* generally maintain that a just war requires the following:

(1) there is a just cause;
(2) war is authorized by a legitimate authority;
(3) those waging the war have just intentions;
(4) the costs incurred by the war are not disproportionate in comparison to the wrongs that justify the waging of war (proportionality);
(5) war is the last resort;

(6)  the war has a reasonable chance of meeting its objectives; and,

(7)  its goal is a fair peace.[4]

Furthermore, standard accounts of *jus in bello* generally tend to maintain that

(1)  the means employed to wage war should not involve disproportionate casualties (proportionality); and,

(2)  intentional attack on non-combatants is wrong (non-combatant immunity).[5]

Lest my claim is misconstrued, it should be stressed that to argue that there is a commonly accepted framework of values does not entail that there is agreement on the meaning, importance, and implications of these values. In the first place, it should, of course, be stressed that different thinkers have interpreted these conditions differently. Consider, for example, the idea of a just cause. Most agree that self-defence is a just cause, but there is disagreement as to whether war may be waged in order to punish aggressors. Hugo Grotius, for example, maintains in *de Jure belli ac Pacis Libri Tres* that '[j]ustifiable causes include defence, the obtaining of that which belongs to us or is our due, and the inflicting of punishment' (1925 [1646]: bk. II, ch. I, sec. II, p. 171). Samuel Pufendorf, by contrast, does not regard punishment as a just cause for waging war (1991 [1673]: bk. II, sec. 16, subsec. 2, p. 168). And Kant explicitly insists in *The Metaphysics of Morals* that states may not wage war to punish another state: 'No war of independent states against each other can be a *punitive war* (*bellum punitivum*). For punishment occurs only in the relation of a superior (*imperantis*) to those subject to him (*subditum*), and states do not stand in that relation to each other' (1996 [1797]: part II, ch. II, sec. 57, p. 117). So there is room for disagreement about some aspects of what constitutes a just cause.

In the second place, to claim that there is a common discourse is not to gainsay the fact that people disagree profoundly in the application of these principles to existing and historical conflicts. There are, of course, vehement disagreements over whether the Gulf war of 1991 or the bombing of Afghanistan in 2001–2 or the 2003 war against Iraq, for example, met these conditions. To attest to a common framework is not to claim that there is homogeneity, either at the theoretical level or at the level at which the theory is employed to judge and guide practice.

## II

Let us turn now to normative analyses of the nature of a just war. I shall begin with Michael Walzer's account. In his celebrated *Just and Unjust Wars* Walzer provides, among other things, an account of both when war may be waged and also how it may be waged (1977: parts II and III). It is worth focusing on Walzer's work in some detail because it is the most sophisticated and extensive modern treatment of warfare and it exemplifies a certain statist conception of justice. Starting with his account of *jus ad bellum*, Walzer presents but modifies what he terms 'the legalist paradigm' (1977: 58, 58–63). This comprises six principles. These maintain the value of a society of states (1); affirm the right of states to their own territory and independence (2); condemn any act of aggression against a state (3); justify war as a response to aggression (4); maintain that war is not justified in any other circumstance (5); and sanction the punishment of aggressors (6) (1977: 61–2). At the heart of this theory is the claim that states have a right to wage war in self-defence. Walzer then adds to this, however, that states may also engage in a pre-emptive strike because there are situations in which an aggressor is about to attack and it is justified to engage in warfare to land the first blow (1977: ch. 5).[6] Walzer's point here is that this can still be seen as an act of self-defence because it is only a matter of time before the enemy attacks and one is entitled to defend against it (1977: 85).

Let us, however, consider Walzer's defence of the right of states to wage war in greater detail. It may seem obvious that states that are invaded or attacked do have a right to engage in war to defend their sovereignty against external aggression. This, indeed, is a core feature of the just war tradition. As we shall see, however, this assumption stands in need of justification and Walzer's arguments do not sustain his conclusions. Let us begin then with Walzer's justification of the claim that states have a right to wage war when attacked. Within Walzer's work we can find three distinct lines of reasoning, the first two of which draw on his general theory of the rights of states (1977: 53–8).

1. Walzer's central justification of a state's right to wage war in self-defence proceeds as follows: states embody the 'common life' of their people (1977: 54). As such they have a moral worth and moral rights. Aggression is, therefore, wrong because it violates these rights. By attacking or invading, an external agent is violating the legitimate rights of the state and the latter is entitled to use force in self-defence (1977: 53–4).

Several points should be made in response to this. The first point is that, even if we work within Walzer's theory, the *unqualified* statement that states have a right to self-defence is inaccurate. To see why we should consider two points. First, Walzer maintains that military intervention in the affairs of another political regime is justified in certain exceptional circumstances. He argues, in particular, that military intervention in a state is justified when: (a) the state does not represent a united community and there is a national liberation movement wishing to secede (1977: 90–2); or (b) another regime has already intervened (1977: 90, 93–101); or (c) a state is engaged in genocide (1977: 90, 101–8). If any one of these situations arises, Walzer says, intervention is justified. To this we should also add—and this is the second step in my argument—that Walzer thinks (quite reasonably) that it cannot be the case that both sides in an armed conflict are in the right (1977: 59). It follows from this that, on Walzer's own analysis, if A intervenes in B, it cannot be right *both* that A is justified in employing force to change the internal affairs of society B and that B is justified in employing force to repel A. But, given both of these points, it follows that it is not true that states necessarily have a right to engage in self-defence when they are invaded. To take one of Walzer's examples, states committing genocide are not entitled to wage war in self-defence. The unqualified statement of the right to employ force in self-defence is, thus, inaccurate *on Walzer's own theory*.[7] The seemingly obvious claim—that states may employ force in self-defence—is thus undermined.[8]

This first point employs Walzer's own criteria as to what constitutes a *legitimate* state. A further problem with his account of *jus ad bellum* is that his standards are too lax and legitimize far too many cruel, unfair, and repressive states. Any state is legitimate on Walzer's account as long as it does not contain a secessionist movement and as long as it does not engage in genocide. It may persecute individuals and minorities; engage in ethnic cleansing; cause opposition members to 'disappear'; deny people the vote; exploit workers and immigrants; and repress women (Doppelt 1978, esp. pp. 6–7, 16, 20–6; 1980: 399–400, 402–3; Luban 1980a: 169–70, 179–80; 1980b: 393–7). It is hard, however, to see why a state that treats its members in these ways possesses a moral status such that it is morally entitled to use violence to defend itself. We would not think that a violent gang or mafia-clan that treated people in these ways possesses the right to wage war in self-defence, so why should we think that a state that does exactly the same things does?

2. Let us consider a second argument that Walzer deploys to defend the right of political regimes to wage war in self-defence. Walzer argues that states are analogous to individuals. He argues, on the basis of this analogy, that since individuals are allowed to defend their rights so political regimes are entitled to defend their sovereignty and their territory: 'given a genuine "contract", it makes sense to say that territorial integrity and political sovereignty can be defended in exactly the same way as individual life and liberty' (1977: 54; see also 1977: 55).[9] He adds later: '[i]f states actually do possess rights more or less as individuals do, then it is possible to imagine a society among them more or less like the society of individuals. The comparison of international to civil order is crucial to the theory of aggression' (1977: 58).[10] This thus represents an additional vindication of the right of states to wage war in defence of their sovereignty.

Again, however, Walzer's argument is flawed. One important problem with his argument is simply that the analogy is deeply unpersuasive. Individuals are disanalogous to states in many morally important ways. It is simply unhelpful to treat states, which are often divided by class, nationality, ethnicity, regional identity, and religion, as if they possessed the sort of unity that individuals possess (Beitz 1999c: 69–71, 74–6, 81; McMahan 1986: 28–30, esp. p. 29).[11] Second, even if we grant the analogy, it is far from clear whether this sustains the conclusion that Walzer seeks. To claim that individuals and states are analogous is actually unhelpful to his case for we are extremely wary about claiming that an individual may kill people whenever someone violates his or her rights. Does it not depend on what rights are being violated, and how grave they are? As many have remarked, there is a strong contrast between, on the one hand, people's vehement condemnation of murder where it is regarded as abhorrent, and, on the other, people's attitudes to killing during war where it is taken to be perfectly normal.[12] The point is nicely made by Tolstoy:

'Enlightened, sensible, good Christian people, who inculcate the principle of love and brotherhood, who regard murder as an awful crime, who, with very few exceptions, are unable to kill an animal—all these people suddenly, provided that these crimes are called war, not only acknowledge the destruction, plunder, and killing of people to be right and legal, but themselves contribute toward these robberies and murders, prepare themselves for them, take part in them, are proud of them.'   (1987 [original date unknown]: 126)

Thus, in analogising the individual and the state Walzer is inadvertently undermining his case. For if we do not think individuals may kill, and if we think that states are akin to individuals, then we should be more reticent than Walzer is about thinking that states may kill people.

Walzer's defence of the right of states to wage war in defence of their rights is thus unpersuasive. His first argument does not sustain the unconditional right of states to engage in warfare; and his second argument relies on an implausible but also self-undermining analogy.

3. The first two arguments have invoked the right of communities to engage in self-defence. Walzer does, however, employ a third line of argument. He argues that waging war is justified in the name of enforcing the law of international society (1977: 59, 62). Thus he writes: '[t]he victim of aggression fights in self-defense, but he isn't only defending himself, for aggression is a crime against society as a whole. He fights in its name and not only in his own' (1977: 59).

This third argument is, however, problematic in three respects. First, Walzer is unclear on the precise nature of the conclusion that he is seeking to derive. In some instances he maintains that his argument shows that states that have not been attacked are morally *permitted* to come to the assistance of a (morally legitimate) state that has been attacked. He writes that, '[o]ther states *can rightfully* join the victim's resistance; their war has the same character as his own, which is to say, they are *entitled* not only to repel the attack but also to punish it. All resistance is also law enforcement' (1977: 59, my emphasis). Again: '[a]nyone *can* come to the aid of a victim, use necessary force against an aggressor' (1977: 62, my emphasis). On other occasions, however, he appears to make a stronger claim, arguing that states that have not been attacked are under a *moral obligation* to come to the assistance of a (morally legitimate) state that has been attacked. For example, he writes that 'it is the tendency of the theory to undermine the right of neutrality and to *require* widespread participation in the business of law enforcement' (1977: 62, my emphasis).

Second, Walzer's argument assumes that unless a state repels an aggressor international society will collapse. But this empirical assumption is hard to sustain. It is perfectly conceivable that one state invades and usurps another, taking it over, and yet the international order of a society of states continues. Of course, the original society of states has been destroyed because there is one less state but to object on these grounds would make his claim tautologous. The important consideration is that the international order, one comprising states, remains intact. One act of aggression by one state has not destroyed and will not destroy that.[13]

A third problem lies in Walzer's unargued assumption that the current international order, consisting of sovereign states, is of such moral value that it must be preserved. It is far from clear that this is so and given the forceful criticisms of the current statist order (outlined in Chapter 5) it does stand in need of justification. In other words, Walzer's argument is incomplete: for his defence of just cause to stand he has to establish that the current international order is valuable enough to generate permissions/duties on the part of states to preserve it.

This concludes my analysis of Walzer's defence of *jus ad bellum*. It is taken as a datum by many that states are entitled to wage war in defence of their sovereignty. In this section I have argued that Walzer's arguments to support this claim are unpersuasive. Neither his appeal to the rights of states nor his appeal to the importance of international society establish that aggression against states is per se a wrong[14] and a wrong that justifies the waging of war.

### III

Let me now move on to consider Walzer's analysis of *jus in bello*, focussing in particular on his account of non-combatant immunity. In chapter 9 of *Just and Unjust Wars* Walzer affirms two key principles. The first maintains that it is always permissible to attack enemy soldiers, except when 'they are wounded or captured' (1977: 138). What of those who are not soldiers who are nonetheless part of the war effort? Walzer makes a persuasive distinction between those whose activities are intrinsically linked to the process of war (like making arms) and those whose activities may assist the waging of war but are not intrinsically linked to the process of war (like for example, farming or healing the sick). The distinction is between what is specifically needed for war and what is generally needed for normal human existence (1977: 146). He then argues that those participating in the production of arms can be attacked only if there are no other ways of preventing them from producing arms. If there are other methods available these should be adopted (1977: 146).

Walzer's second principle states that one cannot attack non-combatants: that is, one cannot intentionally seek to kill non-combatants (1977: 151). Like many others, though, Walzer affirms the principle of double effect which, when applied to warfare, sanctions acts which bring about the death of non-combatants under certain conditions. Walzer presents the following account of double effect. Actions that result in the deaths of non-combatants are justified when

'1) The act is good in itself or at least indifferent, which means, for our purposes, that it is a legitimate act of war.
2) The direct effect is morally acceptable—the destruction of military supplies, for example, or the killing of enemy soldiers.

3) The intention of the actor is good, that is, he aims only at the acceptable effect; the evil effect is not one of his ends, nor is it a means to his ends.
4) The good effect is sufficiently good to compensate for allowing the evil effect; it must be justifiable under Sidgwick's proportionality rule' (1977: 153).

Walzer then argues, however, that (3) needs to be modified for it is too permissive. (3) is insensitive to how many non-combatants die. As long as one is performing an action for the right reason and that is one's only aim and as long as the deaths of the non-combatants are not a means to one's end, then according to (3), it does not matter how many non-combatants die (1977: 153–6). For this reason Walzer argues that (3) should be reformulated to read as follows:

'3) The intention of the actor is good, that is, he aims narrowly at the acceptable effect; the evil effect is not one of his ends, nor is it a means to his ends, and, aware of the evil involved, he seeks to minimize it, accepting costs to himself' (1977: 155).[15]

Its central point, then, is that one has duties to non-combatants and not intending harm to them is insufficient. These two principles thus comprise the key features of Walzer's account of the content of *jus in bello*.

Much later in the book Walzer argues that weighty though these rules of *jus in bello* are, they can be overridden in times of 'supreme emergency' (1977: ch. 16). For Walzer, a supreme emergency is defined in terms of two properties—'the imminence of the danger' and 'its nature' (1977: 252). Supreme emergencies thus exist when there is imminent threat of a morally horrendous outcome. Walzer's example of an acceptable use of the supreme emergency condition is Britain's bombing campaign against Germany during the Second World War. Nazism is clearly evil and since Britain was alone the threat of Nazism was imminent. Accordingly, Britain's use of bombing against civilians was justified in the early stages of the war, although Walzer then goes on to say that it was unjustified later (1977: 255–62). By contrast America's use of an atomic bomb on Hiroshima was not justified under the supreme emergency condition. This is partly because America's insistence on unconditional surrender was inappropriate and partly because the bomb was being used to speed up the end of the war (1977: 263–8).

How adequate is his account of the content and moral significance of *jus in bello*? Walzer's treatment is open to question on both scores. Consider the former. His account of *jus in bello* faces three problems. (i) The first problem is simply that Walzer does not provide any argument for the actual rules he proposes. He simply lays them out and does not adduce any considerations in their defence (Bull 1979: 591, 596–9 (esp. pp. 598–9)). What is lacking in Walzer's account, then, is any actual argument for his rules. (ii) This problem is complicated further because within Walzer's work as a whole there are two distinct, and incompatible, methodological commitments. On some occasions, Walzer invokes universal concepts like human rights and seeks to base his theory on such ideals (1977: xvi, 54). On other occasions, Walzer takes a relativist position affirming that just principles mirror the shared understandings of communities (1983, esp. p. 313) and also arguing that there is no global community (1983: 29–30). These two approaches, however, obviously conflict. Finally, (iii), his account of *jus in bello* and his account of *jus ad bellum* also pull in conflicting directions. Walzer's account of *jus ad bellum*, recall, is strongly communitarian and state-centric. It prioritizes the moral value of states over and above individuals and bestows moral status on states even if they are cruel and repressive and kill individuals (as long as they are not genocidal) (Doppelt 1978, esp. pp. 6–7, 16, 20–6; 1980: 399–400, 402–3; Luban 1980*a*: 169–70, 179–80; 1980*b*: 393–7). His account of *jus in bello*, by contrast, is highly individualistic and prioritizes the rights of individuals: as we have seen, military forces must strive (even at cost to their own safety) not to harm *individual* civilians. It is hard to see, however, how one can square such non-individualistic rules of *jus ad bellum* with such individualistic rules of *jus in bello*. Put otherwise, if Walzer recognizes, as he does in his account of *jus in bello*, the rights of individuals why does he not do so in his account of *jus ad bellum*?[16] The deep problem here is that Walzer adopts what Robert Holmes has termed an 'externalist' account of the relationship between *jus ad bellum* and *jus in bello* (1992: 224).[17] The latter are not derived in any way from the former. There is no logical link between them and hence there is the possibility of conflict. For these three reasons, then, Walzer's account of *jus in bello* is undermotivated and inconsistent with other aspects of his theory.

If we turn now to Walzer's treatment of 'supreme emergencies' we can see that his account of the moral weight of the rules of *jus in bello* is also suspect. First, it is striking that Walzer defends the supreme emergency condition on the grounds that it is needed to defend the 'political community' (1977: 254). He writes, moreover, that:

'it is possible to live in a world where individuals are sometimes murdered, but a world where entire peoples are enslaved or massacred is literally unbearable. For the survival and freedom of political communities—whose members share a way of life, developed by their ancestors, to be passed on to their children—are the highest values of international society. Nazism challenged these values on a grand scale, but challenges more narrowly conceived, *if they are of the same kind*, have similar moral consequences. They bring us under the rule of necessity (and necessity knows no rules)'. (1977: 254)

Killing innocent people is thus needed to preserve 'political communities'. The point is reiterated later when he maintains that attacking non-combatants is justified to prevent 'a defeat likely to bring disaster to a political community' (1977: 268). What is puzzling about this is that it treats political communities as having intrinsic value. Surely though what is wrong with Nazism and other similar phenomena is that they kill individuals. Walzer does, on occasion, recognize that political communities have value only insofar as they protect the rights of individuals (1977: xvi, 54). But then if he accepts this, he should, to be consistent, simply justify the use of the supreme emergency condition in the name of protecting the rights of individuals. Any appeal to the value of 'political communities' is rendered redundant.

The intentions of the political leaders are not really relevant to the question of whether the system is just. Consider examples other than the waging of war. If we accept an egalitarian theory of distributive justice, we think that a distribution is fair if people have equal shares: the intentions of the political authorities are not germane. Theories of distributive justice do not include a 'just intentions' clause stating that a distribution is just only if the politicians responsible for it had the right thoughts and it would be anomalous to claim that just intentions are required for just warfare but not for civil and political justice or distributive justice. If politicians wage war in a way that protects people's rights but some of them do this because they want to be well thought of then this is not pertinent to the question of whether it is just (Moellendorf 2002*a*: 122; cf. also Brown 2002*b*: 108–9). (3) should, thus, be rejected.[28]

Having made these three observations we may now examine the ways in which accepting a cosmopolitan framework requires revisions of the remaining principles—namely (1), (2), and (4).

Let us start with the concept of 'just cause'. Cosmopolitanism has two implications. The first concerns when a regime may wage war in self-defence. Traditional just war theory maintains that *all* states that are attacked have a right to wage war in self-defence. Such a sweeping statement is, however, unsustainable from a cosmopolitan framework because the latter maintains that states (and political systems in general) are legitimate only if they serve the interests or rights of individuals (Barry 1999: sec. IV; Beitz 1994). As we have seen above, states should not be fetishized: they are human institutions and like any other human institution some are wicked, corrupt, repressive, and inhumane. And where they are, there can be no grounds on which to say that they have a *moral right* to defend themselves. This key point is rightly stressed by David Luban in an illuminating discussion of *jus ad bellum* (1980*a*: 160–81).[29] Luban argues that states do not have intrinsic value and that this entails that they do not have an unconditional moral right to defend themselves. The right to wage war in self-defence is a right possessed only by a legitimate state (1980*a*: 164–6).[30] We therefore need a criterion of moral legitimacy. In Luban's view, states are legitimate if they defend human rights and if they enjoy the consent of the people (1980*a*: 167–70).[31] One need not, however, accept Luban's specific (contractarian) account of moral legitimacy. What is crucial here is his point that whether states have the right to wage war in self-defence depends on whether they are legitimate and this is consistent with accepting other cosmopolitan accounts of moral legitimacy (such as, say, a utilitarian approach).

The precise relationship between, on the one hand, the justice of a political system and, on the other hand, whether it has 'just cause' needs to be stated carefully for it can be easily misunderstood. To see this consider two statements about the relationship.

(a) A political regime does not have 'just cause' if it is unjust.
(b) A political regime does not have 'just cause' if it is unjust and waging war does not make it more just than it currently is.

(a) may seem to follow from the reasoning in the previous paragraph and may also seem intuitively plausible. If a regime is unjust how can it claim to have a just cause to defend itself? (b) might also have some appeal. It is affirmed by Moellendorf who, in a discussion of the war to defend Kuwait against Iraq, argues that since Kuwait was unjust and '[s]ince there would be no improvement from the perspective of justice by restoring the Kuwaiti regime to power, the war to do so lacked just cause and was therefore unjust' (2002*a*: 161). However, neither (a) nor (b) is plausible. To see why consider the following example:

> One political regime, X, attacks another political regime, Y. Y is far from being an internally just society. Furthermore, a war defending Y against X's attack (either by Y or by states that come to Y's aid) would not make Y a fairer society. However, if Y (or other states) do not wage war to defend Y against X's attack, and Y is consequently conquered by X, Y will become *even more unjust than it currently is*. As members of a conquered colony they are treated brutally and thoroughly exploited, and suffer even more injustices than they experienced before.

Now according to (a), Y does not have 'just cause' because it is unjust. And according to (b), Y does not have 'just cause' because waging war will not make it a more just society. But this is surely perverse for denying Y (and other states) 'just cause' to defend Y results in an even more unjust state of affairs, one in which there are far more serious rights violations. (a) and (b) result in more injustice. We should, thus, accept a third principle:

(c) A political regime has 'just cause' even if it is unjust (contra (a)) and even if waging war does not make it more just than it currently is (contra (b)) *if waging war produces a more just state of affairs than would be the case if no war is waged and it is conquered without any military resistance.*

The problem with (a) and (b) is that they exclude from their account of 'just cause' the effects on an unjust regime of its being attacked. Once we consider the latter we can see that even unjust political regimes can have just cause. It would be perverse to claim that a regime has no just cause simply because it has a poor human rights record if not waging war would result in an even worse human rights record.

A second way in which cosmopolitanism entails a revised understanding of 'just cause' concerns the question of whether regimes that are not the victims of aggression have a right or duty to wage war in defence of an attacked regime. The conventional understanding of this issue is that (setting aside allies who may have a contractual duty to assist an attacked state), regimes may come to the aid of attacked regimes but are not duty bound to do so.[32] Against this, a cosmopolitan approach maintains that persons have duties to other persons. A corollary of this is that third parties may be under a moral duty to wage war on behalf of the members of a regime that is unjustly attacked.[33] This duty may of course, be balanced against other duties that a regime has (including, notably, duties to its own citizens): the duty is thus overridable. It is nonetheless a genuine duty: a powerful regime that could do something to prevent another regime from being conquered but stands idly by, and thereby allows the institution of an even more unjust state of affairs, is condemned by such a cosmopolitan approach.[34]

If we turn now to the stipulation that just war must be authorized by a legitimate authority, we can see that cosmopolitanism requires a revision in the conventional interpretation of this requirement. Today it is often assumed that this entails that only a *state* can wage a just war. From a cosmopolitan perspective, however, we should not simply assume, without supporting argument, that there should be a world of states and hence that the authority to engage in warfare should rest with states. The existing world order is, no doubt, primarily a state-centric order but it would be wrong to assume that the appropriate legitimate authority is necessarily, in the nature of things, a state. Suppose, for example, that we live in the sort of world order defended in Chapter 5—a world of democratic supra-state authorities. In such an order if one political regime were to attack another, the authority to determine whether force may be used by the latter (and/or others) to repel the former might rest with a supra-state body.[35] For a less extravagant illustration of this argument, consider proposals to pool armed forces—so-called collective security arrangements. Insofar as this occurs, authority passes to supra-state bodies. The central point is that to the extent that we question a purely statist political order we also question whether the right to make war rests with states. Of course, even within our world the recent war against Iraq brought out the fact that many thought that war could have been legitimate only if it was authorized by the United Nations.

At this point it is worth considering a challenge to the claim that war must be sanctioned by a legitimate authority made by Moellendorf. Moellendorf's argument occurs in the context of his discussion of intervention and having identified the principles of a just intervention he then claims that they can be applied to other cases where military force is deployed (2002*a*: 142, 158). It is necessary to bear this in mind to make sense of his argument. His argument has two aspects. First, he argues that legitimate authority has only instrumental value and can only be valued because it results in order. It does not have any intrinsic moral value. Second, he argues that to stipulate that war may only be sanctioned by a legitimate authority may result in outcomes in which people's rights are violated and that a war that could prevent this is forbidden because a legitimate authority has not authorized it. We are faced, then, with a conflict between the value of order and the value of justice and in such cases, claims Moellendorf, we should choose justice (2002*a*: 121).

Since Moellendorf's argument is initially presented in his discussion of intervention, this argument will be discussed more extensively in Chapter 7. However, three points should be made here. First, the second step in Moellendorf's argument is implausible. Why would waiting for a legitimate political institution to authorize war be time-consuming and hence costly? It is hardly likely that a political regime that has been attacked will take an undue amount of time wondering whether it should wage war or not. Here the original context of Moellendorf's argument shows for his assumption about the costs of a 'legitimate authority' principle makes sense in that context (which is not to say that it is correct). It is at least arguable that to require a legitimate authority involves a delay and that that will lead to the unnecessary prolongation of injustice. However, it has little force where A has been attacked and seeks to wage war in self-defence.[36]

Second, Moellendorf's argument overlooks the force of the classical case for legitimate authority. We gain a better understanding of the value of the 'legitimate authority' condition if we consider Aquinas's argument for it. Aquinas reasons that: 'it is not the business of a private individual to declare war, because he can seek redress of his rights from the tribunal of his superior' (1988 [1266–73]: 221). This suggests the following logic: before taking the law into our own hands we must try other more legitimate channels. This is one reason why private individuals cannot wage war. Furthermore, suppose that a wrong is being committed in my regime. I do not have the right to take the law in my own hands because the first option should be to go through the legal channels. Given this the same should be true of using force against an aggressor.[37] The point could be expressed the other way round: since we have justified a set of political institutions with authority to implement principles of justice (in my case the institutional framework specified in Chapter 5) it would be odd not to conclude that it is institutions that have the authority to protect people's rights.[38]

Third, we need to have a legitimate authority because often there is dispute about whether war is justified. Modern societies are not homogeneous; they contain people who hold profoundly different beliefs on when and how war may be waged. To give some obvious examples: there was controversy over the war against Afghanistan. Similarly, the need for a legitimate authority was evident in early 2003 given that there was profound disagreement as to whether war should have been waged against Iraq and, if so, on what grounds. More generally, there is often controversy over whether we have a duty to wage war on behalf of others. There may also be controversy as to what means may be used. And so on. Given such disagreement it is clear that there needs to be an authoritative decision as to what is done: there needs, in other words, to be a legitimate authority. For these three reasons, then, Moellendorf's critique of the idea of legitimate authority is unsuccessful. The principle of legitimate authority stands and the cosmopolitan reformulation of it similarly remains intact.[39]

If we turn now to the concept of proportionality, we can discern a third implication of cosmopolitanism for just war theory. As Jeff McMahan and Robert McKim have persuasively argued, since the concept of 'proportionality' requires one to sum up the costs of war it raises the question of whether one should treat all casualties on a par. To apply the proportionality principle we need to know whether a death of one's own soldier is on a par with the death of an enemy soldier. McMahan and McKim raise this point to argue that it is acceptable to accept some (modest) national partiality (although I think they mean by this a partiality to one's own citizens) (McMahan and McKim 1993: 516–17; McMahan 1996: 87).

Robert Jackson raises a similar point, arguing that a state may adopt some methods (like bombing from a great height) even if it is more likely to result in civilian casualties if it minimizes the chances of the loss of life of one's own airmen and -women. He writes that '[t]he policy of limiting collateral damage—no matter how sincere the combatant's commitment to it, or how precise the available bombing technology—will always come into contact and perhaps conflict with the primary responsibility of all humane commanders: protecting their own people' (2000: 229). He adds later on the same page that this sort of issue constitutes 'a real difficulty with the just-war tradition: it does not come to grips with the ethics of citizenship; it is cosmopolitan in its ethical outlook' (2000: 229). Of course, however, we need not follow McMahan, McKim, and Jackson in this weighting.[40] It is, perhaps, helpful to think here of a continuum, at one end of which is ambitious cosmopolitanism (where this says that all persons—enemy, fellow citizen, or fellow ally—enjoy equal moral weight) and the other end of which is a strong partialism (where this says that enemy combatants and civilians enjoy zero moral weight). Quite how one explicates 'proportionality' depends then on how close one is to the cosmopolitan end of the spectrum. The key point is that one's construal of the principle of proportionality depends on how strong one's commitment is to cosmopolitan principles.

The above considerations provide the bare bones of a cosmopolitan account of *jus ad bellum*. Of course how they are fleshed out depends on what kind of cosmopolitanism one affirms. The point about the above is that it outlines principles of *jus ad bellum* potentially common to all cosmopolitan approaches. Having done this, let us now turn to the contributions that cosmopolitans have made to debates about *jus in bello*.

# VI

We can consider two specific cosmopolitan accounts of *jus in bello*. First to be analysed is a utilitarian approach. It is cosmopolitan in that it treats people as equals; it includes all within its scope; and it recognizes that persons have duties to all other persons (Pogge 1994*a*: 89). What is the utilitarian position on the nature of a just war? The clearest answer to this question is provided by Richard Brandt, who outlines a derivation of utilitarianism and then generates three rules that he thinks should apply to the conduct of war (1972: 145–65).[41]

Let us begin then with his brief derivation of utilitarianism. Brandt reasons as follows: fair principles are those that rational persons would agree to when located behind a veil of ignorance. He then argues that such persons would adopt a qualified form of utilitarianism (1972: 149–50, 152). He contends that egoists will choose utilitarianism because from behind the veil it is the most rational way of maximizing their self-interest and that altruists will choose utilitarianism simply because it maximizes utility (1972: 152). However, he also adds that both will demand that utility be maximized 'subject to the restriction that the rules of war may not prevent a belligerent from using all the power necessary to overcome the enemy' (1972: 152). Persons behind the veil would not 'consent to or follow rules of war which seriously impair the possibility of bringing the war to a victorious conclusion' (1972: 154, cf. more generally pp. 153–4). Brandt's position, then, is that

> correct rules of war are those rules that maximize human happiness subject to the qualification that they must not inhibit people from employing 'all the power necessary' (1972: 152) to win.

Now, using this criterion, Brandt derives rules of war for three distinct types of situation. First, there are, according to Brandt, cases where the observance of moral constraints does not in any way undermine the successful prosecution of the war. In this kind of situation, he argues, utilitarianism requires compliance with these moral constraints. This means, for example, that captured combatants may not be slaughtered and that civilians in occupied territory may not be raped or treated cruelly (1972: 154–5). Second, there are cases where moral constraints are potentially costly to military success (1972: 155). Brandt here argues that one may override a conventional moral constraint if it makes a considerable difference to the successful prosecution of war (1972: 155–60). Stated more precisely he writes that one can disregard the conventional moral restraints if the expected marginal utility that this brings outweighs the expected marginal disutility of this action (1972: 157). Brandt adds that, on this criterion, utilitarianism is likely to condemn bombing civilians because the latter rarely has the (presumably intended) effect of demoralizing civilians and increasing one's chances of victory (1972: 159). Third, there are cases where one might incur military casualties by acting in a humanitarian manner (1972: 160). The sort of issues at stake here include whether one may simply kill prisoners of war given that they will be a drain on one's own resources or whether one can compel civilians in occupied territory to reveal where the enemy is hidden. Brandt argues that the latter would be wrong on utilitarian grounds (1972: 161). The upshot, then, of Brandt's constrained utilitarianism is a vindication of some familiar rules of war—including rules against attacking non-combatants and killing prisoners.

How plausible is this as an account of just war? Brandt's argument is vulnerable to three objections. The first concerns his derivation of utilitarianism. It is far from clear that persons behind a veil of ignorance would choose a principle of maximizing happiness. The reason for doubting this has been stated most forcefully by Rawls who, as is well known, argues that such a choice would be highly irrational. To choose utilitarianism is to risk an outcome in which one could be treated horrendously just because that increases the utility of others (1999c: 135, 138–9). Rawls also invokes what he terms the 'strains of commitment', where these refer to the demands imposed on people by political principles. Rawls makes the point that an agent's commitment to a contract is genuine only if he or she can honour it. That is, a contract can be genuine only if it does not impose unduly demanding 'strains of commitment'. Drawing on this Rawls then reasons that no one can sincerely and genuinely choose utilitarianism for to do so is to choose a principle that he may not be able to honour (1999c: 153–5).[42] Brandt's derivation of utilitarianism is thus suspect.

A second set of problems with Brandt's argument concerns the restriction that he imposes on his utilitarianism. Brandt states, recall, that persons would agree to a utilitarian policy with *the qualification that one can do everything in one's power to win the war (even if it lowers total utility)* (1972: 152). This generates three problems. (i) It is not clear, contra Brandt, that persons would necessarily choose a principle that calls for victory (no matter what the cost). Might some not think that victory (either for them or for the other side) may sometimes come at too high a price? Such a choice seems far from irrational. An overriding blanket commitment to waging war no matter how high the cost to you, to your enemy, or to humanity or large, by contrast, does appear irrational. We simply have no reason to assume that doing everything possible to win a war is in each and every situation the rational choice. (ii) Second, suppose persons choose Brandt's restriction. It is difficult to make sense of this ad hoc qualifier. Adding it runs the risk of rendering Brandt's moral rules of war otiose. It entails that *even if* Brandt's rules of war do follow from his utilitarianism (which I shall call into question shortly) they can be violated whenever doing so prevents one from doing everything in one's power to win the war. In other words, the qualification can sanction policies at variance with Brandt's humanitarian rules, and since it takes priority it sanctions disregard for the rules of war. (iii) Finally, Brandt's ad hoc qualification generates a further problem for he has to explain why, if agents are happy to call for one deviation from utilitarianism, they would not also call for other deviations from utilitarianism. If Brandt allows one impurity in the utilitarian scheme why not others? Why would they not choose a moral theory which is generally consequentialist but which is hedged in by some inviolable rights? Brandt's particular brand of *qualified* utilitarianism is thus implausible.

Further problems surround Brandt's derivation of conventional moral constraints from utilitarian reasoning. One of the commonest criticisms of utilitarianism is, of course, that it sanctions repugnant outcomes. The topic of warfare is, moreover, a rich source of examples in which utilitarian reasoning does appear to generate morally grotesque conclusions. Consider Brandt's third category (1972: 160–1). It is very far from evident that a utilitarian policy does require supplying one's prisoners of war with (possibly scarce) food and medical resources. Brandt reasons that if both sides in a conflict adopted this policy then neither would be worse off. But the opposite is also true: if neither side did it, neither side would be worse off. Each would lose some of their own soldiers who have been captured but then each would also have less of a drain on their food and medical resources. The central point is that it is far from clear that utilitarianism would yield the morally attractive constraints Brandt claims it would.

# VII

Having critically analysed one cosmopolitan analysis of *jus in bello*, let us now consider a second prominent cosmopolitan perspective, namely a deontological approach. Deontological conceptions of civil and political human rights were, of course, examined in Chapter 3. Here I wish to examine the application of deontological principles to just warfare. A number of writers have developed such an account—prominent examples including Elizabeth Anscombe (1981*a*: 51–61; 1981*b*: 62–71) and more recently Richard Norman (1995). This section focuses on the particularly illuminating and powerful treatment provided by Nagel. It will concentrate on his important essay 'War and Massacre' (1972: 123–44) but we should also note that since publishing that essay he has continued to develop and refine the deontological perspective employed in this earlier work (cf. Nagel 1986: 175–85). Nagel's concern is, like Brandt's, exclusively with *jus in bello* and shall be examined as such. In 'War and Massacre' he contrasts utilitarian and deontological (which he terms 'absolutist') approaches to the ethics of war and seeks to motivate support for the deontological approach. The latter emphasizes the evil of performing certain actions and its concern is with the actions one performs rather than the state of affairs that result from those actions. As he puts it: 'what absolutism forbids is *doing* certain things to people, rather than bringing about certain *results*' (1972: 130, cf. more generally pp. 129–31). Absolutism refuses to take an aggregative or maximizing approach. The emphasis is not on the number of bad acts committed but on our not committing them (1972: 131–2). As Nagel again puts it: 'Absolutism requires that we *avoid* murder at all costs, not that we *prevent* it at all costs' (1972: 132).[43]

A deontological (or absolutist) approach, note, is clearly a cosmopolitan account. It includes all persons; stipulates that they must be treated as equals; and generates duties to all individuals (in this case certain negative duties) (Pogge 1994*a*: 89).

Why should we accept this approach? And what rules of war does it generate? Nagel's fundamental thought is that when we are doing something to someone we have to be able to justify what we are doing *to that person* (1972: 134, 136–7). To treat the person with respect we have to be able to give a justification to him or her as to why what we are doing treats them with respect. It requires 'justifying *to the victim* what is being done to him' (1972: 137). Utilitarians will offer 'justifications to the world at large' but this is inadequate for what is required here is a special justification to the person one confronts (1972: 137). Employing this method, Nagel generates two types of moral restrictions (1972: 133). First, it entails that one may not attack non-combatants. To do so would be to use them as a means to an end and not to show them respect (1972: 138–9). His account of who counts as a non-combatant is similar to Walzer's: non-combatants are those not participating in an activity which is solely required to wage war (1972: 139–40).[44] Second, Nagel argues, employing this deontological framework, that one may not use certain weapons—such as starvation or poison—for these attack the person and not simply the soldier (1972: 141, cf. more generally pp. 140–1). One must distinguish 'between the combatant and the human being' and the only appropriate weapons are those that target someone as a combatant and do not target their capacity to be a human being (1972: 141).

Let us now consider Nagel's argument. Nagel's vindication of moral constraints is open to four objections. The first is that it prioritizes and privileges the agent-relative perspective. Let me explain. Consider a case where a soldier is confronted with an instance in which attacking a non-combatant will result in fewer deaths. Consider, for instance, the following example, which is adapted from an example by Richard Norman (1995: 125):

> one is on a commando raid in enemy territory and one's aim is to destroy enemy bomber planes which are used to bomb combatants and civilians in one's own country and in countries of one's allies. Now suppose that one encounters a non-combatant (hereafter $P_i$) who, on seeing you, will inadvertently give away your position. One can prevent this simply by killing her and thereby save the mission. To do otherwise is certain to lead to one's capture and hence to future bombing raids which will kill large numbers of innocent men, women and children ($Q_{i-n}$).

Nagel maintains that one is 'in a special relation' to the agent (1972: 137) and as such one has to be able to justify to her what one does to her.

The problem with this is that it skews everything in her favour. It is surely unfair to say that one has to justify one's action to her but that one does not have an equal obligation to choose a course of action that one can justify to the innocent men, women, and children who will otherwise be killed.[45] Nagel's approach fails, thus, to treat persons *equally* for it privileges and grants unequal moral worth to the person who happens to witness the commando raid. It grants higher moral authority to $P_i$ and effectively demotes the others since no similar justification is, on Nagel's theory, owed to them. A fairer requirement is surely that one treats $P_i$ on all fours with everyone else: to do otherwise is arbitrarily to give some people a lesser moral standing. Nagel's approach does so, moreover, for no reason other than that they have the misfortune not to be the inadvertent witness. Nagel's scheme penalizes some (namely $Q_{i-n}$) who have the misfortune not to be in the agent's position whereas $P_i$ is granted a privileged moral standing simply because of happenstance and sheer fluke.

Second, it is far from clear that Nagel's theoretical apparatus will necessarily yield his absolutist conclusions. More precisely, it is not clear that one *can never* justify policies which call for a rights-violation to the agent whose rights one is about to violate. Why is it not possible to say to a non-combatant: 'look it is only by doing X to you that I can save the lives of many other non-combatants. I recognize that you have rights and that what I am doing violates them but just as much as you have rights so do other men and women and theirs will be violated unless I do X to you. If there were another way I would pursue it but there is not'? Nagel simply asserts that no such justification can be made (1972: 137) but the above is surely cogent. It is moreover a justification directed at the agent in question.

A third problem concerns Nagel's derivation of a ban on certain types of weapons (1972: 140–1). Nagel argues that we can distinguish between attacking the soldier and attacking the human (1972: 141). Weapons such as napalm and flamethrowers, he maintains, are unjust because they harm the person rather than the soldier (1972: 141). Whilst Nagel's distinction does have some intuitive appeal, it can hold up only if we can think of ways of attacking someone as a soldier that do not harm them in any way as a human being. The obvious problem here is that virtually any attack on someone qua-soldier is also an attack on him or her qua-person as well. Take shooting at someone.[46] Nagel allows this as an acceptable way to treat an enemy combatant but surely this represents a fundamental assault on that person as a human being. As Norman expresses the point, '[k]illing an enemy combatant is, if anything is, a case of attacking "the man, not the soldier". It does not just put an end to his soldierly activities, it puts an end to all his activities' (1995: 180).

A final problem stems from a more general problem with deontological moral theories as a class and has already been raised in Chapter 3, Section V. Notwithstanding the intuitive appeal of such theories they are vulnerable to a powerful objection that has proved hard to meet. Simply stated, the charge is that deontological perspectives are 'irrational'.[47] If according to a deontological perspective a certain action (torturing someone) is abhorrent then isn't it even worse if ten people are tortured? The point can be put another way. Deontologists condemn certain actions, but we need to ask what is wrong with these actions (actions like killing innocent people). Surely we condemn such acts because of the impact that they have on people. In other words, certain actions are wrong because of the states of affairs they produce. But, then, if this is the case we should seek to minimize these bad states of affairs: to abstain from one such action, even if performing it would prevent many identical actions, would be perverse.

Nagel's deontological account of *jus in bello*, thus, fails to treat persons as equals. It is unable to generate prohibitions against certain methods of waging war and it is vulnerable to the charge of irrationality.

# VIII

Having criticized two prominent cosmopolitan discussions of *jus in bello*, this section will seek to construct an alternative account that aims to overcome the problems that afflict both the deontological and utilitarian approaches. The account draws on, and is indebted to, Sen's account of rights, notably his essay 'Rights and Agency' (1988). Sen's analysis of rights was employed earlier in Chapter 3, Section V, to criticize deontological analyses of rights but the positive implications of his thought were not fully developed. My aim is to do this here and to apply it to just war theory. Although Sen has not, to my knowledge, discussed 'just war theory' in any of his philosophical writings, his conception of rights nonetheless represents a fruitful approach with which to address the questions surrounding the nature of just warfare.

Let us begin then by outlining his approach. Sen defends what he terms a 'goal rights system', where the latter is defined as '[a] moral system in which fulfilment and non-realization of rights are included among the goals, incorporated in the evaluation of states of affairs, and then applied to the choice of actions through consequential links' (1988: 199). On Sen's approach, then, 'people's enjoyment of their rights' can and should count as one component of a good state of affairs. In this sense, it takes a consequentialist approach to rights. As Sen notes, making this claim is compatible with claiming that rights are intrinsically valuable and/or that their value derives from the benefits they generate (1988: 199–200). What is distinctive about Sen's approach is not the justification he gives of rights (as either intrinsically or instrumentally valuable): it is that persons' ability to exercise their rights is one aspect of a good state of affairs. Thus defined, a goal rights system can be contrasted, to its advantage, with both deontological and utilitarian approaches.

Consider deontological approaches (like Nagel's). The latter, of course, treat rights as 'side-constraints' and issue in negative duties that require us not to perform certain actions.[48] As we saw in Chapter 3 Section V (using Sen's analysis), and has been noted above in the analysis of Nagel, this approach results in irrational outcomes for it will not allow a person to perform an action that will avert a state of affairs containing numerous rights violations (Sen 1988: 190–1, 195–6). A goal rights system, by contrast, is not indifferent to how many people's rights are being protected. In virtue of its sensitivity to consequences, Sen's approach is, therefore, not vulnerable to the charge of irrationality. Consider now utilitarian approaches such as Brandt's. The central problem with this brand of consequentialism is, as we have seen, its indifference to people's rights. Its concern is with maximizing utility and as such it may prove hostile to people's rights. In virtue of its commitment to rights, however, Sen's approach is not vulnerable to this objection (1988: 191–5).[49] A goal rights theory, thus, possesses some intuitive appeal for it combines the virtues of both deontological and utilitarian conceptions and it avoids their vices. Unlike a deontological theory, it does not exclude 'consequential analysis' and, unlike a utilitarian theory, it does not exclude 'non-welfarist evaluation of consequences' (1988: 196).

Now if we accept this cosmopolitan conception of rights it has important implications for our account of *jus ad bellum* and *jus in bello*. To see its relevance to *jus ad bellum* we should return to the point made earlier in Section V, namely that whether a regime is entitled to defend itself, and whether other regimes should come to its aid, depends on whether the attacked state secures the rights of its members and non-members. We need, thus, a more general account of when and why political regimes have moral worth. And Sen's rights-centred framework provides such an account for it implies that whether a regime is morally legitimate depends on the extent to which it realizes the protection of people's individual rights. Accordingly, *if* we accept that what rights regimes have (including the right to wage war in self-defence) depends on their legitimacy (step one) and *if* we accept that the appropriate criterion of legitimacy is the extent to which a regime protects people's rights (step two), it follows that whether a regime has the right to wage war in self-defence, and also whether other regimes ought to come to its aid, depend on whether it satisfactorily protects the rights of its members and non members.

If we turn now to *jus in bello*, it follows from this conception of rights that military forces must observe certain rights. To do otherwise is not to respect persons and their fundamental interests. This conception, it should be noted, *might* allow that in extreme circumstances it is permissible to violate non-combatant immunity if, and to the extent that, this is needed to protect the rights of a larger group of non-combatants. This, however, should not be confused with Walzer's version of the supreme emergency condition. It differs in three crucial respects. First, Walzer's justification of supreme emergency invokes the importance of the integrity of the political community: i.e., not the rights of persons. Second, Walzer sanctions the violation of non-combatant immunity even when lives are not at stake. Third, Walzer's account excludes from consideration the rights and interests of those who are not members of the attacked state. A rights-based account by contrast factors in not simply the rights of the members of the political system facing imminent danger but also the rights and interests of each and everyone.

The above is, of course, very schematic and much more needs to be said in its defence. However, before concluding this section, it is worth drawing attention to two further virtues of the account. First, unlike other theories (notably Walzer's), it can give a unified account of *jus ad bellum* and *jus in bello*. As I argued earlier, Walzer's theory is flawed because he fails to provide an integrated account of the rules of *jus ad bellum* and *jus in bello*. Indeed the principles embodied in his version of *jus ad bellum* conflict with the principles embodied in his version of *jus in bello*.[50] The upshot of this is that the two come into conflict. One advantage of the cosmopolitan account sketched above is that such a conflict cannot arise because both *jus ad bellum* and *jus in bello* are derived from a common source—namely the rights of individuals. Second: although this chapter is not directly concerned with civil war it is nonetheless relevant to note that a cosmopolitan account is better able to provide principles to govern civil war than are statist conceptions of just war. Since the latter derive their conclusions from the practices of states and what states can agree to, it is not at all clear how suitable their principles are for conflict within the state or when there is in effect no state. A cosmopolitan account, by contrast, can simply ascribe the respective principles of *jus ad bellum* and *jus in bello* by drawing on its account of the equal rights of all persons.

# IX

Some are likely to be sceptical of the theories that have been presented thus far. Some thinkers, informed by realist sentiments, are critical of the sorts of values defended by statists like Walzer and Nardin and are yet more critical of cosmopolitan conceptions such as those examined in the previous four sections. Common to these criticisms is a belief that these understate the importance of power politics and the national interest and attribute too significant a role to moral and legal considerations. It is worth noting that even if one rejects realist claims on other issues, realism is perhaps best suited to discussions of warfare. Since many realist prescriptions operate on the assumption that the relations between states are characterized by conflict and mistrust, one might expect realist normative claims to have most force during times of war. In this and the following section I shall therefore examine realist perspectives on just war. As David Mapel observes, we can identify realist perspectives on both *jus ad bellum* and *jus in bello* (Mapel 1996, esp. p. 55; cf. also Wight 1991: 220–1).

Let us begin, then, with *jus ad bellum*. As we have seen throughout this book, what matters from a realist point of view is the promotion of the national interest. A foreign policy that maintains that the state's duty is to further the national interest issues in at least four implications for the rules of *jus ad bellum*.

1. First, as both Mapel and Martin Wight observe, some realists maintain that it justifies pre-emptive strikes or even preventive wars if these can work (Mapel 1996: 59–60; Wight 1991: 220).[51] Consider a state of affairs in which a state is evidently going to attack another state. Given the state's duty to protect its national interest, then there would seem to be a prima facie case for the second state's striking the first blow, rather than waiting until it is attacked and then responding.

2. A second implication pulls in the other direction. Whereas the first implication of a realist perspective is that states should be more warlike than conventional just war theory, a second implication of a commitment to the national interest is that there are occasions in which states should not wage war in self-defence where conventional just war theory would permit it (Mapel 1996: 61). Thus whereas just war theory entails a right of self-defence, realists would sometimes counsel a state not to exercise this right. E. H. Carr provides a clear illustration of this point for in *The Twenty Years's Crisis* he famously argued for appeasing Hitler (Dunne 1998: 44–5, fn. 61). Where an aggressor is powerful and the waging of war is extremely costly, one may best promote the national interest by not fighting but appeasing the enemy. This is not, note, in itself, a contradiction of orthodox just war theory because it is not denying the alleged right. It recommends that states do not seek to defend themselves by waging war and this is consistent with claiming that states have this right.

3. A third implication of the realist perspective on *jus ad bellum* concerns the aims of war. Conventional just war theory, and cosmopolitan approaches, maintain that states should wage war to achieve a just peace. If, however, states should seek solely to further their national interest then they have no reason to aim for justice or peace except insofar as it promotes their national interest.[52]

4. To this we should also add, fourth, that realists would reject out of hand the cosmopolitan claim advanced in Section V that states have a duty to come to

the aid of other states that have been unfairly attacked. If the national interest is the prime value, then states have no reason to assist other beleaguered states unless doing so happens to coincide with its national interest. It is on these lines, for example, that Robert Tucker and David Hendrickson criticize the USA's waging of war against Iraq to liberate Kuwait in 1991. Their argument in *The Imperial Temptation* is that states should promote their own interests and since the USA had no need to wage war against Iraq to protect its interests it should not have done so. War on behalf of others is wrong (Tucker and Hendrickson 1992, esp. p. 16). In the same vein a prominent contemporary neo-realist writes, 'wars should not be fought for idealistic purposes, but instead for balance-of-power reasons' (Mearsheimer 1995: 48).

Underpinning each of these claims is a commitment to prioritizing the national interest over and above any respect for the rights of other states or the members of other states. As such, three points are in order.

1. First, since the rationale for each of these claims depends directly on whether we accept a lexically prime goal of maximizing the national interest, it is worth revisiting the sorts of arguments adduced for privileging the national interest and considering their applicability to questions of warfare. For example, one standard argument for realism maintains that adhering to moral precepts actually makes matters worse and that states achieve (morally) better outcomes if they advance their own interests. Such an argument, however, lacks force when we consider *jus ad bellum*. Given the enormous differences in military capacity, a system in which states sought only their own interests would involve the powerful subjugating the weak.

2. Second, when appraising the claim that states must subordinate all other objectives to their pursuit of the national interest it is worth pondering why the state should enjoy this status. After all we deny this to other human institutions. Why then should we allow states to exempt themselves from working within the bounds of justice? If we do not think that other institutions—like churches or economic firms or trade unions—may further their interests by violating background principles of justice then why should we think the state any different? (Barry 1991*b*: 165; Pogge 1992*a*: 93–4).

3. Third, it is worth considering the realist defence of pre-emptive strikes and preventive wars. This argument suffers from an epistemological and a moral objection. The epistemological problem is that states will rarely, if ever, have certain knowledge that an attack is imminent and there is therefore a high risk of a state attacking when it lacks good reason to do so. The problems that the United States and the United Kingdom have had in establishing that Iraq possessed weapons of mass destruction are a particularly graphic illustration of the difficulties in claiming that one knows that a state is willing and able to attack. The moral problem is that a practice of pre-emptive strikes is highly likely to accelerate conflict.

# X

Having considered realist positions on *jus ad bellum* let us turn now to realist perspectives on *jus in bello*. The realist claim can be described as arguing for what might be termed a *minimizing* effect. By this I mean that realists tend to argue that the role of principles, such as that of non-combatant immunity, should be rejected to the extent that they impede the protection of the national interest and they are more willing to argue that necessity justifies overriding such principles (Mapel 1996: 65–8, 68–73). In Wight's words, one feature 'of the Realist doctrine is the acceptance of unlimited war, of the maximum exercise of strength. . . . War is inherently illimitable and uncontrollable' and hence 'talk of "methods too horrible to employ" is sentimental nonsense' (1991: 220, cf. pp. 220–1). Many realists do not argue that moral considerations should be abandoned: it is rather that traditional just war theory (and cosmopolitan conceptions) grant undue importance to certain 'idealistic' moral considerations and grant insufficient importance to the primacy of the national interest.[53] Realists are thus keener to invoke supreme emergency conditions to override rules of *jus in bello*.

Why should we accept this line of reasoning? The key normative premise in this argument asserts that the extent to which one should comply with moral strictures depends upon, and is proportionate to, the extent to which one can expect others to reciprocate. The idea here is that one would be foolish to comply with rules such as those of non-combatant immunity and the rule to use proportionate force if one's opponent does not. It adds, moreover, that in wartime one can have no guarantee that one's opponent will comply. People will simply not adhere to any proposed rules of just conduct since the state of war is, by its nature, one of violent disagreement. But given this, why should one stick to the rules if one's opponent does not?[54]

There are three possible replies to this line of reasoning. First, one might argue along constructivist lines that the national interest is often defined in moral terms. That is, one might argue that people build into their conception of their national interest certain moral standards and ideals. Hence fulfilling their national interest requires them to conform to certain moral standards. To perform acts like intentionally killing civilians or using disproportionate means may then be to abandon their national interest because it is in contradiction of their self-image as civilized and just. How relevant this point is depends upon two factors. First, it depends on the extent to which a state's conception of its national interest has moral notions built into it. Perhaps they are a subordinate and minor component of it. Second, it is a function of the content of those moral notions. It depends, that is, on whether a state is profoundly committed to human rights or humanitarian virtues or whether it sees such values as signs of weakness. Nonetheless, it is fair to say that for many states it is part of their self-image that they treat both combatants and non-combatants fairly.

A second response to the argument targets the empirical assumption that states will not comply with moral codes during war. Key to the realist argument is the assumption that those in a state of war with each other will not agree to abide by some rules of humanity and cannot trust one another. This too, how-ever, is contestable as a description of relations during war and its scepticism is too sweeping. As a number of writers observe, even in conflict people can agree on certain rules of war (Jackson 2000: 217–18; Walzer 1977: 3–20, esp. pp. 11–20). Indeed, Morgenthau himself argues that states tend to rule out certain courses of action as morally unacceptable (1985: 252–5), although he adds that there has been a decline in observance of rules of *jus in bello*, a decline he thinks results from increasing democratization and nationalism (1985: 256–74). Even though his emphasis is on the decline in standards what his discussion makes clear is that compliance is variable depending on historical and social circumstances. Any sweeping assertion to the effect that during war there can be no common standards should thus be rejected. It may be tempting to think that when there is violent conflict there are no holds barred but such temptation should be resisted.[55]

Finally, and most crucially, we might question the normative assumption made by this argument that a state can be obligated to comply with rules of *jus in bello* only if the state(s) with which it is at war also complies with them. Performance of duties is thus conditional on other parties (most notably one's enemy) reciprocating. This assumption is, however, not self-evidently true. Against it, one might reason that it is the mark of a civilized state not to descend to cruelty and injustice just because its enemy does and that to do so is to forfeit some of its moral standing. The idea here is that one should not stoop to the same low levels as others if one is to retain one's moral integrity and decency. One might, however, reach the same conclusion by another route. Look at it from the point of view of the victims and consider the non-combatant members of a state with which one is at war. Suppose that the enemy initially complies with rules of *jus in bello* but later violates them. The central reason for not harm-ing non-combatants (or for minimizing harm to them) surely stems from their moral standing and dignity as persons. But if this is the case, then does this not remain constant even if one of their military commanders himself commits war crimes? His act does not lower their moral standing or their intrinsic value. Their moral worth and the obligations that one had before surely remain the same as before.

To this one might add that the realist argument gains force if we anthropo-morphize states and treat them as analogous to individuals. Consider a situation where two individuals are in conflict. If one adopts underhand methods then one *might* (notwithstanding the last point) argue that in doing so he or she has relin-quished their right not to have the same done to them. Accordingly, the other is no longer bound by a duty to honour the rules. The realist argument, I want to suggest, acquires any intuitive plausibility it possesses from appealing to this sort of two-person situation. However, war between states is disanalogous to such situations for what is almost always the case is that one person or persons from state A commits a violation against members of state B and then some members of state B commit a violation against some members of state A *who did not commit the initial violation.* So we cannot say that they brought it upon themselves and relinquished their immunity to be treated in this way for the person(s) committing the atrocity and the person(s) suffering the ensuing response are not one and the same. Hence any intuitive appeal that the two-person example has (and I am not arguing that it should be endorsed) cannot be transposed to the international level and employed to legitimize one state transgressing rules of *jus in bello* if its opponent is doing so or has done so.

# XI

This concludes the arguments of this chapter. The aim throughout has been to assess the question of whether political regimes may wage war in response to external wrongs and, if so, when and how may they wage war. More particularly it has argued that

(1) Walzer's account of *jus ad bellum* is flawed and that none of his defences of the right of states to wage war in self-defence is persuasive. He does not, moreover, provide an argument for his rules of *jus in bello* and his account of when and why it may be overridden is too permissive;

(2) Nardin's defence of *jus ad bellum* presupposes a commitment to the society of states and that his derivation of non-combatant immunity and proportionality are unpersuasive.

Having examined two state-centric perspectives, the chapter then turned to cosmopolitanism, and

(3) constructed a general cosmopolitan account of just war, outlining the principles that would be endorsed from a cosmopolitan point of view.

It then proceeded to examine two specific cosmopolitan contributions to just war theory, arguing that

(4) Brandt's utilitarian analysis of *jus in bello* fails because (a) he does not provide a compelling defence of his qualified utilitarianism and (b) he fails to show that morally acceptable rules of war issue from it; and

(5) Nagel's deontological analysis of *jus in bello* fails (a) to treat persons as equals, (b) to explain why certain weapons may not be employed, and (c) to meet the charge of irrationality.

It then

(6) outlined a particular consequence-sensitive account of rights and sought to derive principles of *jus ad bellum* and *jus in bello* from it.

Finally, it critically assessed

(7) realist challenges to orthodox and cosmopolitan conceptions of *jus ad bellum* and *jus in bello,* arguing that none succeed.

One further point that emerges from the analysis in this chapter is the interconnected nature of a global political theory. The analysis of this chapter has shown how an account of just war would be incomplete if it were conducted in isolation from an analysis of other issues in global political theory. This holds for three reasons. First, as we have seen above, many accounts of just warfare argue that aggression is justified in defence of a political regime's rights. For this argument to succeed, however, we need to know what rights such regimes have and what moral standing is possessed by the state that has been attacked (Chapter 5). Second, conventional accounts of *jus in bello* maintain, as we have seen above, that individuals (including both combatants and non-combatants) have rights. It thus rests on an account of persons' civil and political human rights (Chapter 3). Third, an adequate account of just war cannot be divorced from an analysis of the nature and strength of persons' obligations to fellow citizens and to fellow human beings (Chapter 4).[56] The upshot of these considerations then is that analyses of just warfare should not be conducted in isolation from analyses of other issues in global political theory.[57]

## NOTES

1. Here I follow Rawls (1999*b*: 90–105).
2. I should stress that my account cannot claim, in any way, to be exhaustive. It does not, for example, discuss the important contributions to the just war tradition by some distinguished contributors like Paul Ramsey. Nor does it discuss the defences of pacifism given by Christian thinkers like Leo Tolstoy (1987 [original date unknown]), Stanley Hauerwas (1986), and John Howard Yoder (1994) or those by secular thinkers like Robert Holmes (1992). For discussions of Christian pacifism see Cartwright (1996) and Koontz (1996).
3. However, civil war is examined where it bears on the question of whether an external agent may intervene in another regime that is being torn apart by civil war. Civil war almost certainly issues in human rights violations and as such is a potential ground for intervention. As such it is covered by the principles of humanitarian intervention analysed in Ch. 7.
4. The above seven rules are drawn from James Turner Johnson (1999: 28–9). For a similar account see Norman (1995: 118). The only difference between Norman and Johnson is that the former, unlike the latter, includes the principle that there must be a formal declaration of war (1995: 118) and that the latter, unlike the former, requires that war be fought with the intention of attaining peace (1999: 29). For another very similar account of the just war tradition see the United States Catholic Bishops' document 'The Challenge of Peace: God's Promise and Our Response' (1992, esp. pp. 98–101). For a canonical statement of the first three conditions see Aquinas, *Summa Theologiae*, II-II, question 40, 'Of War', First Article (1988 [1266–73]: 221).
5. See, again, Johnson (1999: 29). See also Norman (1995: 119) and US Catholic Bishops (1992: 101, 101–4).
6. This is his first of five modifications to the legalist paradigm. Three other modifications concern the legalist paradigm's absolute prohibition on intervention: as we shall

see, Walzer details three instances in which intervention is acceptable (1977: 90–108). His fifth and final modification concerns the right to punish (1977: ch. 7). Walzer's account of non-intervention is analysed in Ch. 7, Sect. III and VII.

7. Brian Orend claims that '[i]t is crucial to note that, for Walzer, the moral standing of a state *is contingent upon* its protection of its members, both individually and collectively' (2000: 91). My point is that Walzer fails to recognize the implications of thinking a state's moral standing is contingent in this way for his account of *jus ad bellum*. (It should also be stressed that the amount of protection the state needs to provide to have moral standing, for Walzer, is very low).

8. The argument of this paragraph supports the methodological point made in Ch. 1 about the interconnected nature of global political theory since it shows that one's conclusions about the legitimacy of particular states and one's position on the legitimacy of humanitarian intervention should inform one's account of when states may wage war in self-defence. To conduct the different questions in isolation is unacceptable for one's account of when a state may use force in another state (i.e. when it may use aggression) must cohere with one's account of when a state may use force to repel another state (i.e. when it may repel aggression). Otherwise one could generate the contradictory result that both forces had just aims.

9. There is a footnote after the word 'liberty' in which Walzer links the right of states to resist and the duty of citizens to fight (1977: 54–5).

10. See also Walzer's use of the term the 'domestic analogy' (1977: pp. 58, 61). On (1997, p. 58 footnote 9) he cites Bull's two 1966 essays on this: see Walzer (1977, p. 339, footnote 9) and Bull (2000*a*, *b*).

11. This problem is discussed at further length in Ch. 7, Sect. III. For good criticisms of the analogy Walzer deploys see Norman (1995: 132–4, and also pp. 134–8). See, more generally, his probing and comprehensive analysis of Walzer's account of *jus ad bellum* (1995: 132–40, 149–56).

12. This discrepancy is noted by both Glover (1986: 251–2) and Norman (1995: 1, 38–9).

13. Walzer's wording unwittingly concedes this. He writes: 'The rights of the member states must be vindicated, for it is only by virtue of those rights that there is a society at all. If they cannot be upheld (*at least sometimes*), international society collapses into a state of war or is transformed into a universal tyranny' (1977: 59, my emphasis). The clause in brackets appears to concede the possibility that aggression need not always be met with war for international society to survive.

14. Compare Walzer's position with Elizabeth Anscombe's striking statement: '[t]he present-day conception of "aggression," like so many strongly influential conceptions, is a bad one. Why *must* it be wrong to strike the first blow in a struggle? The only question is, who is in the right, if anyone is' (1981*a*: 52).

15. For the application of this principle to two case studies see Walzer (1977: 157–8).

16. This conflict between a collectivist commitment to state sovereignty, on the one hand, and a commitment to individual rights, on the other, surfaces in other aspects of Walzer's analysis of international affairs. For four additional instances see Frost (1996: 133–5).

17. Holmes provides a perspicacious analysis of the relationship between *jus ad bellum* and *jus in bello* in Walzer's work, relating it in particular to Walzer's treatment of supreme emergencies (1992: 217–22, esp. pp. 217, 221–2). Cf. also Walzer (1992: 224–6).

18. Kant (1996 [1797]: part II, ch. II, sec. 60, pp. 118–19).

19. For this point see also Nardin (1983: 302–3).

20. The ideal of a society of states entails not just the right of self-defence. Nardin maintains that it also follows that 'a state may in some circumstances use force to vindicate the rights of other states and their inhabitants' (1983: 287).

21. Nardin's account is framed only for instances where the external aggressor is another state but his argument could be extended to deal with non-state aggressors. The key criterion would be the same, viz., who is a participant in the conflict.

22. There is a footnote after the word 'citizens' which refers to the Roman practice whereby citizens who volunteered to fight did so by taking an oath specifying the particular enemy to be fought (1968 [1762]: bk. I, ch. 4, p. 56).

23. For an earlier version of this argument see Rousseau's discussion in *Fragments on War* (1991*b* [c.1755–1756]: 52).

24. For other interesting accounts of just war which also affirm the idea of a society of states/peoples see Rawls (1999*c*: 331–3; 1999*b*: 37, 89–105). Space precludes an examination of these arguments here.

25. One partial exception to this is Moellendorf who has a chapter on just war (2002*a*: ch. 7; cf. also 2002*b*). However, Moellendorf's treatment is limited in four ways. The first concerns his conception of 'just cause'. Moellendorf's statement of the latter is framed very much in terms of the account of humanitarian intervention that he supplies in an earlier chapter of his book. Throughout he assumes that waging war involves invading a state (2002*a*: 104, 159–60). The same problem is apparent in his official statement of 'just cause'. Moellendorf asserts that a regime has just cause in only two circumstances. In his own words 'just cause for the use of military force exists if and only if the intervention is directed toward advancing justice in the basic structure of the state or the international effects of its domestic policy' (2002*a*: 159). This, however, is radically incomplete for it is silent on whether a regime has just cause to wage war in self-defence when it has been attacked. The first point, then, is that Moellendorf's argument is distorted by its exclusive concern with intervention and overlooks, or perhaps rejects without argument, the claim that war may be waged to defend a just state from attack. A second limitation in Moellendorf's treatment of just war is that he explicitly does not discuss or provide an account of rules of *jus in bello* (2002*a*: 158; 2002*b*: 109). His account of both *jus ad bellum* and *jus in bello* is incomplete. As we shall see below, Moellendorf's account also suffers from two further problems. In particular, a third limitation of his account is that it affirms an unduly narrow account of 'just cause' (2002*a*: 161). Fourth and finally, Moellendorf wrongly rejects the claim that war may only be waged by a legitimate authority (2002*a*: 121).

26. I have omitted a seventh principle that Johnson gives—the statement that the goal of war must be a fair peace (1999: 29)—because this is best understood, not as a separate condition, but as part of what makes a cause just (principle 1).

27. The relevance of this will be apparent in Ch. 7 when we examine military humanitarian intervention. As we shall see there, it is arguable that there are options (such as economic sanctions) which are even worse in their effects than military action. In such cases, (5) is implausible—war is not the last resort and should be resorted to before sanctions—a failing that $(5_i)$ is not vulnerable to.

28. Two further points. First, although Moellendorf is a cosmopolitan, this argument does not, of course, depend on any cosmopolitan assumptions. Second, Moellendorf is not entirely consistent in his eschewal of the significance of the intentions of those

waging war and when exploring the justice of the Gulf War he questions the motives of the allies (2002*a*: 161).

29. See also Norman who writes: 'in deciding whether a community ought to be defended, we cannot escape the need to make *qualitative* judgements about its cultural and political life. We cannot short-cut the argument by appealing to the concept of political sovereignty' (1995: 153).

30. As Luban writes, '[a] legitimate state has a right against aggression because people have a right to their legitimate state' (1980*a*: 166).

31. For Luban's conception of rights see (1980*a*: 174–5). For his rights-based account of 'just cause' see Luban (1980*a*: 175). See further (1980a: 175–6).

32. See, for example, Samuel Pufendorf's discussion. He maintains that '[o]ne may wage war on another's behalf as well as for oneself. This is justified where the party for whom one is going to war has a just cause, and where the party coming to aid has a reasonable ground for conducting hostilities on his behalf against the third party' (1991 [1673]: bk. II, sec. 16, subsec. 11, p. 170). However, reasonable grounds for Pufendorf are that the attacked state is one of 'our subjects' or 'allies' or 'friends' or related to us by 'kinship' (1991 [1673]: bk. II, sec. 16, subsec. 11, pp. 170–1). Where none of these apply there is no duty.

33. This is, I think, briefly recognized in Luban's analysis but he does not develop the point (Luban 1980*a*: 175). (Moreover, in a later publication he retracts his earlier view (2002: 93–4, 111–12, fn. 30)). Cf. also Richard Norman's cautious assent to the idea of using force to defend another (1995: 131–2).

34. Grotius, we should note, maintains that 'kings, and those who possess rights equal to those kings, have the right of demanding punishments not only on account of injuries committed against themselves or their subjects, but also on account of injuries which do not directly affect them but excessively violate the law of nature or of nations in regard to any persons whatsoever' (1925 [1646]: bk. II, ch. XX, sec. XL, pp. 504–6). And he challenges Vitoria and others 'who in justification of war seem to demand that he who undertakes it should have suffered injury either in his person or his state, or that he should have jurisdiction over him who is attacked' (1925 [1646]: bk. II, ch. XX, sec. XL, p. 506).

35. This point is also recognized by Orend (1999: p. 334, fn. 28 and p. 343, fn. 46).

36. A question: what of third parties that are willing to wage war to defend a just political regime that is under attack? To require that such third parties can wage war only if they are authorized to do so might involve a delay. This is true, but the appropriate reply to it is that they need to be authorized because the attacked regime may not want their support. It might not, for example, want to be beholden to the United States.

37. The argument being employed here has some affinities with the idea of 'least awful option'. Whereas the principle of 'least awful option' refers to the kinds of methods employed and insists that military force can only be employed if other less severe methods have been considered first; the principle of 'legitimate authority' refers to the kinds of bodies who can wage war and insists that we should first expect certain legitimate authorities to wage war.

38. Consider again Aquinas's defence of the 'legitimate authority' principle. He writes: 'since the care of the common weal is committed to those who are in authority, it is their business to watch over the common weal of the city, kingdom, or province subject to them. And just as it is lawful for them to have recourse to the sword in defending that common weal against internal disturbances . . . so too it is their business to have

recourse to the sword of war in defending the common weal against external enemies' (1988 [1266–73]: 221). Aquinas here invokes the authority of Augustine citing his *Contra Faustum*, XXII, 75: see Aquinas (1988 [1266–73]: 229, fn. 7).

39. An additional, distinct, argument for the importance of 'legitimate authority' is developed by David Rodin. Rodin argues as follows: war can (only) be defended as an action of law enforcement and punishment (2002: 174–88). The practices of law enforcement and punishment require a legitimate authority (2002: 175). Hence the waging of war must be authorized by a legitimate authority. Rodin also argues that states do not have the authority to wage war in order to enforce international law (2002: 176–9) and argues that such authority should rest with a global state (2002: 179–88).

40. See Ch. 4, Sect. X and also Caney (1996*a*; 1999*a*).

41. See also R. M. Hare (1972: 166–81). Brandt's focus, note, is exclusively on *jus in bello* and his account is silent on *jus ad bellum*.

42. See also Rawls (1999*a*: 229–30).

43. There is a footnote after the word 'costs' in which Nagel reflects on the possibility that non-avoidance of an evil action (e.g. murdering someone) is worse than non-prevention of that action (not stopping a murder) but that it is not prohibited (1972: 132, fn. 6).

44. See also Anscombe (1981*a*: 53).

45. For a related point made from a utilitarian point of view see Hare (1972: 183).

46. Nagel himself raises the question of why shooting is acceptable on his framework (1972: 141, fn. 11).

47. The problem is well-stated by Robert Nozick (1974: 30). Nozick, of course, believes the objection can be met, arguing that deontological injunctions 'express the inviolability of other persons' (1974: 32, cf. more generally pp. 30–3). For an illuminating discussion of this problem see Scheffler (1982: 82–114). See too Norman (1995: 76–7) who reports this consequentialist charge but does not endorse it.

48. The term is Nozick's (1974: 29, 29–35). In *Anarchy, State and Utopia*, Nozick anticipates a moral theory with the structure of Sen's 'goal rights' approach. He refers, for example, to 'a "utilitarianism of rights" ' which he describes as the view that 'violations of rights (to be *minimized*) merely would replace the total happiness as the relevant end state in the utilitarian structure' (1974: 28).

49. As we saw in Ch. 3, Sect. V, Sen's critique of both utilitarianism and deontological moral theories employs an example in which one person, Ali, will get bashed by some racists unless one breaks into someone's room, thereby finds out where Ali is, and consequently warns him (1988: 191–6).

50. Cf. again Holmes (1992, esp. pp. 217–22, 224–6).

51. This, of course, bears on the war against Iraq in 2003 since President George W. Bush defended the war on the grounds that the United States was entitled to engage in preemptive strikes to prevent Iraq from using weapons of mass destruction against it.

52. Consider Schmitt's view: 'The justification of war does not reside in its being fought for ideals or norms of justice, but in its being fought against a real enemy.' (1996 [1932]: 49)

53. Consider, however, Machiavelli's statement in *The Discourses* that 'one's Country should be defended whether it entail Ignominy or Glory, and that it is Good to defend it in any way whatsoever' (1988 [1531]: bk. III, sec. 41, p. 514). He continues in the same section to say 'For when the safety of one's country wholly depends on the decision to be taken, no attention should be paid either to justice or injustice, to kindness or cruelty, or to its being praiseworthy or ignominious. On the contrary, every other

consideration being set aside, that alternative should be wholeheartedly adopted which will save the life and preserve the freedom of one's country' (1988 [1531]: bk. III, sec. 41, p. 515).

54. A version of this argument is given by David Hume in his *An Enquiry Concerning the Principles of Morals*. Arguing that principles of justice derive their validity from being mutually advantageous, Hume writes 'were a civilized nation engaged with barbarians, who observed no rules even of war, the former must also suspend their observance of them, where they no longer serve to any purpose; and must render every action or rencounter as bloody and pernicious as possible to the first aggressors' (1988 [1777]: sec. III, part 1, subsec. 148, pp. 187–8). Hume, note, claims not simply that the 'civilized nation' may suspend their commitment to principles of justice: they 'must' do so as much as 'is possible'.

55. We should also add that even if the enemy is deliberately targeting civilians and even if one thinks along purely rational lines one may have reason to pause before committing a violation if one's state has signed up to the International Criminal Court. If so, one may be prosecuted and one may be prosecuted even if one's enemy also committed rights violations. We should not, perhaps, make too much of this save to note that there may be prudential reasons for compliance even when one's enemy is not complying.

56. For this point see McMahan and McKim (1993: 516–17) and McMahan (1996: 87). (McMahan also argues that the weight of people's duties to fellow citizens is relevant to an account of 'last resort' (1996: 87–8)). On the more general point that just war theories presuppose an account of our duties to foreigners see Nussbaum (2000*b*: 177–8). For pertinent discussions of the weight of persons' duties to their fellow citizens in comparison with the weight of their duties to enemy persons see also Jackson (2000: 229) and Walzer (1977: 158).

57. These are not the only kinds of interdependencies between topics in global political theory. Consider, for example, two additional interconnections between war and distributive justice. First, the existence of warfare raises questions about *to whom* aid should be supplied? Should it, for example, go to aggressors and sustain them in their conduct of an evil war? Do people forfeit their entitlement to receive aid if such aid enables them to wage war unjustly on others (Slim 1997)? Second, and relatedly, any plausible normative account of distributive justice must be sensitive to the causes of poverty. It is sometimes assumed that the causes of poverty are natural calamities like famine but warfare can often cause it. For example, Alex de Waal has persuasively argued that the war waged by the Ethiopian military forces in Tigray and north Wollo in 1980–5 led intentionally to famine in those parts of Ethiopia (1997: 115–21). The military forces destroyed crops, animals, and food reserves, bombed market places and food transportation, prevented trade, food supplies, and mobility of traders and their produce, relocated people, and prevented relief from getting through to rebel areas (1997: 117–120). Given that war can be a cause of famine, some conventional responses to famine (exporting food and medical supplies) are insufficient because they do not tackle the problem at root. If, then, one holds that members of western societies have considerable duties to protect the entitlements of disadvantaged persons in Africa, it follows that fulfilment of this duty requires addressing the causes of war. The central point is that an adequate normative account of global distributive justice cannot be divorced from an empirical analysis of war.

# 7

# Humanitarian Intervention

The voyager reflected: It's always a serious business to intervene decisively in other people's affairs. He was neither a citizen of the penal colony nor a citizen of the state to which it belonged. If he wished to condemn this execution, or even to prevent it, they could say to him: You are a stranger, hold your peace. To that he could make no answer, but simply add that in this instance he was a mystery to himself, for he was voyaging as an observer only, and by no means with any intention of changing other people's judicial systems. But here the circumstances were indeed extremely tempting. The injustice of the procedure and the inhumanity of the execution were beyond all doubt. No one could presume any kind of self-interest on the voyager's part, for the condemned man was unknown to him, was no fellow countryman, and by no means a person who inspired sympathy.

Franz Kafka, *In The Penal Colony* (1992 [1919]: 138)

What does this non-intervention principle in real fact now mean? It means precisely this—Intervention on the wrong side; Intervention by all who choose, and are strong enough, to put down free movements of peoples against corrupt governments. It means co-operation of despots against peoples, but no co-operation of peoples against despots.

Guiseppe Mazzini 'Non-Intervention' in *Life and Writings of Joseph Mazzini*.
(Smith, Elder (1870: vol. vi, pp.305–6) as quoted in Wight (1966b: 114))

The last chapter analysed one kind of injustice—what I termed *external* injustices. This chapter continues to examine non-ideal theory and turns its attention to what I have termed *internal* injustices. What should an external agent do when injustices are taking place within another political society? The chapter addresses the following sorts of question: is state sovereignty inviolable? How morally defensible is Article 2(7) of the United Nations Charter, which affirms the principle of non-intervention? How acceptable is Article 2(4), which proscribes the use of force? May a state or international institution (like the United Nations) intervene in the affairs of another state or international institution? Is there, for example, a case for intervention on humanitarian grounds when a political regime is harming its own citizens? In such cases, is there a right to intervene and do we have an obligation to intervene? It is important to examine these questions because situations frequently arise in which wrongs are taking place within another regime and they prompt the question of whether external agencies (like states or international institutions) are justified in acting to prevent them, and, if so, when and how. Furthermore, we are often faced with occasions when external agencies have engaged in intervention but others have questioned their morality and occasions when external agencies have not intervened but some have thought they should have. In both cases we need to address the moral justifiability of intervention.

There have, in recent years, been many interventions. The United Nations, for example, sought to create 'safe havens' in northern Iraq in April 1991 (Griffiths, Levine, and Weller 1995: 48–50) and to create 'an aerial exclusion zone' in southern Iraq during the summer of 1992 to protect Shiite Muslims (Griffiths, Levine, and Weller 1995: 50). And, of course, the United States of America and Britain have also intervened in Iraq in 2003, giving as one of their justifications the argument that this is needed to protect the human rights of Iraqis.[1] In addition to these interventions, other recent interventions have included the United Nations' intervention in Somalia. This took the form of an arms embargo in January 1992 and then was followed by the United Nations sending in troops to enforce the peace and to defend those supplying aid (Morphet 1995: 222–3).[2] Similarly, in the former Yugoslavia it adopted several measures including applying an arms embargo in 1991, granting UNPROFOR permission to deploy force to defend itself in 1992, and creating safe areas in a number of places including Srebrenica and Sarajevo in 1993 (Griffiths, Levine, and Weller 1995: 53–5). Such activity has not been confined to the UN and single countries have also engaged in acts of intervention: thus India intervened in what was then East Pakistan in 1971 and America intervened in Grenada in 1983. And, of course, NATO waged a bombing campaign in 1999 against the Federal Republic of Yugoslavia in the name of preventing the oppression, slaughter, and ethnic cleansing of Kosovars (on which cf. Wheeler (2000: 257–81, 283–4)).

To address the ethical justifiability of intervention this chapter will begin by analysing how we should define humanitarian intervention (Section I). It will then examine the main cosmopolitan argument for humanitarian intervention (Section II) before then examining four types of counter-arguments (Sections III–VI). Having argued that there is a case for intervention on humanitarian grounds, the chapter will then analyse the conditions that must be satisfied before intervention is attempted (Section VII) as well as the principles that should guide the conduct of an intervention (Section VIII). It concludes by examining whether international law should affirm a right to humanitarian intervention (Section IX).

# I

As in earlier chapters, it is necessary to begin with a clear understanding of the concept to be analysed. We need then to start by addressing the question 'what is humanitarian intervention?' and to answer this I want first to provide a definition of 'intervention' before then analysing the nature of a *humanitarian* intervention. Much has been written on the issue of how to define 'intervention' and a number of different definitions have been proposed.

A good place to start is the definition given by Bull. Intervention, he maintains, is 'dictatorial or coercive interference, by an outside party or parties, in the sphere of jurisdiction of a sovereign state, or more broadly of an independent political community' (1984*b*: 1). Whilst this definition has several virtues it does, however, need to be modified. In particular, its use of the pejorative words 'dictatorial' and 'interference' is unhelpful, suggesting, before any normative considerations have been adduced, that intervention is wrong.[3] What is required, therefore, is a definition which abjures the use of such value-laden words (Caney 1997*a*: 28). In line with this, we can revise Bull's definition as follows: an intervention is a coercive action 'by an outside party or parties, in the sphere of jurisdiction of a sovereign state, or more broadly of an independent political community'. This is, I believe, a plausible and accurate definition.

Three features of this definition should be stressed. First, it is important to note that intervention necessarily involves coercion and thus not all action that alters a state's behaviour counts as intervention. Non-coercive forms of action (like persuasion or diplomacy), on this definition, do not count as interventionary (Brown 1992: 112).[4]

Second, as Bull's definition recognizes, and as others have also stressed, the agents engaging in intervention may be bodies other than states (Hoffmann 1984: 10; McMahan 1986: 25–6; Vincent 1974: 4–5). Intervention can be conducted by a number of different bodies—including, for example, states, associations of states, international institutions, social institutions like churches or even economic enterprises. This is important for two reasons. In the first place, the world we currently live in includes such bodies (like NATO and the United Nations and the European Union) and to restrict intervening agents to states is accordingly inappropriate. Second, it would be unhelpful to define intervention in such a way that the concept could not be applied to the supra-state authorities defended in Chapter 5. Given that Chapter 5 proposed the construction of accountable global political authorities and suggested an increased role for such authorities, it is appropriate to ask whether such bodies, as well as states, may or indeed should intervene.[5]

The third important feature of the definition being proposed is that the entity in which intervention is taking place (what Bhikuh Parekh calls 'the object of intervention' (1997: 53)) need not be a state. Bull refers thus to interventionary action in 'the sphere of jurisdiction of a sovereign state, *or more broadly of an independent political community*' (1984*b*: 1, my emphasis). Interventions can then be directed at political regimes other than states. As with the preceding point, this refusal to define intervention in a wholly statist fashion is important for two reasons. First, in our current world, there are instances which it is natural to describe as interventions but in which a state is absent. The clearest example of this is Somalia—a country in which civil war had broken out and there was no monopoly of power. The United Nations' actions in Somalia (under UNOSOM II) are nonetheless surely interventions. Consider also institutions such as the European Union. It resists categorization as a state but it is clearly a political entity which has its own institutions (such as the European Commission, the Council of Ministers, and the European Parliament) which make political decisions. There is no reason to define intervention in such a way that it could not *by definition* be subject to intervention. A second reason for including political regimes other than states as potential objects of intervention corresponds to a point made above, namely that there is as we have seen a powerful case for instituting powerful global political bodies. It therefore follows that there is little point in providing an analysis of intervention which employs concepts of utility only in a purely statist framework. The terms to be deployed (including most obviously the definition of intervention) should be applicable to the institutional framework defended earlier as well, of course, to the current institutional framework.[6] The object of intervention should thus include political units other than states.

The account of intervention proposed (like the analysis of war in Chapter 6) is therefore designed to be applicable to a wide variety of different international institutional frameworks. It is, for example, applicable to a purely statist order; a system which includes states and supra-state political bodies like the UN (the current situation); and the system defended in Chapter 5 (one with sub-state entities, states, and supra-state authorities). Characterized as such the concept of intervention is relevant to the contemporary international political system (the scenario assumed by almost all discussions of intervention) as well as to the non-statist type of political framework favoured by some cosmopolitans. As in Chapter 6, I shall hereafter generally refer simply to 'political regimes' as the object of intervention to cover these different scenarios.

Several scholars have proposed narrower definitions and it is worth addressing some of these proposals. First, some argue that intervention must necessarily employ force or military power. Donnelly, for example, defines intervention in terms of coercion and then identifies coercion with force (1993: 608–10).[7] As several writers have pointed out, however, this is an unduly narrow definition (McMahan 1986: 25; Vincent 1974: 7–8; Smith 1989: 4).[8] It neglects non-military ways of determining another state's behaviour like economic sanctions or trade embargoes. As Mark Wicclair points out, the misgivings some people have about intervention apply not just to military modes of intervention but also to non-military modes (1979: 143). What is sometimes objected to is the use of coercion—for one state to be determining what happens in another country—but coercion can take different forms and we therefore have no reason to limit intervention to military modes of coercion alone.

A second restriction should also be considered. Some, for example, argue that intervention, by definition, is an action against the interests or wishes of another state (cf., for example, Moellendorf 2002*a*: 103; Wicclair 1979: 143–4). Thus, for A to engage in intervention in state B, A must be acting against B's wishes.

Whilst this is often so, we have no reason to narrow intervention solely to such cases (McMahan 1986: 26–7; Smith 1989: 2, fn. 3). In some cases, for example, a state invites outside agencies to come to its assistance (perhaps to overcome some internal revolutionaries) and it is natural to describe those outside agencies as intervening in that country's affairs. In addition, sometimes an external body is invited in by two parties to a conflict to help resolve the disagreement. In April 1990, for example, the government in El Salvador and the rebels invited the United Nations to intervene to help resolve the conflict (Munck and Kumar 1995: 169–79, esp. p. 170).

A more general point about defining intervention should also be made. As Beitz notes, there is a good case for adopting a wide definition of intervention (1999c: 72–4). A wide definition enables us, when considering the moral legitimacy of intervention, to bear in mind the variety of different methods available and to distinguish between the advantages of different modes of intervention. The wider the definition the more types of action are considered and the fuller picture one gets as to what should be done.[9]

Having defined intervention, we can now analyse what is meant by terming an intervention a 'humanitarian intervention'. In this chapter, I shall define an intervention as a humanitarian intervention if one of its central aims is to protect the welfare of the members of another political regime. Some might demur from this definition, arguing that humanitarian interventions are interventions undertaken for no reason other than to protect the welfare of members of another political regime. As Mason and Wheeler plausibly argue, however, on such a definition there are no humanitarian interventions and there is little point in proposing to define a phenomenon in such a way that it has little, if any, application to our world (1996: 95). Thus, a humanitarian intervention, as I define it, is an intervention which is undertaken in part for humanitarian reasons. Interventions which are undertaken simply in order to increase the intervener's prestige or security interests are therefore not included as humanitarian interventions. In addition, and perhaps more controversially, on this definition, interventions designed to protect one's own nationals residing in a foreign political regime are also not included as humanitarian interventions (Akehurst 1984: 99–104).

Now, combining this account of humanitarianism with the earlier definition of intervention, it follows that humanitarian intervention should be defined as:

coercive action 'by an outside party or parties, in the sphere of jurisdiction of a sovereign state, or more broadly of an independent political community' (Bull 1984b: 1) which is undertaken, partly or exclusively, to protect the welfare of the members of that political community.

Two further points should be made before appraising the justifiability of humanitarian intervention. First, when judging these arguments we should bear in mind whether they address the (weaker) claim that outside agencies have a right to intervene or the (stronger) claim that they have an obligation to intervene. The latter is, clearly, more difficult to establish since it claims not just that they are permitted to intervene but that they ought to do so. In what follows, I shall concentrate on this stronger claim but will draw attention to the weaker claim when it is relevant. Second, it is important to stress that a sound appreciation of the case for and against intervention should note the many forms that intervention can take. Military interventions, for example, can involve the creation of safe havens, or the deployment of troops, or the provision of training and weapons. Alternatively it might involve weapon inspections and the destruction of weapons. Furthermore, as was mentioned earlier, intervention may involve non-military types of coercion including embargoes or sanctions or monitoring elections. All of these are acts that coerce another political regime or the members of another political regime. It is important, however, to note their diversity because some objections to intervention may have force against some types of interventionary behaviour but not others.

## II

Let us now therefore address the normative question of whether humanitarian intervention is justifiable and in particular whether external agencies have an obligation to intervene. Many do believe that humanitarian intervention is sometimes justified. Many, for example, think it right for external agencies to intervene to prevent a state engaging in genocidal policies against some of its own people or if there is widespread human rights abuse. On what grounds, however, can we defend intervention? What kind of internal wrongs would justify humanitarian intervention?

A plausible answer to this question, I believe, cannot be divorced from the issues considered in Chapters 3 and 4. That is, whether one thinks there is a justification for intervention depends, in part, on whether one affirms principles of civil, political, and economic justice and what those principles affirm. It would, in other words, be odd to think that persons have inviolable fundamental human rights but that this should not inform in any way one's judgement of the legitimacy of a political system. The moral justifiability of intervention, it should be stressed, only depends *in part* on whether one accepts human rights for, as we shall see shortly, one might affirm civil or political or economic human rights but nonetheless reject intervention. A commitment to human rights is insufficient to justify humanitarian intervention. Nonetheless, this point is quite compatible with the looser point I want to make here that one should not divorce the question of 'is intervention justified?' from the question of 'what universal principles of justice are there?'

In what follows I want to do two things. I shall first argue that most (if not all) arguments for humanitarian intervention share four crucial premises which jointly justify intervention. The aim here is to set out the abstract features— the bare bones—of any convincing argument for humanitarian intervention. Second, I aim to illustrate and develop these four crucial premises by presenting and defending an argument for intervention that draws on the egalitarian cosmopolitan principles defended in Chapters 3 and 4. The aim here then is to put flesh on the abstract argument and to spell out what I take to be the most plausible argument for humanitarian intervention, namely that which is grounded on cosmopolitan egalitarian liberal principles of civil, political, and distributive justice.

1. *The standard cosmopolitan argument*. Let me begin then with the first of these aims. The standard case for humanitarian intervention rests on four important claims.[10] First, proponents of humanitarian intervention affirm the cosmopolitan claim (made by, amongst others, Barry, Beitz, and Pogge) that individuals have moral interests or a moral status which is worthy of respect.[11] As we have seen in Chapters 3 and 4, some would employ the concept of rights and emphasize people's human rights, say, not to be killed or imprisoned without trial. Others eschew the concept of rights and might emphasize people's needs or interests, arguing that there is a humanitarian case for intervening when people are in great need. Whichever approach is adopted, however, both are united in their commitment to the claim that individuals have a moral worth which should be respected and moral interests which should be protected.

Second, and relatedly, proponents of humanitarian intervention make the further claim that political institutions have value only to the extent that they respect people's moral interests or moral standing. Political regimes do not have a right to rule regardless of their citizens' welfare. Thus not only do individuals have moral standing (assumption 1): political institutions, like states, have moral value only insofar as they respect people's interests (Barry 1999: 35–40; Beitz 1988a: 192; 1994). This claim is familiar from Chapter 5. It can be explicated in a number of ways. Drawing on the analysis in Chapter 5 we can distinguish between at least two possibilities. (i) Some human rights theorists adopt an *instrumental* approach to political institutions, arguing that political regimes treat people with respect and thereby have value only insofar as they act in a just fashion and respect people's rights. If they violate them then external intervention may be justified to rectify this situation (Barry 1998: 153, 160; Barry 1999: 40; Beitz 1999c: 69–92; Doppelt 1980: 398–403; Pogge 1992a; Smith 1998: 76–8). (ii) A different reading of this second premiss is provided by those who adopt an *intrinsic* approach. The latter maintain that political institutions (like states or transnational institutions) treat people with respect and thereby have legitimacy if their members have chosen or would choose to be governed by them. On this intrinsic (or contractarian) approach, therefore, political systems are not legitimate when they do not command the consent of their people (Tesón 1988: 112–13; Wicclair 1980: 293–302).[12] This position is clearly articulated by Luban: '[a]ccording to contract theory, a political community is made legitimate by the consent (tacit or explicit) of its members; it thereby acquires rights which derive from the rights of its members. Thus the rights of political communities are explained by two rather harmless assumptions: that people have rights, and that those rights may be transferred through freely given consent' (1980a: 167). Underlying the differences between these instrumental and intrinsic versions, there is nonetheless the common assumption that political institutions are justified only when they treat persons with respect. They do not have any value in themselves.

These first two assumptions, however, do not establish an obligation to intervene on humanitarian grounds. The latter requires a third assumption, namely that people's rights generate obligations on others (Pogge 1994*a*: 89).[13] That is, external agencies have a duty to ensure that other people's rights are respected. Without this further assumption, one can show at most that humanitarian intervention is permissible, i.e. that people have a right to intervene.[14] To show that people have an obligation to intervene, this further third assumption is required. Here it is appropriate to note that many, but not all, philosophers would conceive of such duties as being positive duties.[15] One exception to this is Pogge who also subscribes to this third assumption but who employs the notion of 'negative' duties: as we have seen earlier, on his account persons have a negative duty not to be part of an oppressive social and political system. He further argues, recall, that given the extent of global interdependence, people have a negative duty not to be part of a global system in which some members' rights are being violated and this entails that one should prevent such actions.[16]

Fourth, and finally, the case for humanitarian intervention rests on the further assumption that acts of humanitarian intervention can work. Clearly this assumption is crucial and if it proved to be the case that humanitarian interventions never succeeded in meeting the appropriate humanitarian ends, there could be no case for such policies. Here, it is appropriate to note that many who are deeply committed to the protection of human rights are wary of humanitarian intervention precisely because they are sceptical of the success of humanitarian interventions. Distinguished cosmopolitan thinkers like Beitz (1980: 390–1) and Booth (1994: 65–70; 1995: 120–1), for example, are critical of military intervention for precisely this reason.

To sum up, therefore, the cosmopolitan case for humanitarian intervention claims that all persons have fundamental interests (assumption 1) and that political institutions do not have value except insofar as they respect these interests (assumption 2). It claims further that external agents have duties to protect people's fundamental interests (assumption 3) and that this obligation sometimes requires external intervention because the latter is an effective way of protecting such interests (assumption 4).[17]

2. *The 'egalitarian liberal' cosmopolitan argument.* The above account is very abstract and needs filling in both to illustrate what it entails and to provide concrete guidance. With this in mind, it may be useful to illustrate and flesh out the abstract argument with the egalitarian liberal cosmopolitan principles defended in Chapters 3, 4, and 5. Let us consider the features of the standard argument for intervention in turn, starting with the first key assumption, that individuals have a moral status which should be respected. The well-being based arguments considered in Chapter 3, Section VI suggest that respect for individuals should

take the form of providing liberal civil and political rights, rights to freedom of worship, conscience, action, and association. In addition, the analysis conducted in Chapter 4 suggests that there is a powerful case for cosmopolitan principles of distributive justice. These include meeting basic needs, granting all persons equality of opportunity, rules of fair trade, and, over and above this, prioritizing the position of the least advantaged. The abstract assumption that individuals have a moral status that should be respected thus should, if the arguments in Chapters 3 and 4 are correct, be elaborated to take the form of egalitarian liberal civil, political, and economic rights. In this respect this argument differs from that presented by other cosmopolitans, like Tesón, who defend intervention to protect civil and political rights but not economic rights (1988: 118–19). The egalitarian cosmopolitanism defended earlier in this book represents one way of explicating this first claim.

Moving on to the second feature of the standard argument for intervention, we can see that, as was argued in Chapter 5, political institutions (like states or transnational institutions) have worth only to the extent that they respect persons and protect their interests. In the context of the egalitarian cosmopolitanism developed in Chapters 3 and 4, this entails that political institutions have value only to the extent that they respect people's fundamental interests and this, in turn, requires that they protect people's civil, political, and economic rights (including their right to determine the social forces that impact on their other rights). Where political institutions are not protecting its members' rights, then, they lack moral standing.

Turning to the next assumption, an egalitarian liberal cosmopolitanism provides an argument for the claim that all persons have a duty to protect human rights. In so doing, as we have seen, it counters the suggestion made by nationalists like Miller that the duty to protect someone's rights falls mainly on that person's fellow nationals (1995: 75–7, 79–80, 108; 1999: 200, 202) (Chapter 4, Sections X and XI). Similarly, it contests the realist claim discussed earlier that outside bodies like states lack a duty to protect human rights overseas and that states are obliged simply to pursue the national interest (Chapter 3 Section XII, and Chapter 4 Sections XII and XIII).[18]

Turning finally to the fourth assumption, the egalitarian liberal cosmopolitanism developed earlier does not have anything specific to say on this matter. As with all variations of the standard argument, it claims simply that there is no case for intervention if it will not work.

Now conjoining these four claims we can see a distinctive egalitarian liberal cosmopolitan version of the standard argument for intervention. It stipulates that persons have political human rights (including rights to freedom of belief, religion, worship, association, and communication) and economic human rights (including rights to have their basic needs met and to be accorded equality of opportunity). It argues further that political institutions—be they states or transnational polities like the European Union or global institutions—have worth only in so far as they protect these values. Thus political institutions lack legitimacy when they fail to protect these rights. Furthermore, given that all persons have duties to respect and protect these human rights (claim 3), it follows that intervention is justified when it could successfully protect these rights (claim 4). Indeed, it is not just morally permissible: it is a duty.

Prior to moving on to consider counter-arguments, it is worth returning to the observation made earlier that both this presentation of the abstract cosmopolitan argument for intervention, and the egalitarian liberal variant of it, confirm and illustrate one of the claims advanced in the introduction of this book, namely that it is arbitrary to separate issues (like 'international distributive justice') from others ('intervention'). As the analysis of the egalitarian cosmopolitan argument for intervention reveals, discussions of intervention draw on analyses of civil and political justice (what civil and political rights, if any, are there?), distributive justice (what economic rights, if any, are there and who has the duty to protect them?), and the sources of the value of institutions (when do institutions have moral standing?).

# III

Many have deep misgivings about humanitarian intervention and the following sections seek to explore some of the most commonly expressed counter-arguments.[19] Attention will be focused, in particular, on four types of counter-argument, namely the arguments that humanitarian intervention is illegitimate because: (a) it fails to respect a people's right to self-government; (b) it is presumptuous and arrogant; (c) it destroys international stability; and (d) it rarely succeeds. The rest of this section will examine (a) before considering the three other types of argument in the next three sections.[20]

One very common counter-argument to intervention invokes a community's right to be self-governing. Those who are sympathetic to the ideal of a society of sovereign states, for example, articulate one version of this argument, claiming that intervention is standardly wrong because it represents an infraction of the rightful autonomy of the state. The most uncompromising version of this argument can be found in the work of Christian Wolff who in his *Jus Gentium Methodo Scientifica Pertractatum* affirms the intrinsic right of states to be independent in order to defend non-intervention. He writes, for example, that 'the law of nations is originally nothing else than the law of nature applied to nations, which are considered as individual persons living in a state of nature' (1934 [1764], ch. II, sec. 156, p. 84). Throughout his work, states are assumed to be analogous to persons and given that the latter should be respected as independent, it follows that states should be as well (1934 [1764], prolegomena, secs. 2 and 3, p. 9). As Wolff writes, 'since by nature nations are bound to each other in the same way as individuals are bound to individuals, every nation also ought to allow to another nation its right' (1934 [1764], ch. II, sec. 264, p. 135). Hence, 'no ruler of a state has the right to interfere in the government of another' (1934 [1764], ch. II, sec. 257, p. 131, cf. also secs. 255–60, pp. 130–3).

The analogy on which this argument depends has already been encountered in Chapter 6, Section II, where it was invoked to defend the right of a state to employ force in self-defence. As we saw there, however, it is not plausible to claim that states are analogous to persons (Beitz 1999c: 69–71, 74–6, 81; McMahan 1986: 28–30, esp. p. 29). They lack the moral properties we attribute to human beings. We therefore have no reason to think that states should be given intrinsic value and Wolff's view that, like persons, states possess independent value—value that is, regardless of how they affect humans—is, as we have seen, highly implausible. The cornerstone of this traditional argument is thus deeply counter-intuitive. It is worth exploring this point further. The argument under scrutiny must overcome three problems. The first is that it must establish that an entity, X, has value independently of whether X has an impact on human beings. Even if this task is met, however, and someone shows that some entities have some value regardless of how they affect humans, this approach faces a second task. She must establish that states are a member of this class of entities. Someone might, for example, accept that some entities have value independently of their effects on persons but think that, whilst works of art or environmental scenes belong in this category, states do not. Suppose, however, that these two problems are overcome and that someone establishes that states have value in and of themselves. This does not establish Wolff's position on non-intervention: one has to show that this value possessed by states overrides the importance of human rights. Otherwise, it is quite possible that states possess independent value but that this does not outweigh the importance of saving human lives from slaughter. To argue therefore that intervention is wrong because it is incompatible with the intrinsic value of state independence is not credible and encounters three severe problems.

There are, however, ways of spelling out the thought that intervention is illegitimate because it violates a people's right to self-government which do not rest on Wolff's implausible assumptions. For instance, some who emphasize the moral value of self-determination object to intervention because it violates the autonomy of *nations* (Miller 1995: 77–8). Similarly, Walzer has developed an argument against intervention which, like the preceding argument, affirms the right of a collectivity in order to oppose intervention but which, unlike the preceding argument, does not attribute independent moral value to states. It appeals instead to the rights of 'communities'.[21] Walzer's argument makes two essential claims. First, he defends what he terms 'communal integrity', reasoning that 'the idea of communal integrity derives its moral and political force from the rights of contemporary men and women to live as members of a historic community and to express their inherited culture through political forms worked out among themselves' (1980: 211). In short: communal self-government is desirable (1980: 225–6).[22] Walzer then argues that those outside a state are unable to judge whether that state represents a form of communal self-government. And since they are ignorant about the internal affairs of another state they should adopt a 'morally necessary presumption . . . [namely] that there exists a certain "fit" between the community and its government and that the state is "legitimate". It is not a gang of rulers acting in its own interests, but a people governed in accordance with its own traditions' (1980: 212). Thus given that communal integrity is valuable and given that external bodies must (because of their ignorance) assume that a state embodies the norms of the community, external bodies should eschew intervention. They do not have a right (let alone an obligation) to intervene.[23]

Walzer's argument is, however, unpersuasive for a number of reasons. One serious problem with it concerns his second claim that external agents are too ill-informed to be able to assess whether there is a 'fit' between a people and a state (and should therefore simply assume that there is). As many have noted, this claim is simply implausible (Beitz 1980: 386; Doppelt 1980: 400; Luban 1980b: 395; McMahan 1986: 42–3). External bodies, like the United Nations, can surely draw on research of another country, survey its infrastructure, socio-economic base, traditions, history, and so on and thereby reach an informed opinion on whether there is 'fit'.

Furthermore, in many cases there is no match between a state and a community, most states being multi-national, multi-ethnic, and multi-cultural (Brown 1993: 517–18). And there are many glaring cases where the political elite does not represent the values of the entire population but only a subsection (Beitz 1980: 385–6). In such cases, to respect the state is to grant protection of one community but in doing so to enable it to persecute other communities (McMahan 1986: 33). A particularly striking example of this is the Federal Republic of Yugoslavia which from 1989 revoked Kosovo's status as an autonomous province and persecuted Kosovan Albanians.

In addition, the very idea at the centre of his argument, that of 'cultural autonomy', is insufficiently precise to do the job required of it. To see this one needs only ask 'which community?' Walzer's argument presupposes that we can identify a clearly marked community but this is an inaccurate and misleading assumption (Smith 1997: 16). Often there is no one clear community. Differing communities exist depending on whether one focuses on religion or language or ethnicity and so on. Different criteria for specifying a community yield different results and this is destructive of the idea of communal autonomy. For these three reasons, then, the ideal of 'communal integrity' provides very little support for state sovereignty and non-intervention.[24]

Thus neither version of the claim that intervention violates a people's right to self-government is persuasive.

# IV

Let us therefore consider a second argument against intervention. One sentiment commonly voiced defends non-intervention on the grounds that to intervene is presumptuous, arrogant, and involves an outside body playing God. What gives us the authority, someone might ask, to determine someone else's affairs (Benn and Peters, 1959: 362)? Isn't intervention presumptuous? Aren't we just imposing our values on someone else?

There are, however, four problems with this argument. The first is that it focuses exclusively on the position of a would-be intervening force but does not apply that question to the political bodies governing that political regime. The question it poses applies in any instance where political power is being exercised. It is thus right to ask of a would-be intervening force 'what gives them the right to exercise political power?' and 'are they just imposing their values on some subject people?' but one should equally ask the same question of existing political regimes. In other words, we have no reason to suppose that the questions being posed count against intervening agents. And we should not simply assume that the currently ruling authorities have the right to rule there. It may be equally presumptuous of them to exercise power. Indeed they may be as alien and foreign as the intervening force.

Second, the argument runs into the following countervailing line of reasoning: in our interdependent world outside bodies inevitably affect what happens within another polity. No political regime is utterly unaffected by the outside world and, consequently, outside bodies cannot fail to make a difference. Put another way: powerful outside agencies cannot avoid playing God because whatever they do will make a difference (Chapter 2, Section XIV). Given this, however, then the question that arises is not 'should we make a difference?' but 'given that we do make a difference, how should we exercise our power?' (Caney 2000c: 545–7). The force of the argument presented in Section II of this chapter is that outside bodies have a duty to exercise this power by intervening when certain conditions arise (including, among many other conditions, considerable rights violations). Nothing that the argument considered in this section has said undermines that reasoning.

One can then add to this, third, that while intervention brings with it risks (such as acting in a presumptuous arrogant fashion and being dismissive of others who espouse different values), non-intervention also brings with it risks (such as indifference and callousness). The decision not to intervene in 1995 when Serbs killed nearly 8000 Muslims at Srebrenica is, certainly, open to the charge of indifference.

Finally, we should note that this argument assumes that one party is foisting its values on others but that this applies only in some instances. It does not, for example, apply in cases where intervention is welcomed and invited by some party. In such a situation, there is no hierarchical relationship in which one party (the intervening force) is telling the other (the country or political system to be intervened in) how the latter should conduct their arrangements. It is simply responding to their claims. In other words, one can have intervention without condescension and arrogance. Whether intervention is regarded as presumptuous would depend, in part, on procedural factors, such as *how* the intervention takes place (whether there is dialogue and consultation with people within the regime being intervened in). It is also reasonable to suppose that it depends also on *who* intervenes and this important issue will be addressed later.

In the meantime, however, the four considerations already cited suggest that humanitarian intervention need not be guilty of the vices of arrogance and immodesty.

## V

Given the failure of the two previous arguments against humanitarian intervention let us consider another critique of such interventions. Many of those sympathetic to the ideal of a society of states advance a third argument against intervention. This argument affirms the importance of a stable international order. It then argues that permitting (or defending) humanitarian intervention encourages other interventions and thereby destroys international order. Intervention should therefore be rejected because to permit it would engender instability. This argument has been stressed by a number of prominent defenders of the 'society of states' including Bull (on which see (Wheeler 1992: 463–77)), Nardin (Nardin 1983: 5, 18–19; Slater and Nardin 1986: 87), and Vincent (1974: 328–33).[25] A particularly clear statement of it is given by Jackson who, in *The Global Covenant*, opposes humanitarian intervention on the grounds that it jeopardizes '[i]nternational order and stability, international peace and security'. He continues '[i]n my view, the stability of international society, especially the unity of the great powers, is more important, indeed far more important, than minority rights and humanitarian protections in Yugoslavia or in other country—if we have to choose between those two sets of values' (2000: 291).

This argument is unpersuasive. First, the argument's empirical assumption that defending intervention will encourage further interventions and thus destabilize the global order is implausible. As Beitz and McMahan note, many interventions have taken place which have not triggered other interventions or in any other way destabilized global politics (Beitz 1988*b*: 187; McMahan 1986: 44).

As McMahan further adds, it is hard to see why reaching a conclusion about the moral justifiability of intervention will affect the conduct of states (1986: 43–4). At this point, it is worth distinguishing the argument under scrutiny from a distinct argument which appears similar but which is importantly different. The argument being considered, recall, states that intervention is morally unjustified because it destroys international order. This claim should, however, be distinguished from the following often made claim: *international law should not include a legal right to intervene because this would destroy international order.* The latter is not a claim about whether intervention is morally right or wrong: it is a claim about whether there should be a legal right to intervene.

This distinction will be explored in more length in Section IX of this chapter but it is worth drawing attention to it here because the concern about instability is more forceful as a critique of the claim that there should be a legal right to intervene than it is of the claim that intervention is morally justified. Whilst it is hard to see why reaching a moral conclusion about the justifiability of intervention will affect the conduct of states, it is not hard to see that creating a legal right to intervene may well affect the conduct of states and that it might conceivably bring about the collapse of the international order. My claim here, I should stress, is not that this empirical thesis is true. (Indeed, as we see in Section IX of this chapter, these dangers can be avoided). It is simply that this argument against the legal right to intervene has more credibility than the argument under scrutiny in this section and that the latter gains illicit plausibility if it is run together with this superficially similar claim. We should, for that reason, distinguish between the two claims.

In addition, even if humanitarian intervention did generate instability this alone does not establish that it is wrong. It would do so only if we attributed supreme importance to preserving the international status quo. We therefore need to know whether the current international system is worth preserving and whether a more attractive alternative is attainable. The value of stability (including international stability) is a function of the value of the current arrangements. Appeals to international order are therefore incomplete and need to be supplemented by an argument showing that the international system is fair and morally legitimate (Beitz 1988b: 187–8; Wicclair 1979: 150). Furthermore, and relatedly, to prioritize stability is to reward the most powerful who—if they cannot get their way—will generate instability. It appeases the most powerful and it disenfranchises the weak who are unable to threaten instability (Caney 1997a: 30). As Rawls expresses the point: 'to each according to his threat advantage is not a principle of justice' (1999c: 122).

Arguments invoking the importance of order are thus incomplete and rest on the dubious assumption that intervention engenders instability.

## VI

For many, however, the problem with humanitarian intervention lies not with its disregard for the rights of states or its alleged propensity to cause disorder. Rather the problem is that, for a number of reasons, intervention does not succeed in its objectives. This is certainly a common response from those who are sympathetic to realist claims about the possibility of effective moral action in the international realm and who accuse such projects of utopianism. Someone might accept assumptions 1, 2, and 3 of the argument for humanitarian intervention but have deep misgivings about the efficacy of humanitarian intervention (i.e. assumption 4). Those who oppose intervention are, thus, not necessarily indifferent to the plight of others.[26] Caroline Thomas, for instance, affirms a pragmatic argument, drawing on examples like Tanzania's intervention in Uganda in 1978–9 and the Vietnamese intervention into Cambodia, to argue that interventions rarely work (1993: 91–103, esp. 93–5). In addition, a recent analysis of UN peacemaking activities concludes that these have standardly proved to be unsuccessful (Diehl, Reifschneider, and Hensel 1996). These empirical examples cast doubt on the case for humanitarian intervention but before we accept them, they need to be supplemented with theoretical explanations, showing why no intervention will further humanitarian ends. A number of reasons have been suggested as to why intervention will not work.[27]

1. *Knowledge.* First, some argue that external agencies are insufficiently well informed about another state and its population to make good decisions (Donnelly 1993: 640). The experience of a number of interventions lends support to this argument. Ioan Lewis and James Mayall record, for example, that the UN intervention in Somalia (UNOSOM) was ill-informed. They argue that

[v]ery few adequately representative Somali advisors were recruited, and UN officials generally could hardly have been more inadequately briefed about Somali society and culture. The huge gap between traditional Somali methods of dealing with foreigners and American high-tech put most of the UN staff at a great disadvantage in their local dealings. This is perhaps most graphically illustrated by US helicopters dropping leaflets on a population with a primarily oral tradition whose sensitivity to radio broadcasting is famous in Africa. (1996: 121)

Similarly, the UN intervention in Cambodia (UNTAC) was afflicted by poor information. Mats Berdal and Michael Leifer, for instance, draw attention to the failure to have an intelligence unit tracking the movements of the Khmer Rouge and Vietnamese troops present in Cambodia (1996: 48–9). They argue, further, that UNTAC's success 'required intimate knowledge of and sensitivity to the host culture. Yet both were in short supply and UNTAC's attempts to control the administration with any effect were wholly unsuccessful' (1996: 43–4).

Nonetheless, as a number of scholars have pointed out, the assumption that external agencies are always insufficiently informed is too sweeping (Adelman 1992: 71; Wicclair 1979: 153). States and international institutions can finance thorough and comprehensive analyses of the socio-economic structure of another society, its political system, and its political culture. Moreover, all the examples above point to technical problems which can be rectified rather than to any deep or fundamental obstacle to one group of people understanding the nature of another society.

2. *Improper motives.* A second reason for doubting whether interventions will further humanitarian objectives is voiced by Stanley Benn and R. S. Peters (1959: 361). They argue that states rarely act out of altruism and contend that they will usually intervene to further their national interest rather than the fundamental rights of people abroad. Similarly, realists are sceptical of the motives of states and hence are sceptical of the likelihood of genuinely humanitarian intervention (Morgenthau 1967: 430). The point is made particularly forcefully by Schmitt:

'When a state fights its political enemy in the name of humanity, it is not a war for the sake of humanity, but a war wherein a particular state seeks to usurp a universal concept against its military opponent. At the expense of its opponent, it tries to identify itself with humanity in the same way as one can misuse peace, justice, progress, and civilization in order to claim these as one's own and to deny the same to the enemy. The concept of humanity is an especially useful ideological instrument of imperialist expansion, and in its ethical humanitarian form it is a specific vehicle of economic imperialism. Here one is reminded of a somewhat modified expression of Proudhon's: whoever invokes humanity wants to cheat'.   (1996 [1932]: 54)

The charge, then, is that humanitarian intervention is just a cover for self-interested action.

Four points, however, should be made about this argument. First, as Wicclair points out, it does not show that interventions will not further humanitarian ends. This would be the case only if we assume that a state's pursuit of its interests never includes policies that also further humanitarian aims (like the observance of human rights or the prevention of starvation). Policies motivated in part by the national interest may also have beneficial outcomes for others. Furthermore, states might acquire prestige and standing through humanitarian acts. A political leader might, for example, seek to enhance his or her reputation through securing a foreign policy success (such as facilitating peace in the Middle East) (Wicclair 1979: 152).

A second problem with this argument lies in its rather crude understanding of the motivations of states. It would be utopian and idealistic to think that states do not seek to further their national interest but it is also unrealistic to think that they are never motivated by other concerns, including ideological commitments (Jervis 1988: 342–3; Waltz 1979: 91–2, 205). Given the definition of humanitarian intervention presented in Section I (which identifies interventions as humanitarian if they are in part motivated by humanitarian concerns) the argument in question works only if we make the extreme assumption that the sole motivations are non-moral considerations. To claim that states are motivated by their own interests is certainly plausible; to claim that they are always only motivated by this is simply inaccurate.

Furthermore, it is artificial to characterize a state's national interest independently of the moral beliefs of its leaders. For many, a state's national interest affirms and embodies certain moral principles and ideals (cf., for example, Murray's (1996) analysis of Morgenthau).[28] Consequently, a state's pursuit of the national interest can include a commitment to humanitarian ideals.[29] It is also important at this point not to lose sight of the point made in Section I that interventions can be undertaken by non-state bodies since non-state bodies, like the United Nations, even more clearly construe their role in moral terms. This is not to claim that such institutions actually do act in a morally decent way. Rather it is to point out that such bodies do not define their goals in a value-neutral way: they construe their ends in moral terms. The institutions of the United Nations, for example, perceive their various roles in terms of certain ideals and it is artificial to separate their 'interests' from their 'values'.

A fourth limitation of this argument is that it fails to take into account the motives of a state towards its own citizens. External agencies, it is true, may seek to further their own interests and therefore not have the interests of those abroad at heart but we should also note that many political elites, too, are not greatly concerned about the welfare of their own people (Tesón 1988: 105). This is particularly likely to be true in non-democratic states where the political leaders have no incentive to respect the rights of their subjects. In addition it is likely to be the case in countries containing ethnic or cultural minorities. In such circumstances it is simply utopian to think that the leaders of a state will always care more for the interests of all of their people than will external agencies.

The concern about power politics is, thus, a salutary one but it does not show humanitarian intervention to be inherently unsuccessful.

3. *Resistance to intervention*. Even if external agencies are suitably well-informed and motivated by the right considerations, humanitarian intervention might not succeed for other reasons. Interventions sometimes flounder simply because they encounter resistance from some of the members of the country which is subject to intervention. UNOSOM, for example, encountered considerable resistance from Somalis once Admiral Howe began to hunt down General Aideed (Lewis and Mayall 1996: 116–18). Furthermore in Cambodia, 'SOC [State of Cambodia] ministries and officials deliberately obstructed UNTAC. It was made impossible, for example, for it to "work as a partner with all existing adminstrative structures charged with public security" as stipulated in the implementation plan' (Berdal and Leifer 1996: 44).

Like the preceding points, this third consideration has a great deal of force and should not be dismissed lightly. Like the others, however, it does not represent an insuperable obstacle to humanitarian intervention. First, we should note that sometimes external agencies are invited in to help resolve a problem and hence there is little resistance to intervention. The UN intervention in El Salvador is perhaps a good example of this: both participants in the civil war agreeing to UN intervention (Munck and Kumar 1995: 170). Second, even where there is local resistance to intervention (say by a tyrannical state) it will not necessarily be more powerful than the intervening authority. Clearly small local forces have often humbled interventionary forces and external agencies have notoriously underestimated the potency of resistance. Nonetheless, we have no reason to assume that those who resist will in all cases prove to be more powerful than those intervening.[30] In short, then: interventions will not always encounter opposition and when they do, those who oppose them are not always powerful enough to thwart the intervention's success. The third consideration thus does not establish that intervention will always prove futile.

4. *Millian considerations*. A further reason for being sceptical about the success of humanitarian intervention has been suggested by J. S. Mill. Mill argues that external interventions will rarely secure long-term success.[31] He argues that a political system will prove viable only if the people are committed to it and, he adds, a people will be committed only if they (and not some outside body) have fought for it. Thus external agency will not secure long-term stability.

As Mill writes 'If a people . . . does not value it [their freedom] sufficiently to fight for it, and maintain it against any force which can be mustered *within* the country, even by those who have the command of the public revenue, it is only a question in how few years or months that people will be enslaved' (1984 [1859]: 122). Again: 'the evil is, that if they have not sufficient love of liberty to be *able to wrest it* from merely domestic oppressors, the liberty which is bestowed on them by other hands than their own, will have nothing real, nothing permanent' (1984 [1859]: 122, emphasis added). So, even where external bodies have the requisite *knowledge, motivation*, and *capability to overcome resistance*, intervention will not work.[32]

Now Mill is right to argue that a political system will thrive only if the people endorse it. This, however, does not justify a blanket repudiation of intervention. The central flaw in the argument is that it is simply incorrect to stipulate that only those able to conquer their oppressors (without outside aid) are committed to their political vision. Put another way: people may be wholly committed to their political ideal (they have 'love of liberty') but are too weak because of a lack of resources and force to be able to overcome a despotic ruler (they are not 'able to wrest' power 'from merely domestic oppressors') (Mill 1984 [1859]: 122). An inability to fight should not be confused with an unwillingness to fight. Mill's argument overlooks the possibility that a people may be willing to fight for a state but be unable to overthrow the current tyranny without external aid (Mason and Wheeler 1996: 105; Wicclair 1979: 151). One can therefore endorse Mill's central point—that people must be committed enough to their political vision to fight for it—and yet also support humanitarian intervention. A people might, for example, be committed to their political vision and also be aided by outside bodies to achieve their political objectives.

In general, then, each of the four considerations raised against humanitarian intervention does have force. But none of them—either alone or combined with others—shows that intervention will never succeed. What is needed is a cautious and nuanced approach which, rather than rejecting intervention outright, bears these weighty factors in mind and analyses the circumstances in which interventions succeed.

Four further general points are also worth bearing in mind. First, when assessing the success of an intervention in meeting humanitarian goals it is important to compare it with other options (including non-intervention) in meeting those same goals. Consider, for example, a military intervention which does not eliminate military conflict but does lessen the loss of human life more than a policy of non-interventionism. In such circumstances it is implausible to criticize humanitarian intervention as 'unsuccessful' when it is more 'successful' in meeting the humanitarian objectives than any of the other courses of action. In 'absolute' terms, it does not meet its objectives but 'relative' to the other options available it is the most successful and, if our concern is to further humanitarian ends, the latter (i.e. 'relative') criterion is the one which we should adopt.

Second, when considering whether interventionism (or non-interventionism) best furthers humanitarian ideals we should take into account *not just* those cases where intervention did not promote the desired objectives as well as other options *but also* cases where a policy of non-intervention was adopted but in which, as a consequence, people suffered or lost their lives. People tend to focus on interventions that do not succeed (either in absolute or relative terms) in furthering humanitarian goals. But they should also consider cases where no intervention takes place and in which such non-interventionism is in relative (or absolute) terms a failure in promoting humanitarian ends. (A possible illustration of this is the decision by the United Nations not to intervene effectively in Rwanda in 1994 when 1,000,000 people were killed in 100 days (Keane 1996: 29)). They should, in other words, consider the good sacrificed (in terms of meeting humanitarian objectives) by non-intervention.

Both of these factors point to ways in which our judgement of the success of humanitarian intervention may be distorted and in which we may wrongly reject intervention when it represents the most successful of all the options available. They may result in our losing sight of the point that a critique of the efficacy of interventions is plausible only when it takes the form of a consequentialist comparison of whether intervention or non-intervention best secures people's rights (a policy that is in line with the 'goal rights system' defended in the last chapter: Chapter 6, Section VIII).

This second point introduced above brings to the fore a third important point that must not be overlooked, namely that two of the factors adduced as to why interventions may fail also apply with force against non-intervention. That is, they show that a policy of non-intervention is also frequently a failure. To see this consider the following chain of reasoning. First, as we have just seen, all the arguments considered in this section appeal to outcomes (arguing that intervention results in unsuccessful outcomes). In claiming that interventions do not in fact save lives, say, they are invoking the relevance of outcomes as an appropriate ethical criterion. Similarly, in defending non-intervention their claim is that this results in better outcomes. Bearing this in mind, we should also note that bad outcomes may result from inaction as well as from action. Furthermore—and this is the important point—the first two factors adduced against a policy of intervention apply equally to a policy of non-intervention. Specifically, they may bring about non-intervention in cases where intervention may have achieved important humanitarian objectives. Consider the first factor: ignorance. This may, it is true, lead intervening forces to blunder and thereby to fail *but* it may also lead external bodies not to intervene (they do not realize how bad things are) and consequently to fail to intervene in cases where they are able to protect rights. As such it contributes to a policy of non-intervention which fails in humanitarian terms. It produces a state of affairs in which people lost their lives, lives which could have been saved were it not for the ignorance of the external agents. Consider also the second factor: self-interest. Again, this may result in unsuccessful humanitarian interventions, *but* it may also result in unsuccessful non-interventions, that is, cases where a state or international institution is able to help but chooses not to do so out of self-interest. Again, therefore, it may produce a state of affairs in which people lost lives, lives which could have been saved were it not for self-interest. The central point then is that from the consequentialist viewpoint adopted by the critics, appealing to ignorance and self-interest is a double-edged sword. Both factors may result in unsuccessful interventions and *unsuccessful non-interventions*. This point is standardly ignored but again it represents an important consideration that should be recognized when assessing the dangers to which intervention (and non-intervention) are susceptible.

Finally, given the problems interventions have routinely faced, there is a need for analyses of the conditions in which interventions are likely to work. Instead, however, of focusing exclusively on the question 'can interventions succeed?' it would be helpful to address questions like 'in what situations can interventions succeed?' and 'how can interventions be rendered more successful?'. The question 'can interventions work?' is perhaps rather misplaced because, as we have seen from the analysis of the four reasons as to why interventions may fail, the answer to that question is that there is no fundamental reason why some interventions cannot work. Given this perhaps the more appropriate question is 'when are they most likely to work?' (a topic addressed by Munck and Kumar 1995: esp. 163–4). To illustrate this point, consider one important factor, namely that the intervening agent be cohesive and well-organized. What is striking is that this condition has often been absent and that many interventions (including interventions in Somalia and Cambodia) are simply poorly organized with no unified overarching authority. In their analysis of the failure of the United Nations intervention in Somalia, for example, Lewis and Mayall point out that the Secretary General of the United Nations and the United States disagreed about how UNOSOM I should be constituted (1996: 110). In addition, the US government itself was internally divided, with the Pentagon and White House opposing the position of the Office for Disaster Relief (1996: 109–10). Lack of coordination also afflicted the intervention in Cambodia. Berdal and Leifer for example report that UNTAC's police force combined personnel from '30 different police forces world-wide' (1996: 44) and that '[i]n Cambodia, several battalions arrived with no knowledge of either French or English' and few were capable of speaking the Khmer language (1996: 50). They further write that '[t]he lack of civil–military integration, in particular, remained a serious problem throughout the entire operation' (1996: 46) and add later that 'the absence of clear and unambiguous chains of command *internal* to UNTAC, as well as proper coordination between the Secretariat in New York and the field, resulted in a loss of operational efficiency' (1996: 50).

# VII

Having analysed both the justification and criticisms of humanitarian intervention and found that none of the objections to humanitarian intervention justifies a blanket rejection, it is important to analyse when intervention is morally defensible.[33] If, as the argument of Section II maintains, there is a case for humanitarian intervention, we need to know what circumstances would justify intervention. A number of different proposals have been made.

Given the prominence of Walzer's discussion of intervention, it is appropriate to begin with his account of when intervention is legitimate. According to Walzer intervention is justifiable in three circumstances:

1. 'When a particular state includes more than one political community, when it is an empire or a multi-national state, and when one of its communities or nations is in active revolt, foreign powers can come to the assistance of the rebels' (1980: 216–17; cf. 1977: 90–2);
2. 'When a single community is disrupted by civil war, and when one foreign power intervenes in support of this or that party, other powers can rightfully intervene in support of the other party' (1980: 217; cf. 1977: 90, 93–101); and
3. 'Interventions can be justified whenever a government is engaged in the massacre or enslavement of its own citizens or subjects' (1980: 217; cf. 1977: 90, 101–8).

Each of these conditions is, however, questionable or in need of revision. To take (1) first: it is not clear why external agencies are always permitted to come to the assistance of a national minority when it is rebelling. Does it not depend on whether the national minority has good cause to rebel? Suppose that it is being treated fairly but rebels nonetheless, why is intervention to aid the rebels justified?

(2) is also suspect. Indeed it suffers from a similar problem to (1) in that it ignores the moral justifiability of those in conflict. It is peculiar to claim that one can always intervene to aid one side if the other side has already received help. Surely, whether one can intervene or not in support of one participant in a conflict should depend in part on their moral legitimacy. It matters whether one party to the conflict is the Khmer Rouge, say, or whether it is a persecuted minority trying to protect their fundamental rights (Doppelt 1978: 13; McMahan 1986: 47; Smith 1989: 15).

Finally, we might also criticize (3). This is the most plausible condition of the three that Walzer affirms but one might reasonably ask why Walzer justifies intervention only when people are being massacred or put into slavery—why not 'political murder or torture' (Slater and Nardin 1986: 91)? Why not when they do not have enough to eat?

When then is humanitarian intervention legitimate? To answer this question, it is important to make two preliminary points. First, a satisfactory account of when humanitarian intervention is legitimate should cohere with the case for humanitarian intervention. An account of *why* humanitarian intervention is legitimate (if it is) should guide our account of *when* it is. The account that follows therefore draws on the case for humanitarian intervention outlined in Section II. Second, when framing the conditions under which humanitarian intervention is appropriate it is worth bearing in mind the principles of just war discussed in the preceding chapter. As Mona Fixdal and Dan Smith point out, discussions of humanitarian intervention rarely make links with the just war tradition and, as they further note, such an omission is somewhat surprising (Fixdal and Smith 1998: 283–312). However, since humanitarian intervention can, and often does, involve military action, one would expect the principles guiding military action employed to address internal wrongs (armed humanitarian intervention) to cohere with the principles guiding military action employed to address external wrongs (just warfare). To this we should, of course, note that humanitarian intervention need not take the form of military action and hence there will not be a perfect correspondence. Nonetheless one would expect the two accounts to be congruent and have some common points.[34] Given this, the discussion that follows seeks to relate the principles arrived at to the principles informing the just waging of war. These principles, recall, state that there must be:

(1) Just cause
(2) Proportionality
(3) A consideration of less awful measures (the least awful option)
(4) Reasonable chance of meeting objectives
(5) Legitimate authority.[35]

With these two methodological points in mind, we can now draw up a list of the circumstances in which humanitarian intervention is justified. Humanitarian intervention is legitimate when

(1*) a political regime violates people's human rights (where this includes rights to a decent standard of living as well as rights against torture, murder, unjust imprisonment, or enslavement) (just cause).[36]

This is a straightforward principle and requires little further comment.[37] A second condition that must be satisfied before humanitarian intervention is justified is:

(2*) the intervention is a proportionate response: by this is meant that the costs incurred as a result of the intervention are not disproportionate in comparison to the internal wrongs which the intervention is supposed to address (proportionality).[38]

This needs to be unpacked. Intervention can generate (at least) two kinds of cost. First, there is the cost to the people in the political regime that is the object of intervention. In the case of armed intervention, these can include the death of soldiers or civilians who are resisting any armed intervention. It should also include instances where the intervention led the government being attacked to step up their oppression (as was alleged to be the case in Kosovo). Second, however, we should not ignore the costs on third parties. We must include in our calculations cases where an intervention has malign effects on outsiders. Suppose, for example, that a humanitarian intervention resulted in the instability of a neighbouring just regime.[39] An appropriate principle of proportionality must factor in such costs and stipulate that humanitarian intervention is justified only if the benefits produced by the intervention exceed the costs (including both the costs to members of the intervened-in state and non-members).[40]

A third principle that follows from the cosmopolitan argument is

(3*) intervention (military or non-military) may be resorted to only having considered less awful options (such as, say, diplomacy) (the least awful option).

Humanitarian interventions, whether military or not, should not be adopted unless other less severe means for achieving the same result have been given due consideration. Four additional comments about this principle are worth making. First, (3*) claims that intervention may be resorted to only if other less awful options have been explored first but this does not of necessity require actually putting these other options into practice and then intervening only if they have not proved successful. It might sometimes require this but if there is overwhelming evidence for believing that another less severe option just will not work then it would be irresponsible, knowing this, to implement it nonetheless (Caney 1997a: 32).[41] Second, it is worth returning to the discussion of (5) and (5ᵢ) in Chapter 6. As we saw there, the conventional principle that military action should be a last resort (principle (5), the *principle of last resort*) depends on a more fundamental moral principle, namely that war may be resorted to only having considered less awful measures (principle (5ᵢ), the *principle of the least awful option*). We can now see the relevance and importance of this distinction because it is possible to argue that some types of non-military intervention are actually more awful than military intervention. And where war is not the very worst option then it should not be regarded as a last resort and should, of course, be regarded as a better option than whatever else it is that is even more awful. One possible illustration of this point is economic sanctions: these may last for many years and can bring about more deaths than a military intervention.[42] In such circumstances, military intervention should not be considered a last resort: rather, sanctions should. Of course, military force often is the worst option, but the point is that whilst this might very often be the case there is no a priori reason to think that it is always the worst option available. The third point is that we should note that there are two aspects to the principle of the least awful option—what we might term the external and the internal aspect. The external aspect compares non-interventionary actions and interventionary actions and mandates the latter only if intervention is a less awful option. The internal aspect compares different kinds of interventionary actions (such as employing sanctions, sending in troops, imposing weapons inspectors), and it mandates that kind (or those kinds) of interventionary actions which are the least awful option(s). For (3*) to be met, the form of intervention adopted must then be a less awful option than both non-interventionary actions (external aspect) and alternative interventionary actions (internal aspect).

Finally, we should note that I have referred to the 'awfulness' of different options without indicating what metric we should use to gauge 'awfulness'. A full account cannot be given here. I think, however, that we can say that any reasonable account must incorporate three elements. First, it must take into account the *nature* of the rights violations. It must, that is, assess the moral significance of the rights that are being violated. Second, it must take into account the *number* of rights violations. How may rights violations have occurred? Third, it must take into account *whose* rights are violated. Is it the rights of combatants or non-combatants? Given these three quite different considerations the application of the principle of the least awful option will require considerable judgement.[43]

If we return to the normative rationale underpinning humanitarian intervention we can also derive a fourth principle, namely:

(4*) the intervention has a reasonable chance of working (reasonable chance of meeting its objectives).[44]

This is an obvious principle although explicating what it requires is more complicated than might at first seem. First, as we saw earlier (Section VI) we need to be careful in specifying what constitutes 'meeting its objectives'. Second, to render this principle more concrete we would need to clarify what is meant by 'reasonable' prospects of working. Does that mean a 50 per cent chance of working? Or 60 per cent? Or something else?[45]

We should also include a fifth principle, namely:

(5*) the intervention is authorized by a legitimate body (legitimate authority).

(5*) also needs a little explanation. Many accounts of humanitarian intervention do not address the question of *who* should engage in humanitarian intervention (cf., for example, Beitz 1988*b*). One might argue, however, that interventions can be legitimate only if they are authorized by a legitimate body. Several considerations support this. First, as we saw earlier in this chapter (Section IV), much resistance to humanitarian intervention draws on this intuition, asking in effect 'what gives you the right to intervene?' Second, there is an important distinction between thinking that a principle is unjust and should be coercively implemented, on the one hand, and thinking that 'we' therefore are authorized to coercively implement this principle, on the other. Consider a domestic example: suppose that a man does not repay a loan he has taken out. Now we think that he should, other things being equal, be made to repay the loan but it does not follow from this that I or any other citizen have the authority to make him pay (and, say, to threaten punishment if he does not comply). The same point applies at the global level: that X should be prevented by force does not establish that I have the authority to employ force (Kymlicka 1995: 165*ff.*, 233, fn. 15). An account of who is authorized to act is required. Third, as we saw in our examination of just war theory (in Chapter 6), many accounts insist that a just war can only be authorized by certain authorities. There is, therefore, a case for bringing discussions of humanitarian intervention into line. Given these first three considerations, then, we need to address the question: 'which *institution or institutions* possesses the *authority* to intervene?' A fourth, and final, consideration which also supports (5*) provides an answer to this question. Let me explain. An additional argument in favour of (5*) starts from the analysis of political institutions in Chapter 5. As we saw there, there is a case for a set of transnational political institutions whose role it is to uphold persons' civil, political, and economic human rights. But then given that they have this role it surely follows that they are *authorized* to act to protect these rights: this is their responsibility. Given this, it would be odd to construct an account of humanitarian intervention which does not accommodate and reflect the fact that some global institutions have been assigned the role of protecting human rights. The best articulation of (5*), then, would attribute the authority to intervene to impartial transnational political authorities.

But what if there are no such institutions? One might suggest that we should normally encourage multilateral interventions in preference to unilateral interventions. Unilateral interventions are, quite reasonably, often perceived to be promoting a state's own ends (Donnelly 1993: 628–9). There is, therefore, a strong case for claiming that interventions should normally be undertaken by an agent incorporating as wide and ecumenical a coalition of support as possible.[46]

The claim that interventions are justified only if they are authorized by a legitimate body is challenged by Moellendorf. His argument was presented in Chapter 6 and need therefore only be briefly restated. He argues thus. First, legitimacy has no intrinsic value. The only possible value it might possess is that it may contribute towards order. Second, to insist that military action (or in this context interventions) must be authorized by a legitimate authority has a cost attached to it. Acquiring the permission would take time and this is time in which people are being killed.[47] In short, then, the value of legitimacy has no intrinsic value and it does have a considerable cost (2002*a*: 121). Although this argument was considered and criticized in Chapter 6 it might, however, be profitably reconsidered here for two reasons. First, as was noted in Chapter 6 Section V, Moellendorf actually makes this claim about (all) military action in his discussion of intervention and his argument may have more relevance to discussions of intervention than it does to war between political regimes. To assemble a military force which enjoys a wide coalition of support does take time. Second, some further points can be made against his argument, points which are especially appropriate in the context of humanitarian intervention.

If we proceed now to evaluate Moellendorf's argument we can see that both steps in his argument are questionable. To take the first step first, Moellendorf's assumption that legitimacy has only instrumental value and, more particularly, that it has value only insofar as it engenders stability, is implausible. If legitimacy had only instrumental value then we would be indifferent between the following two cases. In the first case, a man commits a murder and the political authority with jurisdiction for that area tries and imprisons him. In the second case, a man commits a murder and I try him and imprison him. In both cases, a man has committed a wrong and, *ex hypothesi*, the same treatment is meted out to him. Surely, though, we make a significant moral distinction between the two cases, and we do so because we care not just about outcomes but also whether the decision-making process was legitimate and authoritative. I do not have the authority to imprison people for misdemeanours. This establishes that legitimacy has intrinsic value: we care about how decisions come about and who makes them. That is why we are not indifferent between the two cases above.

To further strengthen this point consider another example. Suppose that a serious wrong is being committed against me. Let us suppose further that someone can prevent this wrong, that the response they will take will be proportionate, and that they will only use force if it is the least bad resort. It is implausible to conclude that they can undertake this action unless they have been authorized to do so, especially by me. Suppose I don't want them to undertake this action and refuse them my consent. Even though the conditions of just cause, proportionality, success, and least awful option are satisfied, they do not have the *authority* to act on my behalf.[48]

A second, *ad hominem*, problem with Moellendorf's argument is that his dismissal of 'legitimate authority' is at variance with what he says elsewhere in *Cosmopolitan Justice*. For he himself recognizes elsewhere that a fair political structure is one to which people consent (2002*a*: 135–6). He refers, for example, to 'the interest of persons in being governed by state structures to which they consent' (2002*a*: 135). But the principle at work here appears to be nothing more than a specific (contractarian) principle of legitimacy.

A third, and related, problem with Moellendorf's analysis is that he argues that if we insist that intervention may only be waged by a legitimate authority we face a clash between order (this is what legitimate authority provides) and justice. But it is a corollary of the first point that this is not the choice. Rather what we face is a choice between two different kinds of justice. On the one hand, we have a procedural ideal of justice: power can only be exercised fairly if the agent exercising it has been authorized to do so. On the other hand, we have a substantive ideal of justice: power is being exercised to protect people's rights. The choice, then, is not one of '[t]rade-offs between order and justice' (2002*a*: 121). Hence, to claim, as Moellendorf does, that we must choose justice does not settle the case against 'legitimate authority'.

The preceding three points have called into question Moellendorf's dismissal of the intrinsic value of legitimacy. We might also question the second step in his argument—the claim that to insist on legitimacy necessarily incurs a cost to human life. The phenomenon that Moellendorf draws attention to is not, however, a reason to abandon the idea of a legitimate authority. It is, rather, a reason to reform existing institutional structures. It would be quite wrong to resign ourselves to 'authorities' who do not defend rights, regard them as a given, and then adjust our behaviour accordingly. Should we not, rather, revise the system? Moellendorf's argument wrongly treats any delays as an unalterable fact and uncritically accepts them. Surely the most suitable course of action would be to improve the system by which decisions about interventions are made. A domestic example illustrates the point. Suppose that the state fails to protect someone's property from constant attack. In such circumstances, we might think that citizens can step in. However, what would surely be best would be to ensure that the state system is better rather than allow it to continue to be unresponsive. We should consider in this light proposals for a United Nations Volunteer Force. Such a force was proposed by, among others, the Commission on Global

Governance (1995: 110–12) and defended in Chapter 5 Section VI. The Commission suggested that there be a 10,000 person volunteer force under the control of the United Nations (1995: 111). Part of the rationale for this is to prevent huge and damaging time delays and also to deal with the fact that countries are frequently reluctant to commit troops (1995: 111). It would thereby address Moellendorf's concerns.

For these four reasons, (5*) remains intact.[49] One final point is in order. The arguments in defence of (5*) adduced above have at several points employed examples from the 'domestic' domain to show that international intervention must be authorized by a legitimate authority. This suggests another way of thinking about (5*). In particular it suggests that a critic of (5*) must show why it is that although we care about legitimate authority in domestic politics we can disregard it when it comes to global politics. The 'domestic' examples employed above, in effect, issue a challenge to those who reject (5*) for they say 'Given that we think that legitimate authority is necessary for the just exercise of power in the domestic realm what reason do we have for thinking that it is not as important in the global realm?' And, given this, a compelling rejection of (5*) requires an excursus into what Chapter 1 termed level-1 analysis and an explanation of how global political theory and domestic political theory may be categorically different on this particular question.

To the above five conditions we should add one further consideration, namely that if we are considering whether external agencies have a binding *obligation* to intervene we should add the further condition:

(6*) intervention does not impose undue costs on the intervening authorities. Here the distinction between a right to intervene and an obligation to intervene is highly pertinent since to establish the former one does not require this sixth condition. People can have a right to intervene even if doing so is costly or dangerous for them. (6*) is, however, extremely relevant if one wishes to argue that people have an overriding obligation to intervene since where the costs are great it is sometimes reasonable to conclude that external bodies are not obligated to intervene (or their obligation is overridden). Of course all interventions will impose some costs on the intervening agent and this does not imply that intervention is not obligatory. (6*) thus refers to 'undue' costs.

To provide an account of undue costs, and thereby an account of when people are obligated to intervene, we need to provide an account of whether persons have special obligations of justice to their fellow nationals or fellow citizens and, if so, how weighty these are (Buchanan 1999a; Mason 2000: 195–7, 199–200). If one takes a wholly cosmopolitan view (what was termed ambitious cosmopolitanism in Chapter 4) one will treat the lives of fellow nationals or fellow citizens on a par with foreigners and hence will be more inclined to endorse humanitarian intervention. One would determine what constitutes 'undue' cost by treating any wrong to a fellow national as the same as a wrong to a foreigner. If, however, one thinks that we have weighty duties of distributive justice to fellow nationals or fellow citizens then one will ascribe greater moral weight to the wrong committed against one's own soldiers and hence will sometimes think that there are occasions in which foreigners' rights are being violated and humanitarian intervention could work but that it is wrong to call for the sacrifice of the lives of fellow nationals even where that would save more lives.

The point made in the last paragraph, it must be noted, presupposes a situation in which a nation-state or state (or group of such states) intervenes in another political system. In these circumstances, the question of whether an intervening nation-state (or state) has special duties of justice to its own people arises. However, it would not arise in a situation in which an intervention is undertaken by a multi-national United Nations Volunteer Force. To be sure the leaders of any such force have a duty of care to the members of the military force: the point, though, is that the issue of whether there are special obligations of justice to fellow-nationals is not a relevant one.

# VIII

Having discussed when humanitarian intervention is justified (the equivalent of *jus ad bellum*), we should now consider what methods may be employed during intervention (the equivalent of *jus in bello*). This topic is almost always neglected and indeed even Fixdal and Smith explicitly abstain from discussing what principles should guide the conduct of humanitarian intervention and whether conventional rules of *jus in bello* apply (1998: 285, 291). It is nonetheless of considerable practical importance. To outline the appropriate principles, it is worth distinguishing here between non-military and military forms of humanitarian intervention and discussing each in turn. In the case of military intervention it is hard to see why there should be any difference between the principles of *jus ad bellum* analysed in Chapter 6 and those appropriate to armed humanitarian intervention. Accordingly, armed humanitarian intervention should be proportionate and should observe non-combatant immunity (as defined in Chapter 6).

Consider now non-military humanitarian interventions, such as economic sanctions. What principles should guide the use of such measures? First, the concept of proportionality is readily applicable to non-military modes of intervention. To give an example: if a political regime commits a minor rights violation it would be quite wrong to respond to this by imposing sanctions that it is known will induce widespread poverty. The latter is both unnecessary and wrong for it imposes a greater harm on the people than the wrong merits. What of non-combatant immunity? At first glance it might seem that this principle is of no relevance for there are no combatants in a non-military humanitarian intervention. Whilst the latter is true, we should not hastily dismiss the principle for the intuitions underlying it have relevance for the conduct of non-military interventions. To see this consider the principle of non-combatant immunity. Roughly stated this maintains that

> It is wrong to deliberately *employ military means* against those who are *non-combatants* (although such action may be justified if it is a product of deliberately targeting *combatants* and one has taken every step to minimize harm to *non-combatants*).[50]

The intuition underlying it (again put very crudely) is that it is wrong deliberately to inflict harm on those who are not party to the conflict. But if this is the rationale, then it suggests the following principle:

> It is wrong to deliberately *employ (non-military) means* against those who are *not perpetrators of injustice* (although such action may be justified if it is a product of deliberately targeting *perpretrators of injustice* and one has taken every step to minimize harm to *non-perpetrators*).

The logical structure of this principle corresponds exactly to the logical structure of the principle of non-combatant immunity. Where the latter refers to 'combatants' it refers to 'perpetrators of injustice', and where the latter refers to 'employing military means' it refers to 'employing non-military means'. If we accept the principle of non-combatant immunity, then, we have good reason to accept the second principle. If it is wrong to deliberately attack non-combatants is it not also wrong to inflict harm on innocent members of another regime who are not committing any wrong?

This principle is, moreover, of considerable practical relevance as an example brings out. Consider the use of economic sanctions. These, so it is often argued, frequently harm the 'wrong' people (such as children or those being oppressed in a country). The implications of the above principle are that sanctions are illegitimate if they deliberately target people who are not perpetrators of injustice. Furthermore, they are illegitimate unless steps have been taken to minimize harm to non-guilty parties. However, sanctions may be justified even if they result in harm to non-guilty persons if the sanctions are not intended to harm the non-guilty, other methods which inflict less harm on the non-guilty have been considered, and the harm to the non-guilty has been minimized.[51]

## IX

The discussion in the earlier sections has focused on the *moral* question of whether intervention is defensible and if so when? In this final section, I want to conclude and complete the analysis by noting briefly that even if we think (as I think we should) that there is sometimes a *moral* case for intervention this does not establish that international law must grant a *legal* right to intervene. This distinction, recall, was briefly introduced earlier in the chapter in the discussion of international order (Section V). The salient point is that it is arguable that intervention is sometimes morally right but that international law should nonetheless disallow it (Slater and Nardin 1986: 95).

Why might one think that there should not be a legal right to intervene?[52] The main, and most powerful, argument is that to entrench a right to humanitarian intervention in international law would in practice allow not just humanitarian interventions but also non-humanitarian interventions. It would enable powerful states to impose their will on powerless states (Brownlie 1973: 146–8; Farer 1973: 152, 155–7). As Frank and Rodley put it, 'if such a right were to receive the sanction of international law and international lawyers, it is likely to remain, in the future as in the past, the prerogative of a few powerful states' (1973: 290).

Granting this legal right would, then, produce worse moral outcomes than simply legally banning it.

As a consequentialist argument this requires a careful consideration of the empirical effects of such a codification. Three points can, I think, be made against this argument. First, one might argue that what the argument shows is not that there should not be a legal right to intervene but rather that it should be tightly circumscribed. One might argue that it is possible to entrench a legal right to intervene that minimizes the problems (Mason and Wheeler 1996: 106). As Chopra and Weiss point out, one can tighten up laws to prevent abuse (1992: 100). One can, for example, seek to restrict the power of superpowers by denying them the right to intervene and allocating that to an international institution and by ensuring that the latter is an independent institution which is not in the thrall of dominant states. Second, this argument dwells on the incentive effects of the legal permission to intervene but one should also bear in mind the incentive effects of a legal prohibition on intervention. If the legal right to intervene encourages some power hungry states to intervene, the legal prohibition on intervention will also by a similar logic encourage some despots to persecute their own subjects in the knowledge that others are prohibited by international law from intervening. Third, to grant a legal right to intervene under certain highly specific circumstances would clarify the legal situation which at present is vague and disputed, and as such would strengthen international law, making it emphatically clear when intervention is illegitimate (Chopra and Weiss 1992: 100–1). Thus, although there is no straightforward relationship between the claim that external bodies have a moral right or obligation to intervene and the claim that such a right or obligation should be affirmed by international law, we have some reason to endorse such a legal right.

## X

This completes the analysis of this chapter. The aim throughout has been to assess the question of whether political regimes may intervene in another political regime to address internal wrongs. More particularly, it has

(1) identified and outlined four key premises underlying all cosmopolitan conceptions of humanitarian intervention;
(2) illustrated the general structure of the cosmopolitan approach by drawing on the principles of justice derived in Chapters 3 and 4 and the institutional analysis of Chapter 5.

It then considered four challenges to cosmopolitan arguments for humanitarian intervention. Accordingly it criticized the claims that intervention is wrong because

(3) it conflicts with the right of political communities to be self-determining;
(4) it is presumptuous;
(5) it destroys international stability; and
(6) it rarely works.

Having rejected all of these counter-arguments it turned to the question of when intervention is justified and drawing on the cosmopolitan arguments presented in Section II and the analysis of just war in Chapter 6, it

(7) defended five preconditions of a right to intervene (adding a sixth that must be met if one is to claim that intervention is an overriding duty);
(8) set out two principles that should guide the ways in which interventions are undertaken; and
(9) raised the question of whether international law should affirm a right (or duty) to intervene, cautiously arguing that it should.

One further point bears stressing. In the same way that Chapter 6 ended by noting how the analysis of just war bore out the claim that it is artificial to analyse different questions in global political theory in isolation from one another, we should note in the closing section of this chapter that our analysis of intervention similarly supports this claim. For what we have seen is that the principles of justice that ground the right and duty to intervene draw on the analysis of civil and political rights in Chapter 3, the principles of distributive justice considered in Chapter 4, and the evaluation of the normative significance of political institutions conducted in Chapter 5. We have seen further that the issue of whether there is a duty to intervene takes us back to Chapter 4's analysis of the claims of fellow nationals. In addition to this the account of when to intervene has drawn on the norms of both *jus ad bellum* and *jus in bello* advanced in Chapter 6.

We should, however, close with the thought that humanitarian intervention is essentially a 'reactive' policy that is adopted after people's needs or rights have been harmed. Given the difficulties to which interventions are susceptible, there is a strong case for tackling the roots of these problems and seeking to prevent them from occurring rather than responding to them once they have arisen (Booth 1995: 121; Parekh 1997: 68; Pogge 1992*a*: 100–1). This, we should note, returns us to the subject matter of Chapter 5 since, as we saw there, institutional structures can influence the extent to which peoples' rights and interests are protected. An adequate analysis of the problems to which intervention is a response should thus impress on us the importance of constructing political institutions that minimize rights violations. It also reminds us that a normative account of intervention articulates remedial principles.

### NOTES

1. Of course, as was noted in Ch. 6, this action was also justified in terms of preventing a future external wrong. That is, it was claimed that it was necessary to destroy weapons of mass destruction which, it speculated, would otherwise have been used against the United States.
2. For further details see Gordon (1994: 550–7), Griffiths, Levine, and Weller (1995: 51–2), Lewis and Mayall (1996: 107–24), and Slim and Visman (1995).

3. Other definitions of intervention also define intervention in terms of 'interference' and hence are also vulnerable to this criticism. For instance, Donnelly defines intervention as 'any coercive *interference* in the internal affairs of a state' (1993: 609, emphasis added). Cf. also Vincent (1974: 13). This point also applies to McMahan's otherwise accurate definition of intervention as 'coercive external *interference* in the affairs of a population organized in the form of a state' (1986: 27, emphasis added). Once the term 'interference' is exchanged for 'action', McMahan's definition is, I think, a plausible one.

4. In this respect, my definition differs from that given by some. Michael Joseph Smith, for example, writes that 'intervention can be defined as discrete acts which try to affect the domestic affairs of another state' (1989: 2). On this definition, non-coercive acts (like one leader trying to persuade another by force of argument) count as intervention.

5. This practice follows that of Ch. 6 where the term 'political regimes' is preferred to the term 'states' so as to accommodate the issues that arise between non-sovereign political systems as well as states.

6. For a contrary position see Parekh (1997: throughout and esp. pp. 49, 56–8). Parekh argues that interventions are, by definition, directed against states. But his reasoning for this conclusion is, I think, suspect. He rightly argues that it is not possible to intervene in a situation in which there are a number of unconnected individuals (1997: 53). This suggests that interventions take place in political communities. It does not follow from this, however, that they necessarily take place in states since there are other types of political community.

7. He does, though, recognize the existence of non-military ways of determining another state's conduct, preferring to call such action 'quasi-intervention': Donnelly (1993: 610).

8. Indeed, in line with his definition (cf. note 4 above), Smith argues against 'trying to delimit intervention according to its means' and includes 'propagandistic broadcasts' as a form of intervention (1989: 4). Whilst I think Smith is right to challenge the claim that intervention requires force, my view is that according to ordinary usage of the term, intervention is partly defined in terms of the means employed and that non-coercive acts should not be deemed to be interventionary.

9. This marks a contrast with the discussion of external wrongs (analysed in Ch. 6). This chapter considers both military and non-military means of response to injustice whereas Ch. 6 focused on military means of response to injustice (although the claim that war should be resorted to only once less awful alternatives have been explored thereby acknowledges the existence of alternative types of response and recognizes their importance).

10. For the moral assumptions underlying those critical of a principle of non-intervention see the following: Beitz (1979: 413–16; 1988b: 182–95; 1999c: 71–92); Doppelt (1980: 398–403); Luban (1980a: 167–70, 173–6, 178–81; 1980b: 392–7); Pogge (1992a); Tesón (1988: 15–16, 111–23).

11. See Barry (1998: 144–5, 153; 1999: sec. IV, esp. pp. 35–6); Beitz (1979: 417–20; 1988a: 191–3; 1994: 123–6); Pogge (1994a: 89–90).

12. Cf. also Wicclair (1979: 147–8).

13. Some, like Gerard Elfstrom, deny that external agents have a duty to protect the rights of others: see Elfstrom (1983, esp. pp. 711–12, 715–16, 718).

14. Some, it should be noted, seek only to argue for this weaker claim: cf. Tesón (1988: 117). Tesón is not denying that there might be a duty. He is sympathetic to this view but wishes to concentrate on establishing the milder claim (1988: 117, fn. 15).

15. Many, of course, criticize such duties: for an important analysis, and defence, of positive duties see Shue (1996: 35–64).
16. For Pogge's analysis of intervention see Pogge (1992*a*). The claim in question rests, of course, on Pogge's institutionalism: see the discussion of the latter in Ch. 4, Sect. III, and the references to his work cited there.
17. My claim is not that every single argument for humanitarian intervention rests on these four assumptions. Rather it is that almost all arguments for humanitarian intervention make these four claims and that all plausible arguments do. It is, thus, possible to construct an argument for humanitarian intervention which does not rest on these four premises. For example someone might argue that communities have a moral standing which is not reducible to the interests of the individual members and argue that intervention against a state or political system is justified to protect the rights of the penalized communities. This more communitarian argument does not rest on the first and second (individualist) assumptions of what I have termed the standard argument. I do not think, though, that it is a promising approach for two reasons. First, its moral claim is highly dubious—a claim developed and argued for more extensively elsewhere in this book. Second, as we shall see when discussing Walzer's theory, this argument makes the false assumption that we can identify clearly defined communities.
18. See, in this context, Buchanan's fine discussion of humanitarian intervention and, in particular, his critical discussion of the claim that states lack a duty to engage in humanitarian intervention because they have a duty to advance the interests of their own citizens. Buchanan effectively criticizes this view—what he terms 'the "discretionary association" view of the state' (1999*a*: 74, cf. further pp. 74–82)— and defends an alternative conception of the role of states according to which states should seek to promote and support just institutions (1999*a*: 82, cf. pp. 82–7).
19. I should stress that there are many other challenges to the case for humanitarian intervention outlined in Sect. II. Some, for example, challenge the idea of universal values like human rights (cf. Chs 2 and 3) and others challenge the mode of philosophical argument employed in Sect. II (Rengger 1993: 187–90).
20. There are a number of excellent discussions of defences of non-intervention, e.g. Beitz (1988*b*) and McMahan (1986). My position is most in keeping with that developed by Wicclair (1979). The latter provides a useful classification of defences of non-intervention and, as we shall see in the text that follows, he makes persuasive critiques of each of them.
21. What are these communities? Walzer is not very clear on this matter, employing terms such as 'a people' (1977: 88) or a 'political community' (1977: 87–9, 93) or just 'communities' *simpliciter* (1977: 90). Moreover, he compounds this unclarity in his treatment of one of his case studies. In his discussion of the Hungarian attempt to gain autonomy from the Austro-Hungarian empire in the nineteenth century, Walzer treats Hungary as a nation entitled to independence under the heading of 'national liberation' (1977: 96). But, and this is the crucial point, he makes clear that Hungary was not in fact actually a nation but also comprised Croats and Slovenes (1977: 92, 96). He even recognizes that Hungarian nationalists were antagonistic toward Croats and Slovenes (1977: 92). In general, then, Walzer appears to equate communities with nations. (From the point of view of his actual argument the relevant community, however, need not necessarily be a nation. It might be an ethnic group, say, or a religious community).

22. As we saw in Ch. 6, Walzer invokes this consideration to defend the right of the state to wage war in self-defence as well as to defend the right of the state not to be intervened in. It is, of course, no surprise that he employs the same consideration to defend the two different conclusions (the right to self-defence and the right to independence) since both have in common a commitment to the value of the sovereignty of the state and this is what the analogy is intended to support.

23. The claim that intervention is objectionable because it conflicts with the ideal of communal self-government has been developed in other distinct ways: cf. Elfstrom (1983, esp. pp. 713, 715–8). Space precludes the examination of these arguments.

24. McMahan provides a more qualified and nuanced version of the 'communal auto- nomy' argument that attempts to avoid some of the problems of Walzer's argument (cf. McMahan 1986: 34–5).

25. As Wheeler points out, Vincent's views evolved and in later work he took a more human rights-sensitive view than Bull and than his own earlier work: (Wheeler 1992: 478–80). Cf. Vincent (1986, esp. pp. 111–28) and Vincent and Wilson (1993, esp. pp. 127–9).

26. We might term such people 'humanitarian bystanders' for they defend standing by and not intervening on humanitarian grounds.

27. For two good surveys of such arguments see Mason and Wheeler (1996: 100–6) and Wicclair (1979: 149–53).

28. I am grateful to Chris Brown for first drawing my attention to this point (and for referring me to Murray's work). The point is also noted by Smith: cf. Smith (1989: 19; 1998: 71–2).

29. This point returns us to the discussion of objective and subjective characterizations of the national interest in Ch. 1, Sect. II.

30. It is important to add here that resistance to intervention and the costs it imposes has moral significance in a number of ways independently of whether it prevents an intervention from achieving its humanitarian ends. See the later discussions of proportionality and whether there is a duty (as opposed to a mere right) to intervene.

31. For a similar argument see Waltz (1979: 188–9).

32. It should be noted that Mill distinguishes between 'civilized' societies and 'barbar- ians'. The argument outlined in the text applies only to 'civilized' societies. Mill maintains that it is legitimate to intervene in barbarian societies. Why this kind of dif- ferential treatment? He reasons that civilized peoples can treat barbarians differently to civilized societies because intervention will be for their own good and they lack a sense of reciprocity (1984 [1859]: 118–20).

33. For other analyses of the moral justifiability of intervention see McMahan (1986), Moellendorf (2002a: 102–27), Rengger (1993: 179–93), Smith (1998), Vincent (1986: 111–28), and Wicclair (1979).

34. Fixdal and Smith tend to identify humanitarian intervention with armed humani- tarian intervention (1998, throughout but especially pp. 285, 291–2, 295–6, 302–4, 306).

35. These principles are the ones arrived at in Ch. 6, Sect. V, which in turn are a cosmopolitan reworking of the standard principles of *jus ad bellum* (as character- ized by Johnson (1999: 28–9)). The order of these has been changed from that in Ch. 6. This order corresponds better to the arguments underpinning humanitarian intervention.

36. Cf. Beitz (1988b: 188).

37. One comment is, however, in order. Someone might point out that not all human rights are of equal moral significance. They might further argue that some rights that persons have qua human beings are not morally absolutely fundamental. In which case, they might argue, (1*) should be recast to refer to 'fundamental' human rights. Otherwise we might be forced to conclude that intervention is required for rather 'insignificant' human rights. In reply: it is perhaps true that some human rights are not morally fundamental. However, (1*) would not sanction intervention for such 'non-fundamental' human rights because of the other conditions, most notably 'proportionality'. Interventions always incur considerable costs and it would therefore not be justified to intervene for minor rights violations. Furthermore, any legitimate authority is highly unlikely to justify intervention except for fundamental rights violations. I am grateful to Andrew Cross for discussion on this point.

38. For a similar principle see Slater and Nardin's discussion (1986). They outline four conditions, one of which maintains that 'indigenous military resistance to humanitarian intervention must be relatively small—relative, that is, to the scale of rights violations that the intervention is intended to end—in order to ensure that the human costs of the intervention are not excessive' (1986: 93).

39. As Beitz writes '[i]ntervention should not do significant harm elsewhere' (1988b: 189).

40. A third type of cost—the cost to the intervening agent, and its members—should also be included in an account of proportionality. This cost is considered below for a separate reason: see the discussion of principle (6*) below.

41. Compare this principle with Slater and Nardin's claim that 'armed intervention to protect human rights be undertaken only after other, less drastic, remedies have been tried and have failed' (1986: 93).

42. A pertinent example of this point is the United Nations sanctions against Iraq, on which see Moellendorf (2002a: 126). Moellendorf too makes the point that sanctions may be more harmful than military action (2002a: 125) although his point is not focused on the principle of last resort but on whether we define sanctions as interventionary (2002a: 125–6). For a fuller empirical discussion see also Eric Herring's analysis (2002).

43. The principle of last resort, by contrast, does not require such difficult judgements. This should not tempt us into abandoning the principle of least awful option for that of the last resort. This for several reasons. First, as has been argued above, the principle of last resort presupposes the principle of the least awful option. It cannot therefore take priority over it. Furthermore, it would be a non sequitur to move from the difficulty in assessing which options are more awful to the conclusion that we should assume that war is. Third, even if we accept that intervention should be a last resort the evaluation of which interventionary actions one should adopt requires an evaluation of the 'awfulness' of each of them when compared to the others. Judgements of awfulness are therefore inescapable.

44. For similar conditions see Beitz (1988b: 189) and Slater and Nardin (1986: 93).

45. The first four conditions are similar to those defended by Moellendorf in *Cosmopolitan Justice*. He writes that intervention is justified when (i) it is 'directed toward advancing justice either in the basic structure of the state or in the international effects of its domestic policies' (2002a: 118). To this he adds that (ii) 'it must be reasonable to believe that the intervention is likely to succeed' (2002a: 119); (iii) intervention must be adopted only as a last resort (2002a: 119–20, 122); and (iv) the 'interventions must be proportional to the injustice occurring' (2002a: 120).

There are, however, differences. First, (1*) differs from (i) because it is concerned with all injustices in another regime and not simply with injustices in its basic structure. Second, Moellendorf's principle of last resort states that 'the intervention is a last resort *after diplomatic means have failed*' (2002a: 122, my emphasis). (3*), however, does not require that one actually try diplomatic means if one has good reason to think that they will fail and if trying is costly. Moellendorf oscillates on this: cf. (2002a: 119–20). Third, as we have seen in Ch. 6, Moellendorf rejects (5*) (2002a: 121).

46. Smith strikes the right note, arguing that in general collective intervention is best but on occasion unilateral intervention is justifiable: Smith (1998: 77–8).

47. Not all interventions involve military force. Nonetheless, Moellendorf's argument, I assume, applies also to non-military interventions. Both steps of his argument—the denial of the value of legitimacy and the claim that acquiring legitimacy has a cost attached to it—apply as much to non-military interventions.

48. This point might explain why some, such as Tesón (1988: 119–21), insist that intervention must be consented to by the intended beneficiaries of the intervention. (Although there are other good reasons as to why this consent matters, such as that such consent renders the success of the intervention more likely and hence is needed for (4*)).

49. For an additional reason see Tesón (1998: 59).

50. This is a highly compressed statement of some aspects of Walzer's position on non-combatants discussed in Ch. 6 (1977: 153–6).

51. Compare Moellendorf's treatment of sanctions (2002a: 126). He condemns sanctions like those described in the text but he does so by appealing to the principle of proportionality. The latter, however, is insufficient to capture all the morally relevant aspects of sanctions for it does not speak to the question of *which groups of persons* may be targeted and *which groups of people* may not be targeted. A principle of proportionality is concerned with the amount of suffering and cannot in itself distinguish between different groups of people. However, this is a problem because we do think it relevant if the effects of sanctions are borne by innocent men and women who are not responsible for any injustices. Interestingly, Moellendorf's argument refers to the wrong done to 'innocents', referring in particular to children (2002a: 126), but the intuition driving this is not a concern for proportionality: it is a concern for *who* is harmed and the thought is surely that it is wrong that the non-guilty are paying the price. Why else refer to the innocent (which Moellendorf does twice on 2002a: 126) and why else refer to children? To articulate this intuition one needs, then, the principle stated in the text.

52. For a brief but good discussion of this question see Chopra and Weiss (1992: 99–101). They challenge the claim that the legal right to intervene would necessarily result in undesirable consequences.

# 8

## Conclusion

> It ought not to be the case that there is one standard of morality for individuals in their relations with one another, a different and a slighter standard for corporations, and a third and still slighter standard for nations. For, after all, what are corporations but groupings of individuals for ends which in the last resort are personal ends? And what are nations but wider, closer, and more lasting unions of persons for the attainment of the end they have in common, i.e., the commonwealth. Yet we are well aware that the accepted and operative standards of morality differ widely in the three spheres of conduct. If a soul is imputed at all to a corporation, it is a leather soul, not easily penetrable to the probings of pity or compunction, and emitting much less of the milk of human kindness than do the separate souls of its directors and stockholders in their ordinary human relations. . . . The standard of international morality, particularly in matters of commercial intercourse, is on a still lower level.
>
> J. A. Hobson (1920: 1–3)

Martin Wight once wrote that there was no international theory (1966a). Whether that was ever so is open to question. But it is now indubitably true that there is a large, expanding, and sophisticated literature on the ethical issues that arise at the global level. My aims in this work have been to defend a cosmopolitan theory (both a specific cosmopolitan theory and also a cosmopolitan perspective more generally) and to analyse and evaluate competing political philosophies. In this conclusion I hope to pull the threads of the previous six chapters together and to offer some more general reflections on different ways of thinking about the ethical issues that arise at the global level. Given that this work has sought to defend a cosmopolitan political programme it will begin by highlighting some key features of the cosmopolitan vision that have emerged from the preceding chapters and then seek to locate where non-cosmopolitan political philosophies dissent from the cosmopolitan vision.

## I

We can begin this process by examining first the specific brand of cosmopolitanism that I have defended and then reflecting more generally on the prevailing family of contemporary cosmopolitan theories. To start with the former: this book has attempted to justify an egalitarian liberal brand of cosmopolitanism. It has defended the thesis that there are universal principles against cultural relativists. Its general strategy has been to show that many critiques of universalism mischaracterize it and that other critiques are simply unpersuasive. It has defended two universal principles of justice in particular. First: it defends a liberal package of civil and political human rights, arguing that these are necessary to respect persons' interests in leading fulfilling lives. In doing so it chronicled five reasons for thinking that liberal civil and political human rights best enable people to flourish. Second: it defends an egalitarian distributive programme, defending subsistence rights, a principle of global equality of opportunity, rules of fair pay, and a commitment to prioritizing the least advantaged. Furthermore, by contrast with many other cosmopolitans (such as Beitz, O'Neill, and Pogge) the argument for these universal principles of distributive justice does not depend on whether there is extensive economic globalization or not (cf. also Caney 2003: 296–7; Caney forthcoming *a*; Buchanan 2003: ch. 2). Drawing on these universal principles of civil, political, and distributive justice, this work then criticized a statist world order and defended a system of global political authorities. The latter includes a reformed United Nations incorporating a democratically elected second assembly. It calls, furthermore, for democratic procedures to be put in place which enable people to hold powerful international institutions (such as the WTO, IMF, and World Bank) to account. It also comprises a UN volunteer force charged with ensuring that people's civil and political rights are upheld. It argued that such institutions are required for two reasons. First, on *instrumental* grounds, they further people's civil, political, and economic rights. Global institutions are needed to ensure compliance with such principles, determine responsibilities, and overcome collective action problems. Second, such a political framework enables persons to exercise control over the transnational processes and institutions that affect the use of their rights. To put it another way, they extend the suffrage beyond the borders of nations or states to ensure that people have a stake in the political and economic forces that impact on their fundamental rights.

Having outlined an ideal theory, the focus then shifted to non-ideal theory and the book sought to develop and defend a cosmopolitan account of how political regimes may respond to external wrongs (Chapter 6) and internal wrongs (Chapter 7). In both cases, it was argued that war and humanitarian intervention, respectively, are justifiable when: there is a just cause (defined in terms of the protection of individual rights); the actions are authorized by a legitimate body; the action is proportionate to the wrongs being perpetrated; less awful options have been considered first; and the prospects of success are good.

We, thus, have a comprehensive egalitarian liberal brand of cosmopolitanism that covers many (although not all) of the fundamental issues a global political theory should address.[1]

## II

Having restated the nature of the specific brand of cosmopolitanism that has been defended I now wish to make some observations about contemporary egalitarian liberal theories of cosmopolitanism in general.[2] Drawing on the previous six chapters, we can identify five fundamental points about contemporary cosmopolitan political analyses.

**II.1.** *Cosmopolitanism and the relationship between global political theory and domestic political theory.* The first point returns to what Chapter 1 termed level-1 analysis. It concerns, that is, cosmopolitanism's account of the relationship between, on the one hand, those principles that should be applied at the domestic level (domestic political theory) and, on the other hand, those principles that should be applied at the global level (global political theory). For what has emerged from the previous six chapters is that one central feature of cosmopolitanism is its suggestion that there is no fundamental morally significant difference between the domestic and global realms *such that the values that are appropriate in the former realm are inappropriate in the latter.* For cosmopolitans, the principles of justice that inform the domestic level should also inform the global realm. To put the point another way, their claim is that the principles to be applied in the global realm should be 'continuous' with those we think appropriate in the domestic realm (Beitz 1999a: 288; P. Jones 2000). This theme recurs throughout the preceding analysis and can be developed in six ways. First, Chapter 2 provided the theoretical foundations for this claim through its discussion and defence of the *General Argument for Universalism.* The latter, recall, argued that persons throughout the world share some morally relevant properties and hence if some moral values apply to some persons then they should, as a matter of consistency, also apply to all. To make this claim, however, is to say that there is no fundamental morally significant difference between domestic and global realms such that the values that inform the former should not ever inform the latter. A second elaboration, and defence, of this claim was developed in Chapter 3. For Chapter 3 defended the scope$_1$ claim, where this states that the standard justifications of rights to civil and political liberties entail that there are *human* rights to these same civil and political liberties. As such, its central thrust is that the content of global principles of justice should flow from the egalitarian liberal accounts of justice that are normally thought to apply within the state. A third instantiation of the claim that the principles of justice that should inform domestic politics should also inform global politics occurred in the analysis of global distributive justice in Chapter 4. There we saw that the scope$_2$ claim held, where the scope$_2$ claim states that the standard justifications of principles of distributive justice entail that there are cosmopolitan principles of distributive justice. The point of the scope$_1$ and scope$_2$ claims, then, is that borders are not of fundamental moral importance. Their core claims are that people's domestic commitments entail global principles. Furthermore, we should recall that both scope claims obtain because the standard arguments for principles of justice (whether that is civil and political justice, or distributive justice) rely on a universalist conception of 'moral personality'. They rely, that is, upon a conception of moral personality that ascribes entitlements to people not in virtue of their membership of any national or state-level political community (a wholly 'domestic' property) but rather in virtue of some universal (that is, 'global') property.

Further confirmation of cosmopolitanism's conception of the relationship between the global realm and the domestic realm is supplied by an analysis of the institutional structures discussed in Chapter 5. Again we saw that a cosmopolitan approach calls into question any fundamental dichotomy between the principles appropriate to the global realm and those appropriate to the domestic realm. This can be seen through an examination of two points. First, one powerful argument for a cosmopolitan political framework with supra-state political authorities takes an *instrumental* form and argues that this kind of global political system is the most effective way of implementing cosmopolitan principles of justice. So exactly the same reasons often employed to defend the role of the state—the need for a body to ensure compliance with rules of justice, uphold rights, secure public goods, and resolve collective action problems—can be used to defend a system of global political authorities. (Here, though, it should be stressed that the idea of a world state was emphatically rejected). Second, as we also saw in Chapter 5, a system of global political authorities is sustained by what was termed a *right-based* perspective. The latter maintains that there is a powerful argument for transposing principles that apply within the domestic context—in this instance, the principle that persons should be able to determine the processes that govern the exercise of their rights—to the world as a whole. The rationale for these democratic principles that are conventionally thought to apply within the state entails, given facts about economic interdependence, that they should be applied at the global level. Put more succinctly, we saw that the scope$_3$ claim was vindicated. Both *instrumental* and *right-based* arguments, then, are cosmopolitan attempts to apply ideals that inform domestic politics (the notions of democratic, accountable, and effective political decision-making) to the world as a whole. Having said this it is crucial to reiterate the point that neither of these two arguments claim that the global realm should be *identical* to the domestic one. They also do not claim that the global realm should be *identical* to the domestic one as it currently exists—that is, one committed to sovereign statehood. Neither of the two arguments support a world government: furthermore, there is good reason to reject such a notion. Rather the point of the two arguments is that the values that motivate democratic and effective government at the domestic level also motivate *some form of democratic and effective global governance.*

For a fifth and further confirmation of the cosmopolitan tenet that a global political theory should be continuous with a domestic political theory we can now turn to cosmopolitanism's treatment of how best to respond to external wrongs (just war). What comes out of the theoretical apparatus employed to deal with such wrongs is not different in kind from that employed within the state. All of its key claims are ones that we think should hold within the domestic context. There we would expect force to be used only if there is a just cause as explicated in terms of individual rights. Similarly, the other necessary conditions—namely, that force may be used only when it has been authorized by a *legitimate authority*, it is a *proportionate* response, it is employed only when it is the *least bad option*, and when *it is likely to work*—are all conditions we would think appropriate within the state as well as in external affairs. The principles applied, then, are no different in nature to those we think appropriate within the domestic arena.

These conclusions are also borne out when we turn to cosmopolitan accounts of the appropriate response to internal wrongs simply because, as we saw in Chapter 7, the most plausible account of how best to respond to internal wrongs is similar in kind to that employed to deal with external wrongs. And, as has just been noted, these guiding principles (the use of force to uphold fundamental rights only when the conditions of *legitimate authority, proportionality, least awful option*, and *probability of success* are met) are ones familiar from, and continuous with, the principles applied within the state.

In all the above ways, then, we can see that a key feature of a cosmopolitan approach—whether its attention is focused on how there could be universal values, the content of civil and political rights, the nature of global principles of distributive justice, the appropriate institutional structure of the world, or the appropriate responses to external and internal wrongs—is that it calls into question the idea that there is any morally fundamental difference between the domestic realm and the global realm. In each case, it argues that the moral values that inform our account of global politics must be cut from the same cloth as the moral values that inform our account of domestic politics.

Before proceeding further it is worth making two clarificatory points. First, the above does not, of course, deny that there are very many differences between the domestic and global realms. Its claim is that the differences are not morally fundamental in such a way as to show that the principles that inform domestic politics should not carry over to the global realm. This leads to a second point for it is crucial to emphasize the importance of the word 'fundamental'. A cosmopolitan might accept that there are some morally significant differences but that they are only of derivative (that is, non-fundamental) moral importance. An example may help to illustrate this point. Suppose that one is a utilitarian. The scope claims observe that the rationale for utilitarianism implies that it should be globalized. However, once we factor in some empirical considerations (such as the absence of a world state and the lack of a sense of solidarity) then, of course, the specific policy prescriptions that utilitarianism prescribes are likely to be different at the global realm. The key point, though, is that at the fundamental theoretical level it is the same theory being applied to both global and domestic realms. And in this respect such cosmopolitan approaches differ from other approaches—such as that taken by Rawls (1999*b*)—which claim that, at the most fundamental level, the principles appropriate for the global realm are categorically different in kind to those appropriate for the domestic realm.

**II.2.** *The varieties of cosmopolitanism.* The first key point has drawn attention to a tendency common to all cosmopolitans. Having noted this point of commonality it is critical to record that different cosmopolitans defend their claim that there is no fundamental morally significant difference between domestic and global realms (and thus the scope$_1$ and scope$_2$ claims) in different ways. Some, of course, ground their cosmopolitan approach by relying on the notions of rights (C. Jones, Pogge, Shue); others invoke hypothetical contracts (Barry, Beitz, Richards); others adopt a consequentialist approach (Singer). But my point is not solely about this diversity in theoretical frameworks. For there is another important area in which contemporary liberal cosmopolitans do not speak with one voice, namely the significance of globalization for the grounding of their claim that there is no fundamental moral difference between global and domestic arenas. Here Pogge's distinction between 'institutionalists' and 'interactionists' (introduced in Chapter 3) is pertinent. For those termed 'institutionalists' the domestic claims apply globally, and the scope claims are sustained, because justice pertains to systems of interdependence and there is global interdependence. Thus for Pogge himself, the existence of human rights with obligations applying on all is dependent on there being global interdependence. For 'interactionists', by contrast, the domestic claims apply globally simply because there are normative rationales for global principles of justice—rationales which are not reliant on any empirical claims about the nature and extent of economic or political globalization (Chapter 4, Section III). Both institutional and interactional perspectives issue then in cosmopolitan conclusions. And both think that although there are very many differences between the domestic and global realms these are not sufficiently *morally significant* to entail that domestic principles should not inform the global realm. But they reach these conclusions relying on quite distinct theoretical assumptions about the scope of justice.

**II.3.** *Cosmopolitan critiques of other approaches.* Having noted two key features of the cosmopolitan political programme, a third point about egalitarian liberal cosmopolitanism that merits emphasis concerns its critique of non-cosmopolitan perspectives. The preceding analysis has shown that such cosmopolitans have (at least) two powerful tools at their disposal. First, and drawing on the scope claims cited above, cosmopolitans can point out that it is incoherent and inconsistent to argue, as so many do, that schemes of civil, political, and distributive justice apply only within a nation or within a state. This is flatly inconsistent, so the scope claims have established, with the standard rationales for these principles. To employ the terminology coined in Chapter 3, the cosmopolitan arguments have shown that non-cosmopolitan theories violate the 'criterion of *domestic-compatibility*' (the second criterion of an adequate theory of global justice as employed in Chapters 3 and 4).[3] To this we might add that the inconsistency that has been exposed is not simply a failure to adhere to some philosophical nicety. It is not merely some logical faux pas: rather to disregard it is to be guilty of double standards. The point is that if the scope claims are true then unless one applies the same principles to all persons one is guilty of treating like cases in a different way. And to do that is to operate with double standards.[4]

A second tool that egalitarian liberal cosmopolitans can (and do) employ against non-cosmopolitan perspectives is targeted specifically against one kind of alternative—namely those that adopt a minimal approach, ascribing some rights to foreigners but not the comprehensive liberal package. The second tool critiques such minimalist approaches by drawing on what Chapter 3 termed the 'criterion of *coherence*' (the third criterion of an adequate theory of global justice as employed in Chapters 3 and 4) and arguing that minimal political theories violate this criterion. As we saw in Chapters 3 and 4, to affirm only minimal rights and to repudiate an egalitarian liberal cosmopolitan approach is theoretically incoherent because the minimal rights are integrally connected to more-than-minimal rights. To affirm the minimal rights tends to require an affirmation of egalitarian liberal cosmopolitan conception of human rights.

Egalitarian liberal cosmopolitans can, therefore, employ two tools to criticize minimal rights theorists. They can argue both that people's domestic policy commitments entail universal egalitarian liberal cosmopolitan rights (*domestic-compatibility*) and also that their foreign policy commitments (comprising some minimal rights) entail universal egalitarian liberal cosmopolitan rights (*coherence*). The full liberal cosmopolitan package can, thus, be defended from two directions and non-cosmopolitan minimalists accordingly faulted on two grounds.[5]

**II.4.** *Cosmopolitanism and special duties.* One natural set of questions that might arise from the preceding discussion and especially the scope claims is: 'what room is there in a cosmopolitan approach for special duties?' and 'do the scope claims maintain that there are no local obligations and that all obligations are universal?' It would be useful, then, to make absolutely clear the cosmopolitan perspective on this issue. To do so it is worth making six points. *First*, it is essential to distinguish between different kinds of special duties. This book has not challenged the idea that persons have special duties to their friends or family or workplace colleagues. These special duties are not in question. However, the claim that persons have special duties to their fellow nationals is not as straightforward. This leads to the *second* point: this book claims that we have yet to see a plausible argument showing that persons have special obligations to fellow nationals. Furthermore, and this is the *third* point, even if there were, it has claimed that there is no reason to accept (and good reason to doubt) that such obligations that are yielded are obligations of distributive justice (Chapter 4, Section X.1). However, to this we should also add, *fourth*, that the scope$_1$ and scope$_2$ claims do not claim that there are no special obligations of justice. What they do claim is that many of the standard arguments for special rights and obligations actually entail universal rights and obligations. They accept that there can be special obligations of justice to locals if there is an argument for them and the moral properties invoked are not universal ones. What they show, however, and this is the *fifth* point, is that many of the attempted justifications of special rights have in fact justified global rights. We have seen that this holds for consequentialist, contractarian, and rights-based arguments for civil, political, and economic principles of justice. The original formulations of the scope$_1$ and scope$_2$ claims, note, were carefully worded. They maintained only that the *standard* rationales for, respectively, civil and political rights and economic rights entailed the universality of these rights (Chapter 3, Section II; Chapter 4, Section II). It was not claimed that all arguments fitted into this mould, although it was argued that we have yet to find arguments for domestic distributive justice that do not also generate global principles of distributive justice. Finally, and *sixth*, we should record that a complete answer to the question concerning special duties requires that we recognize that even if we accept special duties these in turn entail universal ones. This point needs elaboration: the intuitive line of reasoning here is that before people can exercise their special rights they must have some general rights (determining what actions they can perform, what resources they own, and so on). Hence if there are good arguments for special rights (as surely there are) these entail that there must be a set of general rights in place.[6]

Where does this leave special duties? The answer is that there will be special duties to friends, colleagues, family, and so on when and because these relationships possess moral value (and, moreover, the moral property that justifies these obligations is possessed only by the members of these social institutions and hence these duties are special ones rather than universal ones). However, we have yet to see a persuasive argument to the effect that there are special duties of justice to fellow nationals (and indeed fellow citizens). Furthermore, such special duties that do exist are legitimate if they exist within parameters set down by a cosmopolitan theory.

**II.5.** *Criticizing cosmopolitanism.* One point that arises from the preceding analysis of cosmopolitanism (especially point II.1 above) is that those who wish to defend a non-cosmopolitan approach must provide an account of the relationship between the domestic and global realms that delineates morally significant differences between the two realms. In doing so, they can show that borders have a greater moral significance than that which cosmopolitans accord them and hence that one should not apply ideals normally applied in the domestic realm to the global realm. They must, that is, challenge the cosmopolitan's account of level-1 analysis. To use terminology I have applied elsewhere, the critic must come up with a *Disanalogy Argument*. The latter cites a morally significant property that exists at the domestic level (and hence accounts for the applicability of a moral principle there) but which is absent at the global level (and hence accounts for the inapplicability of the same moral principle there)

(Caney 2001*a*: 118).[7] Hereafter the morally significant property that is said to apply in the domestic sphere but not the global sphere will be termed a *disanalogy property*. By employing and defending a *disanalogy argument*, a critic of cosmopolitanism can satisfy the *domestic-compatibility criterion* by showing that it is acceptable to apply different principles in different realms (domestic and global) because the two are quite different in a morally significant way.

With this in mind, and drawing on the preceding chapters, we can identify (at least) three different types of *disanalogy argument*. One argues that the disanalogy arises simply because global political theory includes *independent political communities* (the 'society of states' approach); a second argues that the disanalogy arises because *cooperation and the regulation of power* are possible within the state but not at the global level (a 'realist' approach); and a third argues that the disanalogy arises because sub-global communities (specifically, nations) are united by common ties (*a sense of nationality*) whereas the global realm lacks such common ties (a 'nationalist' approach). What follows expands on these three types of challenge to cosmopolitanism's level-1 analysis, drawing on the analysis of the previous six chapters.

# III

Let us begin then with the first kind of challenge. According to what I have termed the 'society of states' approach, the very fact that the global realm contains states in itself makes it fundamentally different in a morally significant sense from the domestic realm. The existence of states, it is claimed, constitutes a morally significant difference. The *disanalogy property*, then, is simply the existence of states.

However, this reply is obviously incomplete. It simply defers the question for 'society of states' theorists then have to explain exactly why the existence of states is a morally significant fact. Unless this can be established the fact that global political theory has to deal with sovereign states is insufficient to show that it is different in a morally fundamental way from domestic political theory. In the preceding analysis we have seen (at least) four ways of meeting this challenge.

**III.1.** One response to this challenge that we have encountered affirms the *intrinsic* value of political communities such as states. Collective bodies, it asserts, have value independently of their impact on people's lives. This line of reasoning, recall, was seen in both Chapters 6 and 7 and in both we saw that some make an analogy between individuals and states. They rely on this analogy to argue that since individuals possess rights so too do states: hence they are entitled to defend themselves by waging war (Chapter 6) and to affirm a right to non-intervention (Chapter 7). Similarly, as we saw in Chapter 4, some draw on this analogy to suggest that in the same way that individuals are deemed to be responsible and hence not eligible for economic support if they adopt calamitous policies so too states/peoples are not eligible for economic support from outsiders if they adopt calamitous policies.

However, as we saw in the discussions of these claims, this kind of response is an unpromising one. First, there are very many disanalogies between states and individuals: to equate the two is to homogenize states and to ignore the enormous diversity within them. Second, the claim that states have intrinsic value is morally mysterious: why do states (and not other collective entities) enjoy this special moral status? Third, to treat states as possessing intrinsic moral value is to fail to give adequate protection to the individuals that inhabit them.[8]

**III.2.** A second way of responding to this challenge that we have encountered has been proposed by Rawls. In *The Law of Peoples* he explicitly repudiates the cosmopolitan way of conceiving of the relationship between 'global' and 'domestic' political theory. As we noted in Chapters 3 and 4, his claim is that egalitarian liberal principles should apply within the confines of a liberal democratic society but should not govern global politics: rather, we should think of the latter in terms of the principles that liberal 'peoples' and decent well-ordered societies can share. Why? One of Rawls's answers is that whereas cosmopolitanism is concerned with 'the well-being of individuals' we should be concerned simply with 'the justice of societies' (1999*b*: 119). He brings out the difference between the two approaches with an example comprising two societies. Both maximize the conditions of the least well-off within their society but one is wealthier than the other. On a cosmopolitan view, there should be redistribution from the wealthier society to the poorer one because that would further improve the condition of the least well-off person within the world. But, says Rawls, this is not appropriate. There is no case for global redistribution because what matters is justice within societies and not furthering the standard of living of individual persons (1999*b*: 120).

This is a difficult position to maintain. First, we might ask why 'peoples' occupy this special position in his theory in contrast with every other social organization (such as a family or a religious community or a federal unit in a federation)? For example, we would not say that what matters is not the well-being of individuals but the internal justice of families or the internal justice of counties. So why should we say that what matters is not the well-being of individuals but the internal justice of peoples?

Second, we might question whether it is coherent to care about intra-societal justice independently of, and rather than, 'the well-being of individuals'. Can we plausibly say that we are concerned only with internal justice, that it has intrinsic value? Surely we care about justice within a society in part because of its effects on what people can do and the quality of lives they can lead. If so, then it would be irrational to be concerned with internal justice alone. The reasons for caring about internal justice are reasons for caring also about global redistribution that enables the members of peoples to enjoy a higher standard of living.

A third point: one way of making sense of Rawls's claim that what matters is justice within each people is that it articulates the value of the independence of peoples. The thought here is that valuing the self-determination of peoples entails that we should care about distribution within such self-determining peoples. However, unless we justify the importance of self-determination in terms of its impact on individuals (i.e. their interest in belonging to an independent political community) then it is utterly bizarre to hold that 'peoples' should have this moral standing. Why should 'peoples' have value independently of their impact on persons? And, again, we value the independence of families and religious communities (point 1) but this does not lead us to claim that internal justice not individual well-being is the appropriate objective. The Rawlsian move thus does not constitute a persuasive *disanalogy argument*.

We are still looking, then, for an argument that explains why the fact that the world contains independent political communities suffices to show that it is disanalogous in a morally significant way to the domestic realm.

**III.3.** A third way of meeting this challenge appeals to the existence of cultural diversity and pluralism. As we have seen earlier in this book, some contend that a moral consensus exists within the state/nation/people but that once we move beyond the borders of the state/nation/people we encounter profound and intractable moral conflict. And they infer from this that the principles fit for the global realm are different in kind from those fit for the domestic realm. To use the terminology introduced above, the *disanalogy property* according to this argument is 'cultural agreement'. This line of reasoning is developed in a number of different contexts. For example, it underpins some people's repudiation of cosmopolitan civil and political human rights. Second, it underwrites Nardin's rejection of all cosmopolitan conceptions of justice (1983). Of course, it is also one major consideration motivating Rawls's rejection of the cosmopolitan position on civil and political rights and principles of distributive justice (1999b) and it may thus underlie the view that we have just examined. Third, the same thought is played out in discussions of institutional structures for one fear of a cosmopolitan political framework is that it is inimical to liberty and diversity. As we saw in Chapter 5, many (from Kant onwards to Bull and Walzer) reject a world state on the grounds that it would crush pluralism and diversity. Furthermore, and fourth, this same concern—for pluralism—can also be seen in the fears that many have about intervention (Chapter 7).

However, the examination of these arguments has shown that this line of reasoning is intensely problematic. First, in many cases radical disagreement exists within the state/nation/people. The supposed *disanalogy property* is not one possessed by these bodies. Second, it is not clear why the existence of diversity undermines or is in tension with the pursuit of cosmopolitan principles of justice. Why should the fact that people hold different views entail that they cannot be incorporated within the same scheme of distributive justice? Why can principles of distributive justice not include in their scope people of different creeds and cultures? It cannot, for example, be objected that cosmopolitan ideals of distributive justice conflict with the preservation of cultural diversity because the global distribution of wealth enables many individuals and minority cultures to preserve and protect their currently endangered ways of life. Cosmopolitan ideals neither presume nor produce cultural uniformity.

**III.4.** To conclude our analysis it is worth noting that many proponents of the society of states argue that the existence of independent political communities is desirable on consequentialist grounds. Two examples illustrate this line of reasoning. First, as we saw in Chapter 5, Bull defends a society of states, in part, on the grounds that values such as justice, peace, and environmental protection are best protected by a society of states (1977). Second, as we also saw in Chapter 5, Frost argues that the international society of sovereign states has immense value because it is necessary for persons to flourish (1996). Both, thus, accord states a large moral significance in terms of their desirable effects. These are just two examples of a common line of reasoning.

What is interesting about this kind of defence of the society of states is that it does not constitute a fundamental challenge to cosmopolitanism. It accepts the fundamental moral commitments of a cosmopolitan approach—the equal interests of all—and speaks only to the question of how to best further these interests. As such, it constitutes an indirect brand of consequentialism: it avers that the best way to achieve cosmopolitan goals is not to strive directly to attain them and simply collapses into a brand of cosmopolitanism (Mason and Wheeler 1996, esp. pp. 100–6). We can see this further when we realize that this kind of reasoning does not really draw attention to, and defend, a *disanalogy property*. It is instructive to observe this here for it brings out the fact that many of those who defend the society of states do not, at the most basic level, disagree with the cosmopolitan analysis. Or rather they give us no reason to reject it. They further confirm the emerging picture, viz., that 'society of states' theorists do not provide us with reasons to reject cosmopolitanism's level-1 analysis. The 'society of states' approach has yet to establish why states should have fundamental moral importance and their critique of cosmopolitanism remains unsubstantiated.

## IV

To continue in our analysis of challenges to cosmopolitanism let us turn now to a second statist challenge to its level-1 analysis—namely realism. According to realism's level-1 analysis, there is, contra cosmopolitan theories, a key morally significant difference between the domestic and global realms. For realists the key *disanalogy property* is the *possibility of both cooperation in the pursuit of justice and also the impartial exercise of power*.[9] Whereas the domestic realm has a coercive agent that can implement principles of justice and control private exercises of power, the global realm lacks such a power. This disanalogy between the two realms is, so the argument runs, a morally significant one: unless there is an effective authority that can ensure cooperation and regulate the conduct of individuals there can be no justice. Realisms's *disanalogy argument* thus entails a sceptical perspective on the possibility of moral action in the global realm.

The preceding analysis has explored six ways in which this account of the difference between the orderly 'domestic' realm and the 'anarchic' global realm can be said to undermine attempts to apply moral ideals to the global realm. First, as we saw in Chapter 2, one extrapolation of the above realist account is that global or universal moral principles operate as little more than a cover for power politics. This concern also resurfaces in realist critiques of one specific type of universalist principle in particular—namely those endorsing civil and political rights. A foreign policy that seeks to protect civil and political human rights is simply a legitimization of power politics and nothing more. Again, then, global principles are seen, in contrast to domestic ones, as exercises in power politics. Concerns about power surface again, in a third and distinct way, in the context of international distributive justice. For here the argument is that the effective functioning of a scheme of distributive justice requires a coercive agent to enforce the principles and since this is absent in the global realm it subverts the very possibility of implementing global principles of distributive justice. Again, then, we see that a realist account of the disanalogy between the domestic and global realms yields a scepticism about the prospects of moral principles. If we turn now, for a fourth instantiation of the point, to issues of institutional design we can see again how realists emphasize the centrality of power, contending that any supra-state institution will be either ineffective because states retain power or itself is power-driven. Unlike the domestic realm, an orderly global realm that tames the exercise of power (in order to ensure cooperation in the pursuit of justice) is unattainable. For a fifth illustration of the realist point under consideration we can consider issues surrounding war: the argument here is that rules of *jus ad bellum* are beside the point since states act and should act to secure their interests. They have no superior authority to prevent them from doing this and accordingly can act unchecked in their pursuit of their own interests. Again, then, the emphasis is on the lack of cooperation to ensure justice. In addition to this, the lack of cooperation at the global realm generates a scepticism toward notions of *jus in bello*. Finally, the realist stress on power generates the objection that actions to protect the rights of others in the form of humanitarian intervention are never unbiased and altruistic but always serve ulterior goals and interests.

In all the above instances, then, we can see how the realist contention that the domestic realm is markedly different from the global realm (because the global realm is anarchic and power-driven and the domestic realm is not) results in a scepticism about the attainability of a moralized global realm whether the issue is human rights, distributive justice, institutional design, war, or intervention.

To say this, of course, is not to vindicate the realist challenge. And, drawing on the arguments of the previous six chapters we can see that there are three types of problem with the realist challenge to cosmopolitanism.

**IV.1.** The first is that the sorts of problems that are said to afflict moral principles in the global realm also have force in the domestic realm. The alleged disanalogy thus does not hold. To give one example, consider the contention that humanitarian interventions are wrong because intervenors are interested only in pursuing their own selfish interests. As we saw in Chapter 7, Section VI, this line of reasoning is unpersuasive as a critique of cosmopolitan defences of humanitarian intervention in part because exactly the same point can be made about local political elites. They too are often unjust and seek only their own gain (Tesón 1988: 105).

**IV.2.** A second flaw in the realist challenge concerns its contention that cooperation is present domestically but absent at the global level. As we have seen on several occasions above, this charge is overstated. For example, the discussion of the Tobin Tax in Chapter 4, Section XII, showed how it was possible to secure sufficient cooperation to achieve this tax. Second, the analysis of cosmopolitan governance in Chapter 5 pointed out that supra-state authorities could facilitate greater cooperation. Finally, the analysis of the realist critique of orthodox principles of *jus in bello* pointed out how even in conflict it was possible for opposing parties to agree to some constraints on how war can be waged (Chapter 6, Section X). To this we should, of course, add that the domestic realm too is also frequently marked by severe conflict and a total absence of cooperation, ranging from uncontrollable urban ghettos where the police fear to tread, on the one hand, to brutal civil war on the other. The idea, then, that the global realm is devoid of cooperation but that the domestic realm is not is hard to sustain.

**IV.3.** A further flaw in the realist critique of cosmopolitan principles arises from its analysis of the ethical significance of the lack of cooperation. Put at its crudest the assumption is that moral principles can have no place where there is no cooperation. This assumption is, however, mistaken. Consider a country ruled by a cruel and oppressive despot. It may be true that there is no cooperation to overthrow him and institute a fair society; but this does not entail that moral principles are irrelevant. On the contrary, their relevance lies in the fact that they serve as a critique and condemnation of this society. The role of moral principles in such a context is a *negative* one: they serve to point out what is unjust and why it is unjust. Furthermore, they can play this role even where the lack of cooperation means that there is no prospect of these principles playing a *positive* role and outlining the vision to be attained. So even if cooperation is absent at the global level this does not entail the irrelevance of moral principles.

For these three reasons the realist critique of cosmopolitanism's level-1 analysis fails to hold.

## V

Having considered two challenges to cosmopolitanism's level-1 analysis, we can turn finally to a third. As has been seen throughout this book, for some theorists the problem with a cosmopolitan level-1 analysis stems neither from the existence of sovereign states nor from the absence of a world state. Rather it arises because the domestic realm is characterized by a common (national) culture whereas the world as a whole lacks such a sense of social cohesion. This sense of nationality, it is claimed, differentiates the global realm from the domestic one and, moreover, it is a morally significant property. It explains why the principles for the domestic realm are categorically different from those that apply to the global realm. Put otherwise: the relevant *disanalogy property* is the existence of a sense of nationality.

This disanalogy argument can be developed and applied in several ways. First, if we consider issues of distributive justice we can see that for some the existence of national communities generates duties of justice (and thus affects the scope of distributive justice). Nationalists, thus, resist the scope$_2$ claim, arguing that one can not apply theories designed to apply within a nation to the global level (Miller 2000*c*: 174). However, in doing so nationalists do not thereby necessarily violate the condition of domestic-compatibility for their claim is that the national realm is fundamentally different to the global one and hence one cannot import the conclusions that apply to the former to the latter. Second, as we saw in Chapter 5, when we turn to questions of institutional design, we can see another distinct way in which the existence of national communities can be said to have moral significance. For in this context, it achieves significance in two distinct ways: first, it affects motivations (and thus affects the feasibility of supra-national bodies), and, second, it affects people's well-being and thus forms part of a case for national self-determination. Membership of nations thus generates rights as well as duties. The moral salience of national identity is, then, a recurring feature. For a third instance where the existence of national communities exerts a normative influence we should turn to the issue of war for, as we saw in Chapter 6, some contend that the existence of duties to fellow nationals should inform the way in which we interpret the idea of 'proportionality'. The existence of obligations stemming from persons' national identity, it is said, should influence the waging of war. A fourth case where we can see that a sense of nationality is said to play a normative role is humanitarian intervention. This is true in two senses: first, in the hands of Walzer, the notion of a national community is employed to support a general norm of non-intervention. Second, the sense of nationality also affects the question of *who* is duty-bound to protect the rights of those suffering injustice. Drawing on the discussion of distributive justice, the claim is that this responsibility accrues first to fellow nationals rather than outside bodies. This obviously affects the morality of humanitarian intervention. We can, then, see four ways in which the existence of national communities is said to be morally significant and in which the global realm is categorically different from the domestic realm.

**V.1.** How credible is this level-1 analysis? Four points can be made. First, we saw that the positive claim that a sense of nationality generates special duties is suspect and unsupported (Chapter 4, Section X). One way of vindicating the moral relevance of nationality is thus unsuccessful. Second, we saw that the negative claim that obligations cannot extend further than the group of people with whom one identifies, and hence that one cannot have global obligations, was also unsupported (Chapter 4, Section IX). A second way of vindicating the moral relevance of nationality is thus also unsuccessful. Third, we saw that the negative claim that political institutions cannot function without their members being bound together by a national identity is unsubstantiated (Chapter 5, Section XIII). Fourth, we should record that even if the nationalist empirical claims (namely that schemes of justice and political institutions need to be held together by national bonds) are correct they are insufficient to refute cosmopolitanism's level-1 analysis. For they do not establish that national identity has fundamental moral significance: they are empirical considerations that should be added to fundamental moral principles to derive more concrete proposals. But such claims do not call into any question the basic cosmopolitan tenets. They do not show a morally fundamental difference between the global and domestic realms but are, rather, of a similar status to claims like 'middle class folk care more about other members of their class than about the members of the working class'. The latter—if true—is an important consideration that should not be ignored. But it does not attest to any deep fundamental moral principle. We should regard nationalist claims likewise.

**V.2.** Before concluding the evaluation of nationalism's level-1 analysis, it is worth considering a further claim advanced by nationalists. Some contemporary nationalists maintain that much orthodox political theory assumes, but fails to acknowledge, the existence of a national community. Without such assumptions, nationalists allege, conventional political theorists would be compelled to take a cosmopolitan form. Since they do not they must, so the argument goes, rely on the moral relevance of national identity. Their contention, then, is that conventional political theory should come clean and recognize the fundamental moral relevance of nationality (Canovan 1996a, esp. pp. 1–3, 27–30, 32–4, 44, 114; 1996b, esp. pp. 72, 78–9; Miller 1995: 93; Tamir 1993: 10, 117–39). Two points can be adduced against these claims to unmask the nationalist presuppositions of contemporary political theory. First, whilst many contemporary mainstream political thinkers may unthinkingly assume the moral salience of national boundaries it is important to recognize that this has not always been the case. A good example here is J. S. Mill. As a utilitarian he is committed to a fundamentally cosmopolitan framework. However, he thinks that these cosmopolitan principles, when combined with various empirical considerations, yield conclusions that accord some significance to national boundaries. Two examples illustrate this. First, in his essay on 'Coleridge' he writes that workable political systems need a supportive political culture and this is facilitated by nationality (1969 [1840]: 134–6).[10] Second, and relatedly, he thinks that the overthrow of a despot requires not foreign armies but the uprising of the national community because (and here is the empirical point) only in this way will the future polity survive (1984 [1859]). Now the point here is not whether such claims are correct. (Both arguments have been criticized earlier on). The point is that Mill cannot be faulted for unthinkingly smuggling in 'nationalist' normative assumptions: he does not do this. He consciously accepts empirical claims that refer to the national character of social bonds. Although space precludes further analysis, I think that other prominent thinkers have also explicitly sought to explain why the domestic and global realms are disanalogous.[11] The second, philosophically more significant, point is simply that even if people have presupposed national borders this, of course, does not justify that assumption. If Canovan, Miller, and Tamir are right they have un-masked a (nationalist) assumption contained with much conventional political theory. However, this in itself gives us no reason to accept that assumption.

## VI

This concludes the analysis. Needless to say much more needs to be done. More level-1 analysis is required to examine other ways in which the domestic and global realms may be disanalogous in morally significant ways. More level-2 analysis is required to address topics that have been alluded to but which space has prevented us from discussing—topics such as the environment. Finally, much more level-3 analysis is required to enable us to give practical guidance in particular case studies and this, in turn, requires much more integration of political principles with the relevant empirical data. In the meantime, however, what I hope to have done is to outline the rationale for a specific cosmopolitan approach, to indicate the strengths of cosmopolitanism more generally, and to analyse the strengths and weaknesses of the alternatives.

### NOTES

1. One notable omission is the principles of justice that should apply to the environ-ment. I hope to address this issue in subsequent work.
2. It must be emphasized that what follows focuses on contemporary egalitarian liberal cosmopolitan theories. It does so not because cosmopolitanism is necessarily com-mitted to egalitarian liberalism for as was stressed in Chapter 1 there could quite

conceivably be other kinds of cosmopolitanism. Rather it focuses on these kinds of cosmopolitanism simply because almost all contemporary cosmopolitan philosophers (whether the thinker is Barry, Beitz, O'Neill, Pogge, and so on) are in fact egalitarian liberal ones. Moreover, and relatedly, it makes sense to concentrate here on egalitarian liberal cosmopolitan theories given that the cosmopolitan theories examined in the previous six chapters have all been of this type.

3. Few others have invoked what I have termed 'domestic-compatibility'. For one very important and illuminating exception see Brilmayer's *Justifying International Acts* (1989). Brilmayer contends that when the state is in a coercive relationship with a non-citizen then it must treat them in a way that is consistent with the political principles that govern how they treat their own citizens (the vertical thesis) (1989). Brilmayer's project is, however, rather different from that undertaken here. First, unlike *Justice Beyond Borders*, Brilmayer does not embrace a cosmopolitan approach (1989: 30–2). Second, her aim is generally not to put forward her own political theory (1989, esp. pp. 22–3, 82). Third, when she does engage in normative analysis she reaches conclusions different to those reached here. She is, for example, far more chary of positive duties of international distributive justice and pessimistic about the prospect of justifying them (1989: ch. 6, esp. pp. 136, 138). Furthermore, her slant on intervention points in a different direction to mine (1989: ch. 7). (For an earlier discussion of Brilmayer's vertical thesis, and analysis of how it differs from my concept of domestic-compatibility, see Ch. 3 note 7).

4. To give one clear illustration of this point: Pogge persuasively argues that Rawls is culpable of double standards since the sorts of reasons he adduces against a global difference principle and in defence of a very minimal economic principle of global justice would apply with equal force against his domestic difference principle (2002a: 40–2).

5. Note: the second line of reasoning, unlike the first, applies only to those who dissent from cosmopolitan values but who also affirm some minimal rights. It is powerless against those who do not even embrace some minimal human rights.

6. This last point is a highly abbreviated version of an argument developed by Barry (1991c: 195–203; 1991d: 235, 237) and Steiner (1999: 172–6, esp. pp. 172–3). The argument draws on Hart's distinction between special and general rights (1985: 84–8)

7. For an illuminating discussion of different accounts of how the global and domestic contexts differ in morally relevant ways see Beitz (1999b: 521–4; 1999c: 154–161, see also pp. 13–66). For an interesting *disanalogy argument* see Midtgaard (forthcoming).

8. Some argue that this first position is correct because it is backed up by the practices of international society and is embodied in international law. This is a non sequitur. According states intrinsic value may be a practice of international law but it does not confer moral status on it. In this context we might consider Rousseau's caustic appraisal of Grotius. Rousseau writes: 'Grotius denies that all human government is established for the benefit of the governed, and he cites the example of slavery. His characteristic method of reasoning is always to offer fact as a proof of right. It is possible to imagine a more logical method, but not one more favourable to tyrants' (1968 [1762]: bk. I, ch. 2, p. 51). (I have omitted a footnote at the end of the second sentence.)

9. One might say that there is one factor here (the lack of a coercive agent) and that it has two implications: first, it is needed to perform a *positive* role (to bring about and maintain the cooperation needed to bring about a just distribution), and, second, to perform a *negative* role (to prevent private forces from committing injustices).

10. See also the discussion of nationality in Mill (1977*b* [1861]: ch. XVI, esp. pp. 547–8).
11. A second example is provided by the distinguished example of David Hume. In *A Treatise of Human Nature*, Hume explicitly raises the question of why the principles of justice for the domestic realm should be different from those for the global realm. His proposed answer is that principles of justice pertain to a group of people when cooperation is advantageous to them. Drawing on this he claims that people within a state find cooperation absolutely essential (hence principles of justice apply with utmost force) whereas at the international level cooperation is of some benefit but is not essential to the same degree (hence principles of justice apply with less force). Hume's argument, thus, purports to show how the same fundamental moral theory grounds different prescriptions in domestic and international domains (1985 [1739–40]: bk. III, sec. XI, pp. 617–20, esp. p. 619). He makes the same point with pellucid clarity in *An Enquiry Concerning the Principles of Morals* (1988 [1777]: sec. IV, subsection 165, p. 206). I believe that Hume's argument is unsuccessful but that is not the key point here. The key point is that the charge of unthinkingly accepting local boundaries does not apply to Hume.

# References

Ackerman, Bruce (1994). 'Political Liberalisms', *Journal of Philosophy*, 91/7: 364–86.

Adelman, Howard (1992). 'The Ethics of Humanitarian Intervention: The Case of the Kurdish Refugees', *Public Affairs Quarterly*, 6/1: 61–87.

Akehurst, Michael (1984). 'Humanitarian Intervention', in Hedley Bull (ed.), *Intervention in World Politics* (Oxford: Clarendon Press), pp. 95–118.

Alderson, Kai and Andrew Hurrell (2000). 'Part I: Introduction', in Kai Alderson and Andrew Hurrell (eds), *Hedley Bull on International Society* (Basingstoke: Macmillan), pp. 3–73.

An-Na'im, Abdullahi A. (1987). 'Religious Minorities under Islamic Law and the Limits of Cultural Relativism', *Human Rights Quarterly*, 9: 1–18.

—— (1999). 'The Cultural Mediation of Human Rights: The Al-Arqam Case in Malaysia', in Joanne R. Bauer and Daniel A. Bell (eds), *The East Asian Challenge for Human Rights*, (Cambridge: Cambridge University Press), pp. 147–68.

Anscombe, G. E. M. (1981*a*). 'War and Murder', in *The Collected Philosophical Papers of G. E. M. Anscombe Volume Three: Ethics, Religion and Politics* (Oxford: Blackwell), pp. 51–61.

—— (1981*b*). 'Mr Truman's Degree', in *The Collected Philosophical Papers of G. E. M. Anscombe Volume Three: Ethics, Religion and Politics* (Oxford: Blackwell), pp. 62–71.

Appiah, Kwame Anthony (1992). *In My Father's House: Africa in the Philosophy of Culture* (New York: Oxford University Press).

Aquinas, Thomas (1988 [1266–73]). 'Excerpts from the *Summa Theologiae*', edited, with introduction, by William P. Baumgarth and Richard J. Regan, in *On Law, Morality, and Politics* (Indianapolis: Hackett Publishing Company).

Archibugi, Daniele (1995). 'From the United Nations to Cosmopolitan Democracy', in Daniele Archibugi and David Held (eds), *Cosmopolitan Democracy: An Agenda for a New World Order* (Cambridge: Polity), pp. 121–62.

—— and David Held (eds) (1995). *Cosmopolitan Democracy: An Agenda for a New World Order* (Cambridge: Polity).

—— —— , and Martin Köhler (eds) (1998). *Re-imagining Political Community: Studies in Cosmopolitan Democracy* (Cambridge: Polity).

Arendt, Hannah (1957). 'Karl Jaspers: Citizen of the World', in Paul Schilpp (ed.), *The Philosophy of Karl Jaspers* (New York: Tudor Publishing Company), pp. 539–49.

Arestis, Philip and Malcolm Sawyer (1999). 'What Role for the Tobin Tax in World Economic Governance?', in Jonathan Michie and John Grieve Smith (eds), *Global Instability: the Political Economy of World Economic Governance* (London and New York: Routledge), pp. 151–67.

Art, Robert J. and Kenneth N. Waltz (1983). 'Technology, Strategy, and the Uses of Force', in Robert J. Art and Kenneth N. Waltz (eds), *The Use of Force: International Politics and Foreign Policy* second edition (Lanham: University Press of America), pp. 1–32.

Aśoka (1978). *The Edicts of Aśoka*, edited and translated by N. A. Nikam and Richard McKeon. (Chicago: University of Chicago Press).

Bader, Veit (1997). 'Fairly Open Borders', in Veit Bader (ed.), *Citizenship and Exclusion* (London: Macmillan), pp. 28–60.

Baldwin, Thomas (1992). 'The Territorial State', in Hyman Gross and Ross Harrison (eds), *Jurisprudence: Cambridge Essays* (Oxford: Clarendon), pp. 207–30.

Barry, Brian (1987). 'Nationalism', in David Miller (ed.), *The Blackwell Encyclopaedia of Political Thought* (Oxford: Blackwell), pp. 352–5.

—— (1989). *Theories of Justice: A Treatise on Social Justice Volume I* (Hemel Hempstead: Harvester-Wheatsheaf).

—— (1991*a*). 'Self-Government Revisited' in *Democracy and Power: Essays in Political Theory Volume I* (Oxford: Clarendon), pp. 156–86.

—— (1991*b*). 'Can States be Moral? International Morality and the Compliance Problem' in *Liberty and Justice: Essays in Political Theory Volume 2* (Oxford: Clarendon), pp. 159–81.

—— (1991*c*). 'Humanity and Justice in Global Perspective' in *Liberty and Justice: Essays in Political Theory Volume 2* (Oxford: Clarendon), pp. 182–210.

—— (1991*d*). 'Justice as Reciprocity' in *Liberty and Justice: Essays in Political Theory Volume 2* (Oxford: Clarendon), pp. 211–41.

—— (1995*a*). *Justice as Impartiality: A Treatise on Social Justice Volume II* (Oxford: Clarendon).

—— (1995*b*). 'Spherical Justice and Global Injustice', in David Miller and Michael Walzer (eds), *Pluralism, Justice, and Equality* (Oxford: Oxford University Press), pp. 67–80.

—— (1996). 'Nationalism versus Liberalism?', *Nation and Nationalism* vol.2, pp. 430–35.

—— (1998). 'International Society from a Cosmopolitan Perspective', in David Mapel and Terry Nardin (eds), *International Society: Diverse Ethical Perspectives* (Princeton: Princeton University Press), pp. 144–63.

—— (1999). 'Statism and Nationalism: A Cosmopolitan Critique', in Ian Shapiro and Lea Brilmayer (eds), *NOMOS Volume XLI: Global Justice* (New York: New York University Press), pp. 12–66.

—— (2001). *Culture and Equality: An Egalitarian Critique of Multiculturalism* (Cambridge: Polity).

—— and Robert E. Goodin (eds) (1992). *Free Movement: Ethical Issues in the Transnational Migration of People and of Money* (University Park: Pennsylvania State University Press).

Beetham, David (1995). 'What Future for Economic and Social Rights?', *Political Studies*, vol. 43, Special Issue on Politics and Human Rights, pp. 41–60.

Begg, David, Stanley Fischer, and Rudiger Dornbusch (1991). *Economics: Third Edition* (London: McGraw-Hill).

Beitz, Charles (1979). 'Bounded Morality: Justice and the State in World Politics', *International Organisation*, 33/3: 405–24.

—— (1980). 'Nonintervention and Communal Integrity', *Philosophy and Public Affairs*, 9/4: 385–91.

—— (1983). 'Cosmopolitan Ideals and National Sentiment', *Journal of Philosophy*, 80/10: 591–600.

—— (1988*a*). 'Recent International Thought', *International Journal*, vol. XLIII Spring: 183–204.

—— (1988*b*). 'The Reagan Doctrine in Nicaragua', in Steven Luper-Foy (ed.), *Problems of International Justice* (Boulder: Westview), pp. 182–95.

Beitz, Charles (1991). 'Sovereignty and Morality in International Affairs', in David Held (ed.), *Political Theory Today* (Cambridge: Polity), pp. 236–54.

—— (1994). 'Cosmopolitan Liberalism and the States System', in Chris Brown (ed.), *Political Restructuring in Europe: Ethical Perspectives* (London: Routledge) 123–36.

—— (1999a). 'International Liberalism and Distributive Justice: A Survey of Recent Thought', *World Politics*, 51: 269–96.

—— (1999b). 'Social and Cosmopolitan Liberalism', *International Affairs*, 75/3: 515–29.

—— (1999c). *Political Theory and International Relations* (Princeton: Princeton University Press) with a new afterword by the author.

—— (2000). 'Rawls's Law of Peoples', *Ethics*, 110/4: 669–96.

—— (2001). 'Human Rights as a Common Concern', *American Political Science Review*, 95/2: 269–82.

Bell, Daniel (1993). *Communitarianism and its Critics* (Oxford: Clarendon Press).

Bellamy, Richard (1992). 'Liberal Rights, Socialist Goals and the Duties of Citizenship', David Milligan and William Watts Miller (eds), in *Liberalism, Citizenship and Autonomy* (Aldershot: Avebury), pp. 88–107.

—— and Dario Castiglione (1997). 'Building the Union: The Nature of Sovereignty in the Political Architecture of Europe', *Law and Philosophy*, 16/4: pp. 421–45.

Benhabib, Seyla (1992). *Situating the Self: Gender, Community and Postmodernism in Contemporary Ethics* (Cambridge: Polity).

—— (1995). 'Cultural Complexity, Moral Interdependence, and the Global Dialogical Community', in Martha C. Nussbaum, and Jonathan Glover (eds), *Women, Culture, and Development: A Study of Human Capabilities* (Oxford: Clarendon Press), pp. 235–55.

—— (1999). '"Nous" et "les Autres": The Politics of Complex Cultural Dialogue in a Global Civilization', in Christian Joppke and Steven Lukes (eds), *Multicultural Questions* (Oxford: Oxford University Press), pp. 44–62.

Benn, S. I. and R. S. Peters (1959). *Social Principles and the Democratic State* (London: George Allen and Unwin).

Bentham, Jeremy (1962 [1786–89]). 'A Plan for an Universal and Perpetual Peace', *Essay IV* of *Principles of International Law*, in John Bowring (ed.), *The Works of Jeremy Bentham: Volume Two* (New York: Russell and Russell), pp. 546–60.

Beran, Harry (1984). ' A Liberal Theory of Secession', *Political Studies*, 32(1):21–31.

—— (1987). *The Consent Theory of Political Obligation* (London: Croom Helm).

—— (1994). 'The Place of Secession in Liberal Democratic Theory', in Paul Gilbert and Paul Gregory (eds), *Nations, Cultures and Markets* (Aldershot: Avebury), pp. 47–65.

Berdal, Mats and Michael Leifer (1996). 'Cambodia', in James Mayall (ed.), *The New Interventionism 1991–1994: United Nations experience in Cambodia, former Yugoslavia and Somalia* (Cambridge: Cambridge University Press), pp. 25–58.

Berlin, Isaiah (1982a). 'Introduction', in *Four Essays on Liberty* (Oxford: Oxford University Press), pp. ix–lxiii.

—— (1982b). 'Two Concepts of Liberty', in *Four Essays on Liberty* (Oxford: Oxford University Press), pp. 118–72.

—— (1991a). 'The Pursuit of the Ideal', in Henry Hardy (ed.), *The Crooked Timber of Humanity: Chapters in the History of Ideas* (London: Fontana), pp. 1–19.

—— (1991*b*). 'Alleged Relativism in Eighteenth-Century European Thought', in Henry Hardy (ed.), *The Crooked Timber of Humanity: Chapters in the History of Ideas* (London: Fontana), pp. 70–90.

Bielefeldt, Heiner (2000). ' "Western" versus "Islamic" Human Rights Conceptions? A Critique of Cultural Essentialism in the Discussion on Human Rights', *Political Theory*, 28/1: 90–121.

Biersteker, Thomas J. and Cynthia Weber (1996). 'The Social Construction of State Sovereignty', in Thomas J. Biersteker and Cynthia Weber (eds), *State Sovereignty as Social Construct* (Cambridge: Cambridge University Press), pp. 1–21.

Black, Samuel (1991). 'Individualism at an Impasse', *Canadian Journal of Philosophy*, 21/3: pp. 347–77.

Booth, Ken (1994). 'Military Intervention: Duty and Prudence', in Lawrence Freedman (ed.), *Military Intervention in European Conflicts* (Oxford: Blackwell), pp. 56–75.

—— (1995). 'Human Wrongs and International Relations', *International Affairs*, 71/1: pp. 103–26.

—— (1999). 'Three Tyrannies', in Tim Dunne and Nicholas J. Wheeler (eds), *Human Rights in Global Politics* (Cambridge: Cambridge University Press), pp. 31–70.

Boucher, David (1998). *Political Theories of International Relations: From Thucydides to the Present* (Oxford: Oxford University Press).

Boxill, Bernard (1987). 'Global Equality of Opportunity and National Integrity', *Social Philosophy and Policy*, 5/1: 143–68.

Brandt, Richard B. (1972). 'Utilitarianism and the Rules of War', *Philosophy and Public Affairs*, 1/2: 145–65.

Brilmayer, Lea (1989). *Justifying International Acts* (Ithaca and London: Cornell University Press).

—— (1994). *American Hegemony: Political Morality in a One-Superpower World* (New Haven: Yale University Press).

Brink, David O. (1989). *Moral Realism and the Foundations of Ethics* (Cambridge: Cambridge University Press).

Brown, Chris (1992). *International Relations Theory: New Normative Approaches* (Hemel Hempstead: Harvester Wheatsheaf).

—— (1993). 'International Affairs', in Robert Goodin and Philip Pettit (eds), *A Companion to Contemporary Political Philosophy* (Oxford: Blackwell), pp. 515–26.

—— (1995). 'International Theory and International Society: The Viability of the Middle Way?', *Review of International Studies*, 21: 183–96.

—— (1996). 'Cultural Pluralism, Universal Principles and International Relations Theory', in Simon Caney, David George and Peter Jones (eds), *National Rights, International Obligations* (Oxford: Westview Press), 166–82.

—— (1997*a*). 'Universal Human Rights: A Critique', *The International Journal of Human Rights*, 1/2: 41–65.

—— (1997*b*). 'Review Article: Theories of International Justice', *British Journal of Political Science*, 27/2: 273–97.

—— (2000). 'John Rawls, "The Law of Peoples," and International Political Theory', *Ethics and International Affairs*, 14: 125–32.

Brown, Chris (2002*a*). 'The Construction of a "realistic utopia": John Rawls and International Political Theory', *Review of International Studies*, 28/1: 5–21.

—— (2002*b*). *Sovereignty, Rights and Justice: International Political Theory Today* (Cambridge: Polity).

Brownlie, Ian (1973). 'Thoughts on Kind-Hearted Gunmen', in Richard B. Lillich (ed.), *Humanitarian Intervention and the United Nations* (Charlottesville: University Press of Virginia), pp. 139–48.

Brubaker, Rogers (1998). 'Myths and Misconceptions in the Study of Nationalism', in Margaret Mooore (ed.), *National Self-Determination and Secession* (Oxford: Oxford University Press), pp. 233–65.

Buchanan, Allen (1989). 'Assessing the Communitarian Critique of Liberalism', *Ethics*, 99/4: 852–82.

—— (1991). *Secession: the Morality of Political Divorce from Fort Sumter to Lithuania and Quebec* (Boulder: Westview).

—— (1993). 'Secession and Nationalism', in Robert E. Goodin and Philip Pettit (eds), *A Companion to Contemporary Political Philosophy* (Oxford: Blackwell), pp. 586–96.

—— (1998*a*). 'What's so Special about Nations?', in Jocelyne Couture, Kai Nielsen and Michel Seymour (eds), *Rethinking Nationalism* (Calgary, Alberta: University of Calgary Press), pp. 283–309.

—— (1998*b*). 'Democracy and Secession', in Margaret Moore (ed.), *National Self-Determination and Secession* (Oxford: Oxford University Press), pp. 14–33.

—— (1999*a*). 'The Internal Legitimacy of Humanitarian Intervention', *Journal of Political Philosophy*, 7/1: 71–87.

—— (1999*b*). 'Recognitional Legitimacy and the State System', *Philosophy and Public Affairs*, 28/1: 46–78.

—— (2000). 'Rawls's Law of Peoples: Rules for a Vanished Westphalian World', *Ethics*, 110/4: 697–721.

—— (2003). *Justice, Legitimacy, and Self-Determination: Moral Foundations for International Law* (Oxford: Oxford University Press).

Buchheit, Lee (1978). *Secession: The Legitimacy of Self-Determination* (New Haven: Yale University Press).

Bull, Hedley (1977). *The Anarchical Society: A Study of Order in World Politics* (London: Macmillan).

—— (1979). 'Review Article: Recapturing the Just War for Political Theory', *World Politics* 31/4: 588–599.

—— (ed.) (1984*a*). *Intervention in World Politics* (Oxford: Clarendon Press).

—— (1984*b*). 'Introduction', in Hedley Bull (ed.), *Intervention in World Politics* (Oxford: Clarendon Press), pp. 1–6.

—— (1990). 'The Importance of Grotius in the Study of International Relations', in Hedley Bull, Benedict Kingsbury and Adam Roberts (ed.), *Hugo Grotius and International Relations* (Oxford: Clarendon Press), pp. 65–93.

—— (2000*a*). 'Society and Anarchy in International Relations', in Kai Alderson and Andrew Hurrell (eds), *Hedley Bull on International Society* (Basingstoke: Macmillan), pp. 77–94.

—— (2000*b*). 'The Grotian Conception of International Society', in Kai Alderson and Andrew Hurrell (eds), *Hedley Bull on International Society* (Basingstoke: Macmillan), pp. 95–118.

—— (2000c). 'Justice in International Relations: The 1983 Hagey Lectures', in Kai Alderson and Andrew Hurrell (eds), *Hedley Bull on International Society* (Basingstoke: Macmillan), pp. 206–45.

——, Benedict Kingsbury, Adam Roberts (eds) (1990). *Hugo Grotius and International Relations* (Oxford: Clarendon Press).

Campbell, David (1998). *National Deconstruction: Violence, Identity, and Justice in Bosnia* (Minneapolis: University of Minnesota Press).

Caney, Simon (1996a). 'Individuals, Nations and Obligations', in Simon Caney, David George and Peter Jones (eds), *National Rights, International Obligations* (Oxford: Westview), pp. 119–38.

—— (1996b). 'Impartiality and Liberal Neutrality', *Utilitas*, 8/3: 273–93.

—— (1997a). 'Human Rights and the Rights of States: Terry Nardin on Nonintervention', *International Political Science Review*, 18/1: 27–37.

—— (1997b). 'Self-Government and Secession: The Case of Nations', *Journal of Political Philosophy*, 5/4: 351–72.

—— (1999a). 'Nationality, Distributive Justice and the Use of Force', *Journal of Applied Philosophy*, 16/2: 123–38.

—— (1999b). 'Defending Universalism', in Iain Mackenzie and Shane O'Neill (eds), *Reconstituting Social Criticism: Political Morality in an Age of Scepticism* (London: Macmillan), pp. 19–33.

—— (2000a). 'Global Equality of Opportunity and the Sovereignty of States', in Tony Coates (ed.), *International Justice* (Aldershot: Ashgate), pp. 130–49.

—— (2000b). 'Humanitarian Intervention and State Sovereignty', in Andrew Valls (ed.) *Ethics in International Affairs: Theories and Cases* (Lanham: Rowman and Littlefield), pp. 117–33.

—— (2000c). 'Cosmopolitan Justice and Cultural Diversity', *Global Society* 14/4: 525–51.

—— (2000d). 'Human Rights, Compatibility and Diverse Cultures', *Critical Review of International Social and Political Philosophy*, 3/1: 51–76.

—— (2001a). 'Cosmopolitan Justice and Equalizing Opportunities', *Metaphilosophy*, 32/1–2, 113–34.

—— (2001b). 'British Perspectives on Internationalism, Justice and Sovereignty: From the English School to Cosmopolitan Democracy', *The European Legacy*, 6/2: 265–75.

—— (2002a). 'Survey Article: Cosmopolitanism and the Law of Peoples', *Journal of Political Philosophy*, 10/1: 95–123.

—— (2002b). 'Equal Treatment, Exceptions and Cultural Diversity', in Paul Kelly (ed.), *Multiculturalism Reconsidered: Culture and Equality and its Critics* (Cambridge: Polity), pp. 81–101.

—— (2002c). 'Cosmopolitanism, Rawls and the English School', in Mark Bevir and Frank Trentmann (eds), *Critiques of Capital in Modern Britain and America: Transatlantic Exchanges 1800 to the Present Day* (London: Palgrave), pp. 174–94.

—— (2002d). 'A Reply to Miller', *Political Studies*, 50/5: 978–83.

—— (2003). 'Entitlements, Obligations, and Distributive Justice: The Global Level', i n Daniel A. Bell and Avner de-Shalit (eds), *Forms of Justice: Critical Perspectives on David Miller's Political Philosophy* (Lanham: Rowman and Littlefield), pp. 287–313.

Caney, Simon (forthcoming *a*) 'Global Poverty, Human Rights and Obligations', *Global Poverty as a Human Rights Violation*, edited by Thomas Pogge.

—— (forthcoming *b*) 'Cosmopolitan Distributive Justice and Cosmopolitan Democracy'. *Canadian Journal of Philosophy*.

Canovan, Margaret (1996*a*). *Nationhood and Political Theory* (Cheltenham: Edward Elgar).

—— (1996*b*). 'The Skeleton in the Cupboard: Nationhood, Patriotism and Limited Loyalties', in Simon Caney, David George and Peter Jones (eds), *National Rights, International Obligations* (Oxford: Westview), pp. 69–84.

Carens, Joseph H. (1987). 'Aliens and Citizens: The Case for Open Borders', *Review of Politics*, 49/2: 251–73.

Carr, E. H. (1995 [1939]). *The Twenty Years' Crisis 1919–1939: An Introduction to the Study of International Relations* (London: Macmillan).

Cartwright, Michael G. (1996). 'Conflicting Interpretations of Christian Pacifism', in Terry Nardin (ed.), *The Ethics of War and Peace: Religious and Secular Perspectives* (Princeton: Princeton University Press), pp. 197–213.

Cassen, Robert and associates (1994). *Does Aid Work? Report to an Intergovernmental Task Force* (Oxford: Clarendon Press).

Chan, Joseph (1999). 'A Confucian Perspective on Human Rights for Contemporary China', in Joanne R. Bauer and Daniel A. Bell (eds), *The East Asian Challenge for Human Rights* (Cambridge: Cambridge University Press), pp. 212–37.

Chopra, Jarat and Thomas Weiss (1992). 'Sovereignty is no Longer Sacrosanct: Codifying Humanitarian Intervention', *Ethics and International Affairs*, 6: 95–117.

Christie, Kenneth (1995). 'Regime Security and Human Rights in Southeast Asia' *Political Studies*, 43, special issue on Politics and Human Rights edited by David Beetham, pp. 204–18.

Cicero (2001 [44 BC]). *On Obligations*, translated with an Introduction and Notes by P. G. Walsh, (Oxford: Oxford University Press).

Cochran, Molly (1999). *Normative Theory in International Relations: A Pragmatic Approach* (Cambridge: Cambridge University Press).

Cohen, G. A. (1989). 'On the Currency of Egalitarian Justice', *Ethics*, 99/4: 906–44.

Cohen, Joshua (1986). 'Book Review of *Spheres of Justice: A Defense of Pluralism and Equality*', *Journal of Philosophy*, 83/8: 457–68.

Cohen, Marshall (1984). 'Moral Skepticism and International Relations', *Philosophy and Public Affairs*, 13/4: 299–346.

Commission on Global Governance (1995). *Our Global Neighbourhood* (Oxford: Oxford University Press).

Confucius (1979). *The Analects*, translated with an introduction by D. C. Lau, (Middlesex: Penguin).

Connolly, William (1991). 'Democracy and Territoriality', *Millennium*, 20/3: 463–84.

Dagger, Richard (1997). *Civic Virtues: Rights, Citizenship, and Republican Liberalism* (New York: Oxford University Press).

Daniels, Norman (1996). 'An Argument about the Relativity of Justice', in *Justice and Justification: Reflective Equilibrium in Theory and Practice* (Cambridge: Cambridge University Press), pp. 103–19.

Dante, Alighieri (1949 [1313]). *On World-Government: De Monarchia*, translated by Herbert Schneider with an introduction by Dino Bigongiari, (Indianapolis: Bobbs Merrill).

Davidson, Donald (1984). 'On the Very Idea of a Conceptual Scheme', *Inquiries into Truth and Interpretation* (Oxford: Clarendon Press), pp. 183–98.

Derrida, Jacques (2000). *Of Hospitality: Anne Dufourmantelle invites Jacques Derrida to respond*, translated by Rachel Bowlby, (Stanford: Stanford University Press).

—— (2001). *On Cosmopolitanism and Forgiveness*, translated by Mark Dooley and Michael Hughes with a preface by Simon Critchley and Richard Kearney, (London and New York: Routledge).

de-Shalit, Avner (1996). 'National Self-Determination: Political, not Cultural', *Political Studies*, 44/5: 906–20.

de Waal, Alex (1997). *Famine Crimes: Politics and the Disaster Relief Industry in Africa* (African Rights and The International African Institute in association with James Currey, Oxford, and Indiana University Press, Bloomington and Indianapolis).

Diehl, Paul, Jennifer Reifschneider and Paul Hensel (1996). 'United Nations Intervention and Recurring Conflict', *International Organization*, 50/4: 683–700.

Donnelly, Jack (1989). *Universal Human Rights in Theory and Practice* (Ithaca and London: Cornell University Press).

—— (1992). 'Twentieth-Century Realism', in Terry Nardin and David R. Mapel (eds), *Traditions of International Ethics* (Cambridge: Cambridge University Press), pp. 85–111.

—— (1993). 'Human Rights, Humanitarian Crisis, and Humanitarian Intervention', *International Journal*, 48: 607–40.

—— (2000). *Realism and International Relations* (Cambridge: Cambridge University Press).

Doppelt, Gerald (1978). 'Walzer's Theory of Morality in International Relations', *Philosophy and Public Affairs*, 8/1: 3–26.

—— (1980). 'Statism without Foundations', *Philosophy and Public Affairs*, 9/4: 398–403.

Dostoyevsky, Fyodor (1988 [1880]). *The Brothers Karamazov*, translated with an introduction by David Magarshack, (Middlesex: Penguin).

Dower, Nigel (1998). *World Ethics: the New Agenda* (Edinburgh: Edinburgh University Press).

Doyle, Michael W. (1997). *Ways of War and Peace: Realism, Liberalism, and Socialism* (New York and London: Norton).

Dryzek, John S. (2000). *Deliberative Democracy and Beyond: Liberals, Critics, Contestations* (Oxford: Oxford University Press).

Dunne, Timothy (1998). *Inventing International Society: A History of the English School* (Basingstoke: Macmillan).

Dworkin, Ronald (1986a). *Law's Empire* (London: Fontana).

—— (1986b). 'What Justice Isn't' in *A Matter of Principle* (Oxford: Clarendon Press), pp. 214–20.

—— (1996). 'Objectivity and Truth: You'd Better Believe It', *Philosophy and Public Affairs*, 25/2: 87–139.

—— (2000). *Sovereign Virtue: The Theory and Practice of Equality* (Cambridge, Massachusetts: Harvard University Press).

Eichengreen, Barry, James Tobin and Charles Wyplosz (1995). 'Two Cases for Sand in the Wheels of International Finance', *The Economic Journal*, 105/428: 162–72.

Einstein, Albert (1991 [1933]). 'Why War?', in Albert Dickson (ed.), *The Penguin Freud Library: Volume 12 Civilization, Society and Religion: Group Psychology, Civilization and its Discontents and Other Works* (London: Penguin), pp. 345–48.

Elfstrom, Gerard (1983). 'On Dilemmas of Intervention', *Ethics*, 93/4: 709–25.

Fabre, Cécile (2000). *Social Rights under the Constitution: Government and the Decent Life* (Oxford: Clarendon Press).

Falk, Richard (1995). *On Humane Governance: Toward a New Global Politics* (Cambridge: Polity Press).

Farer, Tom J. (1973). 'Humanitarian Intervention: the View from Charlottesville', in Richard B. Lillich (ed.), *Humanitarian Intervention and the United Nations* (Charlottesville: University Press of Virginia), pp. 149–64.

Fishkin, James (1984). 'Defending Equality: A View from the Cave', *Michigan Law Review*, 82/4: 755–60.

Fixdal, Mona and Dan Smith (1998). 'Humanitarian Intervention and Just War', *Mershon International Studies Review*, 42/2: 283–312.

Føllesdal, Andreas (forthcoming). 'Liberal Contractualism—Partial and Particularist, Impartial and Cosmopolitan', in Simon Caney and Percy B. Lehning (eds), *International Distributive Justice: Cosmopolitanism and its Critics* (London: Routledge).

Foot, Philippa (2002). 'Moral Relativism', in *Moral Dilemmas and other Topics in Moral Philosophy* (Oxford: Clarendon Press), pp. 20–36.

Forbes, Ian and Mark Hoffman (1993). *Political Theory, International Relations, and the Ethics of Intervention* (London: Macmillan).

Forst, Rainer (2002). *Contexts of Justice: Political Philosophy Beyond Liberalism and Communitarianism*, translated by John M. M. Farrell, (Berkeley: University of California Press).

Foucault, Michel (1974). 'Human Nature: Justice versus Power', in Fons Elder (ed.), *Reflexive Water: The Basic Concerns of Mankind* (London: Souvenir Press), pp. 133–197. (This is a transcript of a debate between Noam Chomsky and Michel Foucault.)

—— (1997a). 'Sex, Power, and the Politics of Identity', in edited by Paul Rabinow and translated by Robert Hurley and others, *Ethics: Subjectivity and Truth: The Essential Works of Michel Foucault 1954–1984 Volume One* (London: Penguin Press), pp. 163–73.

—— (1997b). 'The Ethics of the Concern of the Self as a Practice of Freedom', in edited by Paul Rabinow and translated by Robert Hurley and others, *Ethics: Subjectivity and Truth: The Essential Works of Michel Foucault 1954–1984 Volume One* (London: Penguin Press), pp. 281–301.

—— (1997c). 'What is Enlightenment?', in edited by Paul Rabinow and translated by Robert Hurley and others, *Ethics: Subjectivity and Truth: The Essential Works of Michel Foucault 1954–1984 Volume One* (London: Penguin Press), pp. 303–319.

—— (2002a). 'Truth and Power', in edited by James D. Faubion and translated by Robert Hurley and others, *Power: Essential Works of Foucault 1954–1984 Volume Three* (London: Penguin), pp. 111–33.

—— (2002b). 'The Subject and Power', in edited by James D. Faubion and translated by Robert Hurley and others, *Power: Essential Works of Foucault 1954–1984 Volume Three* (London: Penguin), pp. 326–48.

—— (2002c). 'Confronting Governments: Human Rights', in edited by James D. Faubion and translated by Robert Hurley and others, *Power: Essential Works of Foucault 1954–1984 Volume Three* (London: Penguin), pp. 474–75.

Franck, Thomas M. (1997). *Fairness in International Law and Institutions* (Oxford: Clarendon Press).

Franck, Thomas and Nigel Rodley (1973). 'After Bangladesh: The Law of Humanitarian Intervention by Military Force', *American Journal of International Law*, 67: 275–305.

Fraser, Nancy (1997). *Justice Interruptus: Critical Reflections on the 'Postsocialist' Condition* (New York and London: Routledge).

Freeman, Michael (1994). 'Nation-State and Cosmopolis: A Response to David Miller', *Journal of Applied Philosophy*, 11/1: 79–87.

—— (2000). 'Universalism, Particularism and Cosmopolitan Justice', in Tony Coates (ed.), *International Justice* (Aldershot: Ashgate), pp. 65–88.

French, Stanley and Andres Gutman (1974). 'The Principle of National Self-determination' in Virginia Held, Sidney Morgenbesser and Thomas Nagel (eds), *Philosophy, Morality, and International Affairs: Essays edited for the Society for Philosophy and Public Affairs* (New York: Oxford University Press), pp. 138–153.

Freud, Sigmund (1991 [1933]). 'Why War?', in Albert Dickson (ed.), *The Penguin Freud Library: Volume 12 Civilization, Society and Religion: Group Psychology, Civilization and its Discontents and Other Works* (London: Penguin), pp. 349–62.

Friedman, Marilyn (1991). 'The Practice of Partiality', *Ethics*, 101/4: 818–35.

Frost, Mervyn (1996). *Ethics in International Relations: A Constitutive Theory* (Cambridge: Cambridge University Press).

Galston, William A. (1991). *Liberal Purposes: Goods, Virtues, and Diversity in the Liberal State* (Cambridge: Cambridge University Press).

Garber, Peter and Mark P. Taylor (1995). 'Sand in the Wheels of Foreign Exchange Markets: A Sceptical Note', *The Economic Journal*, 105/428: 173–80.

Gauthier, David (1994). 'Breaking Up: An Essay on Secession', *Canadian Journal of Philosophy*, 24/3: 357–71.

George, David (1993). 'The Right of National Self Determination', *History of European Ideas*, 16/4–6: 507–13.

—— (1994). 'The Ethics of National Self-Determination', in Paul Gilbert and Paul Gregory (eds), *Nations, Cultures and Markets* (Aldershot: Avebury), pp. 67–82.

Geras, Norman (1983). *Marx and Human Nature: Refutation of a Legend* (London: Verso).

—— (1995). *Solidarity in the Conversation of Humankind: The Ungroundable Liberalism of Richard Rorty* (London: Verso).

Geuss, Raymond (1993). *The Idea of a Critical Theory: Habermas and the Frankfurt School* (Cambridge: Cambridge University Press).

Gewirth, Alan (1994). 'Is Cultural Pluralism Relevant to Moral Knowledge?', in Ellen Frankel Paul, Fred D. Miller and Jeffrey Paul (eds), *Cultural Pluralism and Moral Knowledge* (Cambridge: Cambridge University Press), pp. 22–43.

Gilbert, Paul (1996). 'National Obligations: Political, Cultural or Societal?', in *National Rights, International Obligations* (Oxford: Westview Press), pp. 102–118.

Glover, Jonathan (1986). *Causing Death and Saving Lives* (Middlesex: Penguin Books).

Goldman, Alan H. (1982). 'The Moral Significance of National Boundaries', in Peter A. French, Theodore E. Uehling, Howard K. Wettstein (eds), *Midwest Studies in Philosophy Volume VII Social and Political Philosophy* (Minneapolis: University of Minnesota Press), pp. 437–53.

Goodin, Robert E. (1979). 'The Development-Rights Trade-Off: Some Unwarranted Economic and Political Assumptions', *Universal Human Rights*, 1/2: 31–42.

Goodin, Robert E. (1985). *Protecting the Vulnerable: A Reanalysis of our Social Responsibilities* (Chicago: University of Chicago Press).

—— (1988). 'What is so Special about our Fellow Countrymen?', *Ethics* 98/4: 663–686.

—— (1990). 'Liberalism and the Best-Judge Principle', *Political Studies* XXXVIII/2: 181–95.

—— (1992a). 'Commentary: The Political Realism of Free Movement', in Brian Barry and Robert E. Goodin (eds), *Free Movement: Ethical Issues in the Transnational Migration of People and of Money* (University Park: Pennsylvania State University Press), pp. 248–264.

—— (1992b). *Green Political Theory* (Cambridge: Polity).

Gordon, Ruth (1994). 'United Nations Intervention in Internal Conflicts: Iraq, Somalia, and Beyond', *Michigan Journal of International Law*, 15/2, pp. 519–89.

Graham, Gordon (1986). *Politics in its Place: A Study of Six Ideologies* (Oxford: Clarendon Press).

Graham, Keith (1996), 'Coping with the Many-Coloured Dome: Pluralism and Practical Reason', in David Archard (ed.), *Philosophy and Pluralism: Royal Institute of Philosophy Supplement 40* (Cambridge: Cambridge University Press), pp. 135–46.

Green, Michael J. (1996). 'Review Essay: National Identity and Liberal Political Philosophy', *Ethics and International Affairs*, 10: 191–201.

Griffin, James (1986). *Well-Being: Its Meaning, Measurement, and Moral Importance* (Oxford: Clarendon).

—— (1996). *Value Judgement: Improving our Ethical Beliefs* (Oxford: Clarendon Press).

Griffiths, Martin, Iain Levine and Mark Weller (1995). 'Sovereignty and Suffering', John Harriss (ed.), in *The Politics of Humanitarian Intervention* (London and New York: Pinter), pp. 33–90.

Grotius, Hugo (1925 [1646]). *de Jure Belli ac Pacis Libri Tres* translated by Francis W. Kelsey with the collaboration of Arthur E. R. Boak, Henry A. Sanders, Jesse S. Reeves and Herbert F. Wright and an introduction by James Brown Scott, (Oxford: Clarendon Press).

Gutmann, Amy (1993). 'The Challenge of Multiculturalism in Political Ethics', *Philosophy and Public Affairs*, 22/3: 171–206.

Gyeke, Kwame (1997), *Tradition and Modernity: Philosophical Reflections on the African Experience* (New York: Oxford University Press).

H M Treasury (2001). 'Treasury Note on Tobin Tax for the International Development Select Committee' Annex A of International Development Committee *Third Special Report: Government Response to the First Report from the Committee, Session 2000–01: The Globalisation White Paper*. HC 470. London: Stationery Office Ltd by the authority of the House of Commons, 8 May.

Habermas, Jürgen (1986). *The Theory of Communicative Action: Volume 1 Reason and the Rationalization of Society*, translated by Thomas McCarthy, (Cambridge: Polity).

—— (1987). *The Philosophical Discourse of Modernity: Twelve Lectures* (Cambridge: Polity).

—— (1992a). 'Discourse Ethics: Notes on a Program of Philosophical Justification', in *Moral Consciousness and Communicative Action*, translated by Christian Lenhardt and Shierry Weber Nicholsen, (Cambridge: Polity), pp. 43–115.

—— (1992b). 'Moral Consciousness and Communicative Action', in *Moral Consciousness and Communicative Action*, translated by Christian Lenhardt and Shierry Weber Nicholsen, (Cambridge: Polity), pp. 116–94.

—— (1993). 'Remarks on Discourse Ethics', in *Justification and Application: Remarks on Discourse Ethics*, translated by Ciaran Cronin, (Cambridge Massachusetts: MIT Press), pp. 19–111.

—— (1997*a*). *Between Facts and Norms: Contributions to a Discourse Theory of Law and Democracy*, translated by William Rehg, (Cambridge: Polity).

—— (1997*b*). 'Kant's Idea of Perpetual Peace, with the Benefit of Two Hundred Years' Hindsight', in James Bohman and Matthias Lutz-Bachmann, *Perpetual Peace: Essays on Kant's Cosmopolitan Ideal*, (Cambridge, Massachusetts: MIT Press), pp. 113–53.

—— (2001*a*). 'Learning from Catastrophe? A Look Back at the Short Twentieth Century', in *The Postnational Constellation: Political Essays*, translated, edited, and with an Introduction by Max Pensky, (Cambridge: Polity), pp. 38–57.

—— (2001*b*). 'The Postnational Constellation and the Future of Democracy' in *The Postnational Constellation: Political Essays*, translated, edited, and with an Introduction by Max Pensky, (Cambridge: Polity), pp. 58–112.

Hampshire, Stuart (1983). *Morality and Conflict* (Oxford: Blackwell).

—— (1989). *Innocence and Experience* (London: Penguin).

Harbour, Frances V. (1995). 'Basic Moral Values: A Shared Core', *Ethics and International Affairs*, 9: 155–70.

Hardin, Garrett (1996). 'Lifeboat Ethics: The Case against Helping the Poor', in William Aiken and Hugh La Follette (eds), *World Hunger and Morality* second edition (New Jersey: Prentice Hall), pp. 5–15.

Hare, R. M. (1972). 'Rules of War and Moral Reasoning', *Philosophy and Public Affairs*, 1/2: 166–181.

Harman, Gilbert (1989). 'Is There a Single True Morality?', edited with an introduction by Michael Krausz in *Relativism: Interpretation and Confrontation* (Notre Dame, Indiana: University of Notre Dame Press), pp. 363–86.

Hart, H. L. A. (1985). 'Are There any Natural Rights?', in Jeremy Waldron (ed.), *Theories of Rights* (Oxford: Oxford University Press), pp. 77–90.

—— (1997). *The Concept of Law* (Oxford: Clarendon Press) second edition with a postscript edited by Penelope A. Bulloch and Joseph Raz.

Hauerwas, Stanley (1986). *The Peaceable Kingdom: A Primer in Christian Ethics* (Notre Dame: University of Notre Dame Press).

Hayek, F. A. (1976 [1944]). *The Road to Serfdom* (London and Henley: Routledge and Kegan Paul).

Heater, Derek (1996). *World Citizenship and Government: Cosmopolitan Ideas in the History of Western Political Thought* (Basingstoke: Macmillan).

Held, David (1995). *Democracy and the Global Order: From the Modern State to Cosmopolitan Governance* (Cambridge: Polity).

—— (1998). 'Democracy and Globalization', in Daniele Archibugi, David Held and Martin Köhler (eds), *Re-imagining Political Community: Studies in Cosmopolitan Democracy* (Cambridge: Polity), pp. 11–27.

—— and Anthony McGrew, David Goldblatt and Jonathan Perraton (1999). *Global Transformations: Politics, Economics and Culture* (Cambridge: Polity).

Hendrickson, David C. (1992). 'Migration in Law and Ethics: a Realist Perspective', in Brian Barry and Robert E. Goodin (eds), *Free Movement: Ethical Issues in the Transnational Migration of People and of Money* (University Park: Pennsylvania State University Press), pp. 213–231.

Herring, Eric (2002). 'Between Iraq and a Hard Place: A Critique of the British Government's Case for UN Economic Sanctions', *Review of International Studies*, 28/1, 39–56.

Hinsley, F. H. (1986). *Sovereignty* (Cambridge: Cambridge University Press) second edition.

Hirschman, Albert O. (1970). *Exit, Voice, and Loyalty: Responses to Decline in Firms, Organizations, and States* (Cambridge, Massachusetts: Harvard University Press).

Hirst, Paul and Grahame Thompson (1996). *Globalization in Question: The International Economy and the Possibilities of Governance* (Cambridge: Polity).

Hobbes, Thomas (1996 [1651]). *Leviathan* (Oxford: Oxford University Press) edited with an introduction by J. C. A. Gaskin.

Hobson, J. A. (1920). *The Morals of Economic Internationalism* (Boston and New York: Houghton Mifflin).

Hoffmann, Stanley (1984). 'The Problem of Intervention', in Hedley Bull (ed.), *Intervention in World Politics* (Oxford: Clarendon Press), pp. 7–28.

Holmes, Robert L. (1992). 'Can War be Morally Justified? The Just War Theory', in Jean Bethke Elshtain (ed.), *Just War Theory* (New York: New York University Press), pp. 197–233.

Horowitz, Donald L. (1998). 'Self-Determination: Politics, Philosophy, and Law', in Margart Moore (ed.), *National Self-Determination and Secession* (Oxford: Oxford University Press), pp. 181–214.

Horton, John (1985). 'Toleration, Morality and Harm', in John Horton and Susan Mendus, (eds), *Aspects of Toleration: Philosophical Studies* (London and New York: Methuen), pp. 113–35.

Hume, David (1985 [1739–40]). *A Treatise of Human Nature*, edited with an introduction by Ernest C. Mossner, (Middlesex: Penguin).

—— (1988 [1777]). 'An Enquiry Concerning the Principles of Morals' in *Enquiries Concerning Human Understanding and Concerning the Principles of Morals*, third edition with text revised and notes by P. H. Nidditch, (Oxford: Clarendon Press).

Hurka, Thomas (1993). *Perfectionism* (Oxford: University Press, 1993).

Hurrell, Andrew (2001). 'Global Inequality and International Institutions', *Metaphilosophy* 32/1–2: 34–57.

Hutchinson, John (1994). *Modern Nationalism* (London: Fontana).

Inada, Kenneth (1998). 'A Buddhist Response to the Nature of Human Rights', in Damien V. Keown, Charles S. Prebish and Wayne R. Husted (eds), *Buddhism and Human Rights* (Richmond, Surrey: Curzon Press), pp. 1–13.

Inoue, Tatsuo (1999). 'Liberal Democracy and Asian Orientalism', in Joanne R. Bauer and Daniel A. Bell (eds), *The East Asian Challenge for Human Rights* (Cambridge: Cambridge University Press), pp. 27–59.

International Development Committee (2002). *Financing for Development: Finding the Money to Eliminate World Poverty: Fifth Report of Session 2001–02*. Volumes I and II. HC 785. London: Stationery Office Ltd by the authority of the House of Commons, 24 July.

Jackson, Kevin T. (1998). 'A cosmopolitan court for transnational corporate wrongdoing: why its time has come', *Journal of Business Ethics*, 17/7: 757–83.

Jackson, Robert (1999). 'Sovereignty in World Politics: a Glance at the Conceptual and Historical Landscape', *Political Studies*, 47. Special Issue on Sovereignty at the Millennium: 431–56.

—— (2000). *The Global Covenant: Human Conduct in a World of States* (Oxford: Oxford University Press).

James, Alan (1986). *Sovereign Statehood: The Basis of International Society* (London: Allen and Unwin).

Jenning, Ivor (1956). *The Approach to Self-government* (Cambridge: Cambridge University Press).

Jervis, Robert (1988). 'Realism, Game Theory, and Cooperation', *World Politics*, XL/3: 317–49.

Jetin, Bruno and Suzanne de Brunhof (2000). 'The Tobin Tax and the Regulation of Capital Movements' in Walden Bello, Nicola Bullard and Kamal Malhotra (eds), *Global Finance: New Thinking on Regulating Speculative Capital Markets* (London and New York: Zed Books), pp. 195–214.

Johnson, James Turner (1999). *Morality and Contemporary Warfare* (New Haven and London: Yale University Press).

Jones, Charles (1996). 'Revenge of the Philosophical Mole: Another Response to David Miller on Nationality', *Journal of Applied Philosophy*, 13/1, 73–86.

—— (1999). *Global Justice: Defending Cosmopolitanism* (Oxford: Oxford University Press).

Jones, Peter (1983). 'Political Equality and Majority Rule', in David Miller and Larry Siedentop (eds), *The Nature of Political Theory* (Oxford: Clarendon Press), pp. 155–82.

—— (1990). 'Universal Principles and Particular Claims: from Welfare Rights to Welfare States', in Alan Ware and Robert E. Goodin (eds), *Needs and Welfare* (London: Sage), pp. 34–53.

—— (1994). *Rights* (London: Macmillan).

—— (1996). 'International Human Rights: Philosophical or Political?' in Simon Caney, David George and Peter Jones, *National Rights, International Obligations* (Oxford: Westview), pp. 183–204.

—— (1999). 'Beliefs and Identities', in John Horton and Susan Mendus (eds), *Toleration, Identity and Difference* (London: Macmillan), pp. 65–86.

—— (2000). 'Human Rights and Diverse Cultures: Continuity or Discontinuity?', *Critical Review of International Social and Political Philosophy*, 3/1: 27–50.

Kafka, Franz (1992 [1919]). 'In The Penal Colony' in *The Transformation ('Metamorphosis') and Other Stories*, translated from the German and edited by Malcolm Pasley, (London: Penguin), pp. 127–53.

Kamm, F. M. (1992). 'Non-consequentialism, the Person as an End-in-Itself, and the Significance of Status', *Philosophy and Public Affairs*, 21/4: 354–89.

Kant, Immanuel (1989 [1795]). 'Perpetual Peace: A Philosophical Sketch' in *Kant's Political Writings*, edited with an introduction and notes by Hans Reiss and translated by H. B. Nisbet (Cambridge: Cambridge University Press), pp. 93–130.

—— (1996 [1797]). *Metaphysical First Principles of the Doctrine of Right* in *The Metaphysic of Morals*, translated and edited by Mary Gregor with an introduction by Roger J. Sullivan (Cambridge: Cambridge University Press).

Kausikan, Bilahari (1996). 'Asia's Different Standard', in Philip Alston, (ed.), *Human Rights Law* (Aldershot: Dartmouth), pp. 201–18.

Keane, Fergal (1996). *Season of Blood: A Rwandan Journey* (London: Penguin).

Keck, Margaret E. and Kathryn Sikkink (1998). *Activists Beyond Borders: Advocacy Networks in International Politics* (Ithaca and London: Cornell University Press).

Kedourie, Elie (1996). *Nationalism*, fourth expanded version (Oxford: Blackwell).

Kekes, John (1994). 'Pluralism and the Value of Life', in Ellen Frankel Paul, Fred D. Miller and Jeffrey Paul, (eds), *Cultural Pluralism and Moral Knowledge* (Cambridge: Cambridge University Press), pp. 44–60.

Kenen Peter B. (1996). 'The Feasibility of Taxing Foreign Exchange Transactions', in Mahbub ul Haq, Inge Kaul and Isabelle Grunberg (eds), *The Tobin Tax: Coping with Financial Volatility* (New York: Oxford University Press), pp. 109–28.

Kennan, George F. (1952). *American Diplomacy: 1900–1952* (London: Secker and Warburg).

—— (1954). *Realities of American Foreign Policy* (London: Oxford University Press).

—— (1985/86). 'Morality and Foreign Policy' *Foreign Affairs*, 64/2: 205–18.

Keohane, Robert (1984). *After Hegemony: Cooperation and Discord in the World Political Eonomy* (Princeton: Princeton University Press).

Keown, Damien V., Charles S. Prebish and Wayne R. Husted (eds) (1998). *Buddhism and Human Rights* (Richmond, Surrey: Curzon Press).

Khilnani, Sunil (1997). *The Idea of India* (London: Hamish Hamilton).

Koestler, Arthur (1987 [1940]). *Darkness at Noon* (Middlesex: Penguin).

Kohn, Hans (1967). *The Idea of Nationalism: A Study in its Origins and Background* (New York: Macmillan).

Koontz, Theodore J. (1996). 'Christian Nonviolence: An Interpretation', in Terry Nardin, (ed.), *The Ethics of War and Peace: Religious and Secular Perspectives* (Princeton: Princeton University Press), pp. 169–96.

Krasner, Stephen D. (1983*a*). 'Structural causes and regime consequences: regimes as intervening variables', in Stephen D. Krasner (ed.), *International Regimes* (Ithaca and London: Cornell University Press), pp. 1–21.

—— (ed.) (1983*b*). *International Regimes* (Ithaca and London: Cornell University Press).

Krasner, Stephen (1992). 'Realism, Imperialism, and Democracy: A Response to Gilbert', *Political Theory*, 20/1: 38–52.

Kukathas, Chandran (1992). 'Are There any Cultural Rights?', *Political Theory*, 20/1: 105–39.

Kuper, Andrew (2000). 'Rawlsian Global Justice: Beyond *The Law of Peoples* to a Cosmopolitan Law of Persons', *Political Theory*, 28/5: 640–74.

Kymlicka, Will (1989). *Liberalism, Community and Culture* (Oxford: Clarendon Press).

—— (1993). 'Appendix I: Some Questions about Justice and Community', in Daniel Bell (ed.), *Communitarianism and its Critics* (Oxford: Clarendon Press), pp. 208–21.

—— (1995). *Multicultural Citizenship: A Liberal Theory of Minority Rights* (Oxford: Clarendon).

—— (2001*a*). 'From Enlightenment Cosmopolitanism to Liberal Nationalism', in *Politics in the Vernacular: Nationalism, Multiculturalism, and Citizenship* (Oxford: Oxford University Press), pp. 203–20.

—— (2001*b*). 'Cosmopolitanism, Nation-States, and Minority Nationalism' (co-authored with Christine Straehle), in *Politics in the Vernacular: Nationalism, Multiculturalism, and Citizenship* (Oxford: Oxford University Press), pp. 221–41.

—— (2001*c*). 'Citizenship in an Era of Globalization: Commentary on Held', in *Politics in the Vernacular: Nationalism, Multiculturalism, and Citizenship* (Oxford: Oxford University Press), pp. 317–26.

—— (2002). *Contemporary Political Philosophy: An Introduction*, second edition (Oxford: Clarendon).

Laërtius, Diogenes (1905: original publication date unknown). 'Diogenes' in translated by C. D. Yonge, *The Lives and Opinions of Eminent Philosophers* (London: George Bell and Sons), pp. 224–48.

Landes, David S. (1998). *The Wealth and Poverty of Nations: Why Some are so Rich and Some so Poor* (London: Little, Brown and Company).

Larmore, Charles (1996). *The Morals of Modernity* (Cambridge: Cambridge University Press).

Lehman, Hugh (1986). 'Equal Pay for Equal Work in the Third World', in Anthony Ellis (ed.), *Ethics and International Relations* (Manchester: Manchester University Press), pp. 155–62.

Leff, Carol Skalnik (1997). *The Czech and Slovak Republics: Nation Versus State* (Boulder, Colorado: Westview Press).

Lévinas, Emmanuel (1999 [1974]). *Otherwise than Being, or, Beyond Essence*, translated by Alphonso Lingis (Pittsburg, Pennsylvania: Duquesne University Press).

Lewis, Ioan and James Mayall (1996). 'Somalia', in James Mayall (ed.), *The New Interventionism 1991–1994: United Nations experience in Cambodia, former Yugoslavia and Somalia* (Cambridge: Cambridge University Press), pp. 94–124.

Linklater, Andrew (1996*a*). 'Citizenship and Sovereignty in the Post-Westphalian State', *European Journal of International Relations*, 2/1: 77–103.

—— (1996*b*). 'The Achievements of Critical Theory', in Steve Smith, Ken Booth and Marysia Zalewski (eds), *International Theory: Positivism and Beyond* (Cambridge: Cambridge University Press), pp. 279–98.

—— (1998). *The Transformation of Political Community: Ethical Foundations of the Post-Westphalian Era* (Cambridge: Polity).

Lipschutz, Ronnie D. with Judith Mayer (1996). *Global Civil Society and Global Environmental Governance: The Politics of Nature from Place to Planet* (Albany, New York: State University of New York Press).

Long, Graham (2001). *Relativism and the Foundations of Liberalism* (Phd Thesis, University of Newcastle).

Luard, Evan (1984). 'Collective Intervention' in Hedley Bull (ed.), *Intervention in World Politics* (Oxford: Clarendon Press), pp. 157–79.

Luban, David (1980*a*). 'Just War and Human Rights', *Philosophy and Public Affairs*, 9/2: 160–81.

—— (1980*b*). 'The Romance of the Nation-State', *Philosophy and Public Affairs*, 9/4: 392–97.

—— (2002). 'Intervention and Civilization: Some Unhappy Lessons of the Kosovo War', in Pablo de Greiff and Ciaran Cronin, (eds), *Global Justice and Transnational Politics: Essays on the Moral and Political Challenges of Globalization* (Cambridge, Massachusetts: MIT Press), pp. 79–115.

MacCormick, Neil (1982). 'Nation and Nationalism' in *Legal Right and Social Democracy: Essays in Legal and Political Philosophy* (Oxford: Clarendon Press), pp. 247–64.

—— (1991). 'Is Nationalism Philosophically Credible?', in William Twining (ed.), *Issues of Self-Determination* (Aberdeen: Aberdeen University Press), pp. 8–19.

—— (1996). 'What Place for Nationalism in the Modern World?', in Simon Caney, Peter Jones and David George (eds), *National Rights, International Obligations* (Oxford: Westview), pp. 34–52.

Machiavelli, Niccolò (1986 [1513]). *The Prince*, translated with an introduction by George Bull (Middlesex: Penguin).

—— (1988 [1531]). *The Discourses*, edited with an introduction by Bernard Crick (London: Penguin).

MacIntyre, Alasdair (1984). 'Is Patriotism a Virtue?' (Lindley Lecture: Department of Philosophy, University of Kansas).

—— (1988). *Whose Justice? Which Rationality?* (London: Duckworth).

—— (1990). *Three Rival Versions of Moral Enquiry: Encyclopaedia, Genealogy, and Tradition* (London: Duckworth).

Macmillan, John (1998). '"The Power of the Pen": Liberalism's Ethical Dynamic and World Politics', *Millennium*, 27/3: 643–67.

Maluwa, Tiyanjana (1997). 'Discourses on Democracy and Human Rights in Africa: Contextualising the Relevance of Human Rights to Developing Countries', *African Journal of International and Comparative Law*, 9: 55–71.

Mann, Thomas (1985 [1924]). *The Magic Mountain*, translated by H. T. Lowe-Porter (Middlesex: Penguin).

Mapel, David R. (1996). 'Realism and the Ethics of War and Peace', in Terry Nardin (ed.), *The Ethics of War and Peace: Religious and Secular Perspectives* (Princeton: Princeton University Press), pp. 54–77.

—— and Terry Nardin (1992). 'Convergence and Divergence in International Ethics', in Terry Nardin and David R. Mapel (eds), *Traditions of International Ethics* (Cambridge: Cambridge University Press), pp. 297–322.

Margalit, Avishai and Joseph Raz (1990). 'National Self-determination', *Journal of Philosophy*, LXXXVII/9: 439–61.

Marx, Karl (1988 [1845]). 'Theses on Feuerbach', in David McLellan (ed.), *Karl Marx: Selected Writings* (Oxford: Oxford University Press), pp. 156–8.

Mason, Andrew (1995). 'The State, National Identity and Distributive Justice', *New Community*, 21/2: 241–54.

—— (1997). 'Special Obligations to Compatriots', *Ethics*, 107/3: 427–47.

—— (1999). 'Political Community, Liberal-Nationalism and the Ethics of Assimilation', *Ethics*, 109/2: 261–86.

—— (2000). *Community, Solidarity and Belonging: Levels of Community and their Normative Significance* (Cambridge: Cambridge University Press).

—— and Nick Wheeler (1996). 'Realist Objections to Humanitarian Intervention', in Barry Holden (ed.), *The Ethical Dimensions of Global Change* (London: Macmillan), pp. 94–110.

McCarthy, Thomas (1992). 'Introduction' to Habermas *Moral Consciousness and Communicative Action*, translated by Christian Lenhardt and Shierry Weber Nicholsen, (Cambridge: Polity), pp. vii–xiii.

—— (1994). 'On the Pragmatics of Communicative Reason', in David Couzens Hoy and Thomas McCarthy (eds), *Critical Theory* (Oxford: Blackwell), pp. 63–100.

—— (1997). 'On the Idea of a Reasonable Law of Peoples', in James Bohman and Matthias Lutz-Bachmann (eds), *Perpetual Peace: Essays on Kant's Cosmopolitan Ideal* (Cambridge, Massachusetts: MIT Press), pp. 201–17.

—— (1999). 'Two Conceptions of Cosmopolitan Justice', in Iain MacKenzie and Shane O'Neill (eds), *Reconstituting Social Criticism: Political Morality in an Age of Scepticism* (Basingstoke: Macmillan), pp. 191–214.

McGarry, John (1998). '"Orphans of Secession": National Pluralism in Secessionist Regions and Post-Secession States', in Margaret Moore (ed.), *National Self-Determination and Secession* (Oxford: Oxford University Press), pp. 215–32.

McGreal, Chris (2002). 'Thabo Mbeki's Catastrophe', *Prospect*, March: 42–7.

McGrew, Anthony (1997). 'Democracy beyond Borders?: Globalization and the Reconstruction of Democratic Theory and Politics', in Anthony McGrew (ed.), *The Transformation of Democracy? Globalization and Territorial Democracy* (Cambridge: Polity), pp. 231–66.

—— (1999). 'The World Trade Organization: Technocracy or Banana Republic?', in Annie Taylor and Caroline Thomas, (eds), *Global Trade and Global Social Issues* (London and New York: Routledge), pp. 197–216.

McMahan, Jeff (1986). 'The Ethics of International Intervention', in Anthony Ellis (ed.), *Ethics and International Relations* (Manchester: Manchester University Press), pp. 24–51.

—— (1996). 'Realism, Morality, and War', in Terry Nardin (ed.), *The Ethics of War and Peace: Religious and Secular Perspectives* (Princeton: Princeton University Press), pp. 78–92.

—— (1997). 'The Limits of National Partiality', in Robert McKim and Jeff McMahan (eds), *The Morality of Nationalism* (New York: Oxford University Press), pp. 107–138.

—— and Robert McKim (1993). 'The Just War and the Gulf War', *Canadian Journal of Philosophy*, 23/4: 501–41.

Mearsheimer, John (1990). 'Back to the Future: Instability in Europe After the Cold War', *International Security*, 15/1: 5–56.

—— (1995). 'The False Promise of International Institutions', *International Security*, 19/3: 5–49.

Mei, Yi-Pao (1974 [original date unknown]). *The Ethical and Political Works of Motse* (Taipei: Ch'eng Wen Publishing).

Midtgaard, Søren (forthcoming) 'Rawlsian Stability and The Law of Peoples', in Simon Caney and Percy B. Lehning (eds), *International Distributive Justice: Cosmopolitanism and its Critics* (London: Routledge).

Mill, John Stuart (1969 [1840]). 'Coleridge' in *Essays on Ethics, Religion and Society: Collected Works of John Stuart Mill Volume X*, edited by J. M. Robson with an introduction by F. E. L. Priestley (Toronto: University of Toronto Press), pp. 117–63.

—— (1977*a* [1859]). 'On Liberty' in *Essays on Politics and Society: Collected Works of John Stuart Mill Volume XVIII*, edited by J. M. Robson with an introduction by Alexander Brady (Toronto: University of Toronto Press), pp. 213–310.

—— (1977*b* [1861]). 'Considerations on Representative Government', in J.M. Robson and introduction by Alexander Brady, *Essays on Politics and Society: Collected Works of John Stuart Mill Volume XIX* (Toronto: University of Toronto Press), pp. 371–577.

—— (1984 [1859]). 'A Few Words on Non-Intervention', *Essays on Equality, Law, and Education: Collected Works of John Stuart Mill Volume XXI*, edited by John Robson and introduction by Stefan Collini (Toronto: University of Toronto Press), pp. 111–24.

Miller, David (1988). 'The Ethical Significance of Nationality', *Ethics*, 98/4: 647–62.

—— (1989). 'In What Sense must Socialism be Communitarian?', *Social Philosophy and Policy*, 6/2: 51–73.

—— (1994). 'The Nation-State: a Modest Defence', in Chris Brown (ed.), *Political Restructuring in Europe: Ethical Perspectives* (London: Routledge), pp. 137–62.

—— (1995). *On Nationality* (Oxford: Clarendon Press).

—— (1997). 'Nationality: Some Replies', *Journal of Applied Philosophy*, 14/1: 69–82.

Miller, David (1998). 'The Limits of Cosmopolitan Justice', in David R. Mapel and Terry Nardin (eds), *International Society: Diverse Ethical Perspectives* (Princeton: Princeton University Press), pp. 164–181.

—— (1999). 'Justice and Global Inequality', in Andrew Hurrell and Ngaire Woods (eds), *Inequality, Globalization, and World Politics* (Oxford: Oxford University Press), pp. 187–210.

—— (2000*a*). 'In Defence of Nationality', in *Citizenship and National Identity* (Cambridge: Polity), pp. 24–40.

—— (2000*b*). 'Bounded Citizenship', in *Citizenship and National Identity* (Cambridge: Polity), pp. 81–96.

—— (2000*c*). 'National Self-Determination and Global Justice', in *Citizenship and National Identity* (Cambridge: Polity), pp. 161–79.

—— (2002*a*). 'Two Ways to Think about Justice', *Politics, Philosophy and Economics*, 1/1: 5–28.

—— (2002*b*). 'Caney's "International Distributive Justice": A Response', *Political Studies*, 50/5: 974–77.

Mitrany, David (1933). *The Progress of International Government* (London: Allen and Unwin).

Moellendorf, Darrel (2002*a*). *Cosmopolitan Justice* (Boulder, Colorado: Westview Press).

—— (2002*b*). 'Is the War in Afghanistan Just?', *Imprints*, 6/2: 108–33.

Morgenthau, Hans J. (1951). *In Defense of the National Interest: A Critical Examination of American Foreign Policy* (New York: Alfred Knopf).

—— (1967). 'To Intervene or Not To Intervene', *Foreign Affairs*, 45/3: 425–36.

—— (1979). *Human Rights and Foreign Policy* (New York: Council on Religion and International Affairs).

—— (1985). *Politics Among Nations: The Struggle for Power and Peace*, sixth edition (New York: Alfred Knopf).

Morphet, Sally (1995). 'UN Peacekeeping and Election-Monitoring', in Adam Roberts and Benedict Kingsbury (eds), *United Nations, Divided World: The UN's roles in International Relations*, second edition (Oxford: Clarendon), pp. 183–239.

Munck, Gerardo and Chetan Kumar (1995). 'Civil Conflicts and the Conditions for Successful International Intervention: a comparative study of Cambodia and El Salvador', *Review of International Studies*, 21/2: 159–81.

Murphy, Liam B. (1998). 'Institutions and the Demands of Justice', *Philosophy and Public Affairs*, 27/4: 251–91.

Murray, A. J. H. (1996). 'The Moral Politics of Hans Morgenthau', *Review of Politics* 58/1: 81–107.

Nagel, Thomas (1972). 'War and Massacre', *Philosophy and Public Affairs*, 1/2: 123–44.

—— (1986). *The View from Nowhere* (New York: Oxford University Press).

—— (1995). 'Personal Rights and Public Space', *Philosophy and Public Affairs*, 24/2: 83–107.

—— (1997). *The Last Word* (New York: Oxford University Press).

Nardin, Terry (1983). *Law, Morality, and the Relations of States* (Princeton: Princeton University Press).

—— (1992). 'International Ethics and International Law', *Review of International Studies*, 18/1: 19–30.

Nathanson, Stephen (1989). 'In Defense of "Moderate Patriotism"', *Ethics*, 99/3: 535–52.

Nickel, James W. (1987). *Making Sense of Human Rights: Philosophical Reflections on the Universal Declaration of Human Rights* (Berkeley: University of California Press).

Nielsen, Kai (1988). 'World Government, Security, and Global Justice', in Steven Luper-Foy (ed.), *Problems of International Justice* (Boulder: Westview), pp. 264–82.

—— (1992). 'Global Justice, Capitalism and the Third World', in Robin Attfield and Barry Wilkins (eds), *International Justice and the Third World* (London: Routledge) pp. 17–34.

—— (1993). 'Secession: The Case of Quebec', *Journal of Applied Philosophy*, 10/1: 29–43.

—— (1996–7). 'Cultural Nationalism, Neither Ethnic nor Civic', *Philosophical Forum*, 28/1–2: 42–52.

Noël, Alain and Jean-Philippe Thérien (1995). 'From Domestic to International Justice: The Welfare State and Foreign Aid', *International Organization*, 49/3: 523–53.

Norman, Richard (1995). *Ethics, Killing, and War* (Cambridge: Cambridge University Press).

Nozick, Robert (1974). *Anarchy, State, and Utopia* (Oxford: Blackwell).

Nussbaum, Martha C. (1992). 'Human Functioning and Social Justice: In Defence of Aristotelian Essentialism', *Political Theory*, 20/2: 202–46.

—— (1993). 'Non-Relative Virtues: An Aristotelian Approach', in Martha Nussbaum and Amartya Sen (eds), *The Quality of Life* (Oxford: Clarendon), pp. 242–69.

—— (1996). 'Patriotism and Cosmopolitanism', in Joshua Cohen (eds), *For Love of Country: Debating the Limits of Patriotism* (Boston: Beacon Press), pp. 2–17.

—— (1997). *Cultivating Humanity: A Classical Defense of Reform in Liberal Education* (Cambridge, Massachusetts: Harvard University Press).

—— (1999). *Sex and Social Justice* (New York: Oxford University Press).

—— (2000a). *Women and Human Development: The Capabilities Approach* (Cambridge: Cambridge University Press).

—— (2000b). 'Duties of Justice, Duties of Material Aid: Cicero's Problematic Legacy', *Journal of Political Philosophy*, 8/2: 176–206.

Nussbaum, Martha (2002). 'Capabilities and Human Rights', in Pablo de Greiff and Ciaran Cronin (eds), *Global Justice and Transnational Politics: Essays on the Moral and Political Challenges of Globalization* (Cambridge, Massachusetts: MIT Press), pp. 117–49.

O'Brien, Robert, Anne Marie Goetz, Jan Aart Scholte and Marc Williams (2000). *Contesting Global Governance: Multilateral Economic Institutions and Global Social Movements* (Cambridge: Cambridge University Press).

Okin, Susan Moller (1999). 'Is Multiculturalism Bad for Women?', in Joshua Cohen, Matthew Howard and Martha C. Nussbaum (eds), *Is Multiculturalism Bad for Women?* (Princeton: Princeton University Press), pp. 7–24.

O'Neill, Onora (1986). *Faces of Hunger: An Essay on Poverty, Justice and Development* (London: Allen and Unwin).

—— (1994). 'Justice and Boundaries', in Chris Brown (ed.), *Political Restructuring in Europe: Ethical Perspectives* (London: Routledge), pp. 69–88.

—— (1996). *Towards Justice and Virtue: A Constructive Account of Practical Reasoning* (Cambridge: Cambridge University Press).

—— (2000). *Bounds of Justice* (Cambridge: Cambridge University Press).

—— (2001). 'Agents of Justice', *Metaphilosophy*, 32/1/2: 180–95.

Orend, Brian (1999). 'Kant's Just War Theory', *Journal of the History of Philosophy*, XXXVII/2: 323–53.

Orend, Brian (2000). *Michael Walzer on War and Justice* (Cardiff: University of Wales Press).

Parekh, Bhikhu (1997). 'Rethinking Humanitarian Intervention', *International Political Science Review*, 18/1: 49–69.

—— (2000). *Rethinking Multiculturalism: Cultural Diversity and Political Theory* (Basingstoke: Macmillan).

Parfit, Derek (1998). 'Equality and Priority', in Andrew Mason (ed.), *Ideals of Equality* (Oxford: Blackwell), pp. 1–20.

Pascal, Blaise (1885 [1670]). *The Thoughts of Blaise Pascal*, translated from the text of Auguste Molinier by C. Kegan Paul (London: Kegan Paul, Trench and co.).

Pateman, Carole (1979). *The Problem of Political Obligation: A Critique of Liberal Theory* (Chichester: Wiley).

Perry, Michael J. (1998). *The Idea of Human Rights: Four Inquiries* (New York: Oxford University Press).

Philpott, Daniel (1995). 'In Defense of Self-Determination', *Ethics*, 105/2: 352–85.

—— (1999). 'Westphalia, Authority, and International Society', *Political Studies*, 47 Special Issue on Sovereignty at the Millennium: 566–89.

Plamenatz, John (1976). 'Two Types of Nationalism', in Eugene Kamenka (ed.), *Nationalism: the Nature and Evolution of an Idea* (London: Edward Arnold), pp. 22–36.

Pogge, Thomas W. (1988). 'Moral Progress', in Steven Luper-Foy (ed.), *Problems of International Justice* (Boulder: Westview), pp. 284–304.

—— (1989). *Realizing Rawls* (London and Ithaca: Cornell University Press).

—— (1992a). 'An Institutional Approach to Humanitarian Intervention', *Public Affairs Quarterly*, 6/1: 89–103.

—— (1992b). 'Loopholes in Moralities', *Journal of Philosophy*, 89/2: 79–98.

—— (1994a). 'Cosmopolitanism and Sovereignty', in Chris Brown (ed.), *Political Restructuring in Europe: Ethical Perspectives* (London: Routledge), pp. 89–122.

—— (1994b). 'An Egalitarian Law of Peoples', *Philosophy and Public Affairs*, 23/3: 195–224.

—— (1995). 'How should Human Rights be Conceived?', *Jahrbuch fur Recht und Ethik*, 3: 103–20.

—— (1998a). 'The Bounds of Nationalism', in Joceylne Couture, Kai Nielsen and Michel Seymour (eds), *Rethinking Nationalism* (Calgary, Alberta: University of Calgary Press), pp. 463–504.

—— (1998b). 'A Global Resources Dividend', in David A. Crocker and Toby Linden (eds), *Ethics of Consumption: The Good Life, Justice, and Global Stewardship* (Lanham: Rowman and Littlefield), pp. 501–36.

—— (2000). 'The International Significance of Human Rights', *The Journal of Ethics*, 4: 45–69.

—— (2001a). 'Priorities of Global Justice', *Metaphilosophy*, 32/1–2: 6–24.

—— (2001b). 'Rawls on International Justice', *The Philosophical Quarterly*, 51/203: 246–53.

—— (2001c). 'Achieving Democracy', *Ethics and International Affairs*, 15/1: 3–23.

—— (2001d). 'The Influence of the Global Order on the Prospects for Genuine Democracy in the Developing Countries', *Ratio Juris*, 14/3: 326–43.

—— (2002a). 'Moral Universalism and Global Economic Justice', *Politics, Philosophy and Economics*, 1/1: 29–58.

—— (2002b). 'Eradicating Systemic Poverty: Brief for a Global Resources Dividend', in *World Poverty and Human Rights: Cosmopolitan Responsibilities and Reforms* (Cambridge: Polity), pp. 196–215.

Pufendorf, Samuel (1991 [1673]). *On the Duty of Man and Citizen According to Natural Law*, edited by James Tully and translated by Michael Silverthorne (Cambridge: Cambridge University Press).

Putnam, Hilary (1981). *Reason, Truth and History* (Cambridge: Cambridge University Press).

Putnam, Robert D. (with Robert Leonardi and Raffaella Y. Nanetti) (1993). *Making Democracy Work: Civic Traditions in Modern Italy* (Princeton: Princeton University Press).

Quashigah, E. K. (1998). 'Religious Freedom and Vestal Virgins: The *Trokosi* Practice in Ghana', *African Journal of International and Comparative Law*, 10: 193–215.

Raffer, Kunibert (1998). 'The Tobin Tax: Reviving a Discussion', *World Development* 26/3: 529–38.

Rawls, John (1993*a*). 'The Law of Peoples', in Stephen Shute and Susan Hurley (eds), *On Human Rights: The Oxford Amnesty Lectures 1993* (New York: Basic Books), pp. 41–82.

—— (1993*b*). *Political Liberalism* (New York: Columbia University Press).

—— (1999*a*). 'Some Reasons for the Maximin Criterion', in Samuel Freeman (ed.), *Collected Papers* (Cambridge Massachusetts: Harvard University Press), pp. 225–31.

—— (1999*b*). *The Law of Peoples with 'The Idea of Public Reason Revisited'* (Cambridge Massachusetts: Harvard University Press).

—— (1999*c*). *A Theory of Justice*, Revised edition (Oxford: Oxford University Press).

—— (2001). *Justice as Fairness: A Restatement*, Erin Kelly (ed.), (Cambridge Massachusetts: Harvard University Press).

Raz, Joseph (1986). *The Morality of Freedom* (Oxford: Clarendon).

—— (1989). 'Liberating Duties', *Law and Philosophy*, 8: 3–21.

Regan, Donald H. (1989). 'Authority and Value: Reflections on Raz's *Morality of Freedom*', *Southern California Law Review*, 62: 995–1095.

Rengger, N. J. (1993). 'Contextuality, Interdependence and the Ethics of Intervention', in Ian Forbes and Mark Hoffman (eds), *Political Theory, International Relations, and the Ethics of Intervention* (London: Macmillan), pp. 179–93.

Richards, David A. J. (1971). *A Theory of Reasons for Action* (Oxford: Clarendon Press).

—— (1982). 'International Distributive Justice', in J. Roland Pennock and John W. Chapman (eds), *Ethics, Economics, and the Law: NOMOS XXIV* (New York and London: New York University Press), pp. 275–99.

Ripstein, Arthur (1997). 'Context, Continuity, and Fairness', in Robert McKim and Jeff McMahan (eds), *The Morality of Nationalism* (New York: Oxford University Press), pp. 209–26.

Rittberger, Volker (1993). *Regime Theory and International Relations*, Peter Mayer (ed.), (Oxford: Clarendon Press).

Rodin, David (2002). *War and Self-Defense* (Oxford: Clarendon Press).

Rorty, Richard (1989). *Contingency, Irony, and Solidarity* (Cambridge: Cambridge University Press).

—— (1991*a*). 'Solidarity or Objectivity?', in *Objectivity, Relativism, and Truth: Philosophical Papers Volume 1* (Cambridge: Cambridge University Press), pp. 21–34.

Rorty, Richard (1991*b*). 'On Ethnocentrism: A Reply to Clifford Geertz', in *Objectivity, Relativism, and Truth: Philosophical Papers Volume 1* (Cambridge: Cambridge University Press), pp. 203–10.

—— (1991*c*). 'Cosmopolitanism without Emancipation: A Response to Jean-François Lyotard', in *Objectivity, Relativism, and Truth: Philosophical Papers Volume 1* (Cambridge: Cambridge University Press), pp. 211–22.

Ross, Michael L. (1999). 'The Political Economy of the Resource Curse', *World Politics* 51: 297–322.

Rousseau, Jean-Jacques (1968 [1762]). *The Social Contract*, translated and introduced by Maurice Cranston (Middlesex: Penguin).

—— (1991*a* [1755]). 'Discourse on Political Economy', in Stanley Hoffmann and David P. Fidler (eds), *Rousseau on International Relations* (Oxford: Clarendon Press), pp. 1–32.

—— (1991*b* [c. 1755–56]). 'Fragments on War', in Stanley Hoffmann and David P. Fidler (eds), *Rousseau on International Relations* (Oxford: Clarendon Press), pp. 48–52.

Ruggie, John Gerard (1993). 'Territoriality and Beyond: Problematizing Modernity in International Relations', *International Organization*, 47/1: 139–74.

Sachs, Jeffrey (1999). 'Cancel Debt Burden that Kills and Maims', *The Observer*, 13 June: 8.

Sandel, Michael J. (1982). *Liberalism and the Limits of Justice* (Cambridge: Cambridge University Press).

—— (1996). *Democracy's Discontent: America in Search of a Public Philosophy* (Cambridge Mass.: Harvard University Press).

Saward, Michael (2000). 'A Critique of Held', in Barry Holden (ed.), *Global Democracy: Key Debates* (London: Routledge), pp. 32–46.

Scanlon, Thomas (1982). 'Contractualism and Utilitarianism', in Amartya Sen and Bernard Williams (eds), *Utilitarianism and Beyond* (Cambridge: Cambridge University Press), pp. 103–28.

Scanlon, T. M. (1985). 'Rawls' Theory of Justice', in Norman Daniels (ed.), *Reading Rawls: Critical Studies of A Theory of Justice* (Oxford: Blackwell), pp. 169–205.

—— (1998). *What We Owe to Each Other* (Cambridge Massachusetts: Harvard University Press).

Scheffler, Samuel (1982). *The Rejection of Consequentialism: A Philosophical Investigation of the Considerations Underlying Rival Moral Conceptions* (Oxford: Clarendon Press).

—— (1995). 'Families, Nations, and Strangers' (Lindley Lecture: University of Kansas).

—— (1997). 'Relationships and Responsibilities', *Philosophy and Public Affairs*, 26/3: 189–209.

—— (1999). 'Conceptions of Cosmopolitanism', *Utilitas*, 11/3: 255–76.

Schmitt, Carl (1996 [1932]). *The Concept of the Political*, translated and with an introduction by George Schwab (Chicago and London: University of Chicago Press).

Sen, Amartya (1988). 'Rights and Agency', in Samuel Scheffler (ed.), *Consequentialism and its Critics* (Oxford: Oxford University Press), pp. 187–223.

—— (1993). 'Capability and Well-Being', in Martha Nussbaum and Amartya Sen (eds), *The Quality of Life* (Oxford: Clarendon Press), pp. 30–53.

—— (1996). 'Humanity and Citizenship', in Joshua Cohen (ed.), *For Love of Country: Debating The Limits of Patriotism* (Boston: Beacon Press), pp. 111–18.

—— (1999*a*). 'Human Rights and Economic Achievements', in Joanne R. Bauer and Daniel A. Bell (eds), *The East Asian Challenge for Human Rights* (Cambridge: Cambridge University Press), pp. 88–99.

—— (1999*b*). *Development as Freedom* (New York: Anchor Books).

Shklar, Judith (1990). *The Faces of Injustice* (New Haven and London: Yale University Press).

Shue, Henry (1983). 'Transnational Transgressions', in Tom Regan (ed.), *Just Business: New Introductory Essays in Business Ethics* (Philadelphia: Temple University Press), pp. 271–91.

—— (1988). 'Mediating Duties', *Ethics*, 98/4: 687–704.

—— (1996a). *Basic Rights: Subsistence, Affluence, and U. S. Foreign Policy*, second edition (Princeton: Princeton University Press).

—— (1996b). 'Solidarity among Strangers and the Right to Food', in William Aiken and Hugh LaFollette (eds), *World Hunger and Morality*, second edition (Upper Saddle River, New Jersey: Prentice Hall), pp. 113–32.

Simmons, John A. (1996). 'Associative Political Obligations', *Ethics*, 106/2: 247–73.

Singer, Peter (1972). 'Famine, Affluence, and Morality', *Philosophy and Public Affairs* 1/3: 229–43.

—— (1977). 'Reconsidering the Famine Relief Argument', in *Food Policy: The Responsibility of the United States in the Life and Death Choices*, edited with an introduction by Peter G. Brown and Henry Shue (London: Collier Macmillan), pp. 36–53.

—— (1979). *Practical Ethics* (Cambridge: Cambridge University Press).

—— (2002). *One World: The Ethics of Globalization* (New Haven and London: Yale University Press).

Skinner, Quentin (1988). 'Meaning and Understanding in the History of Ideas', in *Meaning and Context: Quentin Skinner and his Critics*, edited and introduced by James Tully (Cambridge: Polity), pp. 29–67.

Sklair, Leslie (2002). *Globalization: Capitalism and its Alternatives* (Oxford: Oxford University Press).

Slater, Jerome and Terry Nardin (1986). 'Nonintervention and Human Rights', *Journal of Politics*, 48: 86–95.

Slim, Hugo (1997). *Doing the Right Thing: Relief Agencies, Moral Dilemmas and Moral Responsibility in Political Emergencies and War* (Upsala: Swedish International Development Cooperation Agency and Nordiska Afrikainstitutet).

—— and Emma Visman (1995). 'Evacuation, Intervention and Retaliation: United Nations humanitarian operations in Somalia, 1991–1993', in John Harriss (ed.), *The Politics of Humanitarian Intervention* (London and New York: Pinter), pp. 145–66.

Smith, Anthony (1991). *National Identity* (London: Penguin).

—— (1995). *Nations and Nationalism in a Global Era* (Cambridge: Polity).

Smith, Graham (1996). 'Latvia and the Latvians', in Graham Smith (ed.), *The Nationalities Question in the Post-Soviet States*, second edition (London: Longman), pp. 147–69.

Smith, Michael J. (1986). *Realist Thought from Weber to Kissinger* (Baton Rouge and London: Louisiana State University Press).

—— (1989). 'Ethics and Intervention', *Ethics and International Affairs*, 3: 1–26.

—— (1997). 'Growing up with *Just and Unjust Wars*: An Appreciation', *Ethics and International Affairs*, 11: 3–18.

—— (1998). 'Humanitarian Intervention: An Overview of the Ethical Issues', *Ethics and International Affairs*, 12: 63–79.

Steiner, Hillel (1994). *An Essay on Rights* (Oxford: Blackwell).

—— (1996a). 'Territorial Justice', in Simon Caney, David George and Peter Jones (eds), *National Rights, International Obligations* (Oxford: Westview), pp. 139–48.

—— (1996b). 'Impartiality, Freedom and Natural Rights', *Political Studies*, 44/2: 311–13.

Steiner, Hillel (1999). 'Just Taxation and International Redistribution', in Ian Shapiro and Lea Brilmayer (eds), *Global Justice: NOMOS XLI* (New York and London: New York University Press), pp. 171–91.

Sturgeon, Nicholas L. (1994). 'Moral Disagreement and Moral Relativism', in Ellen Frankel Paul, Fred D. Miller and Jeffrey Paul (eds), *Cultural Pluralism and Moral Knowledge* (Cambridge: Cambridge University Press), pp. 80–115.

Tamir, Yael (1991). 'The Right to National Self-Determination', *Social Research*, 58/3: 565–90.

—— (1993). *Liberal Nationalism* (Princeton: Princeton University Press).

Tan, Kok-Chor (2000). *Toleration, Diversity, and Global Justice* (University Park: Pennsylvania State University Press).

Taylor, Charles (1992). 'The Politics of Recognition', in Amy Gutmann (ed.), *Multiculturalism and the 'Politics of Recognition': An Essay by Charles Taylor* (Princeton: Princeton University Press), pp. 25–73.

—— (1998). 'Modes of Secularism', in Rajeev Bhargava (ed.), *Secularism and its Critics* (Delhi: Oxford University Press), pp. 31–53.

—— (1999). 'Conditions of an Unforced Consensus on Human Rights', in Joanne R. Bauer and Daniel A. Bell (eds), *The East Asian Challenge for Human Rights* (Cambridge: Cambridge University Press), pp. 124–44.

Tesón, Fernando R. (1988). *Humanitarian Intervention: An Inquiry into Law and Morality* (New York: Transnational Publishers).

—— (1995). 'The Rawlsian Theory of International Law', *Ethics and International Affairs*, 9: 79–99.

—— (1998). *A Philosophy of International Law* (Oxford: Westview Press).

Thomas, Caroline (1993). 'The Pragmatic Case against Intervention', in Ian Forbes and Mark Hoffman (eds), *Political Theory, International Relations, and the Ethics of Intervention* (London: Macmillan), pp. 91–103.

Thompson, Janna (1992). *Justice and World Order: A Philosophical Inquiry* (London: Routledge).

Tobin, James (1982). 'A Proposal for International Monetary Reform', in *Essays in Economics: Theory and Policy* (Cambridge, Massachsuetts: MIT Press), pp. 488–94.

Todorov, Tzvetan (1993). *On Human Diversity: Nationalism, Racism, and Exoticism in French Thought* (Cambridge Massachusetts: Harvard University Press).

Tolstoy, Leo (1987 [original date unknown]). 'Carthago Delenda Est' in *Writings on Civil Disobedience and Nonviolence*, with introduction by David Albert and Foreword by George Zabelka (Santa Cruz, CA: New Society Publishers), pp. 125–36.

Tucker, Robert W. and David C. Hendrickson (1992). *The Imperial Temptation: The New World Order and America's Purpose* (New York: Council on Foreign Relations Press).

Tully, James (1995). *Strange Multiplicity: Constitutionalism in an Age of Diversity* (Cambridge: Cambridge University Press).

United Nations Development Programme (2002). *Human Development Report 2002: Deepening Democracy in a Fragmented World* (New York: Oxford University Press).

United States Catholic Bishops (1992). 'The Challenge of Peace: God's Promise and Our Response', in Jean Bethke Elshtain (eds), *Just War Theory* (New York: New York University Press), pp. 77–168.

van Parijs, Philippe (1995). *Real Freedom for All: What (if anything) Can Justify Capitalism?* (Oxford: Clarendon Press).

Vincent, Andrew (1997). 'Liberal Nationalism: An Irresponsible Compound?', *Political Studies*, XLV/2: pp. 275–95.

Vincent, R. J. (1974). *Nonintervention and International Order* (Princeton: Princeton University Press).

—— (1986). *Human Rights and International Relations* (Cambridge: Cambridge University Press).

—— and Peter Wilson (1993). 'Beyond Non-Intervention', in Ian Forbes and Mark Hoffman (eds), *Political Theory, International Relations, and the Ethics of Intervention* (London: Macmillan), pp. 122–30.

Wachtel, Howard M. (2000). 'Tobin and Other Global Taxes', *Review of International Political Economy*, 7/2: 335–52.

Waldron, Jeremy (1989). 'Particular Values and Critical Morality', *California Law Review*, 77/3: 561–89.

—— (1990). *The Right to Private Property* (Oxford: Clarendon Press).

—— (1992). 'Minority Cultures and The Cosmopolitan Alternative', *University of Michigan Journal of Law Reform*, 25/3–4: 751–92.

—— (2000). 'What is Cosmopolitan?', *Journal of Political Philosophy*, 8/2: 227–43.

Walker, R. B. J. (1988). *One World, Many Worlds: Struggles for a Just World Peace* (Boulder Colorado: Lynne Rienner).

Waltz, Kenneth (1959). *Man, the State and War: A Theoretical Analysis* (New York: Columbia University Press).

Walzer, Michael (1977). *Just and Unjust Wars: A Moral Argument with Historical Illustrations* (Middlesex: Penguin).

Waltz, Kenneth (1979). *Theory of International Politics* (Reading, Massachusetts: Addison Wesley).

Walzer, Michael (1980). 'The Moral Standing of States: A Response to Four Critics', *Philosophy and Public Affairs*, 9/3: 209–29.

—— (1983). *Spheres of Justice: A Defence of Pluralism and Equality* (Oxford: Blackwell).

—— (1987). *Interpretation and Social Criticism* (Cambridge, Massachusetts: Harvard University Press).

—— (1988). *The Company of Critics: Social Criticism and Political Commitment in the Twentieth Century* (New York: Basic Books).

—— (1990). 'Nation and Universe', in Grethe B. Peterson (ed.), *The Tanner Lectures on Human Values: Volume XI* (Salt Lake City: University of Utah Press), pp. 507–56.

—— (1994). *Thick and Thin: Moral Argument at Home and Abroad* (Notre Dame: University of Notre Dame Press).

Wapner, Paul (1996). *Environmental Activism and World Civic Politics* (Albany, New York: State University of New York Press).

Weber, Eugen (1977). *Peasants into Frenchmen: The Modernization of Rural France 1870–1914* (London: Chatto and Windus).

Weinstock, Daniel (1996). 'Is there a Moral Case for Nationalism?', *Journal of Applied Philosophy*, 13/1: 87–100.

—— (1999). 'National Partiality: Confronting the Intuitions', *The Monist*, 82/3: 516–41.

Welch, David A. (1993). *Justice and the Genesis of War* (Cambridge: Cambridge University Press).

Wellman, Christopher (1995). 'A Defense of Secession and Political Self-Determination', *Philosophy and Public Affairs*, 24/2: 142–71.

Wells, H. G. (1919–20). *The Outline of History: Being a Plain History of Life and Mankind volume two* (London: George Newnes).

—— (1940). *The Rights of Man or What are we Fighting For?* (Middlesex: Penguin).

Wenar, Leif (2001). 'Contractualism and Global Economic Justice', *Metaphilosophy*, 32/1/2: 79–94.

Wendt, Alexander (1999). *Social Theory of International Politics* (Cambridge: Cambridge University Press).

Wheeler, Nicholas J. (1992). 'Pluralist or Solidarist Conceptions of International Society: Bull and Vincent on Humanitarian Intervention', *Millennium*, 21/3: 463–87.

—— (2000). *Saving Strangers: Humanitarian Intervention in International Society* (Oxford: Oxford University Press).

—— and Timothy Dunne (1996). 'Hedley Bull's Pluralism of the Intellect and Solidarism of the Will', *International Affairs*, 72/1: 91–107.

Whelan, Frederick (1983). 'Prologue: Democratic Theory and the Boundary Problem', in J. Roland Pennock and John Chapman (eds), *Liberal Democracy: NOMOS Volume XXV* (New York and London: New York University Press), pp. 13–47.

White, Stephen K. (1992). *Political Theory and Postmodernism* (Cambridge: Cambridge University Press).

Wicclair, Mark (1979). 'Human Rights and Intervention', in Peter G. Brown and Douglas Maclean (eds), *Human Rights and U. S. Foreign Policy: Principles and Applications* (Lexington: D.C. Heath), pp. 141–57.

—— (1980). 'Rawls and the Principle of Nonintervention', in H. Gene Blocker (eds.), *John Rawls' Theory of Social Justice: An Introduction* (Athens: Ohio University Press), pp. 289–308.

Wight, Martin (1966a). 'Why is there no International Theory?', in Herbert Butterfield and Martin Wight (eds), *Diplomatic Investigations: Essays in the Theory of International Politics* (London: George Allen and Unwin), pp. 17–34.

—— (1966b). 'Western Values in International Relations', in Herbert Butterfield and Martin Wight (eds), *Diplomatic Investigations: Essays in the Theory of International Politics* (London: George Allen and Unwin), pp. 89–131.

—— (1991). *International Theory: The Three Traditions*, edited by Gabriele Wight and Brian Porter with an introductory essay by Hedley Bull (London: Leicester University Press).

Williams, Bernard (1972). *Morality: An Introduction to Ethics* (Cambridge: Cambridge University Press).

—— (1985). *Ethics and the Limits of Philosophy* (London: Fontana).

Wiredu, Kwasi (1996). *Cultural Universals and Particulars: An African Perspective* (Indiana: Indiana University press).

Wolff, Christian (1934 [1749]). *Jus Gentium Methodo Scientifica Pertractatum*, translated by Joseph Drake (Oxford: Clarendon).

Wong, David B. (1984). *Moral Relativity* (Berkeley, California: University of California Press).

—— (1989). 'Three Kinds of Incommensurability' in *Relativism: Interpretation and Confrontation*, edited with an introductrion by Michael Krausz (Notre Dame, Indiana: University of Notre Dame Press), pp. 140–58.

Woods, Ngaire (2001). 'Making the IMF and the World Bank more accountable', *International Affairs*, 77/1: 83–100.

Yasuaki, Onuma (1999). 'Toward an Intercivilizational Approach to Human Rights', in Joanne R. Bauer and Daniel A. Bell (eds), *The East Asian Challenge for Human Rights* (Cambridge: Cambridge University Press), pp. 103–23.

Yoder, John (1994). 'The Pacifism of Absolute Principle', in Lawrence Freedman (ed.), *War* (Oxford: Oxford University Press), pp. 156–58.

Young, Iris Marion (2000). *Inclusion and Democracy* (Oxford: Oxford University Press).

Zolo, Danilo (1997). *Cosmopolis: Prospects for World Government*, translated by David McKie (Cambridge: Polity).

# Index

Lightning Source UK Ltd.
Milton Keynes UK
UKOW07f0201160115

244526UK00004B/57/P